NEW HART'S RULES

NEW HART'S RULES

Adapted from
The Oxford Guide to Style
by R. M. Ritter

OXFORD
UNIVERSITY PRESS

OXFORD
UNIVERSITY PRESS

Great Clarendon Street, Oxford OX2 6DP

Oxford University Press is a department of the University of Oxford.
It furthers the University's objective of excellence in research, scholarship,
and education by publishing worldwide in

Oxford   New York

Auckland   Cape Town   Dar es Salaam   Hong Kong   Karachi
Kuala Lumpur   Madrid   Melbourne   Mexico City   Nairobi
New Delhi   Shanghai   Taipei   Toronto

With offices in

Argentina   Austria   Brazil   Chile   Czech Republic   France   Greece
Guatemala   Hungary   Italy   Japan   Poland   Portugal   Singapore
South Korea   Switzerland   Thailand   Turkey   Ukraine   Vietnam

Oxford is a registered trade mark of Oxford University Press
in the UK and in certain other countries

Published in the United States
by Oxford University Press Inc., New York

© Oxford University Press 2005

Database right Oxford University Press (makers)

First published 2005
Adapted from *The Oxford Guide to Style* (2002) by R. M. Ritter

British Library Cataloguing in Publication Data
Data available

Library of Congress Cataloging in Publication Data
Data available

ISBN   978-0-19-861041-0

4

Typeset in Miller
by Alliance Interactive
Printed in China through
Asia Pacific Offset

Contents

Preface

New Hart's Rules is a new guide to style designed for people writing or working with text in English. Its twenty chapters give a full account of such matters as capitalization, hyphenation, abbreviation, italicization, notes and references, work titles, quotations, bibliography, and publishing terms. Advice is given on dealing with scientific and foreign-language material, and on preparing lists, tables, and illustrations. The text is clearly written and laid out, with short paragraphs and many illustrative examples.

Hart's Rules for Compositors and Readers at the University Press, Oxford was first printed in 1893. Horace Henry Hart (1840-1916) was Printer to the University of Oxford and Controller of the University Press between 1883 and 1915. *Hart's Rules* was originally a slim twenty-four-page booklet intended only for staff of the printing house at the Clarendon Press, the learned imprint of Oxford University Press, but Hart decided to publish it for the public after finding copies of it for sale. In all, *Hart's Rules* was published in thirty-nine editions. Over time its size and influence grew, and it came to be regarded as the essential handbook for editors and typesetters. In 2002 a new edition was published under the name *The Oxford Guide to Style*. It revised and expanded *Hart's Rules*, and was published in a larger format. *New Hart's Rules* marks a return to the *Hart's Rules* name and small 'handbook' format that have been renowned for more than a hundred years.

New Hart's Rules has been written for contemporary writers and editors of all kinds. Whereas the original *Hart's* concentrated on style appropriate to academic publications, *New Hart's Rules* responds to the challenge of a wider constituency. Authors, copy-editors, proofreaders, designers, typesetters, and anyone working on newspapers, magazines, reports, theses, or web content will find here the advice they need on the language and presentation of their text.

New Hart's Rules continues to explain the 'house style' traditionally used at Oxford University Press, but it also gives a full account of widely used contemporary practices in all areas of writing and publishing, and makes clear the differences, where they exist, between British and American style.

Most of the illustrative examples in *New Hart's Rules* are taken from the Oxford English Corpus, a database containing hundreds of millions of words of real English, or from the Oxford Reading Programme. The book's spellings and recommendations are consistent with those given in the current range of Oxford dictionaries, and with those in the *New Oxford Dictionary for Writers and Editors*.

New Hart's Rules forms part of a trio of books designed specifically for writers and editors, along with the *New Oxford Dictionary for Writers and Editors* and the *New Oxford Spelling Dictionary*. These three books combine to form the complete reference set for everyone who is concerned to reach the highest standards in producing written works. They are intended to be used alongside a current Oxford dictionary such as the *Concise Oxford English Dictionary* (eleventh edition, 2004) or the slightly larger *Oxford Dictionary of English* (second edition, 2003), which also includes encyclopedic material. For copy-editors the standard reference is Judith Butcher's *Copy-Editing: The Cambridge Handbook for Editors, Authors and Publishers* (fourth edition, 2006).

Many people have helped put together this book, and those most directly involved in the project are listed below. Special thanks are due to Rebecca Kaye of Willoughby & Partners for advice on copyright law and other legal matters. We would also like to thank Val Rice, Jan Baiton, and other members of the Society for Editors and Proofreaders for their interest in and support of the project. Finally, the editors are indebted to the work of *The Oxford Guide to Style* by Robert Ritter.

Editorial team

CHAPTER 1

The parts of a book

1.1 General principles

A book usually consists of three sections: **preliminary matter** (also called **prelims** or **front matter**), the **main text**, and **end matter**. All books have some kind of prelims, all have a text, and most works of non-fiction have end matter. The prelims and end matter usually contain a number of items or sections, subject to a given order and to conventions that control their presentation.

In discussing the parts of a book the following terms are used:

- **spread** or **double-page spread**—the pair of pages (left-hand and right-hand) exposed when the book is opened at random; the term **opening** is also used. The terms are sometimes distinguished, with a 'spread' being a pair of pages that are designed as an entity, for example in a highly illustrated book, and an 'opening' being any pair of facing pages.

- **recto**—the right-hand page of a spread: a recto always has an odd page number.

- **verso**—the left-hand page of a spread: a verso always has an even page number.

The recto is regarded as the 'more important' of the two pages of a spread. The main text always begins on a recto, and in a book divided into parts (Part I, Part II, etc.) a new part begins on a fresh recto, even though the preceding page may be blank. The design of a book may require that a new chapter begin on a fresh recto. The main items or sections in the prelims customarily begin on a fresh recto.

1.2 Preliminary matter

1.2.1 **Constituents**

Preliminary matter is any material that precedes the main text of
the book. Preliminary pages are usually numbered with lower-case
Roman numerals (rather than Arabic numerals) so that any late
changes to the content or extent of the prelims will not affect the
pagination of the main text. Page numbers (called **folios**) are not
shown on every page of the prelims, though every page has its number
(see also 1.5.1).

Prelims will always include some, and may include all, of the following
items or sections, in this order:

half-title page
half-title verso
frontispiece
title page
title page verso
dedication
foreword
preface
acknowledgements
contents
lists of illustrations, figures, and maps
list of tables
list of abbreviations
list of contributors
note to the reader
epigraph

Some but not all of these sections have headings, which are usually set
to the same design as chapter headings.

Besides prelims and end matter, a hardback (or **case-bound**) book
may have **endpapers** at both ends of the book, often of slightly
stronger paper than the text; endpapers consist of a single sheet,
half of it pasted to the inside of the case and half forming a **flyleaf**
or blank page at the beginning or end of the book. Figures, maps, or
other illustrations are sometimes printed on the endpapers; any that
are essential should be repeated within the text, because endpapers
may be obscured or removed altogether in library copies of the book or
when it is reprinted in paperback.

1.2.2 **Half-title**

The half-title page is the first page (p. i) of the book (after a flyleaf, if any) and thus falls on a recto. It contains the main title, and only the main title, of the book (or the title of the volume if the work is in more than one volume).

Not all books now have a half-title, and it may sometimes be dispensed with as a space-saving measure (see 1.8).

1.2.3 **Half-title verso**

The verso of the half-title page (p. ii) is often blank, though it may carry announcements from the publisher such as a list of other books in the series to which the volume belongs, or a list of other works by the same author. Sometimes it will be given over to a frontispiece (see below). The half-title verso falls opposite the title page and may be incorporated into a special design for this important spread.

1.2.4 **Frontispiece**

A frontispiece is an illustration that faces the title page, an important position that is justified by the significance or representative content of the image. In a biography a frontispiece is usually a portrait of the subject, in a work of history it might be a map or a facsimile of a document, and so on.

If the book has integrated illustrations (see 16.1.1), the frontispiece is likely to be printed on text paper like all the other illustrations. If the book has plates, the frontispiece, like other pictures, will usually be printed on glossy art paper; in this case the frontispiece will appear on the verso of a single leaf **tipped in** (that is, inserted and pasted) between the half-title verso and the title page. Note that tipping-in is a costly process and is best avoided if possible.

Like any illustration, a frontispiece will generally be identified by a caption, which may be printed beneath the image or close by (at the foot of the title page verso, for example). The frontispiece is, exceptionally, listed on the contents page (see 1.2.11 below).

As a frontispiece may not always be reproduced in all subsequent editions of a book (a paperback edition, for example), the author should avoid referring to it in the text.

1.2.5 **Title page**

The title page (p. iii) presents at least the following details:

- the complete title and subtitle of the work
- a volume number, if any
- the name of the author or editor
- the publisher's name (called the **imprint**).

It may also include other, similar, information: for example, a series title; the names of other people involved in the book's preparation, such as a translator or an illustrator; the place of publication or the cities in which the publisher has offices; the publisher's logo or **colophon** (device or emblem); and the date of publication.

The roles of people other than the author are defined by an introductory phrase, such as:

> Selected and edited by
> Translated by
> With illustrations by

1.2.6 **Title page verso**

The title page verso (p. iv, also, variously, called the **copyright**, **biblio**, or **imprint** page) contains the essential printing and publication history of the work. It presents at least the following details:

- publisher's imprint
- date of publication
- publishing history
- copyright line
- copyright notice(s)
- assertion of moral rights
- limitations on sales
- cataloguing in publication data
- statements concerning performing rights
- printer's name and location.

Publisher's imprint
The imprint consists of:

- the publisher's name (or the name of a subdivision of the company if this bears a separate name)
- the publisher's full registered postal address
- the place of publication.

It may also include the names of associated companies or offices, and the cities in which they are located.

Date of publication
The date of publication is given on the title page verso, whether or not it appears on the title page. For the first edition of a work the date of publication is usually the same as the copyright date (see below).

Publishing history
The publishing history of the book includes:

- reference to simultaneous co-publications of the work (with the name and location of the co-publishers)
- a description of the current version of the work (for example its edition number, if other than the first, or its status as a reprint)
- the sequence of editions, reprints, and publication in different bindings that has preceded the current version of the work, each of which is dated.

An **edition** is a version of a book at its first publication and at every following publication for which more than minor changes are made: a book goes into a new edition when it is revised, enlarged, abridged, published in a new format, or published in a different binding. A new edition requires a new ISBN (see below).

A **reprint** or **impression** is a republication of a book for which no corrections or only minor corrections are made. The publishing history usually distinguishes between these two states, describing them as 'reprinted' and 'reprinted with corrections'. The publishing history usually details the issuing of multiple reprints in a single year: *Reprinted 2004 (twice)*.

Copyright line
To qualify for protection under the Universal Copyright Convention, and for reasons of best practice, copyright ownership in a work must

be stated in a particular form, giving the copyright holder's name and the year of first publication, preceded by the copyright symbol:

© Ann Jones 2004

A work may have multiple copyright holders, such as co-authors, an illustrator, a translator, or the contributor of an introduction; the rights of each of them must be separately stated.

Copyright may be held by the publisher rather than by the creator(s) of the work, who in this case will have assigned the rights permanently, rather than have licensed them to the publisher.

For guidelines on copyright see Chapter 20.

Copyright notice(s)
Many publishers include one or more copyright notices in their books, explicitly reserving certain rights in the work. Such notices relate to reproduction, electronic storage, transmission in other forms, and rebinding. An example may be seen on the title page verso of this book.

Assertion of moral rights
Under the UK's Copyright Act 1988 certain 'moral rights' in the work are enjoyed by its creator. Of these the right of paternity (the right to be identified as the author of the work) does not exist unless the author has explicitly asserted it. The assertion of this right, or of the author's moral rights in general, is recorded on the title page verso in a form such as:

The author's moral rights have been asserted

For an explanation of moral rights see Chapter 20.

Cataloguing in publication (CIP) data
Some national libraries, notably the British Library and the Library of Congress, compile catalogue records of new books before their publication. Publishers may include such records in full on the title page verso of the book, or may simply note that they are available. CIP data may not be altered in any way, even if it contains errors, without the written permission of the issuing library.

The CIP data is usually the means of stating the **ISBN** (International Standard Book Number), because this number is essential to the catalogue record. If CIP data is not reproduced in full the ISBN must be included elsewhere on the title page verso. The ISBN uniquely identifies the book in the particular edition to which it is attached. A new ISBN is needed for every new edition of the book, including reissue in a different binding. Each volume of a multi-volume work usually has its own ISBN, as may the set as a whole, though in some cases (notably where the volumes are not separately available for sale) a single number may be used for the whole set. By 1 January 2007 the previous ten-digit ISBNs will have been replaced by the new thirteen-digit ISBNs.

A serial publication, such as a journal, magazine, or yearbook, has an **ISSN** (International Standard Serial Number), which is the same for all issues of the work.

The CIP data will often be accompanied by an indication of what impression a particular book represents. This may be a single number, or a series of numbers, the lowest number of which is that of the current impression. So the following line denotes a second impression:

10 9 8 7 6 5 4 3 2

Performing rights agencies
The public performance of dramatic and musical works is generally controlled on behalf of copyright holders by agents whom they empower to license performing rights. A clause stating that the right to perform the work is restricted, and giving the name and address of the agent to whom application must be made for permission to mount a performance, usually appears on the title page verso of printed plays and music.

Printer's name and location
The printer's name and location must be included on the title page verso.

Other information
The title page verso may present further information about the book as a publication. Typical elements include details of the design and production of the book, including the name and size of the typeface used and the name and location of the typesetting firm.

1.2.7 Dedication

The dedication is a highly personal expression on the part of the author. The publisher usually accepts its wording and content unchanged, and its design is usually subject to the author's approval when that of the rest of the book is not. Whenever possible the dedication falls on a recto (usually p. v), but if, for reasons of space, it must be relocated to a verso, one must be chosen that gives it sufficient prominence (for example the last verso preceding the first page of the text).

1.2.8 Foreword

The foreword is a recommendation of the work written by someone other than the author. He or she is usually named at the end of the piece, or in its title, and in the contents list. The distinction between the foreword and the preface (see below) should be noted and the correct title given to each of these sections of the front matter. The foreword usually begins on a fresh recto.

1.2.9 Preface

The preface is the section where the author sets out the purpose, scope, and content of the book. In the absence of a full acknowledgements section, the author may include in the preface brief thanks to colleagues, advisers, or others who have helped in the creation of the work.

In a multi-author work the preface may be written by the work's editor (*Editor's preface*). All works in a series may contain the same preface by the series editor (*Series editor's preface*), which precedes the preface by the author of each work. Successive editions of a work may have their own prefaces, each of which is appropriately titled (for example *Preface to the second edition*). If one or more earlier prefaces are reprinted in a new edition, they follow, in reverse numerical order, the preface belonging to that new edition; for example:

> Preface to the paperback edition
> Preface to the second edition
> Preface to the first edition

The preface usually begins on a fresh recto, as do each of multiple prefaces unless reasons of economy dictate otherwise.

1.2.10 **Acknowledgements**

Acknowledgements (or, in US spelling, *Acknowledgments*) are of two types: those recognizing the ideas, assistance, support, or inspiration of those who have helped the author to create the work; and those listing the copyright holders in material such as figures, illustrations, and quotations reproduced in the book. The first type may, if those acknowledged are few, be included in the preface (see above). The second type relate to the legal requirement to acknowledge the sources of reproduced material and in many cases to gain permission from copyright holders or their licensees for its use, and as such the wording printed should be exactly as required by the copyright holder, even if this is inconsistent with style used elsewhere in the book. (For guidelines on copyright see Chapter 20.)

It is best to separate the two types of acknowledgement. The author's personal thanks follow the preface and are called simply 'Acknowledgements'. The names of those who hold copyright in verbal material (such as epigraphs, quotations, or tables) are listed in a separate section headed 'Copyright acknowledgements'. Acknowledgements relating to illustrations may be included in a list of illustrations (see below) or presented in a separate section. Both kinds of acknowledgement relating to copyright may appear either in the prelims or the end matter.

1.2.11 **Contents**

The list of contents (headed *Contents*) always falls on a recto. It records the title and initial page number of every titled section that follows it in the prelims, part titles, chapter titles, and all sections in the end matter, including the index. It usually includes reference to the frontispiece if one is present (see 1.2.4). Lists in the prelims are referred to on the contents page as *List of Illustrations*, *List of Abbreviations*, etc., even though their own headings are best formulated simply as *Illustrations*, *Abbreviations*, etc.

Part titles, preceded by the word *Part* and a number, are listed in full, and a page number is given unless it is that of the following chapter in the part. The word *Chapter* may, but need not, appear before the number and title of each chapter, though if it is used in the list of contents it should also appear at the head of each chapter in the text. It is customary to use upper-case Roman numerals for part numbers (see 1.3.3) and Arabic numerals for chapter numbers (see 1.3.4).

In complex works, such as textbooks, headings within chapters may be included on the contents page or even as a subsidiary table of contents at the start of each chapter. In a multi-author volume authors' names as well as chapter titles are given in the contents list.

The wording, punctuation, capitalization, use of italics, and form of authors' names in the contents list must match the headings as they appear in the text itself. No full point is needed at the end of any heading, nor are leader dots wanted between titles and page references. The numerals on the contents page at the editing stage will be those of the script, or 'dummies' such as xxx or 000; they should be circled to indicate that they are not to be printed. At page-proof stage the typesetter should have inserted the correct page references, but they must be checked by the proofreader.

The first volume of a multi-volume work published simultaneously or at short intervals should contain a contents list and list of illustrations (if relevant) for the entire set. Each subsequent volume needs lists only for that volume.

1.2.12 Lists of illustrations, figures, and maps

Illustrations numbered sequentially through the work are presented in a single list. Different types of illustrative material, numbered in separate sequences, are presented in separate lists, usually in the order illustrations, figures, maps.

Such a list consists of the captions, which may be shortened if they are discursive, and the sources or locations of the illustrative material where relevant. As with the contents, the correct page numbers for all illustrative material that is integrated with the text (though not those of plates in a separate section) will need to be inserted at page-proof stage. Acknowledgements to copyright holders may be added here or presented in a separate list in the prelims or end matter. It is better not to include credits or even sources in the captions that accompany the illustrations; however, rights holders may insist that acknowledgement be made beside or beneath the illustration.

1.2.13 List of tables

A list of tables is useful only when the work contains many tables of particular interest. The list gives the table headings, shortened if necessary, and page numbers; sources appear in the text beneath each table.

1.2.14 List of abbreviations

The text of a book should be so presented as to 'explain' itself without recourse to external sources of information. Abbreviations that readers may be unable to interpret must be included in a list with the full form spelled out alongside each one. Well-known abbreviations that need no explanation (such as AD, BC, *UK*, and *US*) are not included in the list, nor are any that will be common knowledge to the expected readership of the work. If a term occurs only very rarely in the text it is better to spell it out at each occurrence than to use an abbreviation. The practice of spelling out a short form at the first instance of its use does not obviate the need for inclusion of a list of abbreviations.

If the abbreviations are used in text or notes the list is best placed in the prelims of the book; if, however, abbreviations are used only in the bibliography, endnotes, or appendices, the list may be presented at the head of the relevant section. Arrange the list alphabetically by abbreviated form.

1.2.15 List of contributors

In a multi-author work it is customary to list the contributors and provide relevant information about each one, such as institutional affiliation or post held, a short biography, or details of other publications. The more detailed and discursive the entries are, the more appropriate it will be to place the list in the end matter of the work rather than the preliminary pages.

The list should be ordered alphabetically by contributor's surname (though names are presented in natural order, not inverted), and names should match the form in the contents list and the chapter headings. The presentation of each entry should as far as possible be standardized.

1.2.16 **Epigraph**

An epigraph is a relevant quotation placed at the beginning of a volume, part, or chapter, and is distinguished typographically from other displayed quotations. An epigraph relating to the entire volume is placed on a new page, preferably a recto, immediately before the text or in another prominent position within the prelims. Epigraphs for parts or chapters may be placed on the verso facing the part or chapter title or under the heading of the part or chapter to which they relate. The use of epigraphs and their positioning must be consistent throughout the work.

Epigraph sources are usually ranged right (see 2.5.1) under the quotation. The author's name and the title and date of the work are usually sufficient: further details are not normally included because readers are not expected to want to verify the quotation.

1.2.17 **Other sections**

Many publications need a short explanation of conventions, terminology, or forms of presentation used in the text, or guidance on how to use the book. Such information is best placed as near as possible to the beginning of the text and often carries the title *Note to the reader* or *How to use this book*.

1.3 Text

The text of a work, whether it is in a single volume or multiple volumes, should ideally unfold in a form in which each division is of equivalent scale and consistent construction. As part of marking up the text the copy-editor will need to code the hierarchy of headings that articulate the structure and all displayed elements of the text— those elements such as quotations, lists, text boxes, equations, and so on that need special presentation on the page. The designer specifies an appropriate typographic treatment for the body text and for each displayed element, and the typesetter applies the appropriate design and layout wherever the copy-editor has marked a code.

1.3.1 **Volumes**

It is usual for each volume of a work published in multiple volumes to have its own pagination, index, bibliography, and so on. Even if the numbering of text pages is consecutive from one volume to the next, the preliminary pages of each volume begin with page i. Volumes may be numbered or titled or numbered and titled, as appropriate to the content of the work: each volume in a collection of correspondence or a biography, for instance, may be distinguished by a range of years, the volumes in a complete edition of an author's works by the names of different genres such as *Poems*, *Plays*, *Essays*.

Large scholarly works, especially those published over many years, are sometimes made available in **fascicles** (or **fascicules**) rather than volumes. While fascicles are technically separate works, each with its own ISBN, they are designed to be bound together and are, accordingly, through-paginated. The first fascicle contains preliminary material for the whole publication and the last the index or other end matter; any front matter or end matter included with the intermediate fascicles is discarded when the fascicles are combined into a book or books.

1.3.2 **The introduction**

The introduction is properly part of the text of the book (except in special contexts such as editions of literary texts, where the editor's introduction forms part of the prelims). The Arabic pagination begins with the first page of the introduction, which therefore must fall on a recto. The introduction may be treated (and numbered) as the first chapter of the work, or it may be headed simply *Introduction*, the numbered chapters following thereafter; when an introduction (or conclusion) addresses the work as a whole, it is usually left unnumbered.

1.3.3 **Parts**

It is useful to arrange a long or complex work in parts when the text falls into logical divisions of similar length. Parts should be numbered and may be titled; although Roman numerals are traditionally used for parts (*Part I*, *Part II*), Arabic numerals may be used or numbers spelled out (*Part One*, *Part Two*). The part number and title are best

placed on a recto with a blank verso following; part title pages are
included in the Arabic pagination of the book but the page numbers
are not shown.

Parts are divided into chapters, which are numbered consecutively
throughout the work.

1.3.4 Chapters

Most works in prose are divided into chapters, which usually have
a number (customarily in Arabic numerals) and often—especially in
non-fiction—a title. The use of the word *Chapter* before the number is
optional (see 1.2.11). Chapter titles should be of similar length and
style throughout a work and as succinct as possible—overlong titles
cause design difficulties at chapter openings and may need to be cut
down for running heads (see 1.5.3).

New chapters are usually allowed to begin on either a verso or a recto
(unlike new parts—see above); exceptionally, when chapters are short
or economical setting is required, they may run on—start on the same
page as the end of the preceding chapter—after a specified number of
lines' space. This is more common in fiction than in non-fiction. The
first page of a new chapter lacks a running head, and the **folio** (page
number) is either omitted or appears at the foot of the page (as a **drop
folio**), even when on other pages it falls in the head margin (see 1.5.1).

The first line following the chapter heading is set **full out** (flush with
the left-hand margin), with no paragraph indentation. In some designs large and small capitals are used for the first word or line of a
chapter, as in 'HE was gone'. If the first word is a single capital letter
(for example *I*, *A*), then the second word is printed in small capitals,
with no further capital. If the chapter starts with a personal name,
then the whole name is in capitals and small capitals, not just the first
name or title: 'MR THORNTON had had some difficulty ...'.

1.3.5 Sections and subsections

Chapters may be divided into sections and subsections by the use of
subheadings (or **subheads**). There may be more than one level of
subheading, though only complex works such as textbooks will generally need more than three. Too many levels of subheading are difficult to design and may be more confusing than helpful to the reader.

Sections, subsections, or even individual paragraphs may be numbered if this will be useful to the reader—as it will when the text contains numerous cross-references. As in the present book, section headings are 'double-numbered', with the two numbers closed up either side of a full point; subsection headings are triple-numbered, the number reflecting the different levels of the headings: within Chapter 9 the first A-level heading is numbered 9.1, and the first B-level heading within section 9.1 is numbered 9.1.1, and so on.

The first line after a subheading is set flush with the left-hand margin, with no paragraph indentation. If the first sentence of a new section refers to the subject articulated in the heading it must begin by re-iterating the subject rather than referring back to it with a pronoun. Not:

> **1.3 Text**
> This should ideally unfold in a form in which each division is of equivalent scale and construction.

but

> **1.3 Text**
> The text of a work should ideally unfold in a form in which each division is of equivalent scale and construction.

1.3.6 **Paragraphs**

Paragraphs are units of thought reflecting the development of the author's argument, and no absolute rules control their length. In the most general terms, one-sentence paragraphs are likely to be too short and paragraphs that exceed the length of a page of typeset material are likely to be too long to hold the reader's attention. However, it is inadvisable for an editor to alter the author's delivery by running together short paragraphs or splitting long ones without fully considering the effect on the integrity of the text, and the author should normally be consulted about such changes.

The first line of text after a chapter, section, or subsection heading is set full out to the left-hand margin, with no paragraph indentation. The first line of every subsequent paragraph is normally indented; the style in which paragraphs are separated by a space and the first line of every paragraph is set full out is characteristic of documents and some reference works, and also of material on the Internet. In fictional dialogue it is conventional (though by no means obligatory) to begin a new paragraph with every change of speaker (see 9.2.4).

Complex works, such as textbooks and practitioner texts, sometimes have numbered paragraphs throughout, the numbers being set against headings or simply at the beginnings of paragraphs; this device facilitates all kinds of internal referencing. In this case the double- and triple-numbering system outlined in 1.3.5 above is applied. Numbered paragraphs may also be used when an author wishes to enumerate long points in an argument.

1.3.7 Conclusion, epilogue, afterword

A conclusion sums up the work's findings and puts them in context. It may be numbered and titled as the final chapter of the work or (as with the introduction) headed simply *Conclusion*.

An epilogue or an author's note is nothing more than a short concluding comment on the text. An afterword is much the same, though it is typically written by someone other than the author. Neither of these sections bears a chapter number, though the headings are usually set to the same design as the chapter headings. One would not normally have more than one or two of these concluding sections in any book.

1.4 End matter

End matter (also called **back matter**) consists of any material that supplements the text. Sections in the end matter are, generally speaking, placed in order of their importance to the reader in using and interpreting the text, with the proviso that the index is always placed last. A series of sections might be ordered as follows:

    appendix
    glossary
    endnotes
    bibliography
    notes on contributors
    picture credits
    index

End matter is paginated in sequence with the text, and the sections carry headings that are usually set to the same design as the chapter headings, though the material itself is often set in smaller type than the text, in keeping with its subsidiary position.

1.4.1 **Appendix**

An appendix (or **annex**, as it is sometimes called in the publication of documents) presents subsidiary matter that relates directly to the text but cannot comfortably be accommodated within it, such as a chronology or the texts of documents discussed. Multiple appendices appear under the collective heading *Appendices*, each with its own subheading and title as appropriate. Appendices may be numbered with Arabic or Roman numerals or marked with letters.

1.4.2 **Glossary**

A glossary is an alphabetical list of important terms found in the text, with explanations or definitions. It is not a substitute for explaining terms at their first occurrence in the text. The glossary may simply repeat the textual explanation or it may expand upon it, but in any event the definitions in text and glossary must conform.

Each entry in a glossary begins a new line. Entries may be arranged in two columns (terms on the left and definitions on the right), or the definition may run on from the headword term; in the latter case turnover lines are often indented and entries spaced off from one another to make the headwords more prominent. Bold type is often used for headwords.

1.4.3 **Endnotes**

Endnotes are an alternative to footnotes, used in a single-author work where it is not essential (or customary in the discipline concerned) to position notes on the same page as the text to which they refer. In multi-author volumes, notes and other apparatus are usually placed at the end of each chapter or essay to preserve the integrity of the author's work: it would be inappropriate in these circumstances to position the reference material in a sequence at the end of the work. For the decision to place notes at the foot of the page, the end of the chapter, or the end of the work see 17.2.2; for setting out notes see 17.2.4; for running heads in endnotes see 1.5.3.

1.4.4 **Bibliography**

There are many ways of presenting citations of other works and materials of potential interest to the reader. The simplest is to list them alphabetically by authors' surnames (in which case names are inverted to expose the ordering principle) or, in specialist works that require it, chronologically. In some cases a bibliographic essay is more appropriate—as the name suggests, a discussion of sources with the citations embedded—or an annotated bibliography, in which comments on some or all of the sources are included.

A list that contains only works cited in the book is properly called *References* or *Works cited*. A list called *Bibliography* contains the works cited in the book and additional works of likely interest to the reader. A *Select bibliography* may be limited to works thought important by the author, or works cited multiple times in the text. A list of *Further reading* usually contains works not cited in the text. In general-interest non-fiction works a more seductive heading, such as *Now read on ...*, may be used for a similar list. For choice and preparation of bibliographies see Chapter 18.

1.4.5 **Index**

The index, an alphabetical list of subjects covered in the book, with references to the pages on which discussion occurs, is the last element in the end matter. A single index is preferred unless there is a strong case for subdivision into (say) an *Index of works* and a *General index*. See Chapter 19.

1.5 Folios and running heads

1.5.1 **Introduction**

The term **folio** has two meanings in book production: it is used of the sheets of a script and also of the page number as a designed element on a typeset page. The latter meaning is the one relevant to this section. A **running head** (or **running headline**, **headline**, **header**, or **running title**) is a book title, chapter title, or other heading which appears at the top of every page or spread. Folios and running heads usually fall on the same horizontal line in the head (or top) margin of the page, though the designer may decide to position them in the foot (bottom) margin—in which case the text is called a **running foot** (or **running footline** or **footer**)—or even at the fore-edge (outer margin). They thus appear outside the text area of the page. Another option is to use running heads but to place folios at the foot of the page. Technically the entire line is the running head, but in editorial parlance the term is restricted to the textual material, excluding the folio.

1.5.2 **Folio**

The folio (set in lower-case Roman numerals in the prelims and in Arabic numerals for the text and end matter of the book) usually appears at the outer top edges of the spread, or centred at the foot.

All pages are counted in the pagination sequence, but the folio is not shown on some pages, including some in the prelims, turned pages (that is, those on which material is printed in landscape format), those taken up entirely by illustrations, figures, or tables, and blank pages. On a chapter opening page the folio usually appears in the foot margin (see 1.3.4).

1.5.3 **Running heads**

Running heads are not found in all books: for instance, they may not appear in modern fiction or in highly designed illustrated books.

Running heads, like folios, are omitted from some pages of the book. These include: any section of the prelims that has no section heading (half-title, title, and imprint pages, the dedication and epigraph); part titles; any page on which a chapter heading occurs (including sections in the front matter and end matter); blank pages. They are often omitted on turned pages and on full-page illustrations, figures, or tables.

The content of the running heads depends on the nature of the book. As a general rule, if the same running head is not used on verso and recto, the larger section generates the head on the verso and the smaller that on the recto: for example, the book or part title may be used on the verso, the chapter title on the recto; in a textbook the chapter title might be used on the verso and a numbered subheading on the recto (though running heads that change every few pages should if possible be avoided for the sake of economy). In a multi-author work authors' names normally appear on the verso and chapter

titles on the recto. In encyclopedias it is common to reflect the first
headword on the verso and the last on the recto in the running heads,
whereas dictionaries tend to give the first and last headword on each
page in that page's running head.

Sections in the prelims and end matter generally carry the same running head on the verso and recto. Ideally, however, running heads for
endnotes should change on every page, indicating the text pages or
chapters to which each page of notes refers: for example, *Notes to
pages 157–99*, or *Notes to Chapter 6*, rather than just *Notes*.

Running heads should match the material from which they are derived in every respect—wording, capitalization, and so on. However, if
the book, chapter, or other titles used are very long they must be truncated for the running heads, which should not exceed about forty
characters (including spaces) for most books, as a very rough rule
of thumb.

1.6 Errata slips

An errata slip lists errors and their corrections; if there is only one
correction the correct term is *erratum slip*. A slip inserted loose in a
book should be labelled with the author's name, book title, and ISBN;
alternatively the slip may be tipped (pasted) in. In a later printing or
edition, if the text itself has not been corrected, the errata may be set as
part of the prelims or end matter. When fixed to, or printed in, the
book the errata may be called **corrigenda** (singular *corrigendum*).
Note that errata slips should be used only in the event of there
being serious mistakes or errors of fact in the book.

A list of errata should be as concise as possible, making clear the location, the substance of the error, and the form of the correction. Italic
type is used for editorial directions, and punctuation is included only
where it is part of the error and/or the correction.

> p. 204, line 15: *for* live wire *read* earth wire
> p. 399, line 2: *for* guilty *read* 'not proven'

1.7 Paper and book sizes

1.7.1 **Paper sizes**

The dimensions of a book depend on the dimensions of the sheet (the **quad sheet**) on which it is printed. For many centuries the dimensions of the common sizes of sheet have been proportioned so that they can be folded to produce viable page sizes without wastage (a small allowance is made for trimming the folded sheet). For example, quarto (4to or 4to) and octavo (8vo or 8vo) are obtained by folding standard sizes two and three times respectively. The old sizes are no longer generally used in British publishing, though they are retained in American production. Measured in inches, the sheet and untrimmed page sizes are:

Size	Standard	4to	8vo
imperial	22×30	15×11	$11 \times 7\frac{1}{2}$
elephant	20×27	$13\frac{1}{2} \times 10$	$10 \times 6\frac{3}{4}$
royal	20×25	$12\frac{1}{2} \times 10$	$10 \times 6\frac{1}{4}$
small royal	19×25	$12\frac{1}{2} \times 9\frac{1}{2}$	$9\frac{1}{2} \times 6\frac{1}{4}$
medium	18×23	$11\frac{1}{2} \times 9$	$9 \times 5\frac{3}{4}$
demy	$17\frac{1}{2} \times 22\frac{1}{2}$	$11\frac{1}{4} \times 8\frac{3}{4}$	$8\frac{3}{4} \times 5\frac{5}{8}$
crown	15×20	$10 \times 7\frac{1}{2}$	$7\frac{1}{2} \times 5$
post	$15\frac{1}{2} \times 19$		
	$14\frac{1}{2} \times 18\frac{1}{2}$	('pinched post')	
	$16\frac{1}{2} \times 21$	('large post')	
foolscap	$13\frac{1}{2} \times 17$	$8\frac{1}{2} \times 6\frac{3}{4}$	$6\frac{3}{4} \times 4\frac{1}{4}$
pot	$12\frac{1}{2} \times 15\frac{1}{2}$	$7\frac{3}{4} \times 6\frac{1}{4}$	$6\frac{1}{4} \times 3\frac{7}{8}$

Metric sizes are based on the old dimensions and some of the traditional names are used. Measured in millimetres the common metric paper sizes (untrimmed) are:

Size	Quad sheet	4to	8vo
metric crown	$768 \times 1{,}008$	252×192	192×126
metric large crown	$816 \times 1{,}056$	264×204	204×132
metric demy	$888 \times 1{,}128$	282×222	222×141
metric royal	$960 \times 1{,}272$	318×240	240×159

International paper sizes have been standardized still further by the ISO (International Standards Organization): A is the commonest, used for business correspondence, photocopying, etc.; B is used for posters, wall charts, and similar large items; C is used for envelopes and folders to fit A-series sizes. Measured in millimetres A and B (trimmed) sizes are:

A series		B series	
A0	$841 \times 1{,}189$	B0	$1{,}000 \times 1{,}414$
A1	594×841	B1	$707 \times 1{,}000$
A2	420×594	B2	500×707
A3	297×420	B3	353×500
A4	210×297	B4	250×353
A5	148×210	B5	176×250
A6	105×148	B6	125×176
A7	74×105	B7	88×125
A8	52×74		
A9	37×52		
A10	26×37		

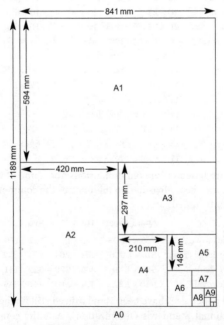

Figure 1.1 **International paper sizes A**

1.7.2 **Book sizes**

The following are the standard octavo trimmed and untrimmed page sizes, and the dimensions of the quad sheets from which they are derived, in millimetres and inches:

Size	Millimetres	Inches
metric crown 8vo		
trimmed	186 × 123	7.32 × 4.84
untrimmed	192 × 126	7.56 × 4.96
quad	768 × 1,008	30.24 × 39.69
metric large crown 8vo		
trimmed	198 × 129	7.80 × 5.08
untrimmed	204 × 132	8.03 × 5.20
quad	816 × 1,056	32.13 × 41.57
metric demy 8vo		
trimmed	216 × 138	8.50 × 5.43
untrimmed	222 × 141	8.74 × 5.55
quad	888 × 1,128	34.96 × 44.41
metric royal 8vo		
trimmed	234 × 156	9.21 × 6.14
untrimmed	240 × 159	9.45 × 6.26
quad	960 × 1,272	37.80 × 50.08
A5		
trimmed	210 × 148	8.27 × 5.83
untrimmed	215 × 152.5	8.46 × 6.00
quad	860 × 1,220	33.86 × 48.03

Dimensions are always given with height before width; for landscape formats reverse the pairs of numbers.

Mass-market paperbacks are often produced in what are known as **A format** and **B format** sizes. The first of these is 178 × 111 mm, B format is 196 × 129 mm.

1.8 Even workings

The pages of the publication are printed on the quad sheet in an order determined by the pattern of folding to be applied to it during the binding process; the arrangement or 'imposition' of the pages on both sides of the sheet is complex, and the editor will usually be asked to check running sheets—a set of unbound pages—to ensure that the correct order results once the quad sheet is folded and trimmed.

Each sheet forms a section or **signature** of the finished book; depending on the size of the sheet and the format of the book, the signature may consist of four, eight, sixteen, thirty-two, sixty-four, or even more pages. In the interests of economy it is desirable to ensure that the entire text of the book fits neatly into an exact multiple of the number of pages in each signature so that there are no blank pages at the end of the final section. At a late stage in the production of a book it may be necessary to restrict the extent of the text in order to fit it exactly, or as nearly as possible, into signatures—that is, to achieve an 'even working'. This must be done without disrupting the pagination of the main text. The usual recourse is to reduce the number of pages in the prelims (which are not part of the main sequence of pages), often by sacrificing the luxury of blank versos and using them for sections that would ideally be placed on rectos; another option is to limit the extent of the end matter, normally by shortening the index or setting it in smaller type.

CHAPTER 2

Preparing copy

2.1 Definitions

2.1.1 **Introduction**

The book in the form in which it is submitted on paper to the publisher, by the author or other creator of the work, is usually called a **typescript** or **script**, though it is unusual now for this to be anything other than a computer printout; the term **manuscript** is sometimes used for this form of the work but is better reserved for copy that is handwritten. The sheets of the typescript are properly **folios** (see 1.2.1 and 1.5.1 for another use of the term *folio*), and should be printed on one side of the paper only.

A book or any other published work is made up of leaves, each side of which forms a page; each leaf consists of a **recto** and a **verso**. The spread or opening consists of the verso of one leaf (on the left) and the recto of the next (on the right).

The technical stages of the production process, which transforms the material from typescript to printed work, are, very generally speaking (and not always in this order):

- copy-editing
- design
- typesetting
- proofreading
- correction (the last two stages may be repeated on successive sets of 'revised proofs')
- proof checking
- final correction
- printing and binding.

Of these, copy-editing, design, and reading and checking of the proofs are the processes traditionally under the control of the publishing house; these are briefly described below. Typesetting, correction, and printing and binding are traditionally specialist operations that the publisher buys in.

2.1.2 Copy-editing

In broad terms the copy-editor is responsible for the technical preparation of the author's material for publication. These responsibilities, at their simplest, comprise:

- identifying and naming all elements of the work that require the designer's attention—that is, headings, displayed quotations, lists, note copy, etc.; the copy-editor applies a 'code' to each type of material and lists the codes for the designer

- integrating extraneous items such as tables, figures, and illustrations to ensure that they are introduced in appropriate places when the typeset pages are assembled

- standardizing the presentation of the material in respect of its 'editorial style' and conventions (see 2.3)

- identifying any special characters (such as symbols or accented letters) or other technical issues of relevance to the designer and typesetter

- cross-checking the material to ensure that elements purporting to be identical or related match each other (for example, that the chapter titles on the contents page match the chapter openings, that the discussion in text relates accurately to the content of pictures and their captions), cross-references lead the reader to the right destination, note numbers refer correctly to the notes themselves, and so on

- monitoring the factual integrity of the material (for example, keeping track of and regularizing the spelling of proper names, ensuring that columns of numerical data add up, checking that the author defines and uses special terms consistently)

- correcting, or raising queries about, the author's spelling, word use, grammar, punctuation, and sentence structure

- marking the typescript clearly (or correcting an electronic file accurately) to ensure that the material can be set in type with minimum difficulty.

The level of responsibility the copy-editor carries for the structure of the material, factual accuracy, clarity of expression, and other authorial concerns is determined, and should be clearly articulated, by the publisher. Dictionaries such as the *Oxford Dictionary of English* or the *Concise Oxford English Dictionary* discuss controversial points of usage, such as the split infinitive and the use of *hopefully* as a sentence adverb, and may usefully be consulted by editors who are uncertain whether an author's phrasing is acceptable English or appropriate to the given context. A copy-editor should also be alert to any material that seems potentially defamatory (see 20.5), that is sexist or racist, or that deals with sensitive areas in an offensive or outmoded way; the current thinking on such topics is dealt with at the relevant entries in the dictionaries mentioned above.

Such matters are outside the scope of this book. Note, however, that it is now generally regarded as old-fashioned or sexist to use *he* in reference to a person of unspecified sex, as in *every child needs to know that he is loved*. The alternative *he or she* is often preferred, and in formal contexts is probably the best solution, but can become tiresomely long-winded when used frequently. Use of *they* in this sense (*everyone needs to feel that they matter*) is becoming generally accepted both in speech and in writing, especially where it occurs after an indefinite pronoun such as *everyone* or *someone*, but should not be imposed by an editor if an author has used *he or she* consistently.

2.1.3 Design

The designer's role is to determine the physical appearance of the material on the printed page. The design instructions are transmitted to the typesetter in the **typographic specification** or **type spec**, which defines the typefaces, type sizes, spacing, and position on the page of all the elements of the material identified and coded by the copy-editor. The coding process allows the designer to specify once and once only the design to be applied to each element, instead of marking the same instructions on the typescript at every occurrence.

One of the designer's responsibilities is choosing an appropriate typeface from the great many available. Briefly, type may be divided into
two broad categories, **serif** and **sans serif**. A serif is a slight projection
finishing off a stroke of a letter: the typeface in which the body of this
book's text is set has serifs, and is called Miller. A sans-serif typeface
lacks these projections, and looks like this: this is an example of a
widely used sans-serif face called Arial. People writing for the Web
should be aware that only certain typefaces are regarded as effective in
this medium: among them are Arial and Times New Roman. For the
choice of typefaces in computing and mathematics see 14.5.2 and
14.6.1.

2.1.4 Typesetting

The marked-up typescript, usually called the **copy**, and the type spec
are sent to the typesetter, generally with the author's disk (see 2.2).
When a work has been edited on screen instead of on paper, the updated file with a clean printout and the type spec are sent to the typesetter. The typesetter produces a **proof**, either by rekeying the material
and applying the design to it in the process, or (as is most often the
case today) by applying the design to the material in the electronic file.

2.1.5 Proofreading

A proof is, as the name suggests, the means of 'proving' (or trying out)
the typesetter's work. Most books today are 'set straight to page' and
the first proof is a **page proof**. However, it may still sometimes be the
case that a very complex work will be set as a **galley proof**, in which
the typographic design is applied but the material is not paginated
and extraneous items such as footnotes, tables, figures, and illustrations are not integrated. The purpose of such a proof is to allow the
textual material to be checked and corrected—that is, to be finalized—
before pages are made up: in a complex or highly designed book the
exact length of the textual material is critical, and corrections to the
text after pagination may cause expensive disruption to the layout.

The proofreader's task is to read and correct the proof. Where there is
a marked-up typescript the proof is read 'against copy'. Where there is
none it is read 'cold' or 'blind' or 'by eye'. In general terms the proofreader's responsibilities comprise:

- checking the accuracy of the typesetter's keying
- ensuring that the transformation of the material into typeset and paginated form has not resulted in poor presentation (such as bad word breaks where words are hyphenated at line endings, a short line at the top of a page, a table, figure, or illustration wrongly positioned, or a running head on a page that should have none)
- checking the integrity of the design—that is, ensuring that all like elements have been set in like manner (the proofreader is not asked to verify the technical implementation of the design, only to check by eye that it has been consistently applied)
- ensuring that page references (for example, on the contents page or in cross-references) have been correctly converted from the numbers of the typescript folios to those of the typeset pages.

The changes marked on the first proof are executed by the typesetter and a revised proof is generated for checking by the proofreader. Several stages of correcting and checking may be needed before the material can be **passed for press** or signed off as ready to be printed and bound.

2.2 Marking copy

Copy-editing practice varies depending on the production method used to turn the author's script into typeset form. When material is edited on paper, a form of markup adapted from the proof-correction symbols is used. Codes identifying the different elements of the text that the designer needs to specify are written in the left-hand margin. Cues locating the position of non-text items, such as illustrations and figures, are best placed in the right-hand margin. Instructions for the setter may be written in any convenient position where the setter will see them before keying the matter to which they relate. Codes, cues, and instructions should all be circled: by convention, circled material is observed by the setter but not itself set in type.

If the script is to be entirely rekeyed, all corrections to the text itself are best positioned in the body of the material, above or (if there is space) on the line of type, so that the setter can readily see how they are to be integrated. It is more usual today to make use of the author's original disk, which obviates the rekeying of the whole script. In this case, the typesetter is sent the author's original electronic files and a printout marked with the copy-editor's changes: the setter does not rekey the material but needs only to intervene where a change is wanted—a task that resembles correcting a proof. In this case, therefore, the copy-editor may make the substance of corrections in the margins and minimal marks in the body of the material, just as with proofreading (see 2.4); or he or she may mark the body of the material as usual but draw attention to minor changes that may be overlooked by the setter by means of a circled cross in the margin.

An example of typescript marked in the body of the text is shown in Figure 2.1.

2.3 Editorial style and house style

2.3.1 **Editorial style and decision-making**

Editorial style controls the way in which words, individual characters, and numbers are presented on the printed (or electronic) page. The essential features of editorial style relate to:

- spelling (including the use of hyphens)
- punctuation
- capitalization
- abbreviations
- treatment of numbers
- use of italic and bold type
- use of quotation marks.

All of these matters are dealt with elsewhere in this book. For spelling and hyphenation see Chapter 3; for punctuation see Chapter 4; for capitalization see Chapter 5; for abbreviations see Chapter 10; for numbers see Chapter 11; for the uses of italic type see Chapter 7; for quotation marks see 4.14 and 9.2.3.

Other conventions that are the subject of editorial decisions include:

- the components and typographic style of bibliographic citations
- the content of notes and in-text references and their relation to bibliographic citations

- the editorial treatment of displayed epigraphs and quotations and their sources
- the punctuation of lists
- the style of in-text references to non-text items such as illustrations, figures, and tables
- the order and contents of prelims and end matter
- the content of running heads.

For coverage of bibliography see Chapter 18; for notes and in-text references see Chapter 17; for quotations see Chapter 9; for lists and tables see Chapter 15; for illustrations and figures see Chapter 16; for prelims, end matter, and running heads see Chapter 1.

Stylistic precepts come into play only where there are alternative solutions of equal or comparable validity. For example, a style decision is needed between 'co-operate' and 'cooperate', each of which is a viable spelling of the word; a choice must be made between 'sine qua non' (roman) and '*sine qua non*' (italic), either of which can be defended. It follows, therefore, that no appeal need be made to stylistic conventions or record kept of them where text is incorrect—for example, a place name beginning with a lower-case letter is not in normal circumstances the subject of a style decision—or where orthodox practice makes a mode of presentation all but incorrect: for example, to style the title of a published book other than in italic in open text would be so unusual as to be tantamount to an error.

It is important to recognize that style decisions are 'made' by leaving text unchanged as well as by changing it; the copy-editor must identify forms that are diagnostic of particular style points and record them explicitly for application throughout the script. The following example contains a number of implicit style decisions:

> In 1539 the monastery was 'dissolved', and the Abbot, in distress of mind— recognising that there was no alternative but to co-operate with the King's officers—blessed his monks (they numbered fifty-seven), prayed with them, and sent them out from the abbey gates to follow their vocation in the world.

If this passage were left unaltered the editor would have 'decided':

- to use single quotation marks
- to capitalize the titles of office holders (*Abbot*, *King*)

- not to capitalize informal references to institutions (*monastery, abbey*)
- to use closed em rules for parenthetical dashes
- to use *-ise* not *-ize* endings
- to spell out numbers (or, at least, those up to 100)
- to use the serial comma.

Stylistic consistency is an important characteristic of published material because it removes one possible cause of interference between the text and the reader. Inconsistent styling, whether of the words themselves or their presentation on the page, may distract or even mislead, and can affect the credibility of a publication, just as a work that is well finished in these respects can project an air of general reliability.

2.3.2 House style

A publisher's house style embodies its preference for how copy is set and laid out on the page. It thus encompasses some elements that control design as well as editorial presentation, including:

- the layout of headings, paragraphs, quotations, lists, and notes
- the make-up of typeset pages
- the application of hyphenation at line endings.

Some or all aspects of the publisher's house style are usually set out in a **style sheet** or **style guide**. Ideally this document will form part of the instructions sent to authors, so that they can follow the house style in creating the work. If this is not done, or if authors follow a different style, it may be necessary for the copy-editor to change the editorial style of the work in the course of editing it.

In some cases—where consistency across multiple publications is important to the integrity of the material—house style or an appropriate adaptation of it should always be imposed; examples include:

- issues of a journal
- individual volumes in a multi-volume publication (including reference works)
- closely integrated series.

How much importance is attached to house style in the case of separate works, however, depends on the policy and traditions of the publisher. In some cases it may be unnecessary or even unwarrantable to impose house style. Where an author has attended carefully and consistently to editorial style and the conventions pose no practical difficulties they may be best left alone: the copy-editor can probably spend editorial time more usefully than in overturning a serviceable and watertight system of editorial decisions, and an imperfect conversion of the author's to the publisher's style will damage rather than improve the work. On the other hand two factors should be noted: it is easier for an experienced copy-editor to impose a familiar house style than to learn an author's style and to check that it has, in fact, been consistently applied; further, those handling the later stages of a book's production may assume that house style has been used and may unwittingly compromise the consistency of the text by making corrections that match house style rather than the author's own style.

Even when house style is in use, it may need to be adapted to the special requirements of particular works. For example, in a historical context modern spellings of place names might be inappropriate; and in a specialist context general practice should not supplant scholarly usage of foreign words or technical terms.

2.3.3 **Editorial style sheets**

No house style, however detailed, will cater for all the editorial or design decisions needed to set a publication in type. Just as the designer needs to create a typographic specification for every book, so the copy-editor needs to record particular decisions on editorial style for every book, sometimes supplementing the house-style guidelines, sometimes preparing a completely new set of 'rules' that govern the text. When the editing task is complete the copy-editor should produce a fair copy of this unique style sheet, setting out the editorial decisions that have been made and applied to the text as a whole. The document has many uses. In its rough form it is, of course, crucial to the copy-editor's own work as a record of decisions that have been made—no editor can hold the minutiae of editorial style in his or her head through an entire script. In its finished form it may be sent to the author as a convenient means of accounting for minor changes made throughout the work. Some publishers send the editorial style sheet to the typesetter for reference. The proofreader ought to receive the style sheet with the proofs so that he or she can tell whether particular style points have been considered and decided by the copy-editor. And the style sheet should be preserved for use by the editor of a future edition of the book or of a related volume.

There are different ways of presenting editorial decisions in a style sheet, but for purposes of easy retrieval and comprehension by those who work on the text after the copy-editor a generic approach is clearest. Under headings such as:

- spelling and hyphenation
- punctuation
- capitalization
- abbreviations
- numbers
- italics
- quotation marks

the copy-editor should record high-level decisions, subordinate decisions, and individual examples. So, for example, the section on spelling and hyphenation might begin with a statement that British English spelling is used and that a particular dictionary is taken as the authority; next, decisions on particular words or groups of words should be recorded (such as those with the suffix *-ize* or *-ise*); and finally a list of examples (ordered alphabetically) will be needed. The section on numbers would start with a general statement about the threshold chosen for changing from words to numerals, and go on to list exceptions (such as dates, round numbers, numbers used with units of measure).

2.4 Marking proofs

The symbols now used to correct proofs in British publishing are those set out in BS 5261, Part 2: 2005. An earlier standard, vestiges of which persist in many authors' and proofreaders' practice, used verbal instructions (such as 'itals' to change the type style to italic) and some different symbols (such as # to indicate a word space). While adherence to the current system is recommended, the only essential

ORIGINAL TYPESCRIPT
COPY

Adapted from Johnson's Typographia (1824), vol.ii, p.216.

Though a variety of opinions exist as to the individual by whom the Art of Printing was first discovered; yet all authorities concur in admitting PETER SCHEOFFER to be the person who invented cast metal types, having learned the art of cutting the letters from the Gutenbergs: he is also supposed to have been the first who engraved on copper plates. The following testimony is preserved in the family by Jo. Fred. faustus of Ascheffenburg:

'Peter Schoeffer of Gernsheim, perceiving his master Faust's design, and being desirous ardently himself to improve the Art, found out (by the good providence of God) the method of cutting (incidendi) the characters on a matrix, that the letters might easily be singly cast, in stead of being cut. He privately cut matrices for the whole alphabet and when he showed his master the letters cast from these matrices faust was so pleased with the contrivance that he promised Peter to give him his only daughter Christina in marriage, a promise which he soon after performed.

But there were as many difficulties at first with these letters, as there had been before with wooden ones; the metal being too soft to support the force of the impression: But this defect was soon remedied by mixing with a substance the metal which sufficiently hardened it.

Figure 2.1 **Marked-up typescript copy**

MARKS USED IN THE CORRECTION OF PROOFS

Adapted from Johnson's Typographia (1824), vol. ii, p. 216.

Though a variety of opinions exists as to the individual by whom the Art of printing was first discovered; yet all authorities concur in admitting PETER SCHOFFER to be the person who inverted *cast metal types*, having learned the art of *cutting* the letters from the Guttenbergs: he is also supposed to have been the first who engraved on copper-plates. The following testimony is preserved in the family by Jo. Fred. Faustus of Ascheffenberg:

'PETER SCHOEFFER of Gernsheim, perceiving his master Faust's design, and being himself ardently desirous to improve the art, found out (by the good providence of god) the method of cutting (*incidendi*) the characters in a *matrix*, that the letters might easily by singly *cast*, instead of being *cut*. He privately cut *matrices* for the whole alphabet: and when he showed his master the letters cast from these matrices, faust was so pleased with the contrivance that he promised Peter to give him only his daughter *Christina* in marriage, a promise which he soon after performed.

But there were as many difficulties as first with these letters as there had been before with wooden ones; the metal being too soft to support the force of the impression: but this defect was soon remedied by mixing the metal with a substance which sufficiently hardened it.'

Figure 2.2 **Proofread proof**

THE PROOFREAD PAGE CORRECTED

Adapted from JOHNSON's *Typographia* (1824),
vol. ii, p. 216.

Though a variety of opinions exist as to the individual by whom the art of printing was first discovered; yet all authorities concur in admitting PETER SCHOEFFER to be the person who invented *cast metal types*, having learned the art of *cutting* the letters from the Guttembergs: he is also supposed to have been the first who engraved on copper-plates. The following testimony is preserved in the family, by Jo. Fred. Faustus of Ascheffenburg:

'PETER SCHOEFFER of Gernsheim, perceiving his master Faust's design, and being himself ardently desirous to improve the art, found out (by the good providence of God) the method of cutting (*incidendi*) the characters in a *matrix*, that the letters might easily be singly *cast*, instead of being *cut*. He privately *cut matrices* for the whole alphabet: and when he showed his master the letters cast from these matrices, Faust was so pleased with the contrivance that he promised Peter to give him his only daughter *Christina* in marriage, a promise which he soon after performed. But there were as many difficulties at first with these letters, as there had been before with *wooden ones*; the metal being too soft to support the force of the impression: but this defect was soon remedied by mixing the metal with a substance which sufficiently hardened it.'

Figure 2.3 **Final proof**

requirement of any correction marks is that they be comprehensible to the setter who must implement the changes they represent. If verbal instructions are used they must be circled.

The task of the proofreader in marking proofs is to attract the type-setter's attention to the presence of a correction, to locate the correction accurately in the body of the material, and to mark the correction clearly in the margin of the proof. A minimal mark is made in the body of the text and the substance of the correction in either margin. Literal errors made by the typesetter should be marked in red, and alterations and instructions made by the editor or proofreader in blue.

Figure 2.2 shows the folio illustrated in Figure 2.1 as a marked proof. Figure 2.3 shows the same page in finalized form.

2.5 Technical issues for the proofreader

2.5.1 Spacing

The height of type and of vertical spaces is measured in **points**. A **pica** is the standard unit of typographic measurement, equal to 12 points; the pica is used particularly to express the total amount of space a text will require, and the text measure (or width of a full line of type) is usually defined in picas.

Vertical spacing

Vertical or interlinear spacing within the body of the text is called **leading** (from the strips of lead formerly inserted between lines of type). The amount of leading affects readability—text that is 'set solid' (that is, without interlinear space) can be tiring to the eye, but too much leading also interferes with ease of reading, and of course takes up more space. The term 'leading' is sometimes also used to refer to the distance from the bottom of one line of type to the bottom of the next, but to avoid confusion it is better to refer to this as the **linefeed**.

The description of the type size is sometimes found on a title page verso. '11 on 12 point' or '11/12 point', for example, indicates that the lines of type are 12 points apart and the text is set in 11 point; in this case, therefore, there is leading of 1 point between the lines of type.

Justification

Copy can be arranged within the text area in one of four ways: **ranged left** (or **flush left**) so that the left-hand side is aligned but the right is uneven (**ragged right** or **unjustified**); **ranged right** so that the right-hand side is aligned and the left ragged; **justified** so that both left- and right-hand sides are aligned to the limits of the 'text measure'; or **centred** so that each line is balanced on the midpoint of the text measure.

Justified copy is produced by evenly varying the spaces between words on each line; spaces that are not permitted to vary in this way are called 'fixed' spaces (such as that between a note cue and the first word of the note) and will be detailed in the type spec. Ragged and centred text has invariable word spacing, as does poetry. Justified text characteristically employs line-end hyphenation to avoid excessive word spacing; ragged text characteristically does not employ it, or uses it to only a limited extent.

Horizontal spacing

An **em** is a unit for measuring the width of printed matter, originally reckoned as the width of a capital roman M. An em space is indicated in markup by the symbol □. The term **pica em** describes the width of a pica, that is, a 12-point space. An **en** is a unit of horizontal space equal to half an em and originally reckoned as the width of a capital roman N. For em rules and en rules see 4.11.

A **thin space** is a fifth of an em space and is usually indicated in markup by the symbol ‡ or ⸮. A **hair space** is a very thin space, thinner (sometimes by half) than a thin space. Both are used in contexts where the visual relationship of characters requires some spacing but not full word spacing (for example, where two punctuation marks follow each other). Both are fixed or invariable, and both are generally non-breaking (that is, the matter preceding and following them cannot be separated at a line ending but is treated as a single 'slug' of text).

A single word space is used after all sentence punctuation (not a double space, as was conventional in typewritten text). The typesetter should use a non-breaking word space between a pair of initials to prevent their being split across a line: for example, *T. S.* | *Eliot* (not *T.* |

S. Eliot). The same device should be used to link abbreviations and numbers that belong together: *3 km, pp. 6-10*, etc.

The first line of a paragraph should be indented (except the first after a heading, epigraph, or section break, which is set full out to the left); the style of setting in which paragraphs are separated by a space and the first line of each new paragraph is set full out to the left is used in reports and other documents and some kinds of reference work.

2.5.2 General principles for typeset matter

Besides checking the accuracy of the typesetter's work, the proof-reader is charged with ensuring that the page is presented so as to be easy to read and pleasing to the eye. To this end some generally accepted rules have become established, though the extent to which they are adhered to depends on circumstances and design consider-ations.

Short lines

Traditionally, printers ensured that the last line of a paragraph did not consist of a single syllable, or numerals alone, or a word of fewer than five characters. This rule is no longer followed strictly, but others controlling the position on the page of short lines are still usually observed. The last line of a paragraph should not fall at the top of a new page or column: this is known as a **widow**. An **orphan**—the first line of a paragraph that falls at the bottom of a page or column—is undesirable, though it is now tolerated in most bookwork.

Line endings

No more than two successive lines should begin or end with the same word. Although practice is now less carefully controlled than for-merly, most publishers set a limit to the number of lines in succession that may end with hyphens (typically, not more than three or four). The last line on a recto page should not end with a hyphen, and trad-itionally should not end with a colon that introduces displayed matter on the following page, although this standard is generally not adhered to today. Columns, lists, etc. should ideally not be split; if they are split the break should be in as unobtrusive a place as possible. For infor-mation on word division see 3.4.

Page depth

Pages should all be the same depth, so that matter aligns across the head and foot of the spread. The same provision applies to columns in multi-column setting. If absolutely necessary to avoid awkward page breaks, facing pages may be made a line short or long. Complete pages of material set in a type size different from that of the main text (appendices, notes, etc.) should be made up to the depth of the text page, to the nearest line.

Vertical spacing

Interlinear spacing between the lines of type should be uniform in normal texts. Where non-text items occur, extra space (or 'style space') is left between the illustration, figure, or table and the surrounding text. In the interests of preserving a constant page depth or avoiding awkward page breaks, style space may be slightly reduced or increased at need. Complex texts such as dictionaries may achieve equal page depth by varying the leading in adjacent columns of pages. See also 2.5.1.

Centred material

Centred displayed material should be set with invariable word spacing and each line should be separately centred. Wherever possible a short single word standing alone on the last line should be avoided.

CHAPTER 3

Spelling and hyphenation

3.1 Spelling

3.1.1 **General principles**

A good dictionary such as the *Concise Oxford English Dictionary* or the *Oxford Dictionary of English* should be consulted on matters of spelling and inflection; for American texts a US dictionary such as the *Oxford American Dictionary* is indispensable. The dictionary will give guidance on recommended spellings and acceptable variants, and cover irregular or potentially problematic inflections. The main rules of spelling and inflection are outlined below.

English has an exceptional tolerance for different spellings of the same word. Some, such as *bannister* and *banister*, are largely interchangeable, although a dictionary will always indicate which is the preferred or dominant version. Other words tend to be spelled differently in different contexts: for instance, *judgement* is spelled thus in general British contexts, but is spelled *judgment* in legal contexts and American English. On the other hand, *accomodation* and *millenium* are commonly encountered in print but are not regarded as correct or acceptable spellings of *accommodation* and *millennium*.

Unless specifically instructed to follow the preferred spellings of a particular dictionary, an editor does not generally need to alter instances where a writer has consistently used acceptable variants, such as *co-operate* or *caviare*, rather than the preferred spellings, which in current Oxford dictionaries are *cooperate* and *caviar*. However, comparable or related words should be treated similarly: for instance, if *bureaus* rather than *bureaux* is used then prefer *chateaus* to *chateaux*, and standardize on -ae- spellings in words such as *mediaeval* if the author has consistently written *encyclopaedia*. For more on house style and editorial style see 2.3.1 and 2.3.2.

3.1.2 **British and American spelling**

Certain general tendencies can be noted in US spelling:

- *e* where British English has *ae* and *oe*: *esthete, ameba, estrogen, toxemia, hemoglobin*
- *-ense* for *-ence*: *defense, offense, pretense, license* (noun and verb)
- *-er* for *-re*: *center, theater, ocher, miter, scepter*
- *f* for *ph*: *sulfur, sulfide, sulfate*
- *k* for *c*: *skeptic, mollusk*
- *-ll* for *-l*: *appall, fulfill, distill, enroll*
- *o* for *ou*: *mold, molt, smolder*
- *-og* for *-ogue*: *analog, catalog* (see 3.1.7)
- *-or* for *-our*: *color, honor, labor, neighbor, harbor, tumor*
- *z* for *s*: *analyze, paralyze, cozy* (but *advise, surprise*).

Further details are given in the following sections.

3.1.3 **Verbs ending in** *-ise* **or** *-ize*

For most verbs that end with *-ize* or *-ise*, either termination is acceptable in British English. The ending *-ize* has been in use in English since the 16th century, and is not an Americanism, although it is the usual form in American English today. The alternative form *-ise* is far more common in British than it is in American English. Whichever form is chosen, ensure that it is applied consistently throughout the text.

Oxford University Press has traditionally used *-ize* spellings. These were adopted in the first editions of the *Oxford English Dictionary*, *Hart's Rules*, and the *Authors' and Printers' Dictionary* (the predecessor of the *Oxford Dictionary for Writers and Editors*). They were favoured on both phonetic and etymological grounds: *-ize* corresponds more closely to the Greek root of most *-ize* verbs, *-izo*.

For some words, however, *-ise* is obligatory: first, when it forms part of a larger word element such as *-cise* (= cutting), *-mise* (= sending), *-prise* (= taking), or *-vise* (= seeing); and second, when it corresponds to nouns with *-s-* in the stem, such as *advertise* and *televise*. Here is a list of the commoner words in which an *-ise* ending must be used in both British and American English:

advertise	advise	apprise	arise
chastise	circumcise	comprise	compromise
demise	despise	devise	disenfranchise
disguise	enfranchise	enterprise	excise
exercise	improvise	incise	merchandise
premise	prise [open]	revise	supervise
surmise	surprise	televise	

In British English, words ending -*yse* (*analyse, paralyse*) cannot also be spelled -*yze*. In American English, however, the -*yze* ending is usual (*analyze, paralyze*).

3.1.4 -*ie*- and -*ei*-

The well-known spelling rule '*i* before *e* except after *c*' is generally valid when the combination is pronounced -*ee*-:

believe	brief	ceiling	conceit	deceive	fiend
hygiene	niece	priest	receipt	receive	siege

There are exceptions, notably *seize*. *Caffeine, codeine,* and *protein* are all formed from elements ending in -*e* followed by -*in* or -*ine*, and *plebeian* is from the Latin *plebeius*.

The rule is not valid when the syllable is pronounced in other ways, as in *beige, freight, neighbour, sleigh, veil, vein,* and *weigh* (all pronounced with the vowel as in *lake*), in *eider, feisty, height, heist, kaleidoscope,* and *sleight* (all pronounced with the vowel as in *like*), and in words in which the *i* and *e* are pronounced as separate vowels, such as *holier* and *occupier*.

3.1.5 -*able* and -*ible*

The rules governing adjectives that end in -*able* or -*ible* relate to etymology: adjectives ending in -*able* generally owe their form to the Latin ending -*abilis* or the Old French -*able*, and words in -*ible* to the Latin -*ibilis*. When new adjectives are formed from English roots they take -*able,* as in *conceivable* and *movable*. New words are not generally formed with the -*ible* suffix.

With some exceptions, words ending in a silent -*e* lose the *e* when -*able* is added:

adorable	excusable	indispensable	movable

However, some words of one syllable keep the final *e* when its loss could lead to ambiguity:

blameable   hireable   likeable   sizeable

In words ending *-ce* or *-ge* the *e* is retained to preserve the soft *c* or *g*:

bridgeable   changeable   knowledgeable
manageable   noticeable   serviceable

whereas if the word ends with a hard *c* or *g* the ending is always *-able*:

amicable   navigable

In American usage, before a suffix beginning with a vowel the final *-e* is often omitted where in British usage it is retained, as in *salable*. But it is always retained after a soft *c* and *g*, as in British usage.

3.1.6 Nouns ending in *-ment*

When *-ment* is added to a verb which ends in *-dge*, the final *e* is retained in British English:

abridgement
acknowledgement
judgement (but note that *judgment* is the usual form in legal contexts)

In American English the form without the *e* is usual (*abridgment*, *acknowledgment*, *judgment*).

3.1.7 Nouns ending in *-logue*

Some—but not all—nouns that end in *-logue* in British English end in *-log* in American English. *Analogue* and *catalogue* usually end in *-log* in America, and *dialogue* has the *-log* form as an accepted variant. Note that *epilogue*, *monologue*, *prologue*, and *travelogue* do not usually take the *-log* form, even in America (though the computing language is spelled *Prolog*).

3.1.8 *-ce* and *-se* endings

Practice is the spelling of the noun in both British and American English, and it is also the spelling of the verb in the US. However, in British English the verb is spelled *practise*. In Britain *licence* is the spelling of the noun and *license* of the verb, whereas in the US both the noun and the verb are *license*.

US spellings of *defence* and *pretence* are *defense* and *pretense*.

3.1.9 *-ae-* in the middle of words

The *-ae-* spellings of *encyclopaedia* and *mediaeval* are being super-
seded by the forms *encyclopedia* and *medieval*, although they are still
acceptable variants. The dated ligature *-æ-* should be avoided, although note that the title of the *Encyclopædia Britannica* is styled
thus. *Archaeology, aeon, haematology* and similar, largely technical
words retain the *-ae-* in British English, but in American English are
spelled *archeology, eon*, etc. The *-e-* spelling is predominant in technical writing, whether British or US in origin.

3.2 Inflection

The chief rules whereby words change form in order to express a
grammatical function are described below. In some cases there are
acceptable variant forms in addition to those forms shown.

3.2.1 Verbs

Verbs of one syllable ending in a single consonant double the consonant when adding *-ing* or *-ed*:

> beg, begging, begged
> rub, rubbing, rubbed

When the final consonant is *w, x,* or *y* this is not doubled:

> tow, towing, towed
> vex, vexing, vexed

When the final consonant is preceded by more than one vowel (other
than *u* in *qu*), or by a diphthong that represents a long vowel, the consonant is not normally doubled:

> appeal, appealing, appealed
> boil, boiling, boiled
> clean, cleaning, cleaned
> conceal, concealing, concealed
> reveal, revealing, revealed

Verbs of more than one syllable ending in a single consonant double
the consonant when the stress is placed on the final syllable:

> allot, allotting, allotted
> occur, occurring, occurred

Verbs that do not have stress on the final syllable do not double the consonant:

> benefit, benefiting, benefited
> focus, focusing, focused
> gallop, galloping, galloped
> offer, offering, offered
> profit, profiting, profited

Exceptions in British English are:

> input, inputting, input *or* inputted
> output, outputting, output *or* outputted
> kidnap, kidnapping, kidnapped
> worship, worshipping, worshipped

US English allows *kidnaping, kidnaped* and *worshiping, worshiped*, although these spellings are variants rather than standard forms.

Verbs ending in *-l* normally double the *l* in British English regardless of where the stress occurs in the word:

> annul, annulling, annulled
> enrol, enrolling, enrolled
> grovel, grovelling, grovelled
> travel, travelling, travelled

Exceptions in British English are:

> parallel, paralleling, paralleled

In American English the final *l* generally doubles only when the stress is on the final syllable. So words such as *annul* and *enrol* inflect the same way in America as they do in Britain, but verbs such as the following are different:

> grovel, groveling, groveled
> travel, traveling, traveled
> tunnel, tunneling, tunneled

Americans sometimes spell the basic form of the verb with *-ll* as well (*enroll, fulfill*).

Note that *install* has a double *l* in both British and American English, but *instalment* has a single *l* in Britain and doubles it in the US.

Verbs generally drop a final silent *e* when the suffix begins with a vowel:

> argue, arguing, argued
> continue, continuing, continued

But a final *e* is usually retained to preserve the soft sound of the *g* in *ageing*, *twingeing*, *whingeing*, *singeing* (from *singe*), and *swingeing*; the latter two are thus distinguished from the corresponding form *singing* (from *sing*) and *swinging* (from *swing*). An *e* is added to *dyeing* (from *dye*) to distinguish it from *dying* (from *die*).

A group of verbs—*burn*, *learn*, *spell*—have an orthodox past tense and past participle ending in *-ed*, but in British English also have an alternative form ending in *-t* (*burnt*, *learnt*, *spelt*). Note that the past of *earn* is always *earned*, never *earnt*, and that of *deal* is *dealt*, not *dealed*, in both British and American English.

3.2.2 Plurals of nouns

Nouns ending in *-y* form plurals with *-ies* (*policy*, *policies*), unless the ending is *-ey*, in which case the plural form is normally *-eys* (*valley*, *valleys*).

Proper names ending in *-y* retain it when pluralized, and do not need an apostrophe:

> the Carys
> the three Marys

Nouns ending in *-f* and *-fe* form plurals sometimes with *-fs* or *-fes*:

> handkerchief, handkerchiefs
> proof, proofs
> roof, roofs
> safe, safes

sometimes *-ves*:

> calf, calves
> half, halves
> knife, knives
> shelf, shelves

and occasionally both *-fs* and *-ves*:

> dwarf, dwarfs *or* dwarves
> hoof, hoofs *or* hooves

Nouns ending in -o

There is no fixed system for the plurals of nouns that end in *-o*. As a guideline, the following typically form plurals with *-os*:

- words in which a vowel (usually *i* or *e*) precedes the final *-o* (*trios*, *videos*)

- words that are shortenings of other words (*demos*, *hippos*)
- words introduced comparatively recently from foreign languages (*boleros*, *placebos*)
- words of many syllables (*aficionados*, *manifestos*)
- proper names used allusively (*Neros*, *Romeos*).

Names of animals and plants normally form plurals with *-oes* (*buffaloes*, *tomatoes*). In other cases practice varies quite unpredictably: *kilos* and *pianos*, *dominoes* and *vetoes* are all correct. With some words a variant is well established; for example, both *mementoes* and *mementos* are used.

Compound nouns

Compound words formed by a noun and an adjective, or by two nouns connected by a preposition, generally form their plurals by a change in the key word:

Singular	Plural
Attorney General	Attorneys General
brother-in-law	brothers-in-law
commander-in-chief	commanders-in-chief
court martial	courts martial *or* court martials
cul-de-sac	cul-de-sacs *or* culs-de-sac
father-in-law	fathers-in-law
fleur-de-lis	fleurs-de-lis
Governor General	Governors General
Lord Chancellor	Lord Chancellors
man-of-war	men-of-war
mother-in-law	mothers-in-law
passer-by	passers-by
Poet Laureate	Poets Laureate *or* Poet Laureates
point-to-point	point-to-points
sister-in-law	sisters-in-law
son-in-law	sons-in-law

Plurals of animal names

The plurals of some animal names are the same as the singular forms, for example *deer*, *grouse*, *salmon*, *sheep*. This rule applies particularly to larger species and especially to those that are hunted or kept by humans. In some contexts the *-s* is optional: the usual plural of lion is *lions*, but a big-game hunter might use *lion* as a plural. For this reason the style is sometimes known as the 'hunting plural': it is never applied to small animals such as mice or rats.

The normal plural of *fish* is *fish*:

> a shoal of fish   he caught two huge fish

The older form *fishes* may still be used in reference to different kinds of fish:

> freshwater fishes of the British Isles

Foreign plurals

Plurals of foreign (typically Latin, Greek, or French) words used in English are formed according to the rules either of the original language:

> alumnus, alumni
> genus, genera
> nucleus, nuclei
> stratum, strata

or of English:

> arena, arenas
> suffix, suffixes

Often more than one form is in use:

> bureau, bureaus or bureaux
> chateau, chateaus or chateaux
> crematorium, crematoriums or crematoria
> referendum, referendums or referenda

Sometimes different plurals are used in different contexts, with the Latinate form typically being more appropriate in technical use. For example, the usual plural of *formula* is *formulas*, but in mathematical or chemical contexts it is *formulae*. In non-technical areas prefer the English form: for example, use *stadiums* rather than *stadia*, and *forums* rather than *fora*, unless dealing with the ancient world. Incidentally, *index* generally has the plural *indexes* in reference to books, with *indices* being reserved for statistical or mathematical contexts; conversely, *appendices* tends to be used for subsidiary tables and *appendixes* in relation to the body part. Always check such words in a dictionary if in any doubt.

Words ending in *-is* usually follow the original Latin form:

> basis, bases
> crisis, crises

3.2.3 **Adjectives**

Adjectives that form comparatives and superlatives through the addition of the suffixes *-er* and *-est* are:

- words of one syllable (e.g. *fast, hard, rich*)
- words of two syllables ending in *-y* and *-ly* (e.g. *angry, early, happy*) and corresponding *un-* forms when these exist (e.g. *unhappy*). Words ending in *-y* change the *y* to *i* (e.g. *angrier, earliest*)
- words of two syllables ending in *-le* (e.g. *able, humble, noble*), *-ow* (e.g. *mellow, narrow, shallow*), and some ending in *-er* (e.g. *clever*)
- some words of two syllables pronounced with the stress on the second syllable (e.g. *polite, profound*)
- other words of two syllables that do not belong to any classifiable group (e.g. *common, pleasant, quiet*).

Words of one syllable ending in a single consonant double the consonant when it is preceded by a single vowel

> glad, gladder, gladdest
> hot, hotter, hottest

but not when it is preceded by more than one vowel or by a long vowel indicated by a diphthong

> clean, cleaner, cleanest
> loud, louder, loudest

Words of two syllables ending in *-l* double the *l* in British English:

> cruel, crueller, cruellest

Adjectives of three or more syllables use forms with *more* and *most* (*more beautiful, most interesting*, etc.).

3.2.4 **Adverbs**

Adverbs ending in *-ly* formed from adjectives (e.g. *richly, softly, wisely*) generally do not have *-er* and *-est* forms but appear as *more softly, most wisely*, etc. Adverbs that form comparatives and superlatives with *-er* and *-est* are:

- adverbs that are not formed with *-ly* but are identical in form to corresponding adjectives (e.g. *runs faster, hits hardest, hold it tighter*)
- some independent adverbs (e.g. *soon, likely*).

3.3 Hyphenation

3.3.1 **General principles**

Since hyphenation often depends on the word's or phrase's role and its position in a sentence, and because it is to an extent dependent on adopted style or personal taste, it cannot be covered fully in a dictionary. This section sets out the basic principles and current thinking on hyphens.

3.3.2 **Soft and hard hyphens**

There are two types of hyphen. The **hard hyphen** joins words or parts of words together to form compounds (e.g. *anti-nuclear, glow-worm, second-rate*). Use of the hard hyphen is described in the rest of this section. The **soft hyphen** indicates word division when a word is broken at the end of a line; for the soft hyphen and word division see 3.4.

3.3.3 **Compound words**

A compound term may be open (spaced as separate words), hyphenated, or closed (written as one word). There is no hard-and-fast rule saying whether, for example, *airstream, air stream,* or *air-stream* is correct: all forms are found in use and none is incorrect. However, there is an increasing tendency to avoid hyphenation for noun compounds: there is, for example, a preference for *airstream* rather than *air-stream* and for *air raid* rather than *air-raid*. There is an additional preference in American English for the form to be one word and in British English for the form to be two words: for example, *end point* tends to be the commoner form in British English, while *endpoint* is commoner in American English.

It is, of course, vital to make sure that individual forms are used consistently within a single text or range of texts. If an author has consistently applied a scheme of hyphenation, an editor need not alter it, although a text littered with hyphens can look fussy and dated. Editors can find the dominant form of a particular compound in a suitable current dictionary such as the *New Oxford Dictionary for Writers and Editors*.

Some compounds are hyphenated where there is an awkward collision of vowels or consonants:

> drip-proof   take-off   part-time

but even here some are now typically written as one word:

> breaststroke   earring

Formerly in British English, a rule was followed whereby a combination of present participle and noun was spaced if the noun was providing the action (*the walking wounded*) but hyphenated if the compound itself was acted upon (*a walking-stick*—that is, the *stick* itself was not *walking*). The so-called 'walking-stick rule' is no longer borne out in common use: *walking stick* and many other such combinations (*clearing house, colouring book, dining room*) are now written as two words.

A combination of a single adjectival noun and the noun it modified was formerly hyphenated (*note-cue, title-page, volume-number*), but this practice too is less common now.

Compound modifiers that follow a noun do not need hyphens:

> the story is well known   the records are not up to date
> an agreement of long standing   poetry from the nineteenth century

but a compound expression preceding the noun is generally hyphenated when it forms a unit modifying the noun:

> a well-known story   up-to-date records
> a long-standing agreement   nineteenth-century poetry

A distinction may be made between compounds containing an adjective, such as *first class* or *low level*, and compound nouns, such as *labour market*: when compounds of the first sort are used before a noun they should be hyphenated (*first-class seats, low-level radioactive waste*), but the second sort need not be (*labour market liberalization*).

Compound adjectives formed from an adjective and a verb participle should be hyphenated whether or not they precede the noun:

> double-breasted suits   Darren was quite good-looking

Where a noun compound is two words (e.g. *a machine gun*), any verb derived from it is normally hyphenated (*to machine-gun*). Similarly, compounds containing a noun or adjective that is derived from a verb are more often hyphenated than ordinary noun or adjective compounds (e.g. *glass-making, nation-builder*).

When a phrasal verb such as *to hold up* or *to back up* is made into a noun a hyphen is added or it is made into a one-word form (*a hold-up, some backup*). Note, however, that normal phrasal verbs should not be hyphenated:

> continue to build up your pension   time to top up your mobile phone

not

> continue to build-up your pension   time to top-up your mobile phone

Do not hyphenate adjectival compounds where the first element is an adverb ending in *-ly*:

> a happily married couple   a newly discovered compound

An exception to this rule is *newly-wed* used as a noun, which is often hyphenated.

Adverbs that do not end in *-ly* should be hyphenated when used in adjectival compounds before a noun, but not after a noun:

> a tribute to the much-loved broadcaster
> Dr Gray was very well known

Do not hyphenate italic foreign phrases unless they are hyphenated in the original language:

> an *ex post facto* decision
> an *ad hominem* argument
> the collected *romans-fleuves*
> a sense of *savoir-vivre*

Once foreign phrases have become part of the language and are no longer italicized, they are treated like any other English words, and hyphenated (or not) accordingly:

> a laissez-faire policy
> a bit of savoir faire

In general do not hyphenate capitalized compounds (although see 4.11.1):

> British Museum staff
> New Testament Greek
> Latin American studies

Compound scientific terms are generally not hyphenated—they are either spaced or closed:

> herpesvirus
> radioisotope
> liquid crystal display
> sodium chloride solution

Capitalizing hyphenated compounds

When a title or heading is given initial capitals, a decision needs to bemade as to how to treat hyphenated compounds. The traditional rule is to capitalize only the first element unless the second element is a proper noun or other word that would normally be capitalized:

> First-class and Club Passengers
> Anti-aircraft Artillery

In many modern styles, however, both elements are capitalized:

> First-Class and Club Passengers
> Anti-Aircraft Artillery

3.3.4 Prefixes and combining forms

Words with prefixes are often written as one word (*predetermine*, *antistatic*), especially in American English, but use a hyphen to avoid confusion or mispronunciation, particularly where there is a collision of vowels or consonants:

anti-intellectual	de-ice	ex-directory	non-negotiable
pre-eminent	pro-life	re-entry	semi-invalid

Note that *cooperate* and *coordinate* are generally written thus, despite the collision of *os*.

A hyphen is used to avoid confusion where a prefix is repeated (*re-release*, *sub-subcategory*) or to avoid confusion with another word (*re-form/reform*, *re-cover/recover*).

Hyphenate prefixes and combining forms before a capitalized name, a numeral, or a date:

> anti-Darwinism   pseudo-Cartesian   Sino-Soviet   pre-1990s

When it denotes a previous state, *ex-* is usually followed by a hyphen, as in *ex-husband*, *ex-convict*. There is no satisfactory way of dealing with the type *ex-Prime Minister*, in which the second element is itself a compound. A second hyphen, e.g. *ex-Prime-Minister*, is not recommended, and rewording is the best option. The use of *former* instead of *ex-* avoids such problems, and is more elegant. Note that in US style an en rule is used to connect a prefix and a compound (*the post–World War I period*).

The prefix *mid-* is now often considered to be an adjective in its own right in such combinations as *the mid nineteenth century*; before a noun, of course, all compounds with *mid* should be hyphenated:

>   a mid-grey tone   a mid-range saloon car

3.3.5 Suffixes

Suffixes are always written hyphenated or closed, never spaced.

The suffixes *-less* and *-like* need a hyphen if there are already two *l*s in the preceding word:

>   bell-less   shell-like

Use a hyphen in newly coined or rare combinations with *-like*, and with names, but more established forms, particularly if short, are set solid:

>   tortoise-like   Paris-like   ladylike
>   catlike   deathless   husbandless

The suffixes *-proof*, *-scape*, and *-wide* usually need no hyphen:

>   childproof   moonscape   nationwide

When a complete word is used like a suffix after a noun, adjective, or adverb it is particularly important to use a hyphen, unless the word follows an adverb ending with *-ly*:

>   military-style 'boot camps'
>   some banks have become excessively risk-averse
>   camera-ready artwork
>   an environmentally friendly refrigerant

There can be a real risk of ambiguity with such constructions: compare

>   a cycling-friendly chief executive
>   rent-free accommodation in one of the pokey little labourer's cottages

with

>   a cycling friendly chief executive
>   rent free accommodation in one of the pokey little labourer's cottages

3.3.6 Numbers

Use hyphens in spelled-out numbers from 21 to 99:

>   twenty-three   thirty-fourth

For a full discussion of numbers see Chapter 11.

3.3.7 **Compass points**

Compass points are hyphenated:

> south-east   south-by-east   south-south-east

but the compound names of winds are closed:

> southeaster   northwesterly

In US usage individual compass points are compound words:

> southeast   south-southeast

Capitalized compounds are not usually hyphenated: note that, for example, *South East Asia* is the prevailing form in British English and *Southeast Asia* in American English.

3.3.8 **Other uses**

Use hyphens to indicate stammering, paused, or intermittent speech:

> 'P-p-perhaps not,' she whispered.
> 'Uh-oh,' he groaned.

Use hyphens to indicate an omitted common element in a series:

> three- and six-cylinder models   two-, three-, or fourfold
> upper-, middle-, and lower-class accents   countrymen and -women

When the common element may be unfamiliar to the reader, it is better to spell out each word:

> ectomorphs, endomorphs, and mesomorphs

Hyphens are used in double-barrelled names:

> Krafft-Ebing's *Psychopathia Sexualis* (*Krafft-Ebing* is one man's name)

In compound nouns and adjectives derived from two names an en rule is usual (*Marxism–Leninism*), although for adjectives of this sort a hyphen is sometimes used (*Marxist-Leninist*). A hyphen, rather than an en rule, is always used where the first element of a compound cannot stand alone as an independent word, as in *Sino-Soviet relations*. See 4.11.1.

3.4 Word division

3.4.1 **General principles**

Words can be divided between lines of printing in order to avoid unacceptably wide spaces between words (in justified setting) or at the end of a line (in unjustified setting). The narrower the column, the more necessary this becomes. Some divisions are better than others, and some are unacceptable because they may mislead or confuse the reader. Rules governing division are based on a combination of a word's construction (i.e. the parts from which it is formed) and its pronunciation, since exclusive reliance on either can yield unfortunate results. The following offers general guidance only; for individual cases, consult the *New Oxford Spelling Dictionary*. See also 2.5.2 for a discussion of the general principles of page layout and proofreading. For word division in foreign languages, see Chapter 12, under the languages concerned.

A hyphen is added where a word is divided at the end of a line. This is known as a **soft hyphen** or **discretionary hyphen**:

> con-
> trary

If a word with a hard hyphen is divided after its permanent (keyed) hyphen, no further hyphen is added:

> well-
> developed

In most texts the hyphens in the examples above (*con-trary* and *well-developed*) will use the same symbol (-). Sometimes, as in dictionaries or other reference works in which it is important for the reader to know whether an end-of-line hyphen is a permanent one or not, a different symbol, such as - (as in this book), is used when words are divided:

> con-
> trary

A tilde (˜) is also occasionally used:

> con˜
> trary

Formerly, a permanent hyphen was sometimes repeated at the start of the following line, thus:

> well-
> -developed

but this is rare nowadays.

In copy to be keyed, add a stet mark (from Latin, 'let it stand', meaning that the original form should be retained) to any permanent (hard) hyphen that falls at the end of a line, to indicate that it must be keyed.

3.4.2 **Principles of word division**

The main principle governing the guidelines that follow is that the word division should be as unobtrusive as possible, so that the reader continues reading without faltering or momentary confusion. All word divisions should correspond as closely as possible to a syllable division:

con-tact   jar-gon

However, syllable division will not be satisfactory if the result is that the first part is misleading on its own and the second part is not a complete recognizable suffix. For example, do not divide *abases*, as neither *aba-ses* nor *abas-es* are acceptable.

An acceptable division between two parts of one word may be unacceptable when applied to the same form with a suffix or prefix: *help-ful* is perfectly acceptable, but *unhelp-ful* is not as good as *un-helpful*.

The *New Oxford Spelling Dictionary* therefore uses two levels of word division—'preferred' divisions (marked |), which are acceptable under almost any circumstances, and 'permitted' divisions (marked ¦), which are not as good, given a choice. Thus *unhelpful* is shown as *un|help¦ful*.

The acceptability of a division depends to a considerable extent on the appearance of each part of the word, balanced against the appearance of the spacing in the text. For instance, even a division that is neither obtrusive nor misleading, such as *con-tact*, may be possible but quite unnecessary at the end of a long line of type, whereas a poorer division, such as *musc-ling*, may be necessary in order to avoid excessively wide word spaces in a narrow line. In justified setting, word spaces should not be so wide that they appear larger than the space between lines of type.

Whether the best word division follows the construction or the pronunciation depends partly on how familiar the word is and how clearly it is thought of in terms of its constituent parts. For instance, *atmosphere* is so familiar that its construction is subordinated to its pronunciation, and so it is divided *atmos-phere*, but the less familiar *hydrosphere* is divided between its two word-formation elements: *hydro-sphere*.

3.4.3 Special rules

Do not divide words of one syllable:

> though   prayer   helped

Do not leave only one letter at the end of a line:

> aground (*not* a-ground)

Avoid dividing in such a way that fewer than three letters are left at the start of a line:

> Briton (*not* Brit-on)
> rubbishy (*not* rubbish-y)

However, two letters are acceptable at the start of a line if they form a complete, recognizable suffix or other element:

> acrobat-ic   clean-er   vivid-ly   out-do

Nearly all words with fewer than six letters should therefore never be divided:

> again   coarse   hero   money

Divide words according to their construction where it is obvious, for example:

- between the elements of a compound word:
  > table-spoon   railway-man
- between the root word and a prefix or suffix:
  > un-prepared   wash-able

except where such a division would be severely at odds with the pronunciation:

> dem-ocracy (*not* demo-cracy)   chil-dren (*not* child-ren)
> archaeo-logical *but* archae-ologist   psycho-metric *but* psych-ometry
> human-ism *but* criti-cism   neo-classical *but* neolo-gism

When the construction of a word is no help, divide it after a vowel, preferably an unstressed one:

> preju-dice   mili-tate   insti-gate

or between two consonants or two vowels that are pronounced separately:

> splen-dour   Egyp-tian   appreci-ate

Divide after double consonants if they form the end of a recognizable element of a word:

> chill-ing   watt-age

but otherwise divide between them:

> shil-ling   soul-less   admit-ting   un-natural

Words ending in *-le*, and their inflections, are best not divided, but the last four letters can be carried over if necessary:

> brin-dled   rat-tled

With the present participles of these verbs, divide the word after the consonant preceding the *l*:

> chuck-ling   trick-ling

or between two identical preceding consonants:

> puz-zling

Divide most gerunds and present participles at *-ing*:

> carry-ing   divid-ing   tell-ing

Avoid divisions that might affect the sound, confuse the meaning, or merely look odd:

> exact-ing (*not* ex-acting)   co-alesce (*not* coal-esce)
> le-gend (*not* leg-end)   lun-ging (*not* lung-ing)
> re-appear (*not* reap-pear)   re-adjust (*not* read-just)

Words that cannot be divided at all without an odd effect should be left undivided:

> cliquey
> sluicing
> breeches
> preaches

Hyphenated words are best divided only at an existing hard hyphen but can, if necessary, be divided a minimum of six letters after it:

> counter-revolution-
> ary

Even where no hyphen is involved, certain constraints must be observed on line breaks:

• Divide abbreviations and dates only after a hard hyphen or an en rule:

> UNESCO
> AFL-|CIO
> 1914–|18

Numbers should not be divided, even at a decimal point: *643.368491*. However, very large numbers containing commas may be divided (but not hyphenated) after a comma, though not after a single digit: *6,493,|000,000.* They cannot be divided at the same places if written with spaces instead of commas: *6 493 000 000.*

- Do not separate numbers from their abbreviated units:

    15 kg   300 BC

- If possible, do not separate a person's initials from their surname, and do not split two initials; a single initial should certainly not be separated from the surname.

- Do not separate a name from a following modifier:

    Louis XIV   Samuel Browne, Jr.

CHAPTER 4

Punctuation

4.1 Introduction

This chapter deals with particular situations where punctuation can be problematic or may be treated in different ways. It does not attempt to give a full account of the ways that punctuation is used in English. Some sections—such as those on the comma splice and on the use of apostrophes to form plurals—give guidance on correct usage, and explain styles that must be followed in order to write good English. Other sections, for example that on the serial comma, describe situations where a number of styles are possible but where a particular one should be adopted in order to produce a consistent text or adhere to a particular house style.

4.2 Apostrophe

4.2.1 **Possession**

Use *'s* to indicate possession after singular nouns and indefinite pronouns (for example *everything, anyone*):

> the boy's job   the box's contents   anyone's guess

and after plural nouns that do not end in *s*:

> people's opinions   women's rights

With singular nouns that end in an *s* sound, the extra *s* can be omitted if it makes the phrase difficult to pronounce (*the catharsis' effects*), but it is often preferable to transpose the words and insert *of* (*the effects of the catharsis*).

Use an apostrophe alone after plural nouns ending in *s*:

> our neighbours' children   other countries' air forces

An apostrophe is used in a similar way when the length of a period of time is specified:

> a few days' holiday   three weeks' time

but notice that an apostrophe is not used in adjectival constructions such as *three months pregnant*.

Use an apostrophe alone after singular nouns ending in an *s* or *z* sound and combined with *sake*:

> for goodness' sake

Note that *for old times' sake* is a plural and so has the apostrophe after the *s*.

Do not use an apostrophe in the possessive pronouns *hers, its, ours, yours, theirs*:

> a friend of yours   theirs is the kingdom of heaven

Distinguish *its* (a possessive meaning 'belonging to it') from *it's* (a contraction for 'it is' or 'it has'):

> give the cat its dinner   it's been raining

In compounds and *of* phrases, use *'s* after the last noun when it is singular:

> my sister-in-law's car   the King of Spain's daughter

but use the apostrophe alone after the last noun when it is plural:

> the Queen of the Netherlands' appeal   Tranmere Rovers' best season

A **double possessive**, making use of both *of* and an apostrophe, may be used with nouns relating to living beings or with personal names:

> a speech of Churchill   a speech of Churchill's

In certain contexts the double possessive clarifies the meaning of the *of*: compare *a photo of Mary* with *a photo of Mary's*. The double possessive is not used with nouns referring to an organization or institution:

> a friend of the Tate Gallery   a window of the hotel

Use *'s* after the last of a set of linked nouns where the nouns are acting together:

> Liddell and Scott's *Greek–English Lexicon*
> Beaumont and Fletcher's comedies

but repeat *'s* after each noun in the set where the nouns are acting separately:

> Johnson's and Webster's lexicography
> Shakespeare's and Jonson's comedies

An *'s* indicates residences and places of business:

> at Jane's   going to the doctor's

In the names of large businesses, endings that were originally possessive are now often acceptably written with no apostrophe, as if they were plurals: *Harrods*, *Woolworths*. This is the case even when the name of the company or institution is a compound, for example *Barclays Bank*, *Citizens Advice Bureau*. Other institutions retain the apostrophe, however, for example *Levi's* and *Macy's*, and editors should not alter a consistently applied style without checking with the author.

An apostrophe and *s* are generally used with personal names ending in an *s*, *x*, or *z* sound:

> Charles's   Dickens's   Marx's   *Bridget Jones's Diary*

but an apostrophe alone may be used in cases where an additional *s* would cause difficulty in pronunciation, typically after longer names that are not accented on the last or penultimate syllable:

> Nicholas' or Nicholas's   Lord Williams's School

Jesus's is the usual non-liturgical use; *Jesus'* is an accepted archaism.

It is traditional to use an apostrophe alone after classical names ending in *s* or *es*:

> Euripides'   Herodotus'   Mars'   Erasmus'

This style should be followed for longer names; with short names the alternative *Zeus's*, for instance, is permissible. When classical names are used in scientific or other contexts their possessives generally require the additional *s*:

> Mars' spear

but

> Mars's gravitational force

Use *'s* after French names ending in silent *s*, *x*, or *z*, when used possessively in English:

> Dumas's   Descartes's

When a singular or plural name or term is italicized, set the possessive *'s* in roman:

> the *Daily Telegraph*'s Brussels correspondent   the *Liberty*'s crew

Do not use an apostrophe in the names of wars known by their length:

> Hundred Years War

It is impossible to predict with certainty whether a place name ending in *s* requires an apostrophe. For example:

Land's End   Lord's Cricket Ground
Offa's Dyke   St James's Palace

but

All Souls College   Earls Court
Johns Hopkins University   St Andrews

Check doubtful instances in the *New Oxford Dictionary for Writers and Editors* or in a gazetteer or encyclopedic dictionary.

4.2.2 **Plurals**

Do not use the so-called 'greengrocer's apostrophe', for example *lettuce's* for 'lettuces' or *video's* for 'videos': this is incorrect. The apostrophe is not necessary in forming the plural of names, abbreviations, numbers, and words not usually used as nouns:

the Joneses   several Hail Marys   three Johns
CDs   the three Rs   the 1990s
whys and wherefores dos and don'ts

However, the apostrophe may be used when clarity calls for it, for example when letters or symbols are referred to as objects:

dot the i's and cross the t's   she can't tell her M's from her N's
find all the number 7's

Such items may also be italicized or set in quotes, with the *s* set in roman outside any closing quote:

subtract all the *x*s from the *y*s
subtract all the '*x*'s from the '*y*'s

4.2.3 **Contraction**

Use an apostrophe in place of missing letters in contractions, which are printed without spaces:

won't   we'll   will-o'-the-wisp   bo'sun

Except when copying older spellings, do not use an apostrophe before contractions accepted as words in their own right, such as *cello*, *phone*, *plane*, and *flu*.

When an apostrophe marks the elision of an initial or final letter or letters, such as *o'*, *'n'*, or *th'*, it is not set closed up to the next character, but rather followed or preceded by a full space:

rock 'n' roll

R 'n' B
it's in th' Bible
how tender 'tis to love the babe that milks me

In contractions of the type *rock 'n' roll* an ampersand may also be used: see 10.2.2.

There is no space when the apostrophe is used in place of a medial letter within a word:

learn'd   ev'ry   ma'am   o'er

Formerly *'d* was added in place of *-ed* to nouns and verbs ending in a pronounced vowel sound:

concertina'd   mustachio'd   subpoena'd   shanghai'd

but a conventional *ed* ending is now usual in such words:

subpoenaed   shanghaied

The *'d* construction is still found, usually in poetry and older typography, especially to indicate that an *-ed* is unstressed—*belov'd, bless'd, curs'd, legg'd*—rather than separately pronounced—*belovèd, blessèd, cursèd, leggèd.*

An apostrophe is still used before the suffix when an abbreviation functions as a verb:

KO's   OK'ing   OD'd

4.3 Comma

4.3.1 Restrictive and non-restrictive uses

There are two kinds of relative clause, which are distinguished by their use of the comma. A **defining** or **restrictive** relative clause cannot be omitted without affecting the sentence's meaning. It is not enclosed with commas:

Identical twins who share tight emotional ties may live longer
The people who live there are really frightened

A clause that adds information of the form *and he/she is, and it was,* or *otherwise known as* (a **non-restrictive** or **non-defining** clause) needs to be enclosed with commas. If such a clause is removed the sentence retains its meaning:

Identical twins, who are always of the same sex, arise in a different way
The valley's people, who are Buddhist, speak Ladakhi

Note that in restrictive relative clauses either *which* or *that* may be used, but in non-restrictive clauses only *which* may be used. Restrictive:

> They did their work with a quietness and dignity which he found impressive
>
> They did their work with a quietness and dignity that he found impressive

Non-restrictive:

> This book, which is set in the last century, is very popular with teenagers

In US English *which* is used only for non-restrictive clauses.

Similar principles apply to phrases in parenthesis or apposition. A comma is not required where the item in apposition is **restrictive** or **defining**—in other words, when it defines which of more than one people or things is meant:

> The ancient poet Homer is credited with two great epics
>
> My friend Julie is absolutely gorgeous

Note, however, that when the name and noun are transposed commas are then required:

> Homer, the ancient poet, is credited with two great epics
>
> Julie, my friend, is absolutely gorgeous

Use a comma or commas to mark off a non-defining or non-restrictive word, phrase, or clause which comments on the main clause or supplies additional information about it. Use a pair of commas when the apposition falls in the middle of a sentence; they function like a pair of parentheses or dashes, though they imply a closer relationship with the surrounding text:

> I met my wife, Dorothy, at a dance
>
> Their only son, David, was killed on the Somme

Ensure that a parenthetical phrase is enclosed in a pair of commas; do not use one unmatched comma:

> Poppy, the baker's wife, makes wonderful spinach and feta pies

not

> Poppy, the baker's wife makes wonderful spinach and feta pies

Do not use a comma when what follows has become part of a name:

> Dave, the builder from down the road, said ...

but

> Bob the Builder

4.3.2 Comma splice

A comma alone should not be used to join two main clauses, or those linked by adverbs or adverbial phrases such as *nevertheless*, *therefore*, and *as a result*. This error is called a comma splice. Examples of this incorrect use are:

> I like swimming very much, I go to the pool every week

or

> He was still tired, nevertheless he went to work as usual

This error can be corrected by adding a coordinating conjunction (such as *and*, *but*, or *so*) or by replacing the comma with a semicolon or colon:

> I like swimming very much, and go to the pool every week
> He was still tired; nevertheless he went to work as usual

4.3.3 After an introductory clause or adverb

When a sentence is introduced by an adverb, adverbial phrase, or subordinate clause, this is often separated from the main clause with a comma:

> Despite being married with five children, he revelled in his reputation as a rake
> Surprisingly, Richard liked the idea

This is not necessary, however, if the introductory clause or phrase is a short one specifying time or location:

> In 2000 the hospital took part in a trial involving alternative therapy for babies
> Before his retirement he had been a mathematician and inventor

Indeed, the comma is best avoided here so as to prevent the text from appearing cluttered. Whichever style is adopted should be implemented consistently throughout.

A comma should never be used after the subject of a sentence except to introduce a parenthetical clause:

> The coastal city of Bordeaux is a city of stone
> The primary reason that utilities are expanding their non-regulated activities is the potential of higher returns

not

> The coastal city of Bordeaux, is a city of stone
> The primary reason that utilities are expanding their non-regulated activities, is the potential of higher returns

When an adverb such as *however, moreover, therefore,* or *already* begins a sentence it is usually followed by a comma:

> However, they may not need a bus much longer
>
> Moreover, agriculture led to excessive reliance on starchy
>   monocultures such as maize

When used in the middle of a sentence, *however* and *moreover* are enclosed between commas:

> There was, however, one important difference

However is, of course, not followed by a comma when it modifies an adjective or other adverb:

> However fast Achilles runs he will never reach the tortoise

4.3.4 Commas separating adjectives

Nouns can be modified by multiple adjectives. Whether or not such adjectives before a noun need to be separated with a comma depends on what type of adjective they are. **Gradable** or **qualitative** adjectives, for example *happy, stupid,* and *large,* can be used in the comparative and superlative and be modified by a word such as *very,* whereas **classifying** adjectives like *black, mortal,* and *American* cannot.

No comma is needed to separate adjectives of different types. In the following examples *large* and *small* are qualitative adjectives and *black* and *edible* are classifying adjectives:

> a large black gibbon native to Sumatra
>
> a small edible fish

A comma is needed to separate two or more qualitative adjectives:

> a long, thin piece of wood
>
> a soft, wet mixture

No comma is needed to separate two or more classifying adjectives where the adjectives relate to different classifying systems:

> French medieval lyric poets
>
> annual economic growth

Writers may depart from these general principles in order to give a particular effect, for example to give pace to a narrative or to follow a style, especially in technical contexts, that uses few commas.

4.3.5 **Serial comma**

The presence or lack of a comma before *and* or *or* in a list of three or more items is the subject of much debate. Such a comma is known as a serial comma. For a century it has been part of Oxford University Press style to retain or impose this last comma consistently, to the extent that the convention has also come to be called the **Oxford comma**. However, the style is also used by many other publishers, both in the UK and elsewhere. Examples of the serial comma are:

> mad, bad, and dangerous to know
> a thief, a liar, and a murderer
> a government of, by, and for the people

The general rule is that one style or the other should be used consistently. However, the last comma can serve to resolve ambiguity, particularly when any of the items are compound terms joined by a conjunction, and it is sometimes helpful to the reader to use an isolated serial comma for clarification even when the convention has not been adopted in the rest of the text. In

> cider, real ales, meat and vegetable pies, and sandwiches

the absence of a comma after *pies* would imply something unintended about the sandwiches. In the next example, it is obvious from the grouping afforded by the commas that the Bishop of Bath and Wells is one person, and the bishops of Bristol, Salisbury, and Winchester are three people:

> the bishops of Bath and Wells, Bristol, Salisbury, and Winchester

If the order is reversed to become

> the bishops of Winchester, Salisbury, Bristol, and Bath and Wells

then the absence of the comma after *Bristol* would generate ambiguity: is the link between Bristol and Bath rather than Bath and Wells?

In a list of three or more items, use a comma before a final extension phrase such as *etc.*, *and so forth*, *and the like*:

> potatoes, swede, carrots, turnips, etc.
> candles, incense, vestments, and the like

It is important to note that only elements that share a relationship with the introductory material should be linked in this way. In:

> the text should be lively, readable, and have touches of humour

only the first two elements fit syntactically with *the text should be*; the sentence should rather be written:

> the text should be lively and readable, and have touches of humour

4.3.6 **Figures**

Use commas to separate large numbers into units of three, starting from the right:

> £2,200
> 2,016,523,354

For more about numbers see Chapter 11.

4.3.7 **Use in letters**

Commas are used after some salutations in letters and before the signature:

> Dear Sir, ...
> Yours sincerely, ...

US business letters use a colon after the greeting. On both sides of the Atlantic, however, punctuation is now often omitted. For more on addresses see 6.2.4.

4.3.8 **Other uses**

A comma is often used to introduce direct speech: see 9.2.2.

Depending on the structure of the sentence as a whole, a comma may or may not be used after *namely* and *for example*:

> The theoretical owners of the firm, namely the shareholders ...
> We categorized them into three groups—namely, urban, rural, or mixed

A comma is generally required after *that is*. To avoid double punctuation, do not use a comma after *i.e.* and *e.g.*

4.4 Semicolon

The semicolon marks a separation that is stronger than a comma but less strong than a full point. It divides two or more main clauses that are closely related and complement or parallel each other, and that could stand as sentences in their own right. When one clause explains another a colon is more suitable.

Truth ennobles man; learning adorns him

The road runs through a beautiful wooded valley; the railway line follows it closely

In a sentence that is already subdivided by commas, use a semicolon instead of a comma to indicate a stronger division:

He came out of the house, which lay back from the road, and saw her at the end of the path; but instead of continuing towards her, he hid till she had gone

In a list where any of the elements themselves contain commas, use a semicolon to clarify the relationship of the components:

They pointed out, in support of their claim, that they had used the materials stipulated in the contract; that they had taken every reasonable precaution, including some not mentioned in the code; and that they had employed only qualified workers, all of whom were very experienced

This is common in lists with internal commas, where semicolons structure the internal hierarchy of its components:

I should like to thank the Warden and Fellows of All Souls College, Oxford; the staff of the Bodleian Library, Oxford; and the staff of the Pierpont Morgan Library, New York

Since it can be confusing and unattractive to begin a sentence with a symbol, especially one that is not a capital letter, the semicolon can replace a full point:

Let us assume that a is the crude death rate and b life expectancy at birth; a will signal a rise in ...

4.5 Colon

The colon points forward: from a premise to a conclusion, from a cause to an effect, from an introduction to a main point, from a general statement to an example. It fulfils the same function as words such as *namely, that is, as, for example, for instance, because, as follows,* and *therefore.* Material following a colon need not contain a verb or be able to stand alone as a sentence:

That is the secret of my extraordinary life: always do the unexpected

It is available in two colours: pink and blue

Use the colon to introduce a list; formerly a colon followed by a dash :— was common practice, but now this style should be avoided unless you are reproducing antique or foreign-language typography:

> We are going to need the following: flashlight, glass cutter, skeleton key, ...
>
> She outlined the lives of three composers: Mozart, Beethoven, and Schubert

The word following a colon is not capitalized in British English (unless it is a proper name, of course), but in American English it is generally capitalized if it introduces a grammatically complete sentence:

> Mr Smith had committed two sins: First, his publication consisted principally of articles reprinted from the *London Review* ...

A colon should not precede linking words or phrases in the introduction to a list, and should follow them only where they introduce a main clause:

> She outlined the lives of three composers, namely, Mozart, Beethoven, and Schubert
>
> She gave this example: Mozart was chronically short of money

Do not use a colon to introduce a statement or a list that completes the sentence formed by the introduction:

> Other Victorian authors worth studying include Thackeray, Trollope, and Dickens

A dash can also be used in a similar way to a colon, but they are not interchangeable: a dash tends to be more informal, and to imply an afterthought or aside (see 4.11.2).

A colon is used after the title of a work to introduce the subtitle. It may be followed by a capital or a lower-case letter (Oxford style uses a capital):

> *Jordan: The Comeback*
> *Monster: The Autobiography of an L.A. Gang Member*

A colon may introduce direct speech: see 9.2.2.

4.6 Full point

The full point is also called **full stop** or, particularly in US use, **period**. Full points are used to mark the end of sentences, and in some classes of abbreviation. Do not use a full point in headings, addresses, or titles of works, even where these take the form of a full sentence:

> *All's Well that Ends Well*
> *Mourning Becomes Electra*

If the full point of an abbreviation closes the sentence, there is no second point:

> a generic term for all polished metal—brass, copper, steel, etc.
> I came back at 3 a.m.

For more on abbreviations see Chapter 10. See 9.2.3 for a discussion of the relative placing of full points and closing quotation marks.

4.7 Ellipses

An ellipsis (plural *ellipses*) is a series of points (...) signalling that words have been omitted from quoted matter, or that part of a text is missing or illegible. Omitted words are marked by three full points (*not* asterisks) printed on the line, with a space around them; they are traditionally separated by normal interword spaces in Oxford style, but today are generally set as a single character with fixed (narrower) spaces between the points (...) and a space either side in running text:

> I will not ... sulk about having no boyfriend
> Political language ... is designed to make lies sound truthful

An ellipsis at the end of an incomplete sentence is not followed by a fourth full point. When an incomplete sentence is an embedded quotation within a larger complete sentence, the normal sentence full point is added after the final quotation mark:

> I only said, 'If we could ...'.

A comma immediately before or after an ellipsis can generally be suppressed, unless it is helpful to the sense. If the sentence before an ellipsis ends with a full point it is Oxford practice to retain the point before the ellipsis, closed up to the preceding text. Every sequence of words before or after *four* points should be functionally complete. This indicates that at least one sentence has been omitted between the two sentences. If what follows an ellipsis begins with a complete sentence in the original, it should begin with a capital letter:

> I never agreed to it. ... It would be ridiculous.

For more details on the use of ellipses in presenting quoted material see 9.3.3.

Sentences ending with a question mark or exclamation mark retain these marks before or after the ellipsis:

Could we ...?
Could we do it? ... It might just be possible ...!

An ellipsis can be used to show a trailing off on the part of a speaker, or to create a dramatic or ironic effect:

The door opened slowly ...
I don't ... er ... understand

It is also used, like *etc.*, to show the continuation of a sequence that the reader is expected to infer:

in 1997, 1999, 2001 ...
the gavotte, the minuet, the courante, the cotillion, the allemande, ...

4.8 Question mark

4.8.1 **Typical uses**

Question marks are used to indicate a direct question. Do not use a question mark when a question is implied by indirect speech:

He wants to know whether you are coming
She asked why the coffee hadn't materialized

Requests framed as questions out of idiom or politeness do not normally take question marks:

May I take this opportunity to wish you all a safe journey
Will everyone please stand to toast the bride and groom

although a question mark can seem more polite than a full point:

Would you kindly let us know whether to expect you?
I wonder if I might ask you to open the window?

Matter following a question mark begins with a capital letter:

You will be back before lunch, right? About noon? Good.

although short questions that are embedded in another sentence are not followed by a capital:

Where now? they wonder

Embedded questions that are not in quotation marks are often not capitalized. The question mark follows the question at whatever point it falls in a sentence:

The question is, what are the benefits for this country? What about the energy?

When the question is presented as direct speech (whether voiced or formulated in someone's mind), it should be capitalized and set in quotation marks:

> 'Why not?' she wondered
> She wondered, 'Why not?'

Note that a question mark at the end of a sentence functions like a full point, and that double punctuation should not be used. For a full account of the use of punctuation with quotation marks see 9.2.3.

4.8.2 Use to express uncertainty

Use a question mark immediately before or after a word, phrase, or figure to express doubt, placing it in parentheses where it would otherwise appear to punctuate or interrupt a sentence. Strictly, a parenthetical question mark should be set closed up to a single word to which it refers, but with a normal interword space separating the doubtful element from the opening parenthesis if more of the sentence is contentious:

> The White Horse of Uffington (? sixth century BC) was carved ...
> Homer was born on Chios(?)

However, this distinction is probably too subtle for all but specialized contexts, and explicit rewording may well be preferable. The device does not always make clear what aspect of the text referred to is contentious: in the latter example it is Homer's birthplace that is in question, but a reader might mistakenly think it is the English spelling (*Chios*) of what is *Khios* in Greek.

A question mark is sometimes used to indicate that a date is uncertain; in this context it may precede or follow the date. It is important to ensure that the questionable element is clearly identified, and this may necessitate the use of more than one question mark. In some styles the exact spacing of the question mark is supposed to clarify its meaning, but the significance of the space may well be lost on the reader, who will not grasp the difference between the following forms:

> ? 1275–1333   ?1275–1333

or

> 1275–1333 ?   1275–1333?

It would be clearer to present the first form with two question marks and the second with one only; and in general the question mark is better placed in the after position:

1275?–1333?   1275?–1333

Similarly, care must be taken not to elide numbers qualified by a question mark if the elision may introduce a false implication: in a context where number ranges are elided, *1883–1888?* makes clear that the first date is certain but the second in question; *1883–8?* suggests that the entire range is questionable.

More refined use of the question mark, with days and months as well as years, is possible but tricky. While *10? January 1731* quite clearly throws only the day into question, *10 January? 1731* could, in theory, mean that the day and year are known but the month is only probable. In such circumstances it is almost always preferable to replace or supplement the form with some explanation:

> He made his will in 1731 on the 10th of the month, probably January (the record is unclear)

or

> He made his will on 10 January? 1731 (the document is damaged and the month cannot be clearly read)

A distinction is usually understood between the use of a question mark and *c.* (*circa*) with dates: the former means that the date so qualified is probable, the latter that the event referred to happened at an unknown time, before, on, or after the date so qualified. (Note that the period implied by *c.* is not standard: *c.*1650 probably implies a broader range of possible dates than does *c.*1653.)

A question mark in parentheses is sometimes used to underline sarcasm or for other humorous effect:

> With friends (?) like that, you don't need enemies

4.9 Exclamation mark

The exclamation mark—called an **exclamation point** in the US—follows emphatic statements, commands, and interjections expressing emotion. In mathematics, an exclamation mark is the factorial sign: $4! = 4 \times 3 \times 2 \times 1 = 24$; $4!$ is pronounced 'four factorial'. In computing it is a delimiter symbol, sometimes called a 'bang'. See Chapter 14.

Avoid overusing the exclamation mark for emphasis. Although often employed humorously or to convey character or manner in fiction, in serious texts it should be used only minimally.

As with a question mark, an exclamation mark at the end of a sentence functions like a full point, and double punctuation should not be used. For a full account of the use of punctuation with quotation marks see 9.2.3.

4.10 Hyphen

For the use of hyphens in compound words and in word division see Chapter 3.

4.11 Dashes

4.11.1 **En rule**

The en rule (–) is longer than a hyphen and half the length of an em rule. (An **en** is a unit of measurement equal to half an em and approximately the average width of typeset characters.) Many British publishers use an en rule with space either side as a parenthetical dash, but Oxford and most US publishers use an em rule.

Use the en rule closed up in elements that form a range:

> pp. 23–36   1939–45   Monday–Saturday   9.30–5.30

In specifying a range use either the formula *from … to …* or *xxxx–xxxx*, never a combination of the two (*the war from 1939 to 1945* or *the 1939–45 war*, but not *the war from 1939–45*). For more on ranges see Chapter 11.

The en rule is used closed up to express connection or relation between words; it means roughly *to* or *and*:

> Dover–Calais crossing   Ali–Foreman match
> editor–author relationship   Permian–Carboniferous boundary

It is sometimes used like a solidus to express an alternative, as in *an on-off relationship* (see 4.13.1).

Use an en rule between names of joint authors or creators to show that it is not the hyphenated name of one person. Thus *the Lloyd-Jones theory* involves two people (en rule), *the Lloyd-Jones theory* one person (hyphen), and *the Lloyd-Jones–Scargill talks* two people (hyphen and en rule).

In compound nouns and adjectives derived from two names an en rule is usual:

> Marxism–Leninism (Marxist theory as developed by Lenin)
> Marxist–Leninist theory

although for adjectives of this sort a hyphen is sometimes used. Note the difference between *Greek–American negotiations* (between the Greeks and the Americans, en rule) and *his Greek-American wife* (American by birth but Greek by descent, hyphen). Elements, such as combining forms, that cannot stand alone take a hyphen, not an en rule: *Sino-Soviet*, *Franco-German* but *Chinese–Soviet*, *French–German*.

Spaced en rules may be used to indicate individual missing letters:

> the Earl of H – – w – – d
> 'F – – – off!' he screamed

The asterisk is also used for this purpose (see 4.15).

4.11.2 Em rule

The em rule (—) is twice the length of an en rule. (An **em** is a unit for measuring the width of printed matter, equal to the height of the type size being used.) Oxford and most US publishers use a closed-up em rule as a parenthetical dash; other British publishers use the en rule with space either side.

No punctuation should precede a single dash or the opening one of a pair. A closing dash may be preceded by an exclamation or question mark, but not by a comma, semicolon, colon, or full point. Do not capitalize a word, other than a proper noun, after a dash, even if it begins a sentence.

A pair of dashes expresses a more pronounced break in sentence structure than commas, and draws more attention to the enclosed phrase than brackets:

> The party lasted—we knew it would!—far longer than planned
> There is *nothing*—absolutely nothing—half so much worth doing as simply messing about in boats

Avoid overuse of the dash in this context and the next; certainly, no more than one pair of dashes should be used in one sentence.

A single parenthetical dash may be used to introduce a phrase at the end of a sentence or replace an introductory colon. It has a less formal, more casual feel than a colon, and often implies an afterthought or aside:

> I didn't have an educated background—dad was a farm labourer
> Everyone understands what is serious—and what is not
> They solicit investments from friends, associates—basically, anyone with a wallet

Do not use it after a colon except in reproducing antique or foreign-language typography.

Use an em rule spaced to indicate the omission of a word, and closed up to indicate the omission of part of a word:

> We were approaching — when the Earl of C— disappeared

Asterisks or two or more en rules are also employed for this purpose (see 4.11.1, 4.15).

An em rule closed up can be used in written dialogue to indicate an interruption, much like an ellipsis:

> 'Does the moon actually—?'
> 'They couldn't hit an elephant at this dist—'

A spaced em rule is used in indexes to indicate a repeated word (see Chapter 19). Two spaced em rules (——) are used in some styles (including Oxford's) for a repeated author's name in successive bibliographic entries (see Chapter 18).

4.12 Brackets

The symbols ( ), [ ], { }, and < > are all brackets. Round brackets ( ) are also called **parentheses**; [ ] are **square brackets** to the British, though often simply called **brackets** in US use; { } are **braces** or **curly brackets**; and < and > are **angle brackets**. For the use of brackets in mathematics see 14.6.5.

4.12.1 **Parentheses**

Parentheses or round brackets are used for digressions and explanations, as an alternative to paired commas or dashes. They are also used for glosses and translations, to give or expand abbreviations, and to enclose ancillary information, references, and variants:

He hopes (as we all do) that the project will be successful
Zimbabwe (formerly Rhodesia)
They talked about power politics (Machtpolitik)
TLS (*Times Literary Supplement*)
£2 billion ($3.1 billion)
Geoffrey Chaucer (1340–1400)

Parentheses are also used in enumerating items in a list (see Chapter 15).

4.12.2 **Square brackets**

Square brackets [ ] are used chiefly for comments, corrections, or translations made by a subsequent author or editor:

They [the Lilliputians] rose like one man
Daisy Ashford wrote The Young Visiters [sic]

For more on the use of brackets in quotations see Chapter 9.

Square brackets are often used on the Internet in place of parentheses (round brackets).

4.12.3 **Braces**

Braces or curly brackets { } are used chiefly in mathematics, computing, prosody, music, and textual notation; their usage varies within each of these fields. A single brace may be used set vertically to link two or more lines of material together:

$$\text{The High Court of Justice} \begin{cases} \text{Queen's Bench} \\ \text{Chancery} \\ \text{the Family Division} \end{cases}$$

4.12.4 **Angle brackets**

Angle brackets $<\ >$, sometimes known as **wide** angle brackets, are used in pairs to enclose computer code or tags. They are used singly in computing, economics, mathematics, and scientific work to show the relative size of entities, the logical direction of an argument, etc. In etymology they are used singly to mean 'from, derived from' ($<$) and 'gives' or 'has given' ($>$):

$<$ Urdu *murġī* hen $<$ *murġ* bird, fowl

In mathematics and science **narrow** angle brackets $\langle\ \rangle$ are used; in these fields $<\ >$ signify 'less than' and 'greater than'. See 14.6.5.

Narrow angle brackets are also used to enclose conjecturally supplied words where a source is defective or illegible:

> He came from *Oxon*: to be ⟨pedagogue⟩ to a neighbour of mine

4.12.5 **Punctuation with brackets**

Rules governing punctuation are the same regardless of the type of bracket used. A complete sentence within brackets is capitalized and ends in a full point unless the writer has chosen to place it within another sentence:

> The discussion continued after dinner. (This was inevitable.)
> The discussion continued after dinner (this was inevitable).

No punctuation precedes the opening parenthesis except in the case of terminal punctuation before a full sentence within parentheses, or where parentheses mark divisions in the text:

> We must decide (*a*) where to go, (*b*) whom to invite, and (*c*) what to take with us

4.12.6 **Nested brackets**

In normal running text, avoid using brackets within brackets. This is sometimes inevitable, as when matter mentioned parenthetically already contains parentheses. In such cases Oxford prefers double parentheses to square brackets within parentheses (the usual US convention). Double parentheses are closed up, without spaces:

> the Chrysler Building (1928–30, architect William van Alen (*not* Allen))
> the album's original title ((*I) Got My Mojo Working* (*But It Just Won't Work on You*)) is seldom found in its entirety

References to, say, law reports and statutes vary between parentheses and square brackets; the prescribed conventions should be followed (see also Chapter 13).

4.13 Solidi and verticals

4.13.1 **Solidus**

The solidus (/, plural *solidi*) is known by many terms, such as the **slash** or **forward slash**, **stroke**, **oblique**, **virgule**, **diagonal**, and **shilling mark**. It is in general used to express a relationship between two or more things. The most common use of the solidus is as a shorthand to denote alternatives, as in *either/or*, *his/her*, *on/off*, *the New York/ New Jersey/Connecticut area* (the area of either New York, New Jersey, or Connecticut, rather than their combined area), *s/he* (she or he). The solidus is generally closed up, both when separating two complete words (*and/or*) and between parts of a word (*s/he*).

The symbol is sometimes misused to mean *and* rather than *or*, and so it is normally best in text to spell out the alternatives explicitly in cases which could be misread (*his or her*; *the New York, New Jersey, or Connecticut area*). An en rule can sometimes substitute for a solidus, as in *an on-off relationship* or *the New York–New Jersey–Connecticut area*. In addition to indicating alternatives, the solidus is used in other ways:

- to form part of certain abbreviations, such as *a/c* (account), *c/o* (care of), *n/a* (not applicable), and *24/7* (twenty-four hours a day, seven days a week)

- to indicate line breaks when successive lines of poetry are run on as a single line, though Oxford traditionally prefers to use a vertical (|) instead (see 4.13.2, 9.4.1)

- to replace the en rule for a period of one year reckoned in a format other than the 1 January to 31 December calendar extent: *49/8 BC*, *the fiscal year 2000/1*

- to separate the days, months, and years in dates: *5/2/99* (see also 11.5)

- to separate elements in Internet addresses: *http://www.oup.com/ oeddicref*.

In scientific and technical work the solidus is used to indicate ratios, as in *miles/day*, *metres/second*. In computing it is called a **forward slash**, to differentiate it from a **backward slash**, **backslash**, or **reverse solidus** (\): each of these is used in different contexts as a separator (see 14.5.3, 14.6.3).

4.13.2 **Vertical**

The vertical rule or line (|), also called the **upright rule** or simply the **vertical**, has specific uses as a technical symbol in the sciences (see 14.5.3, 14.6.5) and in specialist subjects such as prosody. More commonly, it may be used, with a space either side, to indicate the separation of lines where text is run on rather than displayed, for instance for poems, plays, correspondence, libretti, or inscriptions:

The English winter—ending in July | To recommence in August

A solidus may also be used for this purpose. When written lines do not coincide with verse lines it may be necessary to indicate each differently: in such cases use a vertical for written lines and a solidus for verse.

When more than one speaker or singer is indicated in a run-together extract, the break between different characters' lines is indicated by two verticals (set closed up to each other).

In websites, spaced vertical lines are sometimes used to separate elements in a menu:

News | History | Gallery | Music | Links | Contact

The vertical line is used in the syntax of some computing languages and scripts, and is sometimes referred to as a **pipe** (see 14.5.3).

4.14 Quotation marks

Quotation marks, also called **inverted commas**, are of two types: single (' ') and double (" "). Upright quotation marks (' or ") are also sometimes used. People writing for the Internet should note that single quotation marks are regarded as easier to read on a screen than double ones. British practice is normally to enclose quoted matter between single quotation marks, and to use double quotation marks for a quotation within a quotation:

'Have you any idea', he said, 'what "red mercury" is?'

The order is often reversed in newspapers, and uniformly in US practice:

"Have you any idea," he said, "what 'red mercury' is?"

If another quotation is nested within the second quotation, revert to the original mark, either single–double–single or double–single–double.

Displayed quotations of poetry and prose take no quotation marks. In reporting extended passages of speech, use an opening quotation mark at the beginning of each new paragraph, but a closing one only at the end of the last. For more on quotations see Chapter 9, which also covers direct speech and the relative placing of quotation marks with other punctuation.

Use quotation marks and roman (not italic) type for titles of short poems, short stories, and songs (see Chapter 8):

> 'Raindrops Keep Falling on my Head'
> 'The Murders in the Rue Morgue'

Use quotation marks for titles of chapters in books, articles in periodicals, and the like:

> Mr Brock read a paper entitled 'Description in Poetry'

But omit quotation marks when the subject of the paper is paraphrased:

> Mr Brock read a paper on description in poetry

not

> Mr Brock read a paper on 'Description in Poetry'

Quotation marks may be used to enclose an unfamiliar or newly coined word or phrase, or one to be used in a technical sense:

> 'hermeneutics' is the usual term for such interpretation
> the birth or 'calving' of an iceberg
> the weird and wonderful world of fan fiction, or 'fanfic'

They are often used as a way of distancing oneself from a view or claim, or of apologizing for a colloquial or vulgar expression:

> Authorities claim to have organized 'voluntary' transfers of population
> I must resort to a 'seat of the pants' approach
> Kelvin and Danny are 'dead chuffed' with its success

Such quotation marks should be used only at the first occurrence of the word or phrase in a work. Note that quotation marks should not be used to emphasize material.

Quotation marks are not used around the names of houses or public buildings:

> Chequers   the Barley Mow

4.15 Asterisk

A superscript asterisk * is used in text as a pointer to an annotation or footnote, especially in books that have occasional footnotes rather than a formal system of notes (see also 14.1.6). It can also indicate a cross-reference in a reference work:

> Thea *Porter and Caroline *Charles created dresses and two-piece outfits based on gypsy costume

Asterisks may be used to indicate individual missing letters, with each asterisk substituting for a missing letter and closed up to the next asterisk: *that b******!* En rules are also used for this purpose (see 4.11.1).

On websites and in emails asterisks are often used to indicate emphasis, in place of quotation marks, or to show where italicization would normally be used, for example in the titles of books or other works that are mentioned:

> The engagement, the debate, the willingness to engage—*that's* what's important

> Maybe some people can handle these little romances as *harmless fun*, but I can't

Asterisks should not be used in place of dots for ellipsis.

For uses in computing see 14.5.3; for other uses see 10.3.

CHAPTER 5

Capitalization

5.1 General principles

Capital letters in English are used to punctuate sentences, to distinguish proper nouns from other words, for emphasis, and in headings and work titles. It is impossible to lay down absolute rules for all aspects of capitalization; as with hyphenation, the capitalization of a particular word will depend upon its role in the sentence, and also to some extent on a writer's personal taste or on the house style being followed. Also, certain disciplines, especially history, have their own particular styles of capitalization. However, some broad principles are outlined below. Editors should respect the views of authors, except in cases of internal discrepancies. Both authors and editors should strive for consistency: before writing or editing too much of a work, consider the principles that should govern capitalization, and while working through the material create a style sheet showing capitalization choices, and stick to it.

Excessive use of capitals in emails and on bulletin boards is frowned upon (it is regarded as 'shouting'); on websites, words in capitals can be difficult to read, and it is better to use colour for emphasis.

For the use of capitals in work titles see 8.2.2 and 8.8. For capitalization in lists and tables see Chapter 15, in quotations and verse Chapter 9, in legal references 13.2.3, and in bibliographies 18.2.5. Small capitals are discussed at 7.5.2. For capitalization in languages other than English see Chapter 12 under the language concerned.

5.2 Sentence capitals

Capitalize the first letter of a word that begins a sentence, or the first of a set of words used as a sentence:

> This had the makings of a disaster. Never mind.
> Come on. Tell me!

Capitalize the first letter of a syntactically complete quoted sentence. If, as occasionally happens in fiction or journalism, quotation marks are not used, the first word is generally not capitalized:

> Sylvie replied, 'She's a good girl.'
> I thought, 'There goes my theory.'
> The question is, does anyone have an antidote?

Quoted single words or phrases that do not constitute a sentence are not capitalized:

> He'd say 'bye' and run down the wide school steps
> Certain young wines do not 'travel well'

For a full discussion of quotation marks and the punctuation that accompanies them see 9.2.

In British English, matter following a colon begins with a lower-case initial, unless it is a displayed quotation or extract, but in US style a capital letter may be used after a colon if it introduces a complete sentence.

5.3 Use to indicate specific references

5.3.1 **Use to create proper names**

Capital initials mark out the status of words so that the reader interprets them correctly. Ordinary proper names are usually recognizable even when they are set (through error or because of the preference of the person named) with lower-case initials. However, where a proper name consists of common nouns and qualifiers, capital initials are needed to distinguish the specific usage from a general descriptive usage. Consider the difference in meaning, conferred by the application of initial capitals, between the following usages:

> Tate Britain is the national gallery of British art
> the National Gallery contains incomparable examples of British art
> the city of London attracts millions of visitors every year
> the City (London's financial district)
> the sun sets in the west
> nationalist movements which posed a threat to the interests of the
>   West

Some words are capitalized to distinguish their use in an abstract or specific sense. In the names of religious denominations the word *church* is capitalized, as in *the Baptist Church*, but *church* has a lower-case initial in general references to buildings, as in *a Baptist church*. (Note, however, that it would be usual to capitalize the full name of a specific building, as in *Pond Street Baptist Church*.)

Similarly, *State* is capitalized when it is used in an abstract or legal sense, as in *the separation of Church and State*, and in specific names of US states (*New York State*), but a reference to states in general will have a lower-case initial: *seven Brazilian states*. There is no need to capitalize the word *government*, whether it refers to a particular body of persons or to a general concept or body.

Historians commonly impose minimal capitalization on institutional references; this may sometimes appear unconventional and should not be permitted if it will obscure genuine differences in meaning (as, for example, between *the catholic church* and *the Catholic Church*), although readers will seldom misunderstand lower-case forms in context. The style is common in, and appropriate to, much historical work, but editors should not introduce it without consulting with the author and/or publisher.

It is as well, generally, to minimize the use of capital initials where there is no detectable difference in meaning between capitalized and lower-case forms. *Left* and *right* are generally capitalized when they refer to political affiliations, but no reader would be likely to misinterpret the following in a book about British political life:

> He is generally considered to be on the left in these debates

simply because it was not capitalized as

> He is generally considered to be on the Left in these debates

Overuse of capital initials is obtrusive, and can even confuse by suggesting false distinctions.

Capitals are sometimes used for humorous effect in fiction to convey a self-important or childish manner:

> Poor Jessica. She has Absolutely No Idea.
> Am irresistible Sex Goddess. Hurrah!

5.3.2 **Formal and informal references**

When one is referring back, after the first mention, to a capitalized compound relating to a proper name, the usual practice is to revert to lower case:

Cambridge University	their university
the Ritz Hotel	that hotel
Lake Tanganyika	the lake
National Union of Mineworkers	the union
the Royal Air Force	the air force

Capitals are sometimes used for a short-form mention of the title of a specified person, organization, or institution previously referred to in full:

> the Ministry
> the University statute
> the College silver
> the Centre's policy
> the Navy's provisions

This style is found particularly in formal documents. Over the course of a book it is important to keep the practice within bounds and maintain strict consistency of treatment; it is easier to apply the rule that full formal titles are capitalized and subsequent informal references downcased.

Plural forms using one generic term to serve multiple names should be lower case:

> Lake Erie and Lake Huron
> lakes Erie and Huron
> the Royal Geographical Society and Royal Historical Society
> the Royal Geographical and Royal Historical societies
> Oxford University and Cambridge University
> Oxford and Cambridge universities

The rationale for this practice is that the plural form of the generic term is not part of the proper name but is merely a common description and thus ought not be capitalized.

5.4 Institutions, organizations, and movements

Capitalize the names of institutions, organizations, societies, movements, and groups:

the World Bank	the British Museum
the State Department	the House of Lords
Ford Motor Company	the United Nations
the Crown	War Against Want
the Beatles	

Generic terms are capitalized in the names of cultural movements and schools derived from proper names:

the Oxford Movement   the Ashcan School

Notice that the word *the* is not capitalized.

The tendency otherwise is to use lower case unless it is important to distinguish a specific from a general meaning. Compare, for example:

the Confederacy (the Union side in the American Civil War)
confederacy (*as in* 'a federation of states')
Romantic (nineteenth-century movement in the arts)
romantic (*as in* 'given to romance')

Certain disciplines and specialist contexts may require different treatment. Classicists, for example, will often capitalize *Classical* to define, say, sculpture in the fifth century BC as opposed to that of the Hellenistic era; editors should not institute this independently if an author has chosen not to do so.

5.5 Geographical locations and buildings

Capitalize names of geographical regions and areas, named astronomical and topographical features, buildings, and other constructions:

the Milky Way (*but* the earth, the sun, the moon, *except in astronomical contexts and personification*)
New England   the Big Apple   the Eternal City
Mexico City (*but* the city of Birmingham)
London Road (*if so named, but* the London road *for one merely leading to London*)
the Strait of Gibraltar   the Black Forest

the Thames Estuary (*but* the estuary of the Thames)

the Eiffel Tower   Trafalgar Square

the Bridge of Sighs   Times Square

River, *sea*, and *ocean* are generally capitalized when they follow the specific name:

the East River   the Yellow River

the Aral Sea   the Atlantic Ocean

However, where *river* is not part of the true name but is used only as an identifier it is downcased:

the Danube river

When *river* precedes the specific name it can be either upper or lower case, depending on the style adopted:

the River Thames *or* the river Thames

'The River Plate' is always capitalized, being a conventional mistranslation of *Río de la Plata* ('Silver River'). Names of well-known or previously mentioned rivers may be written without the specifying word (*the Amazon, the Mississippi*). A lower-case identifier may be added where some clarification is required—to differentiate between the Amazon river and forest, or the Mississippi river and state.

Capitalize compass directions only when they denote a recognized political or cultural entity:

North Carolina   Northern Ireland (*but* northern England)

the mysterious East   the West End

Usage in this area is very fluid, and terms may be capitalized or downcased depending on context and emphasis. For example, a book dealing in detail with particular aspects of London life might capitalize *North London, South London,* etc., while one mentioning the city merely in passing would be more likely to use *north London* and *south London*. Adjectives ending in -*ern* are sometimes used to distinguish purely geographical areas from regions seen in political or cultural terms: so

Kiswahili is the most important language of East Africa

but

Prickly acacia is found throughout eastern Africa

For treatment of foreign place names see 6.2.

5.6 Dates and periods

Capitalize the names of days, months, festivals, and holidays:

Tuesday	March	Easter
Good Friday	Ramadan	Passover
Thanksgiving	Christmas Eve	the Fifth of November
New Year's Day		

Names of the seasons are lower case, except where personified:

> William went to Italy in the summer
> O wild West Wind, thou breath of Autumn's being

Capitalize historical and geological periods:

the Bronze Age	Early Minoan
the Middle Ages (*but* the medieval period)	the Renaissance
the Dark Ages	

Modern periods are more likely to be lower case; check such instances with the *New Oxford Dictionary for Writers and Editors*:

> the space age
> the age of steam
> the jazz age
> the belle époque

Use lower case for millennia, centuries, and decades (see also 11.6):

> the first millennium   the sixteenth century   the sixties

5.7 Events

Capital initials are generally used for the formal names of wars, treaties, councils, assemblies, exhibitions, conferences, and competitions. The following examples are indicative:

the Crucifixion	the Inquisition
the Reformation	the Grand Tour
the Great Famine	the Boston Tea Party
the Gunpowder Plot	the Great Fire of London
the First World War	the Siege of Stalingrad
the Battle of Agincourt	the French Revolution
the Treaty of Versailles	the Triple Alliance
the Lateran Council	the Congress of Cambrai
the Indian and Colonial Exhibition	the One Thousand Guineas

Note that *war* and equivalent terms are capitalized when forming part of the conventional name of a specific conflict, but are lower case when part of a looser, more descriptive designation:

the Peninsular campaign
the Korean conflict

After the first mention, any subsequent references to *the war* etc. are in lower case.

5.8 Legislation and official documents

The names of laws and official documents are generally capitalized:

the Declaration of Independence   the Corn Laws

Act is traditionally capitalized even in a non-specific reference; *bill* is lower case if it is not part of a name:

a bill banning unlicensed puppy farms
the Bill of Rights
the requirements of the Act
the Factory and Workshop Act 1911

For legal citations see Chapter 13.

5.9 Honours and awards

The full formal names of orders of chivalry, state awards, medals, degrees, prizes, and the like are usually capitalized, as are (in most styles) the ranks and grades of award:

the George Cross
Companion of the Order of the Bath
Dame Commander of the Order of the British Empire
Bachelor of Music
Licentiate of the Royal Academy of Dancing
Fellow of the Royal Society
Nobel Prize for Physics
the Royal Gold Medal for Architecture

Honours relating to a non-English-speaking country usually appear with an initial capital but with all other words in lower case; ranks may be translated or given in the original language, but in either case are best set lower case:

grand officer/*grand officier* of the Légion d'honneur

5.10 Titles of office, rank, and relationship

Words for titles and ranks are generally lower case unless they are used before a name, as a name, or in forms of address:

Tony Blair, the prime minister	Prime Minister Tony Blair
he was elected prime minister	Yes, Prime Minister
the US president	President Bush
the king of England	King Henry
the queen of Castile	Queen Elizabeth
an assembly of cardinals	Cardinal Richelieu
the rank of a duke	the Duke of Wellington
a feudal lord	Lord Byron
a professor of physics	Professor Higgins
Miss Dunn, the head teacher	Head Teacher Alison Dunn
a Roman general	Good evening, General!

Exceptions to this principle are some unique compound titles that have no non-specific meaning, which in many styles are capitalized in all contexts. Examples are:

Advocate General	Attorney General
Chancellor of the Exchequer	Chief Justice
Dalai Lama	Foreign Secretary
Governor General	Holy Roman Emperor
Home Secretary	Lord Chancellor
Prince of Wales	Princess Royal
Queen Mother	

Regardless of their syntactic role, references to specific holders of a rank or title are often capitalized:

> a letter from the Prime Minister
> the Queen and Prince Philip

Use of this style can lead to difficulties in contexts where titles of office appear frequently: in such cases it is generally clearer and more consistent to stick to the rule that the title of office is capitalized only when used before the office-holder's name.

It is usual to capitalize *the Pope*. When it refers to Muhammad, *the Prophet* is capitalized (but note *an Old Testament prophet*).

Historians often impose minimal capitalization, particularly in contexts where the subjects of their writing bear titles: *the duke of Somerset*. This style can be distracting in works for a general readership.

Capitalize possessive pronouns only when they form part of the titles of a holy person, or of a sovereign or other dignitary:

Her Majesty   Their Excellencies   Our Lady   Your Holiness

Personal pronouns referring to the sovereign are capitalized only in proclamations: *We*, *Us*, *Our*, *Ours*, *Ourself*, etc.

Words indicating family relationships are lower case unless used as part of a name or in an address:

he did not look like his father   Hello, Father!
she has to help her mother   Maya tried to argue with Mother
ask your uncle   Uncle Brian

5.11 Religious names and terms

Use capitals for all references to the monotheistic deity:

Allah   the Almighty   God   the Holy Spirit
the Holy Trinity   Jehovah   the Lord   the Supreme Being

Use lower case for pronouns referring to God where the reference is clear, unless the author specifies otherwise. In any event, write *who*, *whom*, *whose* in lower case. Capitalize *God-awful*, *God-fearing*, *God-forsaken*.

Use lower case for the gods and goddesses of polytheistic religions:

the Aztec god of war   the goddess of the dawn

Capitalization of religious sacraments or rites in different religions (and contexts) is not uniform. Note, for example:

a mass   baptism   compline   bar mitzvah

but

the Mass   the Eucharist   Anointing of the Sick

5.12 Personification

Personified entities and concepts are capitalized:

O Freedom, what liberties are taken in thy name!
If the Sun and Moon should doubt, they'd immediately go out

The names of ships and other craft are traditionally female. Formerly, it was also conventional to use *she* of nations and cities in prose contexts, but this is old-fashioned, and the impersonal pronoun is now used:

> Britain decimalized its (*not* her) currency in 1971

The device is still found in poetic and literary writing:

> And that sweet City with her dreaming spires
> She needs not June for beauty's heightening

The names of characters in a play who are identified by their occupation are capitalized in stage directions and references to the text (in the text their names would generally be in small capitals):

> [**First Murderer** appears at the door]

5.13 People and languages

Adjectives and nouns denoting nationality are capitalized:

American	Austrian	French	Catalan
Cornish	Swahili	Aboriginal	

Related verbs tend to retain the capital (*Americanize*, *Frenchify*, *Hellenize*), but note that *anglicize* and *westernize* are usually lower case.

As a very general rule, adjectives based on nationality tend to be capitalized where they are closely linked with the nationality or proper noun, and lower case where the association is remote or merely allusive. For example:

Brussels sprouts	German measles	Irish setter
Turkish delight	Shetland pony	Michaelmas daisy
Afghan hound	Venetian red	

but

venetian blinds	morocco leather	italic script

However, there are many exceptions, such as *Arabic numbers*, *Chinese whispers*, *Dutch auction*, *French kissing*, and *Roman numerals*, and any doubtful instances need to be checked in a dictionary.

Note that in many European languages adjectives of nationality are lower case: the English word 'French' translates as *français* in French and *französisch* in German. See Chapter 12.

5.14 Words derived from proper nouns

Capitals are used for a word derived from a personal name or other proper noun in contexts where the link with the noun is still felt to be alive:

an Adonis	a Casanova	Dantesque	Dickensian
Homeric	Kafkaesque	Orwellian	Shakespearean

Lower case is used in contexts where the association is remote, merely allusive, or a matter of convention:

gargantuan	pasteurize	protean
quixotic	titanic	wellington boots

Some words of this type can have both capitals and lower case in different contexts:

Bohemian (of central Europe) *but* bohemian (unconventional)
Philistine (of biblical people) *but* philistine (tastes)
Platonic (of philosophy) *but* platonic (love)
Stoic (of ancient philosophy) *but* stoic (impassive)

Retain the capital letter after a prefix and hyphen:

pro-Nazi   anti-British   non-Catholic

Use lower case for scientific units and poetic metres derived from names:

ampere	joule	newton	volt
watt	alcaics	alexandrines	sapphics

In compound terms for concepts such as scientific laws the personal name only is capitalized:

Planck's law   Hodgkin's disease   Occam's razor   Halley's comet

5.15 Trade names

Capitalize proprietary terms:

Hoover	Xerox	Biro	Jacuzzi	Persil
Kleenex	Coca-Cola	Levi's	Stilton	

but write related verbs, for example *hoover* and *xerox*, with a lower-case initial.

Some company and proprietary names use unusual configurations of upper- and lower-case letters; these should be followed:

BAe   eBay   PlayStation   PostScript   QuarkXPress

5.16 Ships, aircraft, and vehicles

Capitalize names of ships and vehicles, using italics for individual names but not for types, models, or marques:

> the *Cutty Sark*
> HMS *Dreadnought*
> *The Spirit of St Louis*
> a Boeing 747 Jumbo Jet
> a Supermarine Spitfire Mk 1a
> a Mini Cooper

5.17 Names including a number or letter

It is usual to capitalize names that include a number or letter:

> Route 66   Form 3b   Flight 17   Gate 16   Room 101   Act I

CHAPTER 6

Names

6.1 References to people

6.1.1 **General principles**

Use the form of name individuals are most commonly known by, or known to prefer:

> Arthur C. Clarke (*not* Arthur Clarke *or* Arthur Charles Clarke)
> k. d. lang (*all lower-case*)
> Jimmy Carter (*not* James Earl Carter)
> George Orwell (*not* Eric Arthur Blair)

When mentioned in passing, a person's name usually need appear only in the form by which the bearer is best known. For example, a writer's married name or hereditary title is important only if the person wrote or was known by it. In text, authors need clarify titles and names altered by marriage or by any other means only to avoid confusion or to make a point:

> Michael (later Sir Michael) Tippett
> Laurence (later Lord) Olivier
> George Orwell (born Eric Arthur Blair)
> George Eliot (pseudonym of Mary Ann, later Marian, Evans)

Initials before a surname are separated by full points, with a space after each:

> J. S. Bach   E. H. Shepard   Hunter S. Thompson

although some modern designs, particularly those of newspapers, omit the full points and spaces:

> MR James   PJ Harvey   George W Bush

Normally, names given entirely in initials have points but no spaces (*J.A.S., E.H.S., J.R.R.T.*). When people are commonly known by their free-standing initials, these forms have neither points nor spaces (*FDR, LBJ*).

6.1.2 **Alternative names**

Distinguish between adopted names, pseudonyms, nicknames, and aliases.

- The owner of an **adopted name** uses it for all purposes, and may have adopted it legally. In this case, 'born', 'né(e)', 'formerly', or the like may be used:

  Marilyn Monroe, born Norma Jean Mortensen
  Joseph Conrad (formerly Teodor Józef Konrad Korzeniowski)

- **Né** (feminine form **née**), meaning 'born' in French, is used to indicate a previous forename or surname. In English it is most commonly applied to indicate a married woman's maiden name, after her adopted surname. It is not italicized:

  Susan Wilkinson (née Brown)
  Frances (Fanny) d'Arblay, née Burney
  Baroness Lee of Asheridge, née Jennie Lee

  Do not use 'née' in conjunction with pseudonyms, aliases, or nicknames, but only where the new name is adopted. Some writers differentiate between using 'née' for a married woman's maiden name and 'born' for a person's previous name changed by a process other than marriage. This distinction is acceptable, and should not be changed when consistently applied.

- A **pseudonym** is a name adopted for a specific purpose, such as a pen name or *nom de théâtre*. It can be derived from the bearer's true name, or be wholly distinct from it:

  Boz (Charles Dickens)
  Q (Sir Arthur Quiller-Couch),
  Alain-Fournier (Henri-Alban Fournier)

- A **nickname** can supplement or supplant the owner's original name

  the Sun King (Louis XIV of France)
  the Fat Controller (Sir Topham Hatt)
  Charlie 'Bird' Parker

  Through use it can eventually replace the owner's name, either occasionally (*Old Blue Eyes*, *Il Duce*), partially (*Fats Waller*, *Capability Brown*, *Grandma Moses*, *Malcolm X*), or entirely (*Howlin' Wolf*, *Muddy Waters*, *Meat Loaf*, *Twiggy*). While no rules govern whether a nickname is put in quotation marks, the tendency is for quotation marks to be used when the nickname is inserted

within or precedes another name, and not when used alone.
Sobriquet or **soubriquet** is a more formal term for a nickname.

- An **alias** is a false or assumed name, used with an intention to
  deceive. In law-enforcement reports this is indicated by *aka* ('also
  known as') before the alias.

Nicknames and other familiar terms of address are capitalized:

the Admirable Crichton	Capability Brown	the Famous Five
the Iron Duke	Al 'Scarface' Capone	Uncle Sam

6.1.3 **Identifiers**

Junior and *senior* are added to differentiate a son and father with the
same name. Each has several abbreviations (*Jun.*, *Jnr*, *Jr*; *Sen.*, *Senr*,
Snr, *Sr*). Use the abbreviation *Jr* (with a point in US use) for Americans, prefaced by a comma unless it is known that the bearer of the
name did not use one. In British usage *Jun.* is more common, and the
comma is not usual. In both cases the identifier precedes any abbreviations indicating degrees, honours, or scholarly affiliations. If for
clarity two persons of the same name need to be distinguished, the
younger may be referred to as 'junior': in this case neither a capital
initial nor an abbreviation is normally used.

Unlike *junior*, *senior* never forms part of the bearer's name and is
therefore used only as an ad hoc designation for purposes of clarifying
identities. Although abbreviated forms exist (see above), the spelled-
out form, with a lower-case initial, is normally used.

In French '*fils*' is an ad hoc designation added after a surname to
distinguish a son from a father, as 'Dumas *fils*'; '*père*' does the same
to distinguish a father from a son, as 'Dumas *père*'. Both are italic in
English.

6.1.4 **Titles**

Titles that follow a name are separated from it by a comma. Abbreviated titles of honour, such as *MBE* and *FRS*, are usually in capitals,
with a comma preceding the first and separating each subsequent
title. As with other such abbreviations (see Chapter 10), abbreviated
titles composed of all-capital letters have no full points in modern
style (e.g. *DFC*, *FRA*); those with a combination of upper- and

lower-case letters traditionally do (e.g. *B.Sc.*, *D.Phil.*, *Ph.D.*), but today are often rendered without the points (*BSc*, *DPhil*, *PhD*).

> Mr Joseph Andrews
> Joseph Andrews, Esq.
> Mrs Abigail Andrews
> Dr John Andrews
> Mary Andrews, DPhil
> Admiral of the Fleet Viscount Lamb, GCB, KBE

Do not combine *Mr*, *Mrs*, *Miss*, *Ms*, *Dr*, *Esq.*, etc. with any other title. Note that *Esq.* should not be combined with *Mr*. Formerly *Mr* was used for manual workers or those without a university degree, and *Esq.* for professional men or those with a degree. *Esq.* comes before all other titles that follow a name. For titles of judges see 13.8.

There is no comma in some combinations of titles:

> His Grace the Archbishop of Armagh   His Honour Judge Perkins

Do not use orders, decorations, degrees, or fellowships in title pages, nor normally in text except at first mention—and then only in the proportion required by the subject matter. For example, HRH The Prince of Wales, KG, KT, GCB is more simply styled *Prince Charles*, *the Prince of Wales*, or just *the Prince*.

6.1.5 **Peers**

The peerage of the United Kingdom has five grades: for men, duke, marquess (*not* marquis), earl, viscount, and baron; for women (either in their own right or as the wife, widow, or former wife of a peer), duchess, marchioness, countess, viscountess, and baroness. Note that *count* is not a British title.

Lord is a title given formally to a baron, and is used less formally to refer to a marquess, earl, or viscount, prefixed to a family or territorial name (*Lord Derby*). It is also used, prefixed to a Christian name, as a courtesy title for a younger son of a duke or marquess (*Lord John Russell*). Dukes are not referred to as *Lord* —, but as *the Duke of* —. Baronets (and knights) are entitled to the prefix *Sir*.

The title *Lady* is used in reference to female peers, the female relatives of peers, and the wives and widows of knights.

6.1.6 **Saints' names**

Saints' names can be problematic, as they exist as titles for individuals, as place names, and as surnames.

- In English 'saint' is abbreviated as *St* (*St.* for 'street' is conventionally distinguished by having a full point). It is not hyphenated except from in some personal names such as *St-John*. It is always capitalized in names.

- In French a capital *S* and hyphen are used if the name refers to the name of a place, institution, or saint's day, or is a family name or title: for example, *Saint-Étienne, Sainte-Beuve, Saint-Christophe-en-Brionnais, la Saint-Barthélemy*. A lower-case *s* with no hyphen is used if the reference is to the person of a saint, for example *saint Jean, saint Jeanne d'Arc*. Abbreviations are *S.*, feminine *Ste*, for the persons of saints, in other contexts *St-*, feminine *Ste-*.

- In German, use *Sankt*, abbreviated *St.*; for the saints themselves *hl.* (*heilig*).

- In Italian 'saint' before a consonant in the masculine form is *San* (for example *San Filippo*); before impure *S* (that is, an *s* followed by another consonant), the form is *Santo—Santo Stefano*. The feminine form before a consonant is *Santa*, as in *Santa Maria*. In both genders before a vowel the form is *Sant'* and the words are elided: *Sant'Agostino, Sant'Agnese*.

- In Portuguese 'saint' is masculine *São*, sometimes *Santo* before a vowel; feminine *Santa*.

- In Spanish 'saint' is masculine *San* (before *Do-, To-* it is *Santo*); the feminine is *Santa*.

Abbreviations of names derived from saints' names are generally alphabetized under the full form (that is, *St Andrews* would be found under *Saint* rather than under *St* or *A*).

6.1.7 **Welsh, Scottish, and Irish names**

Welsh names

Surnames were not used in Welsh culture until the Tudor period and became standard practice only from the seventeenth century. Before that both men and women took their names from their fathers. The male patronymic particles are *ap* (preceding a consonant) and *ab* (preceding a vowel), both meaning 'son of'. The female patronymic particle is *ferch*, meaning 'daughter of'. All are lower case. Sometimes the patronymic is doubled, naming the person's father and grandfather in the form 'son/daughter of X son of Y':

> Gruffudd ap Madog
> Llywelyn ab Owain
> Hywel Fychan ap Gruffydd ap Hywel
> Angharad ferch Morgan

Such names must be indexed on the particle rather than the capitalized surname.

Irish and Scottish names

The Irish prefix *O'* means 'grandson of'. In the English form use a closing quotation mark (apostrophe) with no space, as *O'Brien, O'Neill*. In Irish one alternative to this is the capital *O* and full space; another is the more authentic Gaelic *Ó*, followed by a full space: *Ó Cathasaigh, Ó Flannagáin*. Follow the bearer's preference, if known.

Mac means 'son of'. Styling names with *Mac* can lead to problems, depending on whether they are rendered in Gaelic or English forms, or somewhere in between. Spelling rests on the custom of the person bearing the name, and variations in English spelling (*MacDonald, Macdonald, McDonald, M'Donald*, etc.) must be followed, even though they do not reflect any variation in the Gaelic forms. In Irish, names with *Mac* are written as two words, for example *Mícheál Mac Mathúna* (or *Mac Mathghamhna*) 'Michael MacMahon'. As a general rule, leave alone spelling variants found within a text unless you have good reason to believe that the same person's name is being spelled in different ways. However spelled, any name so prefixed is treated as *Mac* in alphabetical arrangement.

6.1.8 Names containing prefixes

With prefixes to proper names such as *de, du, van den*, or *von* (sometimes called **nobiliary particles**), follow the bearer's preference, if known. Within an alphabetical listing supply cross-references where necessary.

de

In accordance with French practice *de* should not have an initial capital (*de Candolle, de Talleyrand-Périgord*), except when anglicized

(*De Quincey*) or at the beginning of a sentence. Before a vowel *d'* is used (*d'Alembert*). Names prefixed with a lower-case *de* or *d'* should be alphabetized under the surname:

Alembert, Jean le Rond d'   Mairan, Jean-Jacques de
Chazelles, Jean-François, comte de

Anglicized names of this form are alphabetized on the prefix.

In Dutch the prefix *de* is generally not capitalized, and does not form the basis for alphabetization, as *Groot, Geert de*. In Flemish the reverse is true, with *De Bruyne, Jan*.

Prefixes in Italian names are capitalized and are the basis for alphabetization:

De Sanctis, Gaetano   Della Casa, Adriana
Del Corno, Francesco   Di Benedetti, Vittorio

An exception is made for aristocratic names beginning *de'*, *degli*, or *di*: *Medici, Lorenzo de'*; these are capitalized under the main name rather than prefix.

In Spanish names *de* is lower case and omitted in bare surname references, and does not form the basis for alphabetization. For example *Luis Barahona de Soto* (alphabetized under *B*), *Diego de Hurtado de Mendoza* (under *H*), *Lope de Vega Carpio* (under *V*). The prefix *del*, as in *del Castillo*, is a contracted form of *de el*.

de la

In modern French the compound particle *de La* has only one capital (*de La Fontaine*). The *de* is dropped in the absence of a forename: *La Fontaine said* ... When anglicized the prefix may deviate from this practice (*de la Mare, De La Warr*); follow established convention or the bearer's preference. Names prefixed with *de La* are alphabetized under *La*: *La Fontaine, Jean de*.

In Spanish *de la* is lower case: *Claudio de la Torre* (alphabetized under *T*).

du

Du normally has an initial capital, and names are alphabetized under *D* accordingly: *Du Deffand, Marie, marquise*. Variations exist with lower-case *du*, with the name alphabetized according to the surname; this is also the case where the surname is actually formed from a title: *Maine, Louise de Bourbon, duchesse du*.

le, la

The definite article is capitalized when it occurs at the beginning of a French surname: *Le Pen*. (Note, however, that it is lower case in place names except at the beginning of a sentence.) In both cases the names are alphabetized on the article.

van, van den, van der

As a Dutch prefix to a proper name *van, van den,* and *van der* are usually not capitalized except at the beginning of a sentence, and therefore are all alphabetized under the main name. In Flemish, however, the reverse is usually true, with a capital *V* used in alphabetizing; Afrikaans employs both conventions. In Britain and the US well-known names of Dutch origin, such as *Vincent Van Gogh*, are usually alphabetized on the prefix: *Van Gogh, Vincent*.

von, von dem, von den, von der, vom

As a Germanic prefix to a proper name *von* usually has no initial capital, except at the beginning of a sentence. In some Swiss names the *Von* is capitalized (*Peter Von der Mühll*). Where the surname stands alone *von* is omitted (*Liebig*, not *von Liebig*), and the name is not indexed on the prefix (*Liebig, Gertrud von*). The related forms *von dem, von den, von der,* and *vom* are usually retained, however, and form the basis for alphabetization.

6.1.9 **Foreign names**

Arabic

Names beginning with the definite article *al* (or variants such as *el, ul,* or *an*) should always be hyphenated: *al-Islām, al-kitāb*. The *a* is capitalized at the start of a sentence but is otherwise lower case. In alphabetizing, the article is ignored and the person is listed under the capital letter of their last name. Thus *Aḥmad al-Jundī* would be listed as *al-Jundī, Aḥmad*, and alphabetized under *J*; the article is not inverted, and can even be deleted if the style is imposed consistently. Compound place names of the type *Shajar al-Durr* would be listed thus, however, not transposed as *al-Durr, Shajar*.

Familial prefix elements such as *abū* (father), *umm* (mother), and *ibn* or *bin* (son) may appear as part of ordinary names. They are then in lower case and do not determine alphabetical position: *Muḥammad bin Aḥmad* would be listed as *Aḥmad, Muḥammad bin*. The prefix elements are not connected to the following name by hyphens. *Ibn* or *bin* is often abbreviated to *b.* in indexes and bibliographical references, and *bint* (daughter) may be abbreviated to *b.* or *bt*. On the other hand, such constructs may appear in established surnames, in which case the prefix should be capitalized and should determine alphabetical position: for example, the medieval author Muḥammad Ibn Saʿd would be listed as *Ibn Saʿd, Muḥammad*.

Transliterated modern Arabic names often employ established westernized spellings that may not follow normal rules of transliteration: *Hussein* rather than *Ḥusayn*, *Nasser* rather than *Nāṣir*, *Naguib* rather than *Najīb*. In each case the most commonly occurring spelling of the bearer's name is acceptable, except in specialist contexts.

Chinese

Chinese personal names normally consist of a single-syllable family name or surname, followed by a two-syllable personal name. In romanization capitals are used for the first letter, both of the family and of the personal name. In the Wade–Giles transliteration system the two elements of the personal name are separated by a hyphen (for example *Mao Tse-tung*), whereas in the Pinyin system they are run together as a single word (*Mao Zedong*). When a form of name has a long-established history, for example *Sun Yat-sen* or *Chiang Kai-shek*, this should be preferred. Names are not inverted for alphabetization.

In pre-modern times two-syllable names were frequently found, for example *Wang Wei*. More recent figures may use a westernized form of surname, giving the initials for the personal name first and placing the family name last, for example *T. V. Soong, H. H. Kung*. In indexing and alphabetizing such names the order should be inverted in Western fashion.

French

The definite article (*le, la*) is capitalized when it occurs at the beginning of a French surname, and the name is alphabetized under *L*. Do not confuse this with the use of an article to refer to a person whose name itself does not incorporate it:

le Guerchin (Guercino)   la Delaporte (Marguerite Delaporte)

Note that the article only accompanies the surname, not the fore-name. See also **de, de la, du** at 6.1.8.

When a first name is abbreviated in a French text, if the second letter of the name is an *h*, the *h* is retained:

    Th. Gautier (Théophile Gautier)   Ch. Mauron (Charles Mauron)

The honorifics *Monsieur* (Mr), *Madame* (Mrs), and *Mademoiselle* (Miss) can be used alone or in conjunction with a surname; in speech these forms precede all appointments and titles: *Madame la docteur*. They are abbreviated as *M*, *Mme*, and *Mlle* (no point).

German

Honorifics are *Herr* (Mr), *Frau* (Mrs), and *Fräulein* (Miss): these are abbreviated as *Hr.*, *Fr.*, and *Frl.* Unmarried women are called *Frau* after a certain age, which in Germany, if not in Austria and Switzer-land, has come down into the teens.

Whether individuals include the *Eszett* (ß) in their names is a matter of personal style in German or Austrian names, though it is rare in Swiss names. See also **von, von dem, von den, von der, vom** at 6.1.8.

Greek

Traditional practice is to write ancient Greek names in a Latinized form (for example *Hercules* rather than *Herakles*), although the Greek form is often used when discussing Greek literature, art, religion, etc. One would discuss the twelve labours of *Herakles* in Greek art and poetry, but in a general context one would refer to the labours of *Her-cules*. A further rule is to give familiar names in their traditional English—that is, Latinized—form, but retain the Greek spelling for less familiar ones. It is difficult to give guidance as to which names are familiar and which are not, but no one should appear in the Greek spelling who is more of a household name than one who is Latinized.

Some scholars differentiate separate bearers of the same name through Latinizing and Hellenizing alone, using *Thucydides* for the historian but *Thoukydides* for his uncle the politician, *Callimachus* for the poet but *Kallimachos* for the Athenian general. Probably no one would call the philosopher *Platon*; on the other hand, a lesser light by that name would normally be called *Platon* by modern scholars. No one would call the philosopher *Aristotle* anything else, though another man of the same name would be *Aristoteles*; similarly with *Homer* and *Hesiod* (*Homeros* and *Hesiodos*).

The following is a basic guide to Latinized forms of Greek names:

Greek	Latin
ai	ae
k	c
kh	ch
ei	i or ei
oi	oe
-os	-us
-ros	-er
ou	u
u	y

Some examples:

Greek	Latin
Achilleus, Akhilleus	Achilles
Aias	Aiax, (*English*) Ajax
Kallimachos, Kallimakhos	Callimachus
Lusandros, Lysandros	Lysander
Odysseus	Ulixes, (*English*) Ulysses
Oidipous	Oedipus
Thoukydides	Thucydides

For transliteration see 12.7.

Hebrew and Jewish

A Hebrew name may be rendered in English in a variety of ways: *Jacob*, for example, may also be *Ya'acov* or *Ya'akov*; similarly *Haim*, *Hayyim*, *Chaim*, and *Chayim* are all variants. Beyond ensuring that the same person is always referred to in the same way, one cannot standardize automatically throughout a text because any variant may represent the personal preference of the individual concerned or an established convention regarding how their name is spelled.

The *ben* that occurs in many Hebrew names means 'son of'; this is the traditional Jewish way of naming Jewish males. The female form is *bat* 'daughter of'. In pre-modern times a man would usually be known simply as the son of his father: *Avraham ben David* (Avraham the son of David). In scholarly works this is often abbreviated to *Avraham b. David*; for works aimed at a more general readership, the full form is probably clearer. The *Ben* that often figures in modern Israeli names represents a different usage: now part of the surname, it should be hyphenated to it and capitalized, as in *David Ben-Gurion*. The un-hyphenated *David Ben Gurion* is wrong, as it suggests that *Ben* is a middle name.

Italian

The forms of address are *Signor* (Mr), *Signora* (Mrs), and *Signorina* (Miss), abbreviated as *Sig.*, *Sig.ra*, and *Sig.na*. *Signor* adds an *-e* when it is not followed by a name. *Dottor* ('Doctor', though used also of any graduate) adds an *-e* in similar circumstances; the feminine form is *Dottoressa*. Those with higher degrees are *Professore* or *Professoressa*. Titles followed by a surname are lower case: *la signora Cappelletti, il dottor Ferro*. See also **de** at 6.1.8.

Japanese

Japanese names usually take the form of a single surname, followed by a personal name: *Itō Hirobumi, Omura Mizuki*. The surname forms the basis for alphabetization. The suffixes *-san* (gender-neutral), *-sama* (polite form), *-chan* (affectionate diminutive), and *-kun* (for addressing an inferior; also used by boys in addressing one another) are used only in speech, or transcriptions of speech.

In Western contexts it is conventional, especially in translations, to transpose the names—*Mizuki Omura*. (The writer known in the West as Kazuo Ishiguro would be Ishiguro Kazuo in Japan.) Well-known artists are often identified only by the personal name element, leaving out any reference to family, for example *Hokusai* rather than *Katsushika Hokusai*. Similarly, writers who are well known by their personal name may be so identified: *Bashō* rather than *Matsuo Bashō*.

Historically, it is common for two elements of a name to be separated by *no*, indicating the subordination of the second element to the first: *Ki no Tsurayuki*. Here, too, the name should appear in direct order.

Korean

In Korean names the surname precedes the personal name, unless a particular individual's name has become westernized. There are five predominant surnames in Korea—*Kim, Yi, Pak, Chŏng*, and *Ch'oe*—and more than a third of people will use one of the first three. Personal names usually consist of two elements separated from one another by a hyphen: *Kim Il-Sung*.

Portuguese and Brazilian

As in Spanish practice, the surname is normally composed of two elements: the mother's maiden name and the father's surname, the latter forming the basis for alphabetization. Unlike Spanish, however, the mother's maiden name comes before the father's surname. Alphabetization is according to the last element in the surname: *Manuel Braga da Cruz* is ordered under *Cruz, Manuel Braga da*.

Standard forms of address are *Senhor* (Mr), *Senhora* (Mrs or Miss), *Minha Senhora* (a more polite form of Mrs), or *Dona* (Mrs or any older woman). *Menina* (Miss) is used only before a given name. Professional or conferred titles normally come after the *Senhor*, *Senhora*, etc.: *Senhor Professor*, *Senhora Doutora*. In Brazilian *Senhorita* is used for 'Miss', and it is considered more polite to use *Senhor* and *Senhora* in conjunction with the first name rather than surname.

Russian

The gender-neutral honorific *tovarishch* (Comrade) is now rarely used; it has been supplanted by the pre-Revolution forms *gospodin* (Mr) and *gospozha* (Mrs or Miss), which are used mostly in writing, and then only with the surname following. Russian names follow the patronymic pattern of given name, father's name with the suffix *-ovich* (son of) or *-ovna* (daughter of), and surname. While the surname is inherited, it is rarely used in speech. Correctly, transliterated abbreviated names with initials composed of two letters, one capital and one lower-case, should not be further reduced, as they are derived from a single Cyrillic letter, for example *Ya.* for Yakov, *Yu.* for Yuri, and *Zh.* for Zhores. For transliteration see 12.15.

Scandinavian

The ancient Scandinavian traditions of alternating patronymic names with each generation—whereby, for example, *Magnus Pálsson* (Magnus, son of Pál) names his son *Pál Magnusson* and his daughter *Björk Magnúsdóttir*—are still found in Iceland, although they have not been used consistently elsewhere for the past one or two centuries; since 1923 only existing surnames have been allowed to be used in Iceland. Icelandic alphabetization is still by given name rather than surname, with *Finnur Jónsson* under *F* and *Vígdís Finnbogadóttir* under *V*.

Spanish

Standard forms of address are *Señor* (Mr), *Señora* (Mrs), *Señorita* (Miss), abbreviated as *Sr*, *Sra*, and *Srta*.

Surnames are usually composed of two elements, the father's family surname followed by the mother's family surname (derived from her father's family name). So if, for example, *Señor Roberto Caballero Díaz* marries *Señorita Isabel Fuentes López*, their son might be *Jaime Caballero Fuentes*. Apart from the change in title from *Señorita* to *Señora*, the wife's surnames normally do not alter with marriage. In unofficial contexts the second half of a married woman's compound surname may be replaced by the husband's first surname and joined to her first surname by the conjunction *de*, although this is becoming rare: in the case above, *Isabel Fuentes López* could be *Isabel Fuentes de Caballero*, or *Señora de Caballero*. (*Señorita* as a form of address is becoming less and less common in everyday contexts, giving way to *Señora*.)

Compound surnames may be joined with a *y*, or in Catalan surnames *i*:

   José Ortega y Gasset   Josep Lluís Pons i Gallarza

The second element may be dropped in everyday use; Cervantes's full name was *Miguel de Cervantes Saavedra*, and prominent figures in Spanish public life may be referred to with only one surname:

   José María Aznar   Javier Solana

In journalistic shorthand they would be referred to as *Aznar* and *Solana*.

Conversely, a person may become known by the second element of their surname, particularly if the expected one is very common: the poet Federico García Lorca is generally known as *Lorca*, the politician José Luis Rodríguez Zapatero is referred to as *Zapatero*, or *Rodríguez Zapatero* (but never just *Rodríguez*), and Pablo Ruiz Picasso, son of José Ruiz Blasco and María Picasso, is known universally as *Picasso*.

Where two elements are used, alphabetization is normally according to the first element in the surname.

6.2 Place names

6.2.1 General principles

Choosing the appropriate spelling of a name for a town, city, country, or geographical feature can be a tricky and sensitive matter. Consulting an authoritative recent atlas, or a dictionary that includes encyclopedic information, such as the *Oxford Dictionary of English* or the *New Oxford Dictionary for Writers and Editors*, will help to establish the currently accepted form, but in many cases a choice must be made between alternative spellings.

Note that place names are always rendered in roman type, even if the form used is a foreign, unnaturalized one with unfamiliar spelling or accents:

rue St-Honoré   Biblioteca Nazionale Centrale di Roma

The modern tendency is to replace English versions of place names by the correct form in the local language, but it is far from being a universal rule: few writers in English would refer to *Roma* or *München* for Rome or Munich, for example. Be aware, also, that some local forms closely resemble their anglicized variant: be wary with *Lyon* and *Lyons*, *Marseille* and *Marseilles*, *Reims* and *Rheims*.

The following list provides examples of current Oxford preference for the names of some foreign cities when given in general—as opposed to specialist or historical—context:

Ankara (*not* Angora)	Beijing (*not* Peking)
Brussels (*not* Bruxelles *or* Brussel)	Florence (*not* Firenze)
Gdańsk (*not* Danzig)	Geneva (*not* Genève)
Livorno (*not* Leghorn)	Lyons (*not* Lyon)
Marseilles (*not* Marseille)	Reims (*not* Rheims)
Sichuan (*not* Szechuan *or* Szechwan)	Vienna (*not* Wien)

It is important to be aware of the sensitivities and contentious issues reflected in choices of name. Some particular points are expanded below:

• The island containing England, Wales, and Scotland is *Britain*; *Great Britain* is more usual when these countries are considered as a political unit. The *United Kingdom* is a political unit that includes these countries and Northern Ireland (but not the Isle of Man and the Channel Islands). The *British Isles* is a geographical term that refers to the United Kingdom, Ireland, and the surrounding islands.

- *America* is a land mass consisting of the continents of North and South America. It should be used to mean 'the United States' only when the context is very clear. *North America* is a continent that contains Canada, the United States, Mexico, and the countries of *Central America* (which is classed as the southernmost part of North America).

- Official names of some Indian cities changed in 1995, with *Mumbai* replacing *Bombay*, *Chennai* superseding *Madras*, and *Kolkata* replacing *Calcutta*. A book about modern India should certainly use the new forms, although if the work is intended for a general readership the names should be glossed with their traditional forms.

- The country between Poland and Russia is *Belarus*, not *Belorussia* or *Byelorussia* and certainly not *White Russia*.

- In contemporary contexts place names in China should be spelled with the Pinyin rather than the Wade–Giles system (see 12.3.3): *Beijing* and *Guangzhou* rather than *Peking* and *Kwangchow*. The old name of the latter, *Canton*, may be felt to be more appropriate in historical contexts.

- The area of the Congo in Africa needs particular care. The country known as Zaire between 1971 and 1997 is the *Democratic Republic of Congo* (capital, Kinshasa), whereas its much smaller neighbour is *Congo* or *Republic of Congo* (capital, Brazzaville); the latter is sometimes distinguished as *Republic of Congo-Brazzaville*.

Names of features such as lakes, oceans, seas, mountains, and rivers can lay traps for the unwary: strictly speaking, a descriptive term should not be added to a name in which it is already present. For example the *meer* in *IJsselmeer* and *mere* in *Windermere* mean 'lake', and the first part of the name of the *Rio Grande* means 'river' in Spanish.

Romanization can cause difficulties with place names; some guidance is given in Chapter 12 under the individual language.

6.2.2 Chronology

Places where the official language has changed owing to historical events may need to be identified or benefit from a gloss: *Breslau (now*

Wrocław). In specialist or historical works the subject, historical period, and prospective readership will govern which language or form is used for a particular place name, though the usage for any given region must be consistent; editors should not automatically change a name given in the text to its modern equivalent. When the place name itself—not merely its linguistic form—has changed, do not use the new name retrospectively: refer to the Battle of *Stalingrad*, even though since 1961 the city has been *Volgograd*. This applies no less when the old name is restored: the *Petrograd Soviet* and the *Siege of Leningrad* should not be placed in *St Petersburg*, though naturally '(now St Petersburg)' may be added if readers are thought to need it.

6.2.3 **Locating places**

It is sometimes necessary to distinguish places of the same name, to identify small places, or to clarify the name of a place when it has changed. In general it would be pedantic to refer to 'Paris, France' on the off-chance that one reader in a million might assume that 'Paris' standing alone referred to the place in Texas. Context will often make plain which of two places of the same name is meant: in a book about English churches it would be unnecessary to refer to 'Boston, Lincolnshire'. However, in the same book, a reference to 'Richmond' would require identification (unless, of course, the surrounding matter located it unambiguously in Surrey or Yorkshire).

A small place may be located by reference to a larger place, a county, a surrounding area, or a country:

> Fiesole near Florence
> Newton, Warwickshire
> St-Julien-de-Jonzy in Burgundy
> Kinshasa, the capital of the Democratic Republic of Congo

It is important to avoid anachronisms in these cases: a modern reference to Hampstead might identify it as 'in north London', but a reference to John Constable's taking a house there in the nineteenth century should identify Hampstead as 'near London' or 'north of London', or 'in Middlesex'. Similarly, care should be taken with historical subject matter not to 'correct' references because they do not conform with modern reality: for example, the town of Abingdon was in Berkshire until boundary changes in 1974 'moved' it to Oxfordshire.

6.2.4 **Addresses**

Use a comma to separate the elements in a run-on postal address:

> Great Clarendon Street, Oxford, OX2 6DP, UK

Commas should be omitted altogether if the address is on separate lines, as on an envelope:

> Great Clarendon Street
> Oxford
> OX2 6DP
> UK

There is no comma after the street number:

> 23 Arnold Road

Postcodes are printed in capitals with no points or hyphens: *OX2 6DP*. Ensure that the letter *O* and the number *0* are distinguished. Postcodes are frequently set in small capitals rather than full capitals.

North American

US addresses have a zip code after the name of the town or city and the postal abbreviation of the state. The standard zip code consists of five numerals (with an optional further code of four more numerals, introduced by a hyphen) and is separated from the state abbreviation by a space:

> 198 Madison Avenue, New York, NY 10016 (*or* 10016-4314)

On an envelope this address would be laid out as:

> 198 Madison Avenue
> New York, NY 10016 (*or* 10016-4314)

Note that the convention for Manhattan addresses is to spell out numbers for avenue names and use figures for street names:

> 25 W. 43 St.
> the corner of Fifth and 59th

In Canadian addresses the postal code is placed on the last line. The postal abbreviation of the province is written on the same line as the town or city name:

> 202 Hanson Street
> Toronto, ON
> Canada
> M4C 1A7

Apartment addresses are written as, for example:

    310-99 Gerard St

or

    99 Gerard St, Apt 310

or

    99 Gerard St, #310

European

The words *rue*, *avenue*, *boulevard*, etc. are not capitalized in French street names:

    56 rue de Rivoli   12 boulevard Louis Pasteur
    place de la République

The definite article in place names is lower case except at the start of a sentence (*le Havre*).

Composite French place names are hyphenated:

    Saint-Étienne-du-Mont   Vitry-le-François
    Saint-Denis-de-la-Réunion   rue du Faubourg-Montmartre

In German, Dutch, and Swedish addresses the equivalent of the word 'road' or 'street' is amalgamated with the name, so the issue of capitalization does not arise. Street numbers follow the name:

    Friedrichsstrasse 10   Eriksgatan

Italian and Spanish street names take lower-case initials, and street numbers follow the name; Portuguese street names take upper-case initials:

    piazza Luigi di Savoia 20   glorieta Puerta de Toledo 4
    Travessa das Amoreiras

CHAPTER 7

Italic, roman, and other type treatments

7.1 General principles

7.1.1 Introduction

In most contexts roman type is the standard typeface used for text matter, but it can be varied, for reasons of emphasis, additional clarity, or common convention, through the use of other typographic styles or forms. Each of these—italic, roman text in quotation marks, bold, capitals and small capitals, and underlining—is used to indicate a departure of some sort from normal text or to alert the reader to interpret the words so distinguished in a particular way. Capital initials are also used to delineate particular classes of word; see Chapter 5.

7.1.2 Punctuation and typography

All internal punctuation within a phrase or work title set in a different type style is set in that style, including colons between titles and sub-titles, and exclamation or question marks that form part of the quoted matter. Punctuation not belonging to the phrase or title is set in roman. Ensure that markup on copy or coding on disk is precise. In

> Have you read *Westward Ho!*?

the exclamation mark is in italics because it is part of the title, but the question mark is in roman because it belongs to the surrounding context. Similarly, the plurals *s* and *es* and the possessive *'s* affixed to italicized or other typographically distinguished words are set in roman:

> several old *Economist*s and *New Yorker*s
> the *Majestic*'s crew

They are set in the variant typography where they form part of the word:

> It's not *John's* fault but *Mary's*
> We fitted several of the *blancs* in our luggage

Occasionally it may be necessary to indicate italics in text that is already italicized, especially in foreign text. In this instance the opposite font—roman type—is chosen:

> *Discuss the principle* caveat emptor *in common-law jurisdictions*
> He hissed, '*Do you have the slightest* idea *how much trouble you've caused*?'

Within italic titles do not convert to roman any material that would be italic in open text (for example ships' names or other work titles):

> *The Voyage of the Meteor* (not *The Voyage of the* Meteor)

Where italic type is shown in typescript by underlining or italic type, editors should indicate the opposite font by circling the word or words and writing 'opposite font' (abbr. 'OF') either between the lines or in the margin.

Some publishers indicate italics in italicized text by putting it within quotation marks:

> *A Study of Dickens's 'Hard Times'*

Use of underlining in this context is not recommended: see 7.6 below. For a further discussion of titles within titles see 8.2.8.

7.2 Italic type

Italic type is used to indicate emphasis or stress; to style titles, headings, indexes, and cross-references; and to indicate foreign words and phrases.

7.2.1 Emphasis and highlighting

Setting type in italics indicates emphasis by setting off a word or phrase from its context:

> An essay's *length* is less important than its *content*
> I don't care *how* you get here, just *get here*
> Such style, such *grace*, is astounding

Employ italics sparingly for emphasis. It may be better to achieve the same effect by making the emphasis clear through the sentence structure, or by using intensifying adjectives and adverbs:

> The actual purpose of her letter remained a mystery

rather than

> The *purpose* of her letter remained a mystery

Italic may also be used to highlight a word, phrase, or character where it is itself the object of discussion:

> the letter *z*   spell *labour* with a *u*   the past tense of *go* is *went*

Quotation marks may also be used in this way (see 7.3 below): decide which will be clearer and more intelligible to the reader, and apply that style consistently in comparable contexts.

Technical or recently coined terms and words being introduced, defined, or assigned a special meaning are often italicized at first mention:

> The unit of cultivation was the *strip* ... a bundle of strips made up what was known as a *furlong*
> a pair of endocrine structures termed the *adrenal glands*

Bold type is also used for this purpose in some contexts (see 7.4 below).

When an author or editor adds italics to a quotation for emphasis, indicate that this has been done by adding 'my italics', 'author's italics', or 'italics added' in square brackets after the italicized word or words, or in parentheses at the end of the quotation or in the relevant footnote or endnote. (Using 'my emphasis' or 'emphasis added' is an acceptable alternative where italics are the only form of emphasis used.)

> The committee had decided not to put it in the petition, 'but intimate it *to the prince*' (BL, Harley MS 6383, fo. 122a: my italics)

7.2.2 Foreign words and phrases

Italic type is used in English texts for words and phrases that are still regarded as foreign or need to be distinguished from identical English forms:

> the *catenaccio* defensive system employed by the Italians
> an *amuse-gueule* of a tiny sardine mounted on a crisp crouton

When a foreign word becomes naturalized into English (that is, no longer regarded as distinctively foreign) it is usually printed in roman like other English words:

> the phrase is repeated ad nauseam throughout the book
> Mortimer describes the scene with characteristic brio

Convention and context rather than logic determine when foreign words are sufficiently assimilated into English to be printed in roman type. In modern English the use of italics for foreign words is less prevalent than it used to be, and newly adopted foreign terms may pass into roman text very quickly. The best advice is to treat any one item consistently within a given text and follow the newest edition of a suitable dictionary, such as the *New Oxford Dictionary for Writers and Editors* or the *Shorter Oxford English Dictionary*. Take into account also the subject's conventions and the intended readers' expectations: if in doubt over the degree of assimilation of a particular word, the more cautious policy is to italicize, but in a work written for specialists whose terminology it may be a part of, it may be wiser not to.

Conversely, consistency or context may require words normally romanized in general English to revert to italicization (or, as in German, capitalization), to avoid their looking out of place among related but less assimilated foreign words. It is also sometimes important to go on italicizing a foreign word, however familiar, where there is an English word with the same spelling, as with *Land* for a province of Germany or *pension* for a Continental boarding house.

When a word is sufficiently assimilated to be printed in roman, it may still retain its accents, as with 'pâté', 'plié', and 'crèche'; or it may lose them, as with 'cafe', 'denouement', 'elite', and 'facade' (these forms are the ones shown in current Oxford dictionaries).

Foreign words assimilated into English tend to lose gender inflections, so that the English 'rentier'—now assimilated into the language in roman type—applies to both male and female, though the French feminine form of *rentier* is *rentière*. While in English the default gender is normally masculine, the dominant anglicized form of some words may be the feminine one: an example is 'blonde', which in British English is the usual form for both sexes, although 'blond' is still sometimes used for a man and is the dominant American form.

The explanation or translation of a foreign word or phrase may be presented in any of a number of ways, using roman type in quotation marks or parentheses, as appropriate:

> *bracchium* means 'arm'
>
> Old French *dangier* is derived from Latin *dominium* 'power',
>   'authority', which is the basic sense of Middle English *daunger*
>
> Napoleon said England was a nation of *boutiquiers* (shopkeepers)

Complicated contexts will require greater diversity: any sensible system is acceptable so long as it is consistently applied and clear to the reader.

Foreign proper names are not italicized, even when cited in their original language:

> rue St-Honoré   Biblioteca Nazionale Centrale di Roma

7.2.3 Titles of works

Work titles are discussed fully in Chapter 8. Use italics for titles of books, periodicals, plays, films, TV and radio series, and albums and CDs:

> *The Electric Kool-Aid Acid Test*   *Past & Present*
> *Look Back in Anger*   *West Side Story*
> *Fawlty Towers*   *La dolce vita*

Italics are used for long poems (those of book length, or divided into books or cantos), but roman in quotation marks is used for shorter poems, songs, articles, and individual episodes in broadcast series. The titles of paintings, sculptures, and other works of art are also italicized, as are titles of operas, oratorios, collections of songs, etc.

7.2.4 Other uses of italic

Italic type is also found in the following contexts:

- stage directions in plays
- dictionaries, for part-of-speech markers, foreign words in etymologies, usage labels, and example sentences
- in some styles, for introducing cross-references as in *see* or *see under*, and other directions to the reader, such as *opposite* and *overleaf*
- enumeration such as (*a*), (*b*), (*c*) in lists
- names of ships, aircraft, and vehicles (see 5.16)

- names of parties in legal cases (see Chapter 13)
- biological nomenclature (see Chapter 14)
- mathematics (see Chapter 14).

7.3 Quotation marks

Quotation marks are discussed at 4.14 and 9.2.3. They are used with roman type in the titles of short poems, songs, chapters in books, articles, and individual episodes in broadcast series; the names of the Bible, the Torah, the Koran, and other religious texts and their subdivisions are written in roman without quotation marks. They are also used to distinguish colloquialisms in formal contexts and to give the implication 'so-called'.

7.4 Bold type

Bold or boldface is a thick typeface **like this**. **Bold type** is indicated in copy by a wavy underline. Where a distinction is to be made between two bold typefaces (e.g. bold and semibold), the convention is to use a double wavy line for bold and a single one for semibold.

Bold may be used instead of italic to highlight a newly introduced term, often one that is going to be defined or explained:

> **Percale** is a fine weave that produces a relatively fine and strong fabric for sheets.
>
> The **Pharisees** were sincere and pious Jews ... The **Sadducees** were a group of aristocratic Jews ... The **Essenes** had serious disagreements with both the Pharisees and the Sadducees.

This device is used particularly in textbooks, guidebooks, and other educational or instructional texts, less so in more literary contexts:

> The village of **Avrolles** (14 km), where the road changes from D943 to D905, has a church with a detached bell tower.

Bold is often used for headwords in dictionaries and encyclopedias; for certain components of citations in bibliographies and reference lists; in indexes to draw attention to types of reference or important references; to indicate cross-referencing generally; and in titles and headings.

Avoid using bold for emphasis in the course of normal printed matter, as the effect is usually too startling in running text; avoid typographical distinction altogether, or prefer instead the less obtrusive italic.

7.5 Capitals

7.5.1 **Full capitals**

Full capitals are usually used for acronyms and other capital abbreviations (see Chapter 10), and for initials (see Chapter 6):

> OPEC   BBC   UNESCO

The use of initial capitals is discussed in Chapter 5.

Full capitals (and small capitals) may be used for displaying text on half-title and title pages, for logos and imprints, and for other types of special presentation and display.

Full capitals are usually too prominent to be used for emphasis in open text, but they are sometimes used, as are small capitals, to mimic inscriptions or to reproduce original orthography:

> The earliest Scandinavian coins, inscribed 'CNVT REX ÆNOR' ('Cnut, king of Danes'), seem to have been struck ... no later than 1015

7.5.2 **Small capitals**

Small capitals are about two-thirds the size of large capitals, as in THIS STYLE OF TYPE, and are indicated in typescript by a <u>double underline</u>. In typography, the term 'even s. caps.' instructs that the word(s) should be set entirely in small capitals, rather than a combination of capitals and small capitals.

Although small capitals are traditionally used in a number of set contexts, which are described below, they are not available in certain typefaces. It is possible to reduce capital letters to the size of small capitals, but for a text which requires a great many small capitals a typeface which already includes them should be selected.

The main uses of small capitals are as follows:

- for specifying eras (AD, BC, BCE; see Chapter 10). In an italic context they may be set in italics; otherwise, small capitals are generally set only in roman type.

- for displayed subsidiary titles and headings, for signatures in printed correspondence, for academic qualifications following names displayed in a list, and sometimes for postcodes.

- for reproduced all-capital inscriptions, headlines, notices, and so forth, if these are not reduced to capital and lower case. Formerly, full-capital abbreviations (such as *BBC*) were often set in even small capitals. While this practice has fallen out of widespread use, it remains a convenient alternative for those disciplines routinely requiring full-capital abbreviations in text, which otherwise can look jarring on the printed page.

- in some styles, for the first word or words of chapters: these may be styled with spaced capital and small capital letters 'THUS' to introduce the text (see 1.3.4).

- for cross-references and indexing:

  sing the praises of see PRAISE

- in some styles, for authors' names in bibliographies.

- for characters' names in plays:

  CECILY When I see a spade I call it a spade.

  GWENDOLEN I am glad to say that I have never seen a *spade*.

- for Roman numerals in references, sigla (letters or symbols used to denote a particular manuscript or edition of a text), and play citations with more than one level.

- for centuries in French and generally in Latin:

  le XIème [*or* XIe] siècle

7.6 Underlining

Underlining text on copy or proofs indicates that it is to be set in italics. When underlining matter in this way, ensure that the underlining includes all matter that is to be italicized, but nothing else. Mistakes are particularly common with internal and surrounding punctuation. Consider

  'The novel <u>Bell, Book, and Candle</u>', *not* 'The novel <u>Bell</u>, <u>Book</u>, <u>and</u> <u>Candle</u>'

  'The colours were <u>red</u>, <u>white</u>, and <u>blue</u>', *not* 'The colours were <u>red,</u> <u>white,</u> and <u>blue</u>'

In typeset material it is undesirable to use underlining, as it cuts through the descenders of the characters and in some typefaces may obscure the identity of similar letters (*g* and *q*, for example). Italic type is preferable as a distinguishing mark, though in some cases underlining is required or is uniquely useful—for example in scientific and mathematical notation, or in the precise reproduction of a manuscript, inscription, or correspondence, where it is needed to approximate underlining in the original.

As underscoring in the copy or proofs indicates to the typesetter that italic is wanted, any instances where underlining is required must be marked in a different way: for example, with a highlighted underscore, which can be explained to the designer and typesetter in a note.

In non-print contexts such as websites it is acceptable to use underlining as a substitute for (or in addition to) italics to indicate work titles, though not usually to show emphasis or for other purposes. The main use of underlining is to indicate a hyperlink:

> For more information, and for a free tour of OED Online, visit
> www.oed.com

CHAPTER 8

Work titles in text

8.1 General principles

The text of one work often contains references to others. They may be discussed at length or mentioned fleetingly in passing, with extended bibliographic information or none at all. Work titles mentioned in the text should be styled according to consistent conventions, which will normally match those used in the notes or bibliography, if these are present.

'Work titles' is a category of convenience whose edges may be fuzzy in places. The works considered here are primarily in written form, but also include broadcast works, film, electronically recorded works, musical works, and works of art. The definition of a title is by no means unproblematic, especially outside the area of printed works, not least because the distinction between a formal title and a description is to some extent a matter of convention and arbitrary decision.

8.2 Titles of written works

8.2.1 **Introduction**

The typography and capitalization of the title of a written work depend on whether or not it was published and on the form in which it was published. Publication is not synonymous with printing: works were widely disseminated before the invention of printing, and material that is printed is not necessarily published.

For capitalization of titles see 8.2.3; for use of 'the' see 8.2.7.

8.2.2 **Typography**

Free-standing publications

The title of a free-standing publication is set in italic type. This category comprises works whose identity does not depend on their being part of a larger whole. Such works may be substantial but they may also be short and ephemeral, if published in their own right. They thus include not only books of various kinds (for example novels, monographs, collections of essays, editions of texts, or separately published plays or poems) but also periodicals, pamphlets, titled broadsheets, and published sale and exhibition catalogues:

> *For Whom the Bell Tolls*
> *Gone with the Wind*
> *The Importance of Being Earnest: A Trivial Comedy for Serious People*
> *Sylvie and Bruno*
> *A Tale of Two Cities*
> *The Merchant of Venice*
> the third canto of *Childe Harold's Pilgrimage*
> *The Economist*
> *Farmer and Stockbreeder*
> a pamphlet, *The Douglas System of Economics*, which found a wide sale
> *Essay toward Settlement*, a broadsheet petition published by 19 September 1659

The names of albums, CDs, and collections of songs are given in italic, whereas those of individual songs are in roman with quotation marks: see 8.6.

The names of sacred texts (see 8.3) are set in roman rather than italic; the names of ancient epic poems are also often in roman, especially when the reference is to the epic in general terms rather than to a particular published text of it, which would be cited in italic.

The titles of works published in manuscript before the advent of printing are italicized. They may be consistently styled like those published in print (it is pointless to ask whether, for example, a medieval work that survives in a unique copy was widely distributed, and irrelevant to inquire whether it has been printed in a modern edition):

> the document we now call *Rectitudines singularum personarum*, which originated perhaps in the mid-tenth century

Items within publications

The title of an item within a publication is set in roman type within single quotation marks. This includes titles of short stories, chapters or essays within books, individual poems in collections, articles in periodicals, newspaper columns, and individual texts within larger editions.

> 'The Monkey's Paw'
> 'The Old Vicarage, Grantchester'
> 'Sailing to Byzantium'
> 'Tam o' Shanter'
> 'Three Lectures on Memory', published in his first volume of essays,
>   *Knowledge and Certainty*
> she began writing a weekly column, 'Marginal Comments', for *The
>   Spectator*

There is room for a degree of flexibility here. In some contexts the title of an individual edited text within a collection or, for example, an individual Canterbury tale may reasonably be italicized:

> the first true editor of the *Canterbury Tales*
> the aristocratic noble love of *The Knight's Tale* gives way to the more
>   earthy passions of *The Miller's Tale* and *The Reeve's Tale*

Series titles

A series of books is not itself a work, and its title is not given the same styling as its component works. The overall title of a series is not normally needed when a book is mentioned, but if given should be set in roman type with the first and principal words capitalized:

> the Rough Guides
> Studies in Biblical Theology
> *The Social Structure of Medieval East Anglia*, volume 9 of Oxford
>   Studies in Social and Legal History

Descriptions of an edition should not be considered series titles and should not be capitalized, but a publisher's named edition of the works of a single author may be treated as a series title:

> the variorum edition of her *Complete Poetry*
> Dent published the Temple Edition of the Waverley Novels in forty-
>   eight volumes

More or less formal titles of series of works of fiction may alternatively be italicized like book titles or set in quotation marks, but loose descriptions of fictional series should not be treated as titles:

> *The Forsyte Saga*   the 'His Dark Materials' trilogy
> the Barsetshire novels

Style the titles of series of works of art like those of series of books (with the exception of series of published prints, which are given italic work titles):

> a series of paintings entitled Guyana Myths
> a series of prints, in issues of six, *Studies from Nature of British Character*

Semi-formal titles

Some authors refer to early works or texts in a style that is midway between a formal title and a description, with roman type and maximal capitalization like a series of books:

> the Life of St John of Bridlington added new accounts
> the Annals of the Four Masters refers to a Munster synod held in 1050

This is a rather illogical compromise, and it is better to refer to a work unambiguously in a descriptive form or by a formal title. An early work may legitimately be known under several titles, which will not necessarily appear in an original manuscript or match that adopted in a modern edition:

> the life of St John of Bridlington added new accounts
> the *Annals of the Four Masters* refers to a Munster synod held in 1050

It is, however, the normal convention to set the name of the Bible and other sacred works in roman rather than italic type (see 8.3).

Unpublished works

The title of an unpublished work is set in roman type within single quotation marks. This category includes titles of such unpublished works as dissertations and conference papers, and longer unpublished monographs. The same styling is applied to provisional titles used for works before their publication and titles of works intended for publication but never published, or planned but never written:

> his undergraduate dissertation, 'Leeds as a Regional Capital'
> 'Work in Progress' (published as *Finnegans Wake*)
> Forster later planned to publish an 'Essay on Punctuation'
> an unpublished short play, 'The Blue Lizard'

This treatment is accorded to unpublished works that are essentially literary compositions. Do not style descriptions of archival items as work titles. References to such material as unpublished personal documents, including diaries and letters, and legal, estate, and administrative records should be given in descriptive form with minimal capitalization:

> Dyve's letter-book is valuable evidence
> the diary of Robert Hooke for 3 April
> the cartulary of the hospital of St John
> the great register of Bury Abbey
> the stewards' accounts in the bursars' book for 1504–5

Capitalized names are sometimes given to certain manuscripts, but these can just as well be styled as lower-case descriptions. It is important to distinguish between names applied to individual manuscripts and the titles of works contained in them.

> poems contained in the Book of Taliesin (a thirteenth-century manuscript then preserved at Peniarth)
> in the book of Leinster, a twelfth-century manuscript
> in addition to the *Gododdin awdlau*, the Book of Aneirin contains four other lays (*gorchanau*) named *Gorchan Tudfwlch*, *Gorchan Addefon*, *Gorchan Cynfelyn*, and *Gorchan Maeldderw*

8.2.3 Capitalization

The capitalization of work titles is a matter for editorial convention; there is no need to follow the style of title pages (many of which present titles in full capitals).

The initial word of a title is always capitalized. The traditional style is to give maximal capitalization to the titles of works published in English, capitalizing the first letter of the first word and of all other important words (for works in other languages see Chapter 12 and 8.8 below). Nouns, adjectives (other than possessives), and verbs are usually given capitals; pronouns and adverbs may or may not be capitalized; articles, conjunctions, and prepositions are usually left uncapitalized. Exactly which words should be capitalized in a particular title is a matter for individual judgement, which may take account of the sense, emphasis, structure, and length of the title. Thus a short title may look best with capitals on words that might be left lower case in a longer title:

> *An Actor and his Time*
> *All About Eve*
> *Six Men Out of the Ordinary*
> *Through the Looking-Glass and What Alice Found There*
> *What a Carve Up!*
> *Will you Love me Always?*

The first word of a subtitle is traditionally capitalized, whatever its part of speech (this is the Oxford style):

> *Small is Beautiful: Economics as if People Mattered*
> *Film Theory: An Introduction*

Alternatively, full capitalization may be applied to the main title while the subtitle has simply the capitalization of normal prose:

> *Rebirth, Reform and Resilience: universities in transition 1300–1700*

In titles containing a hyphenated compound it was formerly standard practice to capitalize only the first part of the compound (*Through the Looking-glass*) unless the second part was a proper name, but today it is more usual to capitalize both parts (*Through the Looking-Glass*); in compounds consisting of more than two parts, all words except conjunctions, prepositions, and articles should generally be capitalized:

> *A Behind-the-Scenes Account of the War in Cuba*

It is possible to give minimal capitalization to very long titles (usually from older sources) while applying full capitalization to most titles:

> *Comfort for an afflicted conscience, wherein is contained both consolation and instruction for the sicke, against the fearfull apprehension of their sinnes, of death and the devill, of the curse of the law, and of the anger and just judgement of God*

And it is usual to apply minimal capitalization to the titles of works, most especially poems or traditional songs, that are in fact their opening words:

> 'Wish me luck as you wave me goodbye'

Of course it is not always possible for an editor to recognize such cases.

If the traditional style is to capitalize the principal words within a work title, a more modern practice—in line with a general tendency to eliminate redundant capitalization—is to capitalize the first word of a title and then to apply the capitalization of normal prose. This style of minimal capitalization, which has long been standard in bibliography, is being adopted more quickly in academic and technical publishing than in general contexts. Even in academic contexts it is applied more frequently to items in roman (such as the titles of articles) than it is to italic titles, and maximal capitalization may be retained for the titles of periodicals after it has been abandoned for the titles of books:

Sheep, their breeds, management and diseases
When champagne became French: wine and the making of a national
  identity
'Inequality among world citizens' in the *American Economic Review*

8.2.4 Spelling

The original spelling of a title in any language should generally be preserved. American spellings should not be replaced by British ones, or
vice versa. However, as with direct quotations from text (see 9.3.1), a
limited degree of editorial standardization may be acceptable where
the exact original orthography is of no particular relevance. Thus in
the titles of early modern works:

- orthographic signs (including the ampersand) and abbreviations
  may be retained or expanded, and superscript letters reproduced or
  brought down, according to editorial preference
- the original's use of the letters *i* and *j*, and of *u* and *v*, may be
  consistently modernized, though it is generally safest to retain the
  printed forms
- a double *v* (*vv*) may be changed to the letter *w*
- the long *s* should always be regularized to *s* (*Perspective Practical*,
  1672, not *Perſpective Practical*).

8.2.5 Punctuation

The original punctuation of work titles should generally be retained.
However, some punctuation may be inserted to articulate a title in
a way that is achieved on a title page by means of line breaks. In
addition, title page forms may be made to run more smoothly by
amending archaic semicolons and colons to commas; similarly, full
points within a title may be changed to commas, semicolons, or
colons:

The Great Arch
English State Formation as Cultural Revolution

on a title page may be rendered in text as

The Great Arch: English State Formation as Cultural Revolution

and

The mathematicall divine; shewing the present miseries of
  Germany, England and Ireland: being the effects portended by
  the last comet

may be rendered as

> *The mathematicall divine, shewing the present miseries of Germany,*
> *England and Ireland, being the effects portended by the last comet*

Similarly,

> *A treatise of the bulk and selvedge of the world. Wherein the greatness,*
> *littleness, and lastingness of bodies are freely handled*

may be rendered as

> *A treatise of the bulk and selvedge of the world, wherein the greatness,*
> *littleness, and lastingness of bodies are freely handled*

Two other changes should be made systematically:

- Use a colon to separate the main title from a subtitle (replace a dash or rule of any kind in this position with a colon).

- Place a comma before and after the word *or* (or its equivalent in any language) between parallel alternative titles. The second title should be given an initial capital, whether maximal or minimal capitalization is employed:

> *The Construction of Nationhood: Ethnicity, Religion and*
> *Nationalism*
> *Parkinson's law, or, The pursuit of progress*
> *Senarius, sive, De legibus et licencia veterum poetarum*

8.2.6 **Truncation**

A long title may be silently truncated, with no closing ellipsis, provided the given part is grammatically and logically complete (use a trailing ellipsis if the shortened title is grammatically or logically incomplete). Do not insert the abbreviation *etc.* or a variant to shorten a title (but retain it if it is printed in the original). Use an ellipsis to indicate the omission of material from the middle of a title.

Opening definite or indefinite articles may be omitted from a title to make the surrounding text read more easily. More severely shortened forms are acceptable if they are accurately extracted from the full title and allow the work to be identified; this is particularly helpful if a work is mentioned frequently and a full title given at its first occurrence.

8.2.7 **Use of *the***

It is a common convention in referring to periodicals to include an initial capitalized and italicized *The* in titles which consist only of the

definite article and one other word, but to exclude the definite article
from longer titles. Even when this convention is adopted the definite
article is best omitted from some constructions:

> *The Economist*
> the *New Yorker*
> he wrote for *The Times* and the *Sunday Times*
> he was the *Times* correspondent in Beirut
> in the next day's *Times*

In the name of the Bible and other sacred texts the definite article is
lower case.

8.2.8 **Titles within titles**

When the title of one work includes that of another this should be
indicated with a minimum of intervention in the styling of the main
title. If titles are fully capitalized the subsidiary title is sometimes
placed within single quotation marks:

> *The History of 'The Times'*

In some styles a subsidiary title can be adequately flagged by giving it
an initial capital:

> *Knowledge and the good in Plato's Republic*
> *The history of The Times*

Underlining text to distinguish it is not recommended: see 7.6.

If there is doubt as to whether the second work is referred to by its
exact title or a paraphrase it is safest not to style it as a title:

> Berington rejected the more radical philosophical tendencies of his
> earlier opinions in *Letters on materialism, and Hartley's theory of
> the human mind* (1776)

When the main title is roman within quotation marks, a subsidiary
title may be italicized and given an initial capital:

> 'The *Cronica de Wallia* and the Welsh legal system'

When one Latin title is incorporated in another the subsidiary title
will be fully integrated grammatically into the main title, and there
should be neither additional capitalization nor quotation marks:

> *In quartum librum meteorologicorum Aristotelis commentaria*

8.2.9 **Italics in titles**

Within italic titles containing a reference that would itself be italic
in open text (for example ships' names), do not revert to roman:

The Voyage of the Meteor (not *The Voyage of the* Meteor)

See 7.1.2.

8.2.10 Editorial insertions in titles

See 4.12.2 for a discussion of square brackets. Use square-bracketed insertions in titles very sparingly. The editorial *sic* should be used only if it removes a real doubt; *sic* is always italic, while the brackets adopt the surrounding typography:

> his *Collection of [Latin] nouns and verbs ... together with an English syntax*
>
> one of them, 'A borgens [bargain's] a borgen', setting a text written in a west-country dialect
>
> *The seven cartons [sic] of Raphael Urbin*

8.2.11 Bibliographic information and locations

A work mentioned in text may or may not be given a full citation in a note; in either case bibliographic detail additional to its title may be included in the text. Broadly speaking, the elements that are given in the text should be styled according to the conventions that govern citations in the notes or bibliography, but some minor variation may be appropriate (an author's full forename, for example, may be used rather than initials). Dates of publication are sometimes useful in text, and may be given in open text or in parentheses. Do not include place of publication routinely, but only if relevant to the discussion. Likewise STC (short-title catalogue) numbers may be given in specialist contexts or if helpful in the identification of a rare early work.

Bibliographic abbreviations and contractions used in the notes (like *edn, vol., bk, pt, ch.*) are generally acceptable in parenthetical citations in text but should be given in full in open text (*edition, volume, book, part, chapter*). Do not capitalize words representing divisions within works (*chapter, canto, section,* and so on). Abbreviations used for libraries or archival repositories in notes may be retained in parenthetical citations but should be extended to full forms in open text.

Locations within works can be described in a variety of ways in open text ('in the third chapter of the second book'; 'in chapter 3 of book 2'; 'in book 2, chapter 3'). Parenthetical references may employ the more abbreviated styles used in notes. In some contexts, for example where a text is discussed at length, short citations (for example 2.3.17 to represent book 2, chapter 3, line 17) may be acceptable even in open text. In such forms the numbers should be consistently either closed up to the preceding points or spaced off from them. The text should follow the conventions of the notes as to the use of Arabic or Roman numerals for the components of locations, for example acts, scenes, and lines of plays, or the divisions of classical or medieval texts. In the absence of parallel citations in the notes it is best to employ Arabic numerals for all elements.

8.3 Sacred texts

8.3.1 The Bible

General considerations

It is the normal convention to set the title of the Bible and its constituent books in roman rather than italic type, with initial capitals. Terms for parts or versions of the Bible are usually styled in the same way (the Old Testament, the Pentateuch, the Authorized Version). Specific modern editions of the Bible (for example the *New English Bible*) should be given italic titles. Terms like *scripture* or *gospel* should not be capitalized when used generically, but may be either upper or lower case when applied to a particular book of the Bible. It is not necessary to capitalize the adjective *biblical*, or the word *bibles* used of multiple copies of the Bible:

> the Acts of the Apostles   the Gospel of St Luke
> a commentary on one of the gospels

Formerly, biblical references to chapters and verses used lower-case Roman numerals for chapter, followed by a full point, space, and verse number in Arabic (ii. 34). Modern practice is to use Arabic numerals for both, separated by a colon and no space (Luke 2:34). Fuller forms (the second epistle of Paul to the Corinthians) are generally more appropriate to open text, and more or less abbreviated citations (2 Cor. or 2 Corinthians) to notes and parenthetical references in text, but the degree of abbreviation acceptable in running text will vary with context.

Versions of the Bible

The Bible traditionally used in Anglican worship, called the Authorized Version (AV), is an English translation of the Bible made in 1611.
The Vulgate, prepared mainly by St Jerome in the late fourth century,
was the standard Latin version of both the Old Testament (OT) and
New Testament (NT). Two modern English versions are the *New English Bible* (*NEB*), published in 1961–70, and the *New International
Version* (*NIV*), published in 1973–8. The Roman Catholic Bible was
translated from the Latin Vulgate and revised in 1592 (NT) and 1609
(OT); the *Jerusalem Bible* is a modern English translation (1966).

The Septuagint (LXX) is the standard Greek version of the Old Testament, originally made by the Jews of Alexandria but now used (in
Greek or in translation) by the Orthodox Churches. Neither Septuagint nor Vulgate recognizes the distinction between 'Old Testament'
and 'Apocrypha' made by Protestants.

Books of the Bible

Names of books of the Bible are conventionally abbreviated as follows:

Old Testament

Genesis	Gen.
Exodus	Exod.
Leviticus	Lev.
Numbers	Num.
Deuteronomy	Deut.
Joshua	Josh.
Judges	Judg.
Ruth	Ruth
1 Samuel	1 Sam.
2 Samuel	2 Sam.
1 Kings	1 Kgs
2 Kings	2 Kgs
1 Chronicles	1 Chr.
2 Chronicles	2 Chr.
Ezra	Ezra
Nehemiah	Neh.
Esther	Esther
Job	Job
Psalms	Ps. (*pl.* Pss.)
Proverbs	Prov.
Ecclesiastes	Eccles.
Song of Songs (*or* Song of Solomon)	S. of S.
Isaiah	Isa.

Jeremiah	Jer.
Lamentations	Lam.
Ezekiel	Ezek.
Daniel	Dan.
Hosea	Hos.
Joel	Joel
Amos	Amos
Obadiah	Obad.
Jonah	Jonah
Micah	Mic.
Nahum	Nahum
Habakkuk	Hab.
Zephaniah	Zeph.
Haggai	Hag.
Zechariah	Zech.
Malachi	Mal.

The first five books are collectively known as the Pentateuch (Five Volumes), or the books of Moses. Joshua to Esther are the Historical books; Job and Psalms are the Didactic books. The remainder of the Old Testament contains the Prophetical books. The major prophets are Isaiah, Jeremiah, and Ezekiel; the minor prophets are Hosea, Joel, Amos, Obadiah, Jonah, Micah, Nahum, Habakkuk, Zephaniah, Haggai, Zechariah, and Malachi.

New Testament

Matthew	Matt.
Mark	Mark
Luke	Luke
John	John
Acts of the Apostles	Acts
Romans	Rom.
1 Corinthians	1 Cor.
2 Corinthians	2 Cor.
Galatians	Gal.
Ephesians	Eph.
Philippians	Phil.
Colossians	Col.
1 Thessalonians	1 Thess.
2 Thessalonians	2 Thess.
1 Timothy	1 Tim.
2 Timothy	2 Tim.
Titus	Titus
Philemon	Philem.
Hebrews	Heb.
James	Jas.

1 Peter	1 Pet.
2 Peter	2 Pet.
1 John	1 John
2 John	2 John
3 John	3 John
Jude	Jude
Revelation	Rev.

Apocrypha

1 Esdras	1 Esdras
2 Esdras	2 Esdras
Tobit	Tobit
Judith	Judith
Rest of Esther	Rest of Esth.
Wisdom	Wisd.
Ecclesiasticus	Ecclus.
Baruch	Baruch
Song of the Three Children	S. of III Ch.
Susanna	Sus.
Bel and the Dragon	Bel & Dr.
Prayer of Manasses	Pr. of Man.
1 Maccabees	1 Macc.
2 Maccabees	2 Macc.

8.3.2 Other sacred texts

As with the Bible, the names of Jewish and Islamic scriptures, and of other non-Christian sacred texts, are cited in roman rather than italic.

In references to the texts of Judaism and Islam, as with the Bible, there are alternative conventions for naming, abbreviating, and numbering the various elements. The forms adopted will depend on the nature of the work and on authorial and editorial preference.

Jewish scriptures

The Hebrew Bible contains the same books as the Old Testament, but in a different arrangement. The Torah or Law has Genesis, Exodus, Leviticus, Numbers, Deuteronomy; Prophets has Joshua, Judges, Samuel, Kings, Isaiah, Jeremiah, Ezekiel, the Twelve; Writings or Hagiographa has Psalms, Proverbs, Job, Song of Songs, Ruth, Lamentations, Ecclesiastes, Esther, Daniel, Ezra, Nehemiah, Chronicles. Though nowadays divided as in Christian Bibles, Samuel, Kings, and Chronicles were (and still may be) each traditionally counted as one book; similarly Ezra–Nehemiah.

The Talmud is the body of Jewish civil and ceremonial law and legend, comprising the Mishnah and the Gemara. The Talmud exists in two versions: the Babylonian Talmud and the Jerusalem Talmud. In most non-specialist works only the former is cited.

Islamic scriptures

The Islamic sacred book is the Koran, believed to be the word of God as dictated to Muhammad by the archangel Gabriel. The spelling 'Koran' is still acceptable in non-specialist contexts, though 'Quran' and 'Qur'ān' are becoming more common even there. The Koran is divided into 114 unequal units called 'suras' or 'surahs'; each sura is divided into verses. Every sura is known by an Arabic name; this is sometimes reproduced in English, sometimes translated, for example 'the Cave' for the eighteenth. The more normal form of reference is by number, especially if the verse follows: 'Sura 18, v. 45', or simply '18. 45'. References to suras have Arabic numbers with a full point and space before the verse number, though the older style of a Roman numeral or colon is also found.

The Sunna or Sunnah is a collection of the sayings and deeds of the Prophet; the tradition of these sayings and deeds is called Hadith.

8.4 References to Shakespeare

The standard Oxford edition of Shakespeare is *The Complete Works*, edited by Stanley Wells and Gary Taylor (Oxford University Press, 1986, compact edn 1988). No single accepted model exists for abbreviating the titles of Shakespeare's plays and poems, although in many cases the standard modern form by which the work is commonly known may be thought to be abbreviated already, since the complete original titles are often much longer. For example, *The First Part of the Contention of the Two Famous Houses of York and Lancaster* is best known as *The Second Part of King Henry VI*, and *The Comical History of the Merchant of Venice, or Otherwise Called the Jew of Venice* as *The Merchant of Venice*. The table below shows the more commonly found forms used by scholars. Column two gives the forms used in the *Shorter Oxford English Dictionary* and the *Oxford English Dictionary*; column three gives those specified for the Oxford editions series. Column four lists still shorter forms, which are useful where

space is at a premium and in the references of specialist texts where
familiarity with the conventions is assumed.

Title of work	Standard abbreviations		Short abbrev.
All's Well that Ends Well	All's Well	All's Well	AWW
Antony and Cleopatra	Ant. & Cl.	Antony	Ant.
As You Like It	AYL	As You Like It	AYL
The Comedy of Errors	Com. Err.	Errors	Err.
Coriolanus	Coriol.	Coriolanus	Cor.
Cymbeline	Cymb.	Cymbeline	Cym.
Hamlet	Haml.	Hamlet	Ham.
The First Part of King Henry IV	1 Hen. IV	1 Henry IV	1H4
The Second Part of King Henry IV	2 Hen. IV	2 Henry IV	2H4
The Life of King Henry V	Hen. V	Henry V	H5
The First Part of King Henry VI	1 Hen. VI	1 Henry VI	1H6
The Second Part of King Henry VI	2 Hen. VI	2 Henry VI (Contention)	2H6
The Third Part of King Henry VI	3 Hen. VI	3 Henry VI (True Tragedy)	3H6
The Famous History of the Life of King Henry VIII	Hen. VIII	Henry VIII (All Is True)	H8
The Life and Death of King John	John K.	John	Jn.
Julius Caesar	Jul. Caes.	Caesar	JC
King Lear	Lear	Lear	Lr.
A Lover's Complaint	Compl.	Complaint	LC
Love's Labour's Lost	LLL	LLL	LLL
Macbeth	Macb.	Macbeth	Mac.
Measure for Measure	Meas. for M.	Measure	MM
The Merchant of Venice	Merch. V.	Merchant	MV
The Merry Wives of Windsor	Merry W.	Merry Wives	Wiv.
A Midsummer Night's Dream	Mids. N. D.	Dream	MND
Much Ado about Nothing	Much Ado	Much Ado	Ado
Othello	Oth.	Othello	Oth.
Pericles	Per.	Pericles	Per.
The Passionate Pilgrim	Pilgr.	P. Pilgrim	PP
The Phoenix and the Turtle	Phoenix	Phoenix	Ph.T.
The Rape of Lucrece	Lucr.	Lucrece	Luc.
The Tragedy of King Richard II	Rich. II	Richard II	R2

The Tragedy of King Richard III	*Rich. III*	*Richard III*	*R3*
Romeo and Juliet	*Rom. & Jul.*	*Romeo*	*Rom.*
Sonnets	*Sonn.*	*Sonnets*	*Son.*
The Taming of the Shrew	*Tam. Shr.*	*Shrew*	*Shr.*
The Tempest	*Temp.*	*Tempest*	*Tmp.*
Timon of Athens	*Timon*	*Timon*	*Tim.*
Titus Andronicus	*Tit. A.*	*Titus*	*Tit.*
Troilus and Cressida	*Tr. & Cr.*	*Troilus*	*Tro.*
Twelfth Night	*Twel. N.*	*Twelfth Night*	*TN*
The Two Gentlemen of Verona	*Two Gent.*	*Two Gentlemen*	*TGV*
The Two Noble Kinsmen	*Two Noble K.*	*Kinsmen*	*TNK*
Venus and Adonis	*Ven. & Ad.*	*Venus*	*Ven.*
The Winter's Tale	*Wint. T.*	*Winter's Tale*	*WT*

'F1' and 'F2' are sometimes used to mean the First Folio and Second Folio respectively, and 'Q' to mean the Quarto edition.

8.5 Films and broadcast works

The titles of films and broadcast works (both individual programmes and series) are set in italic. The titles of episodes in series are set in roman in quotation marks. They are commonly given full capitalization, though minimal capitalization is acceptable if applied consistently. If necessary further information about the recording may be included in open text or within parentheses:

> *Look Back in Anger*
> *West Side Story*
> the film *A Bridge Too Far* (1977)
> his first radio play, *Fools Rush In*, was broadcast in 1949
> the Granada TV series *Nearest and Dearest*
> the American television series *The Defenders* ('The Hidden Fury', 1964)
> the video *Stones in the Park* (1969)

8.6 Musical works

8.6.1 **General principles**

The styling of musical work titles is peculiarly difficult because of the diversity of forms in which some titles may be cited, issues related to language, and longstanding special conventions. The most comprehensive source for the correct titles of musical works and appropriate styling is *The New Grove Dictionary of Music and Musicians*, 2nd edition, edited by Stanley Sadie and John Tyrrell (London, 2001).

8.6.2 Popular music and traditional songs

Song titles in English are set in roman type with quotation marks, capitalized according to the style adopted for titles in general:

> 'Three Blind Mice'   'Brown-Eyed Girl'

This is irrespective of whether the title forms a sentence with a finite verb:

> 'A Nightingale Sang in Berkeley Square'
> 'Papa's Got a Brand New Bag'

In contrast, traditional ballads and songs, which draw their titles directly from the first line, may follow the rules for poetry. Here, only the first and proper nouns are capitalized:

> 'Come away, death'   'What shall we do with the drunken sailor?'

The names of albums, CDs, and collections are given in italic, with no quotation marks:

> *A Love Supreme*   *Forever Changes*
> *Younger Than Yesterday*   *In the Land of Grey and Pink*

This results in the combination of, for example, 'Born to Run', from *Born to Run* (roman in quotation marks for song, italic for album).

8.6.3 True titles

A distinction is usually made between works with 'true' titles and those with generic names. The boundary between the two types of title is not always clear, but, as with all other difficult style decisions, sense and context provide guidance, and consistency of treatment within any one publication is more important than adherence to a particular code of rules.

True titles are set in italic type with maximal or minimal capital initials according to the prevailing style of the publication:

> Britten's *The Burning Fiery Furnace*   Elgar's *The Apostles*
> Tippett's *A Child of our Time*

Foreign-language titles are usually retained (and styled according to the practice outlined in 8.8 below). By convention, however, English publications always refer to some well-known works by English titles, especially when the original title is in a lesser-known language:

>Berlioz's *Symphonie fantastique*   Schubert's *Die schöne Müllerin*
>Liszt's *Années de pèlerinage*

but

>Berg's *Lyric Suite*
>Bartók's *Music for Strings, Percussion and Celesta*
>Stravinsky's *The Rite of Spring*

Operas and other dramatic works may be named in the original language or in English according to any sensible and consistent system—for example, in the original language if the reference is to a performance in that language, in English if the reference is to a performance in translation. A translated title may be given if the reader may not otherwise recognize the work:

>Mozart's *The Magic Flute*
>Janáček's *Z mrtvého domu* ('From the house of the dead')

Some works, however, are by convention always named in the original language:

>Puccini's *La Bohème*   Weber's *Der Freischütz*

The titles of individual songs, arias, anthems, and movements are styled in roman in quotation marks, as are nicknames (that is, those not provided by the composer):

>'Skye Boat Song'
>'Dove sono' from *The Marriage of Figaro*
>the sacred madrigal 'When David heard that Absalom was dead'
>the 'Rigaudon' from *Le Tombeau de Couperin*
>the 'Jupiter' Symphony
>the 'Enigma Variations'

It is customary to use minimal capital initials for titles derived from the words of a song (see 8.6.2).

8.6.4 **Generic names**

Titles derived from the names of musical forms are set in roman type with initial capitals. Identifying numbers in a series of works of the same form, opus numbers, and catalogue numbers are all given in Arabic numerals; the abbreviations 'op.' and 'no.' may be capitalized or not, while the capital abbreviations that preface catalogue numbers are often set in small capitals without a full point and closed up to the numeral (though Oxford style is to use full capitals and a full point and

to space off the numeral). The names of keys may use musical symbols
♯ and ♭ or the words 'sharp' and 'flat'. Note the capitalization, punctuation, and spacing in the examples below:

> Bach's Mass in B minor *or* B Minor Mass
> Brahms's Symphony no. 4/Fourth Symphony
> Handel's Concerto Grosso in G major, op. 3, no. 3
> Mozart's Piano Trio, к496
> Beethoven's String Quartet in C sharp minor, op. 131 *or* ... C♯ minor, op.
> 131

Tempo marks used as the titles of movements are also set in roman
type with initial capitals, as are the sections of the mass and other
services:

> the Adagio from Mahler's Fifth Symphony
> the Credo from the *Missa solemnis*
> the Te Deum from Purcell's Morning Service in D

8.6.5 **Hybrid names**

Certain titles are conventionally styled in a mixture of roman and
italic type. They include works that are named by genre and title
such as certain overtures and masses:

> the Overture *Portsmouth Point*   the Mass *L'Homme armé*

Note, however, that in other styles the generic word is treated as a
descriptor:

> the march *Pomp and Circumstance*, no. 1   the *Firebird* suite

Instrumentation that follows the title of a work may be given descrip-
tively in roman with lower-case initials, or as part of the title. A number
of twentieth-century works, however, include their instrumentation
as an inseparable part of the title.

> *Three Pieces* for cello and piano

but

> *Serenade for Strings*   *Concerto for Orchestra*

8.7 Works of art

8.7.1 **General principles**

The formal titles of works of visual art, including paintings, sculptures,
drawings, posters, and prints, are set in italic. Full capitalization is still

usual, though with longer titles there may be difficulties in deciding which words should be capitalized:

> Joseph Stella, *Brooklyn Bridge*
>
> *The Mirror of Venus*
>
> the etching *Adolescence* (1932) and the painting *Dorette* (1933)
>
> the huge chalk and ink drawing *St Bride's and the City after the Fire, 29th December 1940*
>
> the wartime poster *Your Talk may Kill your Comrades* (1942)

Consistently minimal capitalization is also possible for works of art:

> Petrus Christus's *Portrait of a young man*

Works may be referred to either by a formal title or by a more descriptive form:

> he painted a portrait entitled *James Butler, 2nd duke of Ormonde, when Lord Ossory*
>
> he painted a portrait of James Butler (later second duke of Ormonde) when he was Lord Ossory

Titles bestowed by someone other than the artist or sculptor are usually given in roman with no quotation marks:

> La Gioconda   the Venus de Milo

Works that discuss numerous works of art need consistent conventions and abbreviations for the parenthetical presentation of such information as the medium, dimensions, date of creation or date and place of first exhibition, and the current ownership or location of the works mentioned:

> *Andromeda* (bronze, *c.*1851; Royal Collection, Osborne House, Isle of Wight)
>
> *The Spartan Isadas* (exh. RA, 1827; priv. coll.)

8.7.2 **Series of works of art**

Place the titles of series of unique works of art in roman type with maximal capitalization and without quotation marks. Series of published prints may be given italic titles:

> a series of paintings of children, Sensitive Plants, with such names as *Sweet William* and *Mary Gold*
>
> his finest series of prints, *Gulliver's Travels* and *Pilgrim's Progress*

8.8 Non-English work titles

For general guidance on works in languages other than English see Chapter 12. The rules governing the capitalization of titles in some languages, such as French, are complex, and in less formal contexts it is acceptable to treat foreign-language titles in the same way as English ones.

Take care to distinguish the title, date of publication, and author of the original from the title, date, and translator of an English version. Ideally the title of the translation should not be used as if it were the title of the original work, but this rule may be relaxed in some contexts.

English titles may be used for works performed in English translation. The common English titles of classical works may be used in place of the Greek or Latin originals, and common English or Latin titles may be used for ancient or medieval works originally written in Greek, Arabic, or Persian:

> he translated from the Spanish a biography by Miguel de Luna, published in 1627 as *Almansor the learned and victorious king*
> in *The Marriage of Figaro* at Covent Garden
> Virgil's *Eclogues*
> Avicenna's *Canon of Medicine*
> Aristotle's *De caelo et mundo*

The title in the original language may be accompanied by an English translation, especially if its sense is not implied by the surrounding text. Place such translations in quotation marks within parentheses (square brackets are sometimes used), in roman type with an initial capital on the first word. The true titles of published translations are set in italics, like those of other publications.

> *Auraicept na n-éces* ('The primer of the poets')
> the lament 'O, Ailein duinn shiùbhlainn leat' ('Oh, brown-haired Allan, I would go with you')
> a translation of Voltaire's *Dictionnaire philosophique* (as *A Dictionary of Philosophy*, 1824)

Except in specialist contexts the titles of works in non-Roman alphabets are not reproduced in their original characters but are transliterated according to standard systems (with minimal capitalization) or replaced by English translations. Words actually printed in transliteration in a title are rendered as printed, not brought into line with a more modern style of transliteration:

> Ibn Sīnā's *Kitāb shifā' al-nafs*
>
> Chekhov's *The Cherry Orchard*
>
> his translation of the Bhagavadgita was published in London (as *The Bhagvat-geeta*) in 1785

8.9 Integration of titles into text

Integrate the title of a work syntactically into the sentence in which it is mentioned.

Do not separate an author's name from a work title simply by a comma; where appropriate employ a possessive form. An initial definite or indefinite article may be omitted from a title if this helps the sentence to read more smoothly.

Always treat the title of a work as singular, regardless of its wording:

> his *Experiences of a Lifetime* ranges widely

Phrasing that places the title of a work as the object of the prepositions *on* or *about* (as in the third of the following examples) should be avoided. The style should be:

> a paper on the origins of the manor in England
>
> a paper, 'The origins of the manor in England'

not

> a paper on 'The origins of the manor in England'

When part or all of a book's title or subtitle, or any other matter from the title page, is quoted it should be styled as a quotation, not as a work title, that is in roman not italic type and with the original punctuation and capitalization (unless full capitals) preserved:

> *The Enimie of Idlenesse*, printed in 1568, was presented as a manual 'Teaching the maner and stile how to endite, compose, and write all sorts of Epistles and Letters'

CHAPTER 9

Quotations and direct speech

9.1 General principles

A direct quotation presents the exact words spoken on a particular occasion or written in a particular place. It can be of any length, but there are legal restrictions on how much of another's work one may repeat; for more on copyright see Chapter 20. Quoted direct speech and dialogue are most often found in fiction and journalism.

A direct quotation or passage of direct speech should be clearly indicated and, unlike a paraphrase, should exactly reproduce the words of the original. While the wording of the quoted text should be faithfully reproduced, the extent to which the precise form of the original source is replicated will vary with context and editorial preference.

Quotations from early manuscripts may call for more or less complex and specialist conventions that are not discussed here.

9.2 Layout of quoted text

9.2.1 **Displayed and run-on quotations**

Quotations can be run on in text or broken off from it. A prose quotation of fewer than, say, fifty words is normally run on (or **embedded**) and enclosed in quotation marks, while longer quotations are broken off without quotation marks. But there is no firm rule, and the treatment of particular quotations or groups of quotations will depend on editorial preference, context, and the overall look of the page. A passage that contains multiple quotations, for example, may be easier to read if all are displayed, even if some or all of them contain fewer than fifty words. Or it may be thought helpful to display a single short quotation that is central to the following argument.

Quotations that are broken off from text (called **displayed** or **block** quotations, or **extracts**) begin on a new line, and can appear in various formats: they may be set in smaller type (usually one size down from text size), or in text-size type with less leading (vertical space between the lines); set to the full measure, or to a narrower measure; set with all lines indented from the left, or block centred (indented left and right); or set justified or unjustified. A commonly encountered style is shown below; the text is indented one em left and right:

> Most of those who came in now had joined the Army unwillingly, and there was no reason why they should find military service tolerable. The War had become undisguisedly mechanical and inhuman. What in earlier days had been drafts of volunteers were now droves of victims. I was just beginning to be aware of this.

Traditional Oxford University Press practice in academic books is to set displayed quotations one size down, full measure, and justified, as shown here:

> This morning, the British Ambassador in Berlin handed the German government a final Note stating that, unless we heard from them by eleven o'clock that they were prepared at once to withdraw their troops from Poland, a state of war would exist between us. I have to tell you now that no such undertaking has been received, and that consequently this country is at war with Germany.

Displayed quotations should not be set entirely in italic type (though individual words may of course be italicized). If two or more quotations that are not continuous in the original are displayed to follow one another with none of the author's own text intervening, the discontinuity is shown by extra leading.

More than one line of quoted verse is normally displayed, line by line. Some other material, for example lists, whether or not numbered, and quoted dialogue, is suitable for line-by-line display. For verse quotations see 9.4 below; for extracts from plays see 9.5.

Because displayed quotations are not enclosed by quotation marks any quoted material within them is enclosed (in British style) by single quotation marks, not double. A quotation within a run-on quotation is placed within double quotation marks:

> These visits in after life were frequently repeated, and whenever he found himself relapsing into a depressed state of health and spirits, 'Well', he would say, 'I must come into hospital', and would repair for another week to 'Campbell's ward', a room so named by the poet in the doctor's house.

Chancellor was 'convinced that the entire Balfour Declaration policy had been "a colossal blunder", unjust to the Arabs and impossible of fulfillment in its own terms'.

If a section consisting of two or more paragraphs from the same source is quoted, but not displayed, quotation marks are used at the beginning of each paragraph and the end of the last one, but not at the end of the first and intermediate paragraphs.

9.2.2 Introducing quotations and direct speech

When quoted speech is introduced, interrupted, or followed by an interpolation such as *he said*, the interpolation is usually separated from the speech by commas:

> 'I wasn't born yesterday,' she said.
> 'No,' said Mr Stephens, 'certainly not.'
> A voice behind me says, 'Someone stolen your teddy bear, Sebastian?'

A colon may also be used before the quoted speech. A colon is typically used to introduce more formal speech or speeches of more than one sentence, to give emphasis to the quoted matter, or to clarify the sentence structure after a clause in parentheses:

> Rather than mince words she told them: 'You have forced this move upon me.'
> Philips said: 'I'm embarrassed. Who wouldn't be embarrassed?'
> Peter Smith, general secretary of the Association of Teachers and Lecturers, said: 'Countries which outperform the UK in education do not achieve success by working teachers to death.'

Very short speeches do not need any introductory punctuation:

> He called 'Good morning!'

and neither does a quotation that is fitted into the syntax of the surrounding sentence:

> He is alleged to have replied that 'our old college no longer exists'.

The words *yes* and *no* and question words such as *where* and *why* are enclosed in quotation marks where they represent direct speech, but not when they represent reported speech or tacit paraphrasing:

> She asked, 'Really? Where?'
> He said 'Yes!', but she retorted 'No!'
> The governors said no to our proposal.
> When I asked to marry her, she said yes.

9.2.3 **Quotation marks**

Modern British practice is normally to enclose quoted matter between single quotation marks, and to use double quotation marks for a quotation within a quotation:

> 'Have you any idea', he said, 'what "red mercury" is?'

The order is often reversed in newspapers, and uniformly in US practice:

> "Have you any idea," he said, "what 'red mercury' is?"

If another quotation is nested within the second quotation, revert to the original mark, either single–double–single or double–single–double.

Quotation marks with other punctuation

When quoted speech is broken off and then resumed after words such as *he said*, a comma is used within the quotation marks to represent any punctuation that would naturally have been found in the original passage. Three quoted extracts—with and without internal punctuation—might be:

> Go home to your father.
> Go home, and never come back.
> Yes, we will. It's a good idea.

When presented as direct speech these would be punctuated as follows:

> 'Go home', he said, 'to your father.'
> 'Go home,' he said, 'and never come back.'
> 'Yes,' he said, 'we will. It's a good idea.'

The last example above may equally be quoted in the following ways:

> He said, 'Yes, we will. It's a good idea.'
> 'Yes, we will,' he said. 'It's a good idea.'
> 'Yes, we will. It's a good idea,' he said.

In US practice, commas and full points are set inside the closing quotation mark regardless of whether they are part of the quoted material (note in the US example the double quotation marks):

> No one should 'follow a multitude to do evil', as the Scripture says.
> *American*: No one should "follow a multitude to do evil," as the Scripture says.

This style is also followed in much modern British fiction and journalism. In the following extract from a British novel the comma after 'suggest' is enclosed within the quotation marks even though the original spoken sentence would have had no punctuation:

> 'May I suggest,' she said, 'that you have a bath before supper?'

Traditional British style would have given:

> 'May I suggest', she said, 'that you have a bath before supper?'

When a grammatically complete sentence is quoted, the full point is placed *within* the closing quotation mark. The original might read:

> It cannot be done. We must give up the task.

It might then be quoted as

> He concluded, 'We must give up the task.'
> 'It cannot be done,' he concluded. 'We must give up the task.'

When the quoted sentence ends with a question mark or exclamation mark, this should be placed within the closing quotation mark, with no other mark outside the quotation mark—only one mark of terminal punctuation is needed:

> He sniffed the air and exclaimed, 'I smell a horse!'

When the punctuation mark is not part of the quoted material, as in the case of single words and phrases, place it outside the closing quotation mark:

> Why does he use the word 'poison'?

When a quoted sentence is a short one with no introductory punctuation, the full point is generally placed outside the closing quotation mark:

> *Cogito, ergo sum* means 'I think, therefore I am'.
> He believed in the proverb 'Dead men tell no tales'.
> He asserted that 'Americans don't understand history', and that 'intervention would be a disaster'.

9.2.4 Dialogue

Dialogue is usually set within quotation marks, with each new speaker's words on a new line, indented at the beginning:

> 'What's going on?' he asked.
> 'I'm prematurely ageing,' I muttered.

In some styles of writing—particularly fiction—opening quotation marks are replaced with em rules and closing quotation marks are omitted:

> —We'd better get goin', I suppose, said Bimbo.

— Fair enough, said Jimmy Sr.

In other styles, marks of quotation are dispensed with altogether, the change in syntax being presumed sufficient to indicate the shift between direct speech and interpolations:

> Who's that? asked Russell, affecting not to have heard.
> Why, Henry, chirped Lytton.

Dialogue in fiction is often not introduced with 'say' or any other speech verb:

> I decide it's Spencer's fault, and sit up grumpily.
> 'Who let you in?'

Thought and imagined dialogue may be placed in quotation marks or not, so long as similar instances are treated consistently within a single work.

9.2.5 Sources

The source of a quotation, whether run on or displayed, is normally given in a note if the work uses that form of referencing, or it may be presented in an author–date reference. The source of a displayed prose quotation may be given in the text. It may, for example, follow the end of the quotation in parentheses after an em space, or be ranged right on the measure of the quotation, either on the line on which the quotation ends, if there is room, or on the following line:

> Troops who have fought a few battles and won, and followed up their victories, improve on what they were before to an extent that can hardly be counted by percentage. The difference in result is often decisive victory instead of inglorious defeat.   (*Personal Memoirs*, 355)

> He brought an almost scholarly detachment to public policy—a respect for the primacy of evidence over prejudice; and in retirement, this made him a valued and respected member of the scholarly community. Those of us privileged to know him will always remember him as an exemplar of standards and qualities in public life.   *The Times*, 8 Nov. 1999

9.3 Styling of quoted text

9.3.1 Spelling, capitalization, and punctuation

In quotations from printed sources the spelling, capitalization, and punctuation should normally follow the original. However:

- Such obvious errors as a missing full point or unclosed parentheses or quotation marks may be silently corrected.
- Forms of punctuation that differ from house style may be silently regularized. Thus foreign forms of question mark or quotation mark (for example « » or „ ") should be replaced, and the use of double and single quotation marks and of em rules, en rules, and hyphens standardized.
- It is acceptable to change a capital on the first word of a quotation to lower case in order to integrate it into the surrounding sentence, although this is not preferred Oxford practice.
- Orthographic signs (including the ampersand) and abbreviations may be retained or expanded, and superscript letters reproduced or brought down, according to editorial preference.
- The original's use of the letters *i* and *j*, and of *u* and *v*, may be consistently modernized, though it is generally safest to retain the printed forms.
- A double *v* (*vv*) may be changed to the letter *w*.
- The long *s* (roman ſ, italic ſ) is a variant form rather than a distinct letter and is always regularized to *s*.
- Text that is printed in full caps may be rationalized to upper and lower case (or caps and small caps).

Preserve if possible the Old and Middle English letters ash (æ), eth (ð), thorn (þ), yogh (ȝ), and wyn (ƿ) in quotations from printed sources (see 12.13.1). Ligatured œ and æ in quoted text may be retained or printed as two separate letters according to editorial policy.

9.3.2 **Interpolation and correction**

Place in square brackets any words interpolated into a verbatim quotation that are not part of the original. Use such interpolations sparingly. Editorial interpolations may be helpful in preserving the grammatical structure of a quotation while suppressing irrelevant phrasing, or in explaining the significance of something mentioned that is not evident from the quotation itself. The Latin words *recte* (meaning 'properly' or 'correctly') and *rectius* ('more properly') are rare but acceptable in such places:

> he must have left [Oxford] and his studies

> as though they [the nobility and gentry] didn't waste enough of your
> soil already on their coverts and game-preserves
>
> the Duke and Duchess of Gloucester [*recte* Cumberland] are often
> going to a famous painters in Pall Mall; and 'tis reported that he
> [Gainsborough] is now doing both their pictures

The Latin word *sic* (meaning 'thus') is used to confirm an incorrect or
otherwise unexpected form in a quotation; it is printed in italics
within square brackets. Do not use *sic* simply to flag erratic spelling,
but only to remove real doubt as to the accuracy of the quoted text. Do
not use [!] as a form of editorial comment:

> Bulmer established his Shakspeare [*sic*] Press in London at Cleveland
> Row

In some contexts editorial policy may allow the silent correction of
trivial errors in the original, judging it more important to transmit the
content of the quoted matter than to reproduce its exact form.

9.3.3 **Omissions**

Mark the omission of text within a quotation by an ellipsis (...). Do not
place an ellipsis at the start or end of a quotation, even if this is not the
beginning or end of a sentence; the reader must accept that the source
may continue before and after the text quoted. See 4.7 for a full discussion of ellipsis.

Punctuation immediately before or after an ellipsis can generally be
suppressed unless it is helpful to the sense, as might be the case with
a question or exclamation mark; style in similar contexts should be
consistent within a work. It may, however, be retained in some
contexts—for purposes of textual analysis, for example, or where the
author has some other particular reason for preserving it. If the preceding sentence ends with a full point it is Oxford practice to retain the
point before the ellipsis, closed up to the preceding text:

> Writing was a way of understanding ... world events.
>
> Where is Godfrey? ... They say he is murdered by the papists.
>
> Presently a misty moon came up, and a nightingale began to sing. ... It
> was strange to stand there and listen, for the song seemed to come
> all the more sweetly and clearly in the quiet intervals between the
> bursts of firing.

Do not delete an ellipsis that is part of the original text if the words on
either side of it are retained in the quotation. In a quotation that

contains such an original ellipsis any editorial ellipsis should be distinguished by being placed within square brackets:

> The fact is, Lady Bracknell [...] my parents seem to have lost me ... I don't actually know who I am [...] I was ... well, I was found.

An ellipsis can mark an omission of any length. In a displayed quotation broken into paragraphs mark the omission of intervening paragraphs by inserting an ellipsis at the end of the paragraph before the omission. For omissions in verse extracts see 9.4.3 below.

9.3.4 Typography

A quotation is not a facsimile, and in most contexts it is not necessary to reproduce the exact typography of the original. Such features as change of font, bold type, underscoring, ornaments, and the exact layout of the text may generally be ignored. Italicization may be reproduced if helpful, or suppressed if excessive.

9.4 Poetry

9.4.1 Run-on verse quotations

More than one line of quoted verse is normally displayed line by line, but verse quotations may also be run on in the text. In run-on quotations it is traditional Oxford style to indicate the division between each line by a vertical bar (|) with a space either side, although a solidus (/) is also widely used:

> 'Gone, the merry morris din, | Gone the song of Gamelyn', wrote Keats in 'Robin Hood'

When set, the vertical or solidus must not start a new line. See also 4.13.

9.4.2 Displayed verse

In general, poetry (including blank verse) should be centred on the longest line on each page; if this is disproportionately long the text should be centred optically. Within the verse the lines will generally range on the left, but where a poem's indentation clearly varies the copy should be followed: this is particularly true for some modern poetry, where correct spacing in reproduction forms part of the copyright. In such instances it is useful to provide the typesetter with a photocopy of the original to work from. It is helpful to indent turn-overs 1 em beyond the poem's maximum indentation:

> Pond-chestnuts poke through floating chickweed on the green
>   brocade pool
> A thousand summer orioles sing as they play among the roses
> I watch the fine rain, alone all day,
> While side by side the ducks and drakes bathe in their crimson
>   coats

Do not automatically impose capitals at the beginnings of lines. Modern verse, for example, sometimes has none, and the conventions commonly applied to Greek and Latin verse allow an initial capital to only a few lines (see 12.8.5, 12.12.3).

9.4.3 Omissions

Omissions in verse quotations run into text are indicated like those in prose. Within displayed poetry the omission of one or more whole lines may be marked by a line of points, separated by 2-em spaces; the first and last points should fall approximately 2 ems inside the measure of the longest line:

> Laboreres þat haue no lande, to lyue on but her handes,
> Deyned nouȝt to dyne a-day, nyȝt-olde wortes.
>
> .   .   .   .
>
> Ac whiles hunger was her maister, þere wolde none of hem chyde,
> Ne stryve aȝeines his statut, so sterneliche he loked.

Use an ellipsis when the end of a line of displayed verse is omitted; indicate the omission of the start of the first line of displayed verse by ranging (usually right with the next line):

>   a great beau
> that here makes a show
> and thinks all about him are fools

9.4.4 Sources

If there is sufficient room a short source—such as a book, canto, or line number, or a short title—can be placed in parentheses on the same line as the last line of verse. Oxford practice is to begin the reference 1 em to the right of the end of the quotation's longest line:

> The world was all before them, where to choose

> Their place of rest, and providence their guide:
> They hand in hand with wandering steps and slow
> Through Eden took their solitary way   (xii. 648–9)

If the source is longer place it on the next line down, ranged to the right with the end of the quotation's longest line:

> They hand in hand with wandering steps and slow
> Through Eden took their solitary way
>   *Paradise Lost*, xii. 648–9

9.5 Plays

Publishers have their own conventions for the presentation of plays, quotations from which may be treated as run-on quotations, or as prose or poetry extracts, with no strict regard to the original layout, spacing, or styling of characters' names. Any sensible pattern is acceptable if consistently applied. If a speaker's name is included in the quotation it is best printed as a displayed extract.

To follow Oxford's preferred format in extracts from plays, set speakers' names in small capitals, ranged full left. In verse plays run the speaker's name into the first line of dialogue; the verse follows the speaker's name after an em space and is not centred; indent subsequent lines by the same speaker 1 em from the left. Indent turnovers 2 ems in verse plays, 1 em in prose plays:

> Her reply prompts Oedipus to bemoan his sons' passivity:
>
> OEDIPUS But those young men your brothers, where are they?
> ISMENE Just where they are—in the thick of trouble.
> OEDIPUS O what miserable and perfect copies have they grown to be of
>   Egyptian ways!
>   For there the men sit at home and weave while their wives go out to win
>   the daily bread.
>
> This is apparent in the following exchange between them:
>
> WIPER We've had ballistics research on this. No conceivable injury
>   could from this angle cause even the most temporary failure of the
>   faculties.
> BUTTERTHWAITE You can't catch me. I've read me Sexton Blake. I
>   was turned the other way.
> WIPER Are you in the habit, Alderman, of entering your garden
>   backwards?

Particularly in verse plays a single line is sometimes made up of the speeches of more than one character and is set as more than one line of type. The parts are progressively indented, with an interword space clear to the right of the previous part's end, repeating as necessary. Ideally this layout should be preserved in the quoted extract, as in the following extreme example:

KING JOHN   Death.
HUBERT   My lord.
KING JOHN   A grave.
HUBERT   He shall not live.
KING JOHN   Enough.

Do not include stage directions in extracts from plays unless they are relevant to the matter under discussion (in which case their styling in the original may be preserved or adapted). Similarly, line numbers should not normally be included.

9.6 Epigraphs

In publishing, an epigraph is a short quotation or saying at the beginning of a book or chapter. Publishers will have their own preferences for the layout of epigraphs. In Oxford's academic books they are set in small type, verse epigraphs being treated much like displayed verse quotations and optically centred. A source may be placed on the line after the epigraph, ranged right on the epigraph's measure:

To understand history the reader must always remember how small is the proportion of what is recorded to what actually took place.

Churchill, *Marlborough*

An epigraph's source does not usually include full bibliographic details, or even a location within the work cited (though such information can be given in a note if it seems helpful). The date or circumstances of the epigraph, or the author's dates, may be given if they are thought to be germane:

You will find it a very good practice always to verify your references, sir!

Martin Joseph Routh (1755–1854)

9.7 Non-English quotations

Quotations from languages other than English are commonly given in
English translation, but they are sometimes reproduced in their original language, for example when their sense is thought to be evident,
in specialist contexts where a knowledge of the language in question is
assumed, or where a short quotation is better known in the original
language than it is in English:

> *L'État c'est moi* ('I am the State')
> *Après nous le déluge* ('After us the deluge')
> *Arbeit macht frei* ('Work liberates')

Quotations in other languages follow the same rules as those in English. The wording, spelling, punctuation, capitalization, and layout of
non-English quotations should be treated like those in English, and
omissions, interpolations, and sources presented in the same way:

> Asked about the role of the new Spanish government in his release, Raúl
> Rivero replied:
>
> Tengo un sentimiento de gratitud con el Gobierno de [José María] Aznar
> por lo que hizo cuando caí preso. Pero, efectivamente, me parece que la
> nueva política española ha sido más efectiva. La confrontación nunca en
> política resuelve nada. Creo que el cambio sí ha favorecido ... que en Cuba
> hubiera más receptividad en las autoridades cubanas.
>
> *El País*, 1 Dec. 2004, 33e
>
> *Le Monde* reported that 'Raúl Rivero a exprimé sa "gratitude éternelle"
> envers le gouvernement espagnol'.

In the second example the original wording, including the French
rendering of a Spanish name, has been reproduced exactly, but
French quotation marks and italicization of quotations (*«gratitude
éternelle»*) have been adapted to British conventions.

Sometimes it seems desirable both to retain the original—perhaps because its exact sense or flavour cannot be captured by a translation—
and to provide an English version for readers unfamiliar with the
language in question. It is always worth asking in such cases
whether the original is genuinely helpful to the reader. The English
equivalent may take the form of an explanation or paraphrase, but if
it too is presented as a direct quotation, whether loose or literal, it
should be enclosed in quotation marks and will normally be placed
within parentheses after the original. Alternatively the translation
may be given first, followed by the original in quotation marks

within parentheses. If sources of quotations are given in parentheses, a source may follow a translation within a single set of parentheses, separated from it by a comma, semicolon, or colon, according to house style:

> It provided accommodation for 'candidatos às magistraturas superiores das Faculdades', those eligible for senior posts in the university.
>
> The cyclist Jean Bégué was 'de ces Jean qu'on n'ose pas appeler Jeannot' ('one of those men named John one dare not call Johnny').
>
> He poses the question 'Wie ist das Verhältnis des Ausschnitts zur Gesamtheit?' ('What is the relationship of the sample to the whole group?': Bulst, 'Gegenstand und Methode', 9).
>
> Inter needed to develop 'a winning attitude and an attractive style of play' ('un identità vincente e un bel gioco').

Where a displayed translation is followed by a displayed original—or vice versa—place the second of the two quotations in parentheses. Where the second of the two displayed quotations is the original, some authors prefer to have it set in italics. A displayed verse original may be followed either by a verse translation set in lines or by a displayed prose translation:

> Rufus naturaliter et veste dealbatus
> Omnibus impatiens et nimis elatus
> (Ruddy in looks and white in his vesture,
> Impatient with all and too proud in gesture)   Wright, i. 261

> Gochel gwnsel a gwensaeth
> a gwin Sais, gwenwyn sy waeth
> (Beware the counsel, fawning smile and wine of the Englishman—it is worse than poison)

In most contexts quotations from other languages should be given in translation unless there is a particular reason for retaining the original. On occasion it is helpful to include within a translation, in italics within parentheses, the untranslated form of problematic or specially significant words or phrases:

> Huntington, 'obsessed with the idea of purity, does not recognize the cardinal virtue of ... Spanish: the virtue of coexistence and intermixing (*mestizaje*)'.

Isolated non-English words or phrases generally look best italicized rather than placed in quotation marks (see 7.2.2), especially if they are discussed as set terms rather than quotations from a particular

source. For inflected languages this has the advantage of allowing the
nominative form of a word to be given even when another case is used
in the passage cited. The non-English term may be used untranslated
or with an English equivalent (perhaps on its first occurrence only if it
is used frequently):

> This right of common access (*Allemansrätten*) is in an old tradition
> As early as 1979 the status of *denominação de origem controlada* was
>   accorded to Bairrada
> In this document he is styled *magister scolarum*
> Montella was *capocannoniere* (top scorer), with eleven goals

In some works appropriate conventions will be needed for quotations
transliterated from non-roman alphabets and for the rendering of
German Fraktur type. The German *Eszett* (ß) can normally be regularized as double *s* (ss). For advice on transliteration see Chapter 12.

CHAPTER 10

Abbreviations and symbols

10.1 General principles

Abbreviations fall into three categories. Strictly speaking, only the first of these is technically an abbreviation, though the term loosely covers them all, and guidelines for their use overlap. There is a further category, that of symbols, which are more abstract representations.

- **Abbreviations** in the strict sense are formed by omitting the end of a word or words (*Lieut.*, *cent.*, *assoc.*).

- **Contractions** are formed by omitting the middle of a word or words (*Dr*, *Ltd*, *Mrs*, *Revd*, *St*). Informal contractions (*I've*, *he's*, *mustn't*) are widely used but are not appropriate in all contexts (see 10.2.3).

- **Acronyms** are formed from the initial letters of words. Acronyms are sometimes defined specifically as words formed from the initial letters of other words and pronounced as words themselves (*AWOL*, *NATO*), as opposed to **initialisms**, which are formed from the initial letters of words but not pronounced as words (*BBC*, *CND*). Another class of words originated as acronyms but are now treated as orthodox nouns and written as lower-case forms: examples include *laser* (from *l*ight *a*mplification by *s*timulated *e*mission of radiation) and *Nimby* (*n*ot *i*n *m*y *b*ack *y*ard); *AIDS* (*acquired immune deficiency syndrome*) is today becoming a noun rather than an acronym, and is often written as *Aids*. Oxford dictionaries, in particular the *New Oxford Dictionary for Writers and Editors*, give the meanings of a great many abbreviations. (See also 10.2.4.)

- **Symbols** or **signs** may be letters assigned to concepts (π, Ω), or special typographical sorts (%, +, #). They are typically used in conjunction with words, numbers, or other symbols (πr^2, £100, © Oxford University Press), although they may be used on their own as, for example, note markers.

In work for a general audience do not use abbreviations or symbols in open text (that is, in the main text but not including material in parentheses) unless they are very familiar indeed (*US*, *BBC*, *UN*), space is scarce, or terms are repeated so often that abbreviations are easier to absorb. Abbreviations are more appropriate in parentheses and in ancillary matter such as appendices, bibliographies, captions, figures, notes, references, and tables, and rules differ for these.

Use only those shortened forms likely to be familiar to the intended audience. In writing aimed at a technical or specialist readership shortened forms are widespread, but in all contexts it is helpful to spell out the rarer ones at first mention, adding the abbreviation in parentheses after it:

the Economic and Social Research Council (ESRC)

Normally it is not necessary to repeat this process in each chapter unless the book is likely to be read out of sequence, as in a multi-author work or a textbook. If this is the case, or simply if many abbreviations are used, including a list of abbreviations or a glossary is a good way to avoid repeatedly expanding abbreviations (see 1.2.14). Titles of qualifications and honours placed after personal names are an exception to the general rule that initialisms should be spelled out; many forms not familiar to most people are customarily cited:

Alasdair Andrews, Bt, CBE, MVO, MFH

For more on titles see 6.1.4.

It is possible to refer to a recently mentioned full name by a more readable shortened form, rather than—or in addition to—a set of initials: *the Institute* rather than *IHGS* for the Institute of Heraldic and Genealogical Studies. (See also 5.3.2.)

As a general rule, avoid mixing abbreviations and full words of similar terms, although specialist or even common usage may militate against this, as in *Newark, JFK, and LaGuardia airports*.

For lists of abbreviations see 1.2.14; for legal abbreviations see 13.2.2; for abbreviations in or with names see 6.1.1. For Latin bibliographic abbreviations such as 'ibid.' see 17.2.5.

10.2 Punctuation and typography

10.2.1 **Full points?**

Traditionally, abbreviations end in full points while contractions do not, so that we have *Jun.* and *Jr* for Junior, and *Rev.* and *Revd* for Reverend. This rule is handy and in general is borne out, although there are some exceptions: for example *St.* (= Street) is often written with a point to avoid confusion with *St* for Saint. Note that everyday titles like *Mr*, *Mrs*, and *Dr*, being contractions, are written without a point, as is *Ltd*; editors need not attempt to establish how a particular company styles *Ltd* in its name. US style uses more points than British style does (see 10.2.4), even with contractions, thus giving *Jr.* instead of *Jr* (no point).

A problem can arise with plural forms of abbreviations such as *vol.* (volume) or *ch.* (chapter): these would strictly be *vols* and *chs*, which are contractions and should not end with a point. However, this can lead to the inconsistent-looking juxtaposition of *vol.* and *vols* or *ch.* and *chs*, and so in some styles full points are retained for all such short forms. Similarly, *Bros*, the plural form of *Bro.* 'brother', is often written with a point.

Technical and scientific writing uses less punctuation than non-technical English. Metric abbreviations such as *m* (metre), *km* (kilometre), and *g* (gram) do not usually have a full point, and never do in scientific or technical writing. Purely scientific abbreviations (*bps* = bits per second; *mRNA* = *messenger ribonucleic acid*) tend to be printed without full points.

There are other exceptions to the principle that abbreviations have full points. For example, abbreviations for eras, such as AD and BC (traditionally written in small capitals), have no points. Arabic and Roman numerical abbreviations take no points (*1st, 2nd, 3rd*); similarly, monetary amounts (*£6 m, 50p*) and book sizes (*4to, 8vo, 12mo*) do not have points. Note also that there are no points in colloquial abbreviations that have become established words in their own right, such as *demo* (demonstration) or *trad* (traditional).

If an abbreviation ends with a full point but does not end the sentence, other punctuation follows naturally: *Gill & Co., Oxford*. If the full point of the abbreviation ends the sentence, however, there is no second full point: *Oxford's Gill & Co.*

10.2.2 **Ampersands**

Avoid ampersands except in established combinations (e.g. *R & B*, *C & W*) and in names of firms that use them (*M&S, Mills & Boon*). There should be spaces around the ampersand except from in company names such as *M&S* that are so styled; in journalism ordinary combinations such as *R & B* are frequently written with no spaces.

In informal contexts ampersands may occasionally be convenient for clarification: in *cinnamon & raisin and onion bagels are available* the ampersand makes clear there are two rather than three types on offer.

10.2.3 **Apostrophes**

Place the apostrophe in the position corresponding to the missing letter or letters (*fo'c's'le, ha'p'orth, sou'wester, t'other*), but note that *shan't* has only one apostrophe. Informal contractions such as *I'm, can't, it's, mustn't,* and *he'll* are perfectly acceptable in less formal writing, especially fiction and reported speech, and are sometimes found even in academic works. However, editors should not impose them except to maintain consistency within a varying text.

There are no apostrophes in colloquial abbreviations that have become standard words in the language, such as *cello, flu, phone,* or *plane*. Retain the original apostrophe only when archaism is intentional, or when it is necessary to reproduce older copy precisely. Old-fashioned or literary abbreviated forms such as *'tis, 'twas,* and *'twixt* do need an opening apostrophe, however: make sure that it is set the right way round, and not as an opening quotation mark.

10.2.4 **All-capital abbreviations**

Abbreviations of a single capital letter normally take full points (*G. Lane, Oxford U.*) except when used as symbols (see 10.3 below); abbreviated single-letter compass directions have no points, however: *N, S, E, W.*

Acronyms or initialisms of more than one capital letter take no full points in British and technical usage, and are closed up:

TUC   MA   EU   NE   SW   QC   DFC

US English uses points in such contexts:

U.S.A.   L.A.P.D.   R.E.M.

In some house styles any all-capital proper-name acronym that may be pronounced as a word is written with a single initial capital, giving *Basic*, *Unesco*, *Unicef*, etc.; some styles dictate that an acronym is written thus if it exceeds a certain number of letters (often four). Editors should avoid this rule, useful though it is, where the result runs against the common practice of a discipline or where similar terms would be treated dissimilarly based on length alone.

Where a text is rife with full-capital abbreviations, they can be set all in small capitals to avoid the jarring look of having too many capitals on the printed page. Some abbreviations (e.g. BC, AD) are always set in small capitals (see 7.5.2).

For treatment of personal initials see 6.1.1; for postcodes and zip codes see 6.2.4.

10.2.5 Lower-case abbreviations

Lower-case abbreviations are traditionally written closed up with points after each letter (*b.h.p.*), although they are increasingly written with no points (*mph*), especially in scientific contexts. Note that *plc* (public limited company) has no points.

In running text lower-case abbreviations cannot begin a sentence in their abbreviated form. In notes, however, a group of exceptions may be allowed: '*c.*', '*e.g.*', '*i.e.*', '*l.*', '*ll.*', '*p.*', '*pp.*' are lower case even at the beginning of a note.

Write *a.m.* and *p.m.* in lower case, with two points; use them only with figures, and never with *o'clock*. See 11.3 for more on times of day.

Short forms of weights and measures are generally not written with a point, with the exception of forms such as *gal.* (gallon) and *in.* (inch) that are not in technical use; note that *min.* and *sec.* have a point in general contexts but not in scientific work:

oz   lb   g   dwt
pt   qt   ft   m (miles *or* metres)

When an abbreviated unit is used with a number there is a space between them:

a unit of weight equal to 2,240 lb avoirdupois (1016.05 kg)

although in computing contexts it is usual for the abbreviated unit to follow the number without a space:

    3.0GHz   512kB   1024MB

10.2.6 Upper- and lower-case abbreviations

Contracted titles and components of names do not require a full point:

Dr	Mr	Mrs	Ms
Mme	Mlle	Ft (= Fort)	Mt (= Mount)

St. meaning 'street' is traditionally written with a point to distinguish it from *St* meaning 'saint'.

Shortened forms of academic degree traditionally have points (*Ph.D.*, *M.Litt.*), but today are often written without punctuation (*PhD*, *MLitt*).

British counties with abbreviated forms take a full point (*Berks.*, *Yorks.*), with the traditional exceptions *Hants*, *Northants*, and *Oxon*, whose abbreviations were derived originally from older spellings or Latin forms.

Names of days and months should generally be shown in full, but where necessary, as in notes and in order to save space, they are abbreviated thus:

Sun.	Mon.	Tue.	Wed.	Thur.	Fri.	Sat.
Jan.	Feb.	Mar.	Apr.	May	June	July
Aug.	Sept.	Oct.	Nov.	Dec.		

Only *May*, *June*, and *July* are not abbreviated.

10.2.7 Work titles

Italic text (e.g. titles of books, plays, and journals) usually produces italic abbreviations:

> *DNB* (*Dictionary of National Biography*)
> Arist. *Metaph.* (Aristotle's *Metaphysics*)

Follow the forms familiar in a given discipline; even then permutations can exist, often depending on the space available or on whether the abbreviation is destined for running text or a note.

For legal references see Chapter 13.

10.3 Symbols

Symbols or signs are a shorthand notation signifying a word or concept. They may be special typographical sorts, or letters of the alphabet. Symbols are a frequent feature of scientific and technical writing, but many are also used in everyday contexts, for example to denote copyright (©), currencies (£, $, €), degrees (°), feet and inches (′, ″), and percentages (%).

Do not start a sentence with a symbol: spell out the word or recast the sentence to avoid it:

> Sixteen dollars was the price   The price was $16
> Section 11 states ...   As §11 states, ...

Symbols formed from words are normally set close up before or after the things they modify (*GeV*, *Σ⁺*), or set with space either side if standing alone for words or concepts (*a W chromosome*). Symbols consisting of or including letters of the alphabet never take points. Abstract, purely typographical symbols follow similar rules, being either closed up (° # ¿ » %) or spaced. In coordinates, the symbols of measurement (degrees, seconds, etc.) are set close up to the figure, not the compass point:

> 52° N 15° 7′ 5″ W

Authors should provide good examples of any unusual sorts that they cannot achieve satisfactorily on copy; editors should ensure that these are clearly labelled for setting.

As an alternative to superior numbers the symbols *, †, ‡, §, ¶, ‖ may be used as reference marks or note cues, in that order.

The signs + (plus), − (minus), = (equal to), > ('larger than', in etymology signifying 'gives' or 'has given'), < ('smaller than', in etymology signifying 'derived from') are often used in biological and philological works, and not only in those that are scientific or arithmetical in nature. In such instances +, −, =, >, < should not be printed close up, but rather separated by the normal space of the line. (A thin space is also possible, providing it is consistently applied.)

The use of symbols can differ between disciplines. For example, in philological works an asterisk (*) prefixed to a word signifies a reconstructed form; in grammatical works it signifies an incorrect or non-standard form. A dagger (†) may signify an obsolete word, or 'deceased' when placed before a person's name.

The distinction between abbreviation and symbol may sometimes be blurred in technical contexts: some forms which are derived directly from a word or words are classed as symbols. Examples are chemical elements such as *Ag* (silver) from *argentum* and *U* from *uranium*, and forms such as *E* from *energy* and *m* from *mass* which are used in equations rather than running text. For the use of symbols in science, mathematics, and computing see Chapter 14.

10.4 The indefinite article with abbreviations

The choice between *a* and *an* before an abbreviation depends on pronunciation, not spelling. Use *a* before abbreviations beginning with a consonant sound, including an aspirated *h* and a vowel pronounced with the sound of *w* or *y*:

a BA degree	a KLM flight	a BBC announcer
a YMCA bed	a U-boat captain	a UNICEF card

Use *an* before abbreviations beginning with a vowel sound, including unaspirated *h*:

an MCC ruling	an FA cup match	an H-bomb
an IOU	an MP	an RAC badge
an SOS signal		

This distinction assumes the reader will pronounce the sounds of the letters, rather than the words they stand for (*a Football Association cup match*, *a hydrogen bomb*). *MS* for manuscript is normally pronounced as the full word, *manuscript*, and so takes *a*; *MS* for multiple sclerosis is often pronounced *em-ess*, and so takes *an*. 'R.' for rabbi is pronounced as *rabbi* ('a R. Shimon wrote').

The difference between sounding and spelling letters is equally important when choosing the article for abbreviations that are acronyms and for those that are not: *a NASA launch* but *an NAMB award*.

10.5 Possessives and plurals

Abbreviations form the possessive in the ordinary way, with an apostrophe and *s*:

> a CEO's salary   MPs' assistants

Most abbreviations form the plural by adding *s*; an apostrophe is not needed:

> CDs   MCs   SOSs   VIPs

In plural forms of a single letter an apostrophe can sometimes be clearer:

> A's and S's
> the U's

When an abbreviation contains more than one full point, put the *s* after the final one:

> Ph.D.s   M.Phil.s   the d.t.s

For abbreviations with one full point, such as *ed.*, *no.*, and *Adm.*, see 10.2.1.

A few abbreviations have irregular plurals (e.g. *Messrs* for *Mr*), sometimes stemming from the Latin convention of doubling the letter to create plurals:

> ff. (folios *or* following pages)   pp. (pages)
> ll. (lines)   MSS (manuscripts)

Weights and measures usually take the same form in both singular and plural (*oz*, *lb*), but insert the plural *s* in *hrs*, *yrs*.

10.6 e.g., i.e., etc., et al.

Do not confuse 'e.g.' (from Latin *exempli gratia*), meaning 'for example', with 'i.e.' (Latin *id est*), meaning 'that is'. Compare

> hand tools, e.g. hammer and screwdriver

with

> hand tools, i.e. those able to be held in the user's hands

Although many people employ 'e.g.' and 'i.e.' quite naturally in speech as well as writing, prefer 'for example', 'such as' (or, more informally, 'like'), and 'that is' in running text. Conversely, adopt 'e.g.' and 'i.e.' within parentheses or notes, since abbreviations are preferred there.

A sentence in text cannot begin with 'e.g.' or 'i.e.'; however, a note can, in which case they remain lower case.

Take care to distinguish 'i.e.' from the rarer 'viz.' (Latin *videlicet*, 'namely'). Formerly some writers used 'i.e.' to supply a definition or paraphrase, and 'viz.' to introduce a list of items. However, it is Oxford's preference either to replace 'viz.' with 'namely' or to prefer 'i.e.' in every case.

Write 'e.g.' and 'i.e.' in lower-case roman, with two points and no spaces. In Oxford's style they are not followed by commas, to avoid double punctuation; commas are often used in US practice. A comma, colon, or dash should precede 'e.g.' and 'i.e.' A comma is generally used when there is no verb in the following phrase:

> different fruits, e.g. apples, oranges, bananas, and cherries
> part of a printed document, e.g. a book cover

Use a colon or dash before a clause or a long list:

> palmtop computers have the advantage of being solid-state devices—
> i.e. they don't have moving parts

In full 'etc.' is *et cetera*, a Latin phrase meaning 'and other things'. 'Et al.' is short for Latin *et alii*, 'and others'. In general contexts both are lower-case roman, with a full point, though 'et al.' is sometimes italicized in bibliographic use. Do not use '&c.' for 'etc.' except when duplicating historical typography. 'Etc.' is preceded by a comma if it follows more than one listed item: *robins, sparrows, etc.*; it is best to avoid using 'etc.' after only one item (*robins etc.*), as at least two examples are necessary before 'etc.' in order to establish the relationship between the elements and show how the list might go on. The full point can be followed by a comma or whatever other punctuation would be required after an equivalent phrase such as *and the like*— but not by a second full point, to avoid double punctuation.

Use 'etc.' in technical or scholarly contexts such as notes and works of reference. Elsewhere, prefer *such as*, *like*, or *for example* before a list, or *and so on*, *and the like* after it; none of these can be used in combination with 'etc.' It is considered rude to use 'etc.' when listing individual people; use 'and others' instead; use 'etc.' when listing *types* of people, however. In a technical context, such as a bibliography, use 'et al.':

> Daisy, Katie, Alexander, and others

duke, marquess, earl, etc.

Smith, Jones, Brown, et al.

Do not write 'and etc.': 'etc.' includes the meaning of 'and'. Do not end a list with 'etc.' if it begins with 'e.g.', 'including', 'for example', or 'such as', since these indicate that the list is to be incomplete. Choose one or the other, not both.

10.7 Abbreviations with dates

In reference works and other contexts where space is limited the abbreviations 'b.' (born) and 'd.' (died) may be used. Both are usually roman, followed by a point, and printed close up to the following figures:

Amis, Martin (Louis) (b.1949), English novelist ...

An en rule may also be used when a terminal date is in the future:

The Times (1785–)   Jenny Benson (1960–)

A fixed interword space after the date may give a better appearance in conjunction with the closing parenthesis that generally follows it:

The Times (1785–)   Jenny Benson (1960–)

For people the abbreviation 'b.' is often preferred, as the bare en rule may be seen to connote undue anticipation.

The Latin *circa*, meaning 'about', is used in English mainly with dates and quantities. Set the italicized abbreviation *c.* close up to any figures following (*c.*1020, *c.*£10,400), but spaced from words and letters (*c.* AD 44). In discursive prose it is usually preferable to use *about* or *some* when describing quantities:

about eleven pints   some 14 acres

With a span of dates *c.* must be repeated before each date if both are approximate, as a single abbreviation is not understood to modify both dates:

Philo Judaeus (*c.*15 BC–*c.* AD 50)

Distinguish between *c.* and ?: the former is used where a particular year cannot be fixed upon, but only a period or range of several years; the latter where there are reasonable grounds for believing that a particular year is correct. It follows therefore that *c.* will more often be used with round numbers, such as the start and midpoint of a decade, than with numbers that fall between. See 4.8.2.

A form such as '*c*.1773' might be used legitimately to mean 'between 1772 and 1774' or 'between 1770 and 1775'. As such, it is best in discursive prose to indicate the earliest and latest dates by some other means. Historians employ a multiplication symbol for this purpose: *1996* × *1997* means 'in 1996 or 1997, but we cannot tell which'; similarly, *1996* × *2004* means 'no earlier than 1996 and no later than 2004'. Figures are not generally contracted in this context:

> the architect Robert Smith (b.1772 × 1774, d.1855)

The Latin *floruit*, meaning 'flourished', is used in English where only an approximate date of activity for a person can be provided. Set the italicized abbreviation *fl.* before the year, years, or—where no concrete date(s) can be fixed—century, separated by a space:

> William of Coventry (*fl.* 1360)   Edward Fisher (*fl.* 1627-56)
> Ralph Acton (*fl.* 14th c.)

CHAPTER 11

Numbers and dates

11.1 Numbers: general principles

11.1.1 **Typographical and design issues**

In typography, two different varieties of type are used to set Arabic numerals. The older style, called **old-style**, **non-ranging**, or **non-lining**, has descenders and a few ascenders: 0123456789. The newer style, called **ranging** or **lining**, has uniform ascenders and no descenders: 0123456789. In general do not mix non-ranging and ranging figures in the same book. There are, however, contexts in which mixing is a benefit. For example, ranging figures are particularly suitable for tables, and are often used for this purpose in works that otherwise feature non-ranging figures. For Roman numerals see 11.4 below.

11.1.2 **Figures or words?**

The main stylistic choice to be made when dealing with numbers is whether to express them in figures or in words. It is normal to determine a threshold below which numbers are expressed in words and above which figures are used; depending on the context, the threshold may vary. In non-technical contexts, Oxford style is to use words for numbers below 100; in technical contexts numbers up to and including ten are spelled out. In specialist contexts the threshold may, with good reason, be different: in some books about music, for example, numbers up to and including twelve are spelled out (there being twelve notes in the diatonic scale). The threshold provides only a general rule: there are many exceptions to it, as described below. On the Internet different rules may apply: figures tend to be used more than words.

Large round numbers may be expressed in a mixture of numerals and words (*6 million*; *1.5 million*) or entirely in words (*six million*; *one and a half million*). In some contexts it makes better sense to use a rounded number than an exact one, such as *a population of 60,000* rather than *of 60,011*. This is particularly true if the idea of approximation or estimation is expressed in the sentence by such words as *some*, *estimated*, or *about*. Rounded approximations may be better expressed in words if the use of figures will confer a false sense of exactitude:

> about a thousand *not* about 1000
> some four hundred *not* some 400

Particularly where quantities are converted from imperial to metric (or vice versa), beware of qualifying a precise number with *about*, *approximately*, etc.: *about three kilometres* should not be converted to *about 1⅞ miles*.

Note that in expressing approximate figures *more than* is traditionally preferred to *over* in phrases such as *she is paid more than £15 million a movie*. Use *over* in reference to age, however: *someone who is over 21*.

Use words in informal phrases that do not refer to exact numbers:

> talking nineteen to the dozen
> I have said so a hundred times
> she's a great woman—one in a million
> a thousand and one odds and ends

When a sentence contains one or more figures of 100 or above, a more consistent look may be achieved by using Arabic numerals throughout that sentence: for example, *90 to 100* (not *ninety to 100*) and *30, 76, and 105* (not *thirty, seventy-six, and 105*). This convention holds only for the sentence where this combination of numbers occurs: it does not influence usage elsewhere in the text unless a similar situation exists.

In some contexts a different approach is necessary. For example, it is sometimes clearer when two sets of figures are mixed to use words for one and figures for the other, as in *thirty 10-page pamphlets* or *nine 6-room flats*. This is especially useful when the two sets run throughout a sustained expanse of text (as in comparing quantities):

> the manuscript comprises thirty-five folios with 22 lines of writing,
> twenty with 21 lines, and twenty-two with 20 lines

Anything more complicated, or involving more than two sets of quantities, will probably be clearer if presented in a table.

Spell out ordinal numbers—*first, second, third, fourth*—except when quoting from another source. In the interests of saving space they may also be expressed in numerals in notes and references (see also 11.6.2 below). Use words for ordinal numbers in names, and for numerical street names (apart from avenue names in Manhattan—see 6.2.4):

the Third Reich	the Fourth Estate	a fifth columnist
Sixth Avenue	a Seventh-Day Adventist	

It is customary, though not obligatory, to use words for numbers that fall at the beginnings of sentences:

Eighty-four different kinds of birds breed in the Pine Barrens
'How much?' 'Fifty cents'

In such contexts, to avoid spelling out cumbersome numbers, recast the sentence, writing for example *The year 1849* ... instead of *Eighteen forty-nine* ...

Use figures for ages expressed in cardinal numbers, and words for ages expressed as ordinal numbers or decades:

a girl of 15	a 33-year-old man
between her teens and twenties	in his thirty-third year

In less formal or more discursive contexts (especially in fiction), ages may instead be spelled out, as may physical attributes:

a two-year-old   a nine-inch nail

Words can supplement or supersede figures in legal or official documents, where absolute clarity is required:

the sum of nine hundred and forty-three pounds sterling (£943)
a distance of no less than two hundred (200) yards from the plaintiff

Figures are used for:

- parts of books, including chapters, pages, and plates (*p. 14, Chapter 7*)
- numbers of periodicals (*Language* 61)
- scores of games and sporting events (*a 3–1 defeat, 37 not out*)
- distances of races (*the 400 metres*)
- house or building numbers (*47 Marston Street*)
- road or highway numbers in a national system (*A40, M25, Route 66*).

11.1.3 **Punctuation**

When written in words, compound numbers are hyphenated (see 11.1.6 for fractions):

> ninety-nine   one hundred and forty-three
> in her hundred-and-first year

In non-technical contexts commas are generally used in numbers of four figures or more:

> 1,863   12,456   1,461,523

In technical and foreign-language work use a thin space (see 14.1.3):

> 14 785 652   1 000 000   3.141 592

In tabular matter, numbers of only four figures have no thin space, except where necessary to help alignment with numbers of five or more figures.

There are no commas in years (with the exception of long dates such as 10,000 BC), page numbers, column or line numbers in poetry, mathematical workings, house or hotel-room numbers, or in library call or shelf numbers:

> 1979   1342 Madison Avenue
> Bodl. MS Rawl. D1054   BL, Add. MS 33746

11.1.4 **Number ranges**

Numbers at either end of a range are linked with an en rule. For a span of numbers it is usual to elide to the fewest figures possible:

> 30–1   42–3   132–6   1841–5

However, in some editorial styles numbers that begin with a multiple of ten are not elided:

> 30–32   100–101

It is not incorrect to preserve all digits in number ranges: in more formal contexts, such as titles and headings, and in expressing people's vital dates number ranges are often left unelided:

> Charles Dickens (1812–1870)
> *The National Service of British Seamen, 1914–1918*
> Turbulent years, 1763–1770

In any event, do not elide digits in (or ending with) the group 10 to 19:

> 10–12   15–19   114–18   310–11

Dates that cross the boundary of a century should not be elided: write *1798–1810*, *1992–2001*. Spans in BC always appear in full, because an elided second date could be misread as a complete year: *185–22 BC* is a century longer than *185–122 BC*, and dates for, say, Horace (*65–8 BC*) might appear to the unwary to express a period of three rather than fifty-seven years.

When referring to events known to have occurred between two dates, historians often employ a multiplication symbol: *1225 × 1232* (or in some styles *1225 × 32*) means 'no earlier than 1225 and no later than 1232'. The multiplication sign is also useful where one element in a range is itself a range: *1225 × 32–1278*.

In specifying a range use either the formula *from xxxx to xxxx* or *xxxx–xxxx*; take care to avoid the mistake of combining the two. It is *the war from 1939 to 1945* or *the 1939–45 war*, never *the war from 1939–45*. The same applies to the construction 'between … and …': *the period between 1998 and 2001* or *the period 1998–2001*, but not *the period between 1998–2001*.

When describing a range in figures, repeat the quantity as necessary to avoid ambiguity:

> 1000–2000 litres   1 billion to 2 billion light years away.

The elision *1–2000 litres* means that the amount starts at only 1 litre, and *1 to 2 billion light years away* means that the distance begins only 1 light year away.

A solidus replaces the en rule for a period of one year reckoned in a format other than the normal calendar extent: *49/8 BC*, *the tax year 1934/5*. A span of years in this style is joined by an en rule as normal: *1992/3–2001/2*.

Use a comma to separate successive references to individual page numbers: *6, 7, 8*; use an en rule to connect the numbers if the subject is continuous from one page to another: *6–8*.

11.1.5 Singular or plural?

Whether they are written as words or figures, numbers are pluralized without an apostrophe (see also 4.2.2):

> the 1960s   the temperature was in the 20s
> they arrived in twos and threes   she died in her nineties

Plural phrases take plural verbs where the elements enumerated are considered severally:

> Ten miles of path are being repaved
> Around 5,000 people are expected to attend

Plural numbers considered as single units take singular verbs:

> Ten miles of path is a lot to repave
> More than 5,000 people is a large attendance

When used as the subject of a quantity, words like *number, percentage*, and *proportion* are singular with a definite article and plural with an indefinite:

> The percentage of people owning a mobile phone is higher in Europe
> A proportion of pupils are inevitably deemed to have done badly

The numerals *hundred, thousand, million, billion, trillion*, etc. are singular unless they refer to indefinite quantities:

> two dozen   about three hundred
> some four thousand   more than five million

but

> dozens of friends   hundreds of times
> thousands of petals   millions of stars

Note that a **billion** is a thousand million (1,000,000,000 or 10^9), and a **trillion** is a million million (10^{12}). In Britain a billion was formerly a million million (10^{12}) and a trillion a million million million (10^{18}); in France, Germany, and elsewhere these values are still used.

11.1.6 Fractions and decimals

Spell out simple fractions in running text. When fractions are spelled out they are traditionally hyphenated:

> two-thirds of the country   one and three-quarters
> one and a half

although they are increasingly written as open compounds (*three quarters*). Note, however, that a distinction is often observed between a fraction that expresses proportion and one that expresses number:

> He gave away two-thirds of his inheritance

but

> He kept a third for himself and gave the other two thirds to his sister
> and brother

Hyphenate compounded numerals in compound fractions such as *nine thirty-seconds*; the numerator and denominator are hyphenated unless either already contains a hyphen. Do not use a hyphen between a whole number and a fraction: *one and seven-eighths* rather than *one-and-seven-eighths.* Combinations such as *half a mile* and *half a dozen* should not be hyphenated, but write *a half-mile* and *a half-dozen.*

In statistical matter use specially designed fractions where available (½, ¾, etc.), which have a diagonal bar. Alternatively, the traditional British form of fraction uses a horizontal bar (e.g. $\frac{19}{100}$), but this is in less frequent use today. In non-technical running text, set complex fractions in text-size numerals with a solidus between (*19/100*).

Decimal fractions may also be used: *12.66* rather than *12 2/3*, *99.9* rather than *99 and 9/10.* Decimal fractions are always printed in figures. They cannot be plural, or take a plural verb. For values below one the decimal is preceded by a zero: *0.76* rather than *.76*; exceptions are quantities (such as probabilities) that never exceed one.

Decimals are punctuated with the full point on the line. In the UK decimal currency was formerly treated differently, with the decimal point set in medial position (*£24·72*), but this style has long been out of favour.

Note that European languages, and International Standards Organization (ISO) publications in English, use a comma to denote a decimal sign, so that *2.3* becomes *2,3.*

For the use of decimals in tables see Chapter 15.

11.2 Numbers with units of measure

11.2.1 General principles

Generally speaking, figures should be used with units of measurement, percentages, and expressions of quantity, proportion, etc.:

> a 70–30 split
> 6 parts gin to 1 part dry vermouth
> the structure is 83 feet long and weighs 63 tons
> 10 per cent of all cars sold

Note that *per cent* rather than % is used in running text.

Use figures, followed by a space, with abbreviated forms of units, including units of time, and with symbols:

> winds gusted to 100 mph   250 BC   11 a.m.   13 mm

11.2.2 **Singular and plural units with numbers**

Note that units of measurement retain their singular form when part of hyphenated compounds before other nouns:

> a five-pound note   a two-mile walk
> a six-foot wall   a 100-metre race

Elsewhere, units are pluralized as necessary, but not if the quantity or number is less than one:

> two kilos *or* 2 kilos   three miles *or* 3 miles
> 0.568 litre   half a pint

For a fuller discussion of scientific units see Chapter 14.

11.2.3 **Currencies**

Amounts of money may be spelled out in words with the unit of currency, but are more often printed in numerals with the symbols or abbreviations:

> twenty-five pounds   thirteen dollars   seventy euros
> £25 $13   €70

Round numbers lend themselves to words better than do precise amounts, though even these may need to be spelled out where absolute clarity is vital, as in legal documents. For amounts of millions and above, and for thousands in financial contexts, it is permissible to combine symbols, numerals, words, and abbreviations, according to the conventions of the context in which they appear: *£5 million, US$15 billion.*

Where symbols or abbreviations are used, such as *£* (pounds), *$* (dollars), *€* (euros), *Rs.* (rupees), they precede the figures. There is no space after symbols, but some styles use a space after abbreviations; this is acceptable if imposed consistently within a work:

> £2,542   £3 m $4,542   €11.47 m

Use *00* after the decimal point only if a sum appears in context with other fractional amounts:

> They bought at £8.00 and sold at £11.50

Amounts in pence, cents, or other smaller units are set with the numeral close up to the abbreviation, which has no full point: *56p or 56¢* rather than *£0.56 or $0.56*. Mixed amounts do not include the pence/cent abbreviation: *£15.30* rather than *£15.30p*.

Amounts in pre-decimal British currency (before February 1971) are expressed in pounds, shillings, and pence—*£.s.d.* (italic); a normal space separates the elements:

> Income tax stood at 8*s.* 3*d.* in the £
> The tenth edition cost 10*s.* 6*d.* in 1956

11.3 Times of day

The formulation of times of day is a matter of editorial style, and different forms are more or less appropriate to particular contexts. It is customary to use words, and no hyphens, with reference to whole hours and to fractions of an hour:

> four (o'clock)   half past four   a quarter to four

Use *o'clock* only with the exact hour, and with time expressed in words: *four o'clock*, not *half past four o'clock* or *4 o'clock*. Do not use *o'clock* with *a.m.* or *p.m.*, but rather write, for example, *eight o'clock in the morning*. Use figures with *a.m.* or *p.m.*: *4 p.m.* Correctly, *12 a.m.* is midnight and *12 p.m.* is noon; but since this is not always understood, it may be necessary to use the explicit *12 midnight* and *12 noon*. The twenty-four-hour clock avoids the use of *a.m.* and *p.m.*: *12.00* is noon, *24.00* is midnight.

Use figures when minutes are to be included: *4.30 p.m.* For a round hour it is not necessary to include a decimal point and two zeros: prefer *4 p.m.* to *4.00 p.m.* In British English use a full point, but omit the full point if a further decimal is included, for example *0800.02 hours*. In North America, Scandinavia, and elsewhere the full point is replaced by a colon: *4:30 p.m.*

11.4 Roman numerals

The base numerals are I (1), V (5), X (10), L (50), C (100), D (500), and M (1,000). The principle behind their formation is that identical numbers are added (II = 2), smaller numbers after a larger one are added (VII = 7), and smaller numbers before a larger one are subtracted (IX = 9). The I, X, and C can be added up to four times:

> I, II, III, IV, V, VI, VII, VIII, IX, X (10)
> XI, XII, XIII, XIV, XV, XVI, XVII, XVIII, XIX, XX (20)
> CCCCLXXXXVIIII (499)

If possible, avoid eliding Roman numerals. To save space in certain circumstances two consecutive numerals may be indicated by *f.* for 'following': *pp. lxxxvii–lxxxviii* becomes *pp. lxxxvii f.*

Roman numerals can be difficult to interpret and may cause design problems because of the variable number of characters needed to express them. For example, they may be best avoided in tabulated lists, such as contents pages, because the alignment of the numerals and the following matter can produce excessive white space on the page:

```
I       ...
II      ...
III     ...
IV      ...
V       ...
VI      ...
VII     ...
VIII    ...
IX      ...
X       ...
```

Oxford's use of Roman numerals is described below:

- Capital Roman numerals are used for the chapters and appendices of a book, for acts of plays or sections of long poems, and for volume numbers of multi-volume works:

  Act I of *The Tempest*   Book V
  Chapters III–VIII   Volume XVI Soot–Styx

- The division label (part, book, chapter, appendix, etc.) is styled in the same height as the numeral, capital with capital, lower case with lower case, and small capital with small capital. Thus *Chapter XI*, *chapter xi*, CHAPTER XI.

- Lower-case Roman numerals are used to number the preliminary pages in a book, and for scenes of plays:

  pp. iii–x   *Hamlet*, Act I, sc. ii

- When Roman numerals are used in references, they are lower case if there is only one level, small capital and lower case in that order if there are two (II. i), full capital, small capital, and lower case in that order if there are three (*III. II. i*).

- Capital Roman numerals are used after the names of monarchs and popes: *Henry VIII* (no full point). The number should not be written as an ordinal (*Henry the VIIIth*), although the style *Henry the Eighth* is an acceptable alternative to figures in running text.

- Capital Roman numerals are similarly used in American personal names, where the male of a family bears the same name: *Adlai E. Stevenson III, Daniel P. Daly V*. A male bearing his father's name is styled *Jr*, whereas a male bearing his grandfather's name—but not his father's—is styled *II*.

- Roman numerals in manuscript sometimes have a final or single *i* replaced by a *j*, for example *ij, viij*. This style need be retained only when reproducing copy in facsimile.

- In editions of Latin texts, Roman numerals should generally be set in small capitals. Classical scholars tend to make little use of Roman numerals, both in classical reference (*Ovid*, Amores *3.1.15* not *III.i.15*) and in volume numbers of books.

11.5 Date forms

Figures are used for days and years in dates. Use cardinal numbers not ordinal numbers for dates:

> 12 August 1960   2 November 2003

Do not use the endings -*st*, -*rd*, or -*th* in conjunction with a figure, as in *12th August 1960*, unless copying another source: dates in letters or other documents quoted verbatim must be as in the original. Where less than the full date is given, write *10 January* (in notes *10 Jan.*), but *the 10th*. If only the month is given it should be spelled out, even in notes. An incomplete reference may be given in ordinal form:

> They set off on 12 August 1960 and arrived on the 18th

In British English style dates should be shown in the order day, month, year, without internal punctuation: *2 November 2003*. In US style the order is month, day, year: *November 2, 2003*.

A named day preceding a date is separated by a comma: *Tuesday, 2 November 1993*; note that when this style is adopted a terminal second comma is required if the date is worked into a sentence:

> On Tuesday, 2 November 1993, the day dawned frosty

There is no comma between month and year: *in June 1831*. Four-figure dates have no comma—2001—although longer dates do: *10,000 BC*.

Abbreviated all-figure forms are not appropriate in running text, although they may be used in notes and references. The British all-figure form is *2/11/03* or *2.11.03* (or the year may be given in full). In US style the all-figure form for a date, which is always separated by slashes rather than full points, can create confusion in transatlantic communication, since *11/2/03* is 2 November to an American reader and 11 February to a British one. Note that the terrorist attacks of 11 September 2001 are known by the shorthand *September 11* or *9/11* not only in the US but also in Britain and around the world.

The dating system promoted by the ISO is year, month, day, with the elements separated by hyphens: *2003-11-02*. This style is preferred in Japan and increasingly popular in technical, computing, and financial contexts. Another alternative, common on the Continent and elsewhere, is to use (normally lower-case) Roman numerals for the months (*2. xi. 03*). This system serves to clarify which number is the day and which the month in all contexts—a useful expedient when translating truncated dates into British or American English.

For precise dates in astronomical work, use days (*d*), hours (*h*), minutes (*m*), and seconds (*s*) (*2001 January 1d 2h 34m 4.8s*) or fractions of days (*2001 January 1.107*).

For abbreviations of days and months see 10.2.6.

11.6 Decades, centuries, and eras

11.6.1 **Decades**

References to decades may be made in either words or figures:

> the sixties   in his seventies   the 1960s   in his 70s

Write either *the sixties* or *the 1960s*, not *the '60s*. Similarly, when referring to two decades use *the 1970s and 1980s*, even though *the 1970s and '80s* transcribes how such dates may be read out loud.

When the name of a decade is used to define a social or cultural period it should be written as a word (some styles use an initial capital). The difference between labelling a decade *the twenties* and calling it *the 1920s* is that the word form connotes all the social, cultural, and political conditions unique to or significant in that decade, while the numerical form is simply the label for the time span. So, *the frivolous, fun-loving flappers of the twenties*, but *the oyster blight of the 1920s*.

11.6.2 **Centuries**

Depending on the editorial style of the work, refer to centuries in words or figures; Oxford style is to use words:

the nineteenth century   the first century BC

Centuries may be abbreviated in notes, references, and tabular matter; the abbreviation may be either *c.* or *cent.*: *14th c., 21st cent.* Both spelled-out and abbreviated forms require a hyphen when used adjectivally:

an eighth-century (*or* 8th-c.) poem
the early seventeenth-century (*or* 17th-c.) dramatists

In dating medieval manuscripts, the abbreviation *s.* (for *saeculum*, pl. *ss.*) is often used instead: *s. viii.*

Centuries BC run backwards, so that the fifth century BC spanned 500–401 BC. The year 280 BC was in the third century BC.

Conventions for numbering centuries in other languages vary, though for the most part capital Roman numerals are used, with two common exceptions: French uses small capitals in roman, full capitals in italic. In either case the figures are followed by a superior *e* or *ème* to indicate the suffix: *le XVIIe siècle, le XVIIème siècle*. German uses Arabic numerals followed by a full point: *das 18. Jahrhundert*. Occasionally capital Roman numerals are used; these too must be followed by a full point.

11.6.3 **Eras**

The two abbreviations most commonly used for eras are BC and AD. Both are written in small capitals. The abbreviation BC (before Christ) is placed after the numerals, as in *72 BC*, not *BC 72*; AD (*anno domini*, 'in the year of our Lord') should be placed before the numerals, as in *AD 375* (not *375 AD*). However, when the date is spelled out it is normal to write *the third century AD* rather than *AD the third century*.

Some writers prefer to use AD for any date before the first millennium. While this is not strictly necessary, it can be handy as a clarifying label: *This was true from 37* may not instantly be recognized as referring to a year. Any contentious date, or any year span ranging on either side of

the birth of Christ, should be clarified by BC or AD: *this was true from
43 BC to AD 18*. Conversely, a date span wholly in BC or AD technically
needs no clarification, since *407–346* is manifestly different from
346–409, though it is customary to identify all BC dates explicitly.

The following eras should be indicated by the appropriate abbreviation before the year:

- *a.Abr.* (the year of Abraham), reckoned from 2016 BC and used in
  chronicles by Eusebius and Jerome; not written AA.

- AH (*anno Hegirae*, 'in the year of the Hegira'), the Muslim era,
  reckoned from 16 July 622 (the date of Muhammad's departure
  from Mecca).

- AM (*anno mundi*, 'in the year of the world') will normally represent
  the Jewish era, reckoned from 7 October 3761 BC.

- AS (*anno Seleuci*), the Seleucid era, variously reckoned from
  autumn 312 BC and spring 311 BC, formerly current in much of the
  Near East.

- AUC (*anno Urbis conditae*, 'in the year of the foundation of the
  City'), the supposed Roman era from 753 BC. This was actually used
  only rarely by the Romans (who had several different dates for the
  foundation of Rome, and designated the year by the names of the
  consuls).

The following eras should be indicated by the appropriate abbreviation after the year:

- BCE (Before Common Era) and CE (Common Era) are used instead
  of BC and AD, mainly by writers who wish to avoid specifying dates
  in Christian terms.

- BP (Before Present) is used by geologists and palaeontologists for
  dates not accurate within a few thousand years; AD 1950 is fixed as
  the conventional 'present'. It is customary to use BP when
  discussing periods before 10,000 years ago. Some authors favour
  BP as a matter of course, since it does not presuppose any Christian
  reckoning on the reader's part. This is acceptable, provided BP is
  not intermingled with BC and other references of this kind within
  the same text.

For all era abbreviations other than *a.Abr.*, use unspaced small capitals, even in italic.

11.7 Regnal years

Regnal years are marked by the successive anniversaries of a sovereign's accession to the throne. Consequently they do not coincide with calendar years, which up to 1751 in England and America—though not in Scotland—began legally on 25 March. All Acts of Parliament before 1963 were numbered serially within each parliamentary session, which itself was described by the regnal year or years of the sovereign during which it was held. Regnal years were also used to date other official edicts, such as those of universities.

Regnal years are expressed as an abbreviated form of the monarch's name followed by a numeral. The abbreviations of monarchs' names in regnal-year references are as follows:

Car. *or* Chas. (Charles)
Hen. (Henry)
Steph. (Stephen)
Edw. (Edward)
Jac. (James)
Will. (William)
Eliz. (Elizabeth)
P. & M. (Philip and Mary)
Wm. & Mar. (William and Mary)
Geo. (George)
Ric. (Richard)
Vic. *or* Vict. (Victoria)

The names of John, Anne, Jane, and Mary are not abbreviated. See 13.5.1 for details of citing statutes including regnal years.

11.8 Calendars

11.8.1 **Introduction**
The following section offers brief guidance for those working with some less familiar calendars; fuller explanation may be found in Bonnie Blackburn and Leofranc Holford-Strevens, *The Oxford Companion to the Year* (Oxford University Press, 1999).

Dates in non-Western calendars should be given in the order day, month, year, with no internal punctuation: *25 Tishri AM 5757*, *13 Jumada I AH 1417*. Do not abbreviate months even in notes.

11.8.2 **Old and New Style**

The terms **Old Style** and **New Style** are applied to dates from two
different historical periods. In 1582 Pope Gregory XIII decreed that,
in order to correct the calendar then used—the **Julian calendar**—the
days 5–14 October of that year should be omitted and no future cen-
tennial year (e.g. 1700, 1800, 1900) should be a leap year unless it was
divisible by 400 (for example 1600, 2000). This reformed **Gregorian
calendar** was quickly adopted in Roman Catholic countries, more
slowly elsewhere: in Britain not till 1752 (when the days 3–13 September were omitted), in Russia not till 1918 (when the days 16–28
February were omitted). Dates in the Julian calendar are known as
Old Style, while those in the Gregorian are New Style.

Until the middle of the eighteenth century not all states reckoned the
new year from the same day: whereas France adopted 1 January from
1563, and Scotland from 1600, England counted from 25 March in
official usage as late as 1751. Thus the execution of Charles I was officially dated 30 January 1648 in England, but 30 January 1649 in
Scotland. Furthermore, although both Shakespeare and Cervantes
died on 23 April 1616 according to their respective calendars,
23 April in Spain (and other Roman Catholic countries) was only
13 April in England, and 23 April in England was 3 May in Spain.

Confusion is caused on account of the adoption, in England, Ireland,
and the American colonies, of two reforms in quick succession: the
adoption of the Gregorian calendar and the change in the way the
beginning of the year was dated. The year 1751 began on 1 January in
Scotland and on 25 March in England, but ended throughout Great
Britain and its colonies on 31 December, so that 1752 began on 1 January. So, whereas 1 January 1752 corresponded to 12 January in most
Continental countries, from 14 September onwards there was no discrepancy. Many writers treat the two reforms as one, using *Old Style*
and *New Style* indiscriminately for the start of the new year and the
form of calendar. In the interests of clarity *Old Style* should be reserved for the Julian calendar and *New Style* for the Gregorian; the
1 January reckoning should be called 'modern style', that from
25 March 'Annunciation' or 'Lady Day' style.

It is customary to give dates in Old or New Style according to the
system in force at the time in the country chiefly discussed. Any

dates in the other style should be given in parentheses with an equals sign preceding the date and the abbreviation of the style following it: *23 August 1637 NS* (= *13 August OS*) in a history of England, or *13 August 1637 OS* (= *23 August NS*) in one of France. In either case, *13/23 August 1637* may be used for short. On the other hand, it is normal to treat the year as beginning on 1 January: modern histories of England date the execution of Charles I to 30 January 1649. When it is necessary to keep both styles in mind, it is normal to write *30 January 1648/9*; otherwise the date should be given as *30 January 1648* (= *modern 1649*).

11.8.3 Greek calendars

In the classical period years were designated by the name of a magistrate or other office-holder, which meant nothing outside the city concerned. In the third century BC a common framework for historians was found in the Olympiad, or cycle of the Olympic Games, held in the summer every four years from 776 BC onwards. Thus 776/5 was designated the first year of the first Olympiad; 775/4 the second year; and 772/1 the first year of the second Olympiad. When modern scholars need to cite these datings, they are written *Ol. 1, 1*, *Ol. 1, 2*, and *Ol. 2, 1* respectively.

11.8.4 French Republican calendar

The Republican calendar was introduced on 5 October 1793, and was discontinued with effect from 1 January 1806. On its introduction it was antedated to begin from the foundation of the Republic (22 September 1792). The months of the new calendar were named according to their seasonal significance. Though difficult to translate, approximations are included in parentheses:

Autumn	Winter	Spring	Summer
vendémiaire (vintage)	nivôse (snow)	germinal (seed time)	messidor (harvest)
brumaire (mist)	pluviôse (rain)	floréal (flowers)	thermidor (heat)
frimaire (frost)	ventôse (tempest)	prairial (meadows)	fructidor (fruit)

The months are not now capitalized in French, though they were at the time and may still be so in English. Years of the Republican calendar are printed in capital Roman numerals: *9 thermidor An II*; *13 vendémiaire An IV*; in English *Year II, Year IV*.

11.8.5 **Jewish calendar**

The Jewish year consists in principle of twelve months of alternately 30 and 29 days; in seven years out of nineteen an extra month of 30 days is inserted, and in some years either the second month is extended to 30 days or the third month shortened to 29 days. The era is reckoned from a notional time of Creation at 11.11 and 20 seconds p.m. on Sunday, 6 October 3761 BC.

11.8.6 **Muslim calendar**

The Muslim year consists of twelve lunar months, so that thirty-three Muslim years roughly correspond to thirty-two Christian ones. Years are counted from the first day of the year in which the Prophet made his departure, or Hegira, from Mecca to Medina, namely Friday, 16 July AD 622.

CHAPTER 12

Languages

12.1 General principles

This chapter provides guidelines on the editing and presentation of material in foreign languages and Old and Middle English. Languages are listed alphabetically, either separately or, for clarity and convenience, with related languages: for instance, there is one section for Slavonic languages rather than separate sections for Belarusian, Bosnian, Bulgarian, etc.

The sections stress common pitfalls and conundrums in spelling, punctuation, accents, syntax, and typography, and are intended to offer guidance to users across a broad spectrum of familiarity with the languages. This book cannot give a full account of each language; rather, it seeks to aid authors and editors who are dealing with foreign-language material within English-language contexts. Overall, those languages most often met with in English-language publishing are covered in greatest depth, though not all languages of equal frequency are—or can usefully be—addressed equally: with editorial concerns foremost, distinctions between related languages have been highlighted. Help is given on setting non-Roman alphabets in English-language texts, as well as on transliteration and romanization.

For information on foreign personal names and place names see Chapter 6.

12.2 Arabic

12.2.1 **Alphabet**

Arabic is written from right to left in a cursive script consisting of twenty-eight letters, all representing consonants; their form varies according to position within the word, and several are distinguished only by dots. Some letters cannot be joined to the next even within a word; the space between them should be smaller than that between words, and unbreakable. A horizontal extender on the baseline is often added to a letter that would otherwise seem too close to the next. In verse it is conventional to give all lines the same visual length, so that the rhyming letter is aligned on the left throughout.

The same script, with additional letters, is or has been employed for other languages spoken by Muslims, such as Persian, Pashto, Urdu, Turkish, and Malay; these last two are now written in the Roman alphabet.

There is no standard system of transliterating Arabic. Vowel marks and other guides to pronunciation are used in editions of the Koran, in schoolbooks, and usually in editions of classical poetry; otherwise they are omitted except where a writer thinks they are needed to resolve ambiguity.

12.2.2 **Accents and punctuation**

Strict philological usage requires the underline in *ḏ*, *ṯ*; the under-dot in *ḥ*, *ṣ*, *ḍ*, *ṭ*, *ẓ*; the over-dot in *ġ*; the inferior semicircle in *ḫ*; the háček in *ǧ* (often written *j*) and *š*, and the macron in *ā*, *ī*, *ū* (do not use the acute or circumflex instead). Less learned systems will dispense with some or all of these diacritics. There are also two independent characters, ʿayn ʿ and hamza ʾ (corresponding to Hebrew ʿayin and aleph) which should be used if available; if not, substitute Greek asper (ʽ) and lenis (ʼ) respectively. These should be distinguished from the apostrophe, mainly found before *l-*, e.g. in *ʿAbdu 'l-Malik*; insert a hair space between them and quotation marks.

The definite article *al* or *'l-* (or regional variants such as *el-* and *ul-*) is joined to the noun with a hyphen: *al-Islām*, *al-kitāb*. Do not capitalize the *a* except at the beginning of a sentence; it should not be capitalized at the start of a quoted title.

12.2.3 **Word division**

In Arabic script words should not be divided even at internal spaces; if the spacing of the line would otherwise be too loose, use extenders within words. In transliteration, avoid dividing except at the hyphen following the article; if absolutely necessary, take over no more than

Table 12.1 **Arabic alphabet**

Alone	Final	Medial	Initial			Alone	Final	Medial	Initial		
ا	ﺍ			'alif	'	ض	ﺽ	ﻀ	ﺿ	ḍād	ḍ
ب	ﺏ	ﺒ	ﺑ	bā'	b	ط	ﻂ	ﻄ	ﻃ	ṭā'	ṭ
ت	ﺕ	ﺘ	ﺗ	tā'	t	ظ	ﻆ	ﻈ	ﻇ	ẓā'	ẓ
ث	ﺙ	ﺜ	ﺛ	thā'	th	ع	ﻊ	ﻌ	ﻋ	'ayn	'
ج	ﺝ	ﺠ	ﺟ	jīm	j	غ	ﻎ	ﻐ	ﻏ	ghayn	gh
ح	ﺡ	ﺤ	ﺣ	ḥā'	ḥ	ف	ﻒ	ﻔ	ﻓ	fā'	f
خ	ﺥ	ﺨ	ﺧ	khā'	kh	ق	ﻖ	ﻘ	ﻗ	qāf	q
د	ﺪ			dāl	d	ك	ﻚ	ﻜ	ﻛ	kāf	k
ذ	ﺬ			dhāl	dh	ل	ﻞ	ﻠ	ﻟ	lām	l
ر	ﺭ			rā'	r	م	ﻢ	ﻤ	ﻣ	mīm	m
ز	ﺯ			zāy	z	ن	ﻦ	ﻨ	ﻧ	nūn	n
س	ﺲ	ﺴ	ﺳ	sīn	s	ه	ﻪ	ﻬ	ﻫ	hā'	h
ش	ﺵ	ﺸ	ﺷ	shīn	sh	و	ﻭ			wāw	w
ص	ﺺ	ﺼ	ﺻ	ṣād	ṣ	ى	ﻯ	ﻴ	ﻳ	yā'	y

one consonant. In loose transcription, note that *dh kh sh th* may represent either the single consonants strictly transliterated *ḍ*, *ḥ*, *š*, and *ṭ* respectively, or combinations of *d k s t* plus *h*. When in doubt, do not divide.

12.3 Chinese

12.3.1 Introduction

The forms of Chinese spoken in areas occupied by those of Chinese origin differ so widely from one another that many may be deemed to constitute languages in their own right. The principal dialects are Northern Chinese (Mandarin), Cantonese, Hakka, the Wu dialect of Suzhou, and the dialect of Min (Fukien). All of these, however, share a common written language consisting of thousands of separate ideographs or 'characters'. The language traditionally used for the compilation of official documents is totally unlike the spoken language, as is the language in which the classic texts of Chinese literature are expressed. For these, also, the same script is used.

12.3.2 Scripts

The structure of individual ideographs can sometimes be very complicated in script, involving the use of as many as twenty-eight separate strokes of the brush or pen. A code of simplified characters is in use on the mainland, but more traditional forms are found in Hong Kong, Taiwan, Singapore, and areas beyond Chinese jurisdiction.

The language is monosyllabic, one ideograph representing a syllable. Each ideograph is pronounced in a particular inflection of voice, or 'tone'. The National Language (the standard spoken form of modern Chinese) uses four separate tones, Cantonese, nine. The National Language is derived from the pronunciation of northern China (notably that of the Beijing area), which has traditionally been adopted for the transaction of official business—hence the term 'Mandarin', which is sometimes used to categorize it. Alternative names for it are *putonghua* ('speech in common use') or *Kuo-yü* (otherwise *Guoyu*, 'National Language').

The many thousand Chinese characters are traditionally written from top to bottom in vertical columns running right to left across the page, but nowadays, especially in mainland China, are printed in left-to-right lines like the Western alphabet. This has always been the practice when Chinese phrases are set within a Roman text.

12.3.3 Transliteration

Although the pronunciation of characters varies markedly from dialect to dialect (the surname pronounced *Wu* in Mandarin is *Ng* in Cantonese), romanization is normally based on Beijing ('Mandarin') usage. There are two main systems: **Wade–Giles**, formerly the norm in English-language publications, and **Pinyin**, the official transliteration in the People's Republic. The name, in Wade–Giles, would be spelled *P'in-in*. Wade–Giles gives forms such as T'ien-tsin and *Mao Tse-tung*, whereas Pinyin gives Tianjin and *Mao Zedong*.

Wade–Giles separates the syllables of compounds with hyphens; Pinyin runs them together, with an apostrophe where the break would not be obvious (*Xi'an* = Wade–Giles *Hsi-an*, since *Xian* would be read as Wade–Giles *Hsien*). Wade–Giles distinguishes aspirated from unaspirated consonants with a Greek asper ('), which is sometimes replaced by an opening quote or an apostrophe, and is often omitted in popular writing; Pinyin uses different letters. Wade–Giles uses *ü* more often than Pinyin, which requires it only in the syllables *lü* and *nü*; only Wade–Giles uses *ê* (e.g. *jên* = Pinyin *ren*) and *ǔ* (*ssǔ* = Pinyin *si*). Neither consistently indicates the syllabic tone, despite its importance; when they do so, Wade–Giles writes a superior figure after the syllable (i^1 i^2 i^3 i^4), Pinyin an accent on the vowel (*yī yí yǐ yì*; note the need to combine these with the umlaut).

12.4 Dutch and Afrikaans

12.4.1 Introduction
Dutch is the language of the Netherlands. The Dutch spoken in northern Belgium, formerly called Flemish, is now officially called Dutch (*Nederlands* in Dutch). Afrikaans is one of the official languages of South Africa, and was derived from the Dutch brought to the Cape by settlers in the seventeenth century.

12.4.2 Dutch

Alphabet
The alphabet is the same as English, but *q* and *x* are used only in foreign loanwords. In dictionaries *ij* precedes *ik*; in directories and encyclopedias it is sometimes treated as equivalent to *y*. The apostrophe occurs in such plurals as *pagina's* ('pages'), but not before *s* in the genitive.

Accents
The acute is used to distinguish *één* ('one') from een ('a'), and *vóór* ('before') from *voor* ('for'). The only other accent required—except in foreign loanwords—is the diaeresis:

     knieën 'knees'   *provinciën* 'provinces'   *zeeën* 'seas'

Punctuation and capitalization

Punctuation is less strict than in, for example, German. Capitals are used for the pronouns *U* 'you' and *Uw* 'your', for terms indicating nationality (*Engelsman* 'Englishman', *Engels* 'English'), and for adjectives derived from proper nouns, but not for days or months; in institutional names capitalize all words except prepositions and articles.

The abbreviated forms of *des* and *het* ('*s* and '*t* respectively) take a space on either side except in the case of towns and cities, where a hyphen follows: '*s-Gravenhage*. When a word beginning with an apostrophe starts a sentence, it is the following word that takes the capital: '*t Is*.

Word division

Do not divide the suffixes -*aard*, -*aardig*, -*achtig*, and any beginning with a consonant. This applies to the diminutive suffix -*je*, but note that a preceding *t* may itself be part of the suffix: *kaart-je* ('ticket'), but *paar-tje* ('couple').

Take over single consonants; the combinations *ch*, *sj*, *tj* (which represent single sounds) and *sch*; and consonant + *l* or *r* in loanwords. Take over the second of two consonants (including the *g* of *ng* and the *t* of *st*); when more than three come together take over those combinations that may begin a word. Do not divide double vowels or *ei*, *eu*, *ie*, *oe*, *ui*, *aai*, *eei*, *ieu*, *oei*, *ooi*.

12.4.3 **Afrikaans**

Alphabet, accents, and spelling

There is no *ij* in Afrikaans, *y* being used as in older Dutch; *s* is used at the start of words where Dutch has *z*, and *w* between vowels often where Dutch has *v*.

The circumflex is quite frequent; the grave is used on paired conjunctions (*òf ... òf*, 'either ... or') and a few other words. The acute is found in the demonstrative *dié* to distinguish it from the article *die*, and in certain proper nouns and French loan-words. There is no diaeresis with *ae* (*dae* 'days').

Capitalization

As in Dutch, when a word beginning with an apostrophe starts a sentence in Afrikaans, the following word is capitalized. This rule is important, since the indefinite article is written '*n*:

> '*n Man het gekom*, 'A man has come'

The pronoun *ek* 'I' is not capitalized.

12.5 French

12.5.1 Accents

The acute (´), the most common accent in French, is used only over *e*; when two *e*s come together the first always has an acute accent, as in *née*. The grave (`) is used mainly over *e*, but also on final *a*, as in *voilà*, and on *u* in *où* ('where'), but not *ou* ('or'). The circumflex (^) may be used over *a, e, i, o*, and *u*. The cedilla *c* (*ç*) is used only before *a, o*, and *u*. The diaeresis (¨) is found on *i, e*, and *y*.

Although they are recommended by the Académie française, accents on capital letters are often omitted in everyday French, except when they are needed to avoid confusion:

> *POLICIER TUÉ* 'Policeman killed'
> *POLICIER TUE* 'Policeman kills'

12.5.2 Orthographic reform

Les Rectifications de l'orthographie, drafted by the Conseil Supérieure de la Langue Française, was published in 1990. It is a controversial document and ignored by many. From an editor's point of view the main changes are those affecting circumflex accents and hyphens. Since the document recommends the removal of the circumflex on *i* and *u*, except in verb endings and a few words where it distinguishes meaning, the lack of this accent may indicate the author's support for the reform, and it would be wise to ascertain whether or not this is the case.

12.5.3 Abbreviations

As in English, place a full point after an abbreviation (*chap.*, *ex.*) but not after a contraction (*St, Mlle*). Retain the hyphen when a hyphenated form is abbreviated:

J.-J. *Rousseau* (Jean-Jacques Rousseau)
P.-S. (post-scriptum)

Some common examples of abbreviations in French:

abrév.	abréviation
apr.	après
av.	avant
c.-à-d.	c'est-à-dire
chap.	chapitre
Cie, Cie	compagnie
conf.	confer (Lat.)
d^o	dito
Dr	docteur
éd.	édition
etc.	et cætera
ex.	exemple
f^o	folio
Ier, 1er	premier
IIe, 2e, IIème, 2ème	deuxième
ill.	illustration
in-4°	in-quarto
in-8°	in-octavo
inéd.	inédit
in-f^o	in-folio
in pl.	in plano (Lat.)
l.c.	loc. cit. (Lat.)
liv.	livre
M.	monsieur
Me, M^e	maître
Mlle, Mlle	mademoiselle
MM.	messieurs
Mme, Mme	madame
ms.	manuscrit
mss.	manuscrits
n^o	numéro
p.	page
p., pp.	pages
P.-S.	post-scriptum
qqch	quelque chose
qqn	quelqu'un
s., ss., suiv.	suivant
s.d.	sans date
s.l.	sans lieu
t.	tome
TVA	taxe à la valeur ajoutée
v.	voyez, voir
Vve	veuve

12.5.4 **Capitalization**

Capitalize only the first element (or first element after the article) in compound proper names. If the first element has a following adjective linked by a hyphen, capitalize the adjective also:

> *l'Académie française*   *la Comédie-Française*
> *le Palais-Royal*   *la Légion d'honneur*
> *le Conservatoire de musique* *Bibliothèque nationale*

Note that a following adjective is lower case, while an adjective preceding the noun is capitalized:

> *Le Nouveau Testament*   *les Saintes écritures*
> *l'écriture sainte*

Use lower-case letters for: days of the week; names of months; the cardinal points (*le nord*, *le sud*, etc.); languages; adjectives derived from proper nouns (*la langue française*); ranks, titles, regimes, religions, adherents of movements, and their derivative adjectives (*calvinisme, chrétien(ne), le christianisme, humaniste, les sans-culottes, le socialisme, les socialistes*).

In names for geographical features common nouns such as *mer* ('sea') are lower case, but there are traditional exceptions:

> *le Bassin parisien*   *le Massif central*   *le Massif armoricain*
> *la Montagne Noire*   *le Quartier latin*

12.5.5 **Punctuation**

Hyphen

Use hyphens to connect cardinal and ordinal numbers in words under 100:

> *vingt-quatre*   *trois cent quatre-vingt-dix*

but when *et* joins two numbers no hyphen is used:

> *vingt et un*   *cinquante et un*   *vingt et unième*

Quotation marks

Texts set wholly in French should use quotation marks called **guillemets** (« »); these need not be used for French text in English-language books. A normal word space (sometimes a thin space) is inserted inside the guillemets, separating the marks from the matter they contain.

A guillemet is repeated at the head of every subsequent paragraph belonging to the quotation. In conversational matter guillemets are sometimes put at the beginning and end of the remarks, and the individual utterances are denoted by a spaced dash:

> « — Nous allons lui écrire, dis-je, et lui demander pardon.
> — C'est une idée de génie. »

Many modern authors dispense with guillemets altogether, and denote the speakers by a dash only, although this is officially frowned upon.

English-style inverted commas are often used to mark a quotation within a quotation.

Where guillemets are used, only one » appears at the end of two quotations concluding simultaneously.

12.5.6 Work titles

Capitalize the initial letter of the first word of a title and of a following noun, if the first word is a definite article:

> *Les Femmes savantes*   *Au revoir les enfants*

Where the title occurs within a sentence, a lower-case *l* for the definite article (*le, la, les*) beginning a title may be used; the article is construed with the surrounding sentence:

> *La mise en scène de la Bohème* 'The production of *La Bohème*'

If a noun following an initial definite article is itself preceded by an adjective, capitalize this also:

> *Le Petit Prince*   *Les Mille et Une Nuits* (two adjectives)

but downcase any following adjective:

> *Les Mains sales*

If the title begins with any word other than *le, la, les*, or if the title forms a complete sentence, downcase the words following, unless they are proper nouns:

> *Une vie*
> *A la recherche du temps perdu*
> *La guerre de Troie n'aura pas lieu*
> *Les dieux ont soif*

A parallel title is treated as a title in its own right for the purposes of capitalization:

> *Emile, ou, De l'éducation*

As these rules are complex, some English styles merely capitalize the first word and any proper nouns.

12.5.7 Word division

Divide words according to spoken syllables, and in only a few cases according to etymology. A single consonant always goes with the following vowel (*amou-reux*, *cama-rade*); *ch*, *dh*, *gn*, *ph*, *th*, and groups consisting of consonant + *r* or + *l* count as single consonants for this purpose.

Other groups of consonants are divided irrespective of etymology (*circons-tance*, *tran-saction*, *obs-curité*) but divide a prefix from a following *h* (*dés-habille*). Always divide *ll*, even if sounded *y*: *travaillons*, *mouil-lé*. Do not divide between vowels except in a compound: *anti-aérien*, *extra-ordinaire* (but *Moa-bite*). In particular, vowels forming a single syllable (*monsieur*) are indivisible. Do not divide after a single letter (*émettre*) or before or after an intervocalic *x* or *y* (*soixante*, *moyen*, *Alexandre*), but divide after *x* or *y* if followed by a consonant: *dex-térité*, *pay-san*. Do not divide abbreviated words (*Mlle*), within initials (la *CRS*), or after an abbreviated forename (*J.-Ph.* Rameau) or personal title (le *Dr* Suchet).

Do not divide after an apostrophe within compound words (*presqu'île*, *aujour-d'hui*). Divide interrogative verb forms before *-t-*: *Viendra-|t-il?*

12.5.8 Numerals

Use words for times of day if they are expressed in hours and fractions of hour:

six heures 'six o'clock'   *trois heures et quart* 'a quarter past three'

but use figures for time expressed in minutes: *6 h 15*, *10 h 8 min 30 s*.

Set Roman numerals indicating centuries in small capitals:

le xième siècle   xie siècle

but they should be in full capitals when in italic:

le XIème siècle   XIe siècle

Use upper-case Roman numerals for numbers belonging to proper nouns (*Louis XIV*), but Arabic numerals for the numbers of the arrondissements of Paris: *le 16e arrondissement*.

In figures use thin spaces to divide thousands (*20 250*), but do not space dates, or numbers in general contexts (*l'an 1466*, *page 1250*).

Times of day written as figures should be spaced as *10 h 15 min 10 s* (10 hrs 15 min. 10 sec.); formerly this was also printed *10^h 15^m 10^s*.

12.6 Gaelic

12.6.1 Alphabet and accents

Both Irish and Scots Gaelic are written in an eighteen-letter alphabet with no *j, k, q, v, w, x, y, z* (except in some modern loanwords); in Irish the lower-case *i* is sometimes left undotted. Until the middle of the twentieth century Irish (but not Scots Gaelic) was often written and printed in **insular** script, a medieval form of Latin handwriting, in which a dot was marked over aspirated consonants. In Roman script aspirated consonants are indicated by the addition of *h* after the letter. Irish marks vowel length with an acute accent (*á, é, í, ó, ú*), Scots Gaelic with the grave (*à, è, ì, ò, ù*). Apostrophes are frequent in Scots Gaelic, less so in Irish.

12.6.2 Mutations

In Irish Gaelic, as in Welsh, initial consonants are replaced by others in certain grammatical contexts, in a process called **mutation**. In Irish the mutation known as **eclipsis** is indicated by writing the sound actually pronounced before the consonant modified: *mb, gc, nd, bhf, ng, bp, dt*. If the noun is a proper name, it retains its capital, the prefixed letter(s) being lower case:

> *i mBaile Átha Cliath* 'in Dublin' (*Baile Átha Cliath = Dublin*)
> *na bhFrancach* 'of the French'

The same combination of initial lower-case letter followed by a capital occurs when *h* or *n* is prefixed to a name beginning with a vowel—*go hÉirinn* 'to Ireland', *Tír na nÓg* 'the Land of the Young'—or *t* is prefixed to a vowel or *S*: *an tAigéan Atlantach* 'the Atlantic Ocean', *an tSionnain* 'Shannon'. Before lower-case vowels, *h* is prefixed directly (*na hoíche* 'of the night'), as is *t* before *s* (*an tsráid* 'the street'), but *n* and *t* take a hyphen before a vowel (*in-áit* 'in a place', *an t-uisce* 'the water'). Except in dialects, eclipsis is not found with consonants in Scots Gaelic. Prefixed *h-, n-,* and *t-* always take a hyphen:

> *an t-sràid* 'the street'   *Ar n-Athair* 'Our Father'
> *na h-oidhche* 'of the night'   *na h-Eileanan an Iar* 'the Western Isles'

12.7 German

12.7.1 Accents and special sorts

German uses the diacritics *Ä, Ö, Ü, ä, ö, ü,* and the special sort *Eszett* (ß) (see 12.7.2): *Eszett* differs from a Greek beta (β), which should not be substituted for it.

12.7.2 Orthographic reform

A new orthography agreed by the German-speaking countries came into force on 1 August 1998. The seven-year transitional period, during which both systems were official, ended on 31 July 2005, and the older orthographic forms are now considered incorrect, although they are still widely used. The reform's main tendency is to eliminate irregularities that caused difficulty for the native speaker. At the same time, more variations are permitted than under the old rules, though these options are restricted: it is not acceptable to mix and match old and new spellings at will.

Under the new orthography, certain words were adjusted to resemble related words, so that, for instance, the verbs *numerieren* and *plazieren* become *nummerieren* and *platzieren* to coincide with the related nouns *Nummer* ('number') and *Platz* ('place').

In verbal compounds, nouns and adjectives regarded as retaining their normal functions are written separately:

> *radfahren* → *Rad fahren* 'to ride a bicycle'

but

> *irreführen* ('to mislead') and *wahrsagen* ('to predict')

Long-established loanwords have been Germanized (*Tip* → *Tipp*, 'tip'), and *ee* substituted for *é* in such words as *Varietee* for *Varieté* ('music hall').

The optional use of *f* for *ph* is extended: *Delfin* ('dolphin'), *Orthografie* ('orthography'), but not to words deemed more learned: *Philosophie* ('philosophy'), *Physik* ('physics').

The *Eszett* was traditionally used in place of a double *s* at the end of a syllable, before a consonant (whatever the vowel), and after long vowels and diphthongs. The new rules allow the ß only after a long vowel (including *ie*) or diphthong:

Fuß, Füße 'foot, feet'

after a short vowel *ss* is to be used:

Kuss, Küsse 'kiss, kisses'

but:

ihr esst, ihr aßt 'you [pl.] eat, ate'
wir essen, wir aßen 'we eat, ate'

The *Eszett* is considered an archaism in Swiss German, *ss* being preferred in all circumstances. No corresponding capital and small capital letters exist for *ß*, and *SS* and *ss* are used instead; in alphabetical order *ß* counts as *ss* and not *sz*.

In the absence of specific instructions to the contrary, or of evidence from the nature of the text itself, the new rules should be applied in all matter not by native speakers of German. Quotations from matter published in the old spelling should follow the old style (except in respect of word division), but new editions will normally modernize.

The new orthography's effects in other areas are mentioned under the headings below.

12.7.3 Abbreviations

Use a full point:

- after an abbreviation that would be read out in full; a space after any points within it is optional:

    d. h. (*das heißt*, 'that is')
    Dr. (*Doktor*, 'Dr')
    Prof. (*Professor*, 'Prof.')
    usw. (*und so weiter*, 'and so on')
    z. B. (*zum Beispiel*, 'for example')

- after numerals used for days of the month and ordinal numbers:

    Montag, den 12. August 'Monday, 12 August'
    der 2. Weltkrieg (*der Zweite Weltkrieg*, 'the Second World War')

Do not use points in abbreviations that are pronounced as such:

DM (*die Deutsche Mark*, 'the German mark')
KG (*Kommanditgesellschaft*, 'limited partnership')

Some common examples of abbreviations in German:

a. a. O.	am angeführten Ort
Abb.	Abbildung
Abt.	Abteilung

Anm.	Anmerkung
Aufl.	Auflage
Ausg.	Ausgabe
Bd., Bde.	Band, Bände
bes.	besonders
bzw.	beziehungsweise
d. h.	das heißt
d. i.	das ist
ebd.	ebenda, ebendaselbst
Erg. Bd.	Ergänzungsband
etw.	etwas
Hft.	Heft
hrsg.	herausgegeben
Hs., Hss.	Handschrift, Handschriften
Lfg.	Lieferung
m. E.	meines Erachtens
m. W.	meines Wissens
Nr.	Nummer
o.	oben
o. Ä.	oder Ähnliche(s)
o. O.	ohne Ort
R.	Reihe
s.	siehe
S.	Seite
s. a.	siehe auch
s. o.	siehe oben
sog.	sogenannt
s. u.	siehe unten
u. a.	und andere(s), unter anderem
u. Ä.	und Ähnliches
usf., u. s. f.	und so fort
usw., u. s. w.	und so weiter
verb.	verbessert
Verf., Vf.	Verfasser
vgl.	vergleiche
z. B.	zum Beispiel
z. T.	zum Teil

12.7.4 Capitalization

All nouns in German are written with initial capital letters, as are other words (adjectives, numerals, and infinitives) that are used as nouns:

> *Gutes und Böses* 'good and evil'
> *Die Drei ist eine heilige Zahl* 'Three is a sacred number'

The basic rule of capitalizing nouns remains untouched by the orthographic reform, but whereas all nouns used as adverbs were previously lower case, some changes have been implemented: for example, *heute abend* ('tonight') is now *heute Abend, morgen abend* ('tomorrow evening') becomes *morgen Abend,* and *gestern morgen* ('yesterday morning') becomes *gestern Morgen.*

Adjectives used as nouns are capitalized with fewer exceptions than before: *alles übrige* becomes *alles Übrige* ('everything else').

In the new rules the familiar forms of the second person pronouns *du, dich, dir, dein, ihr, euch, euer* are not (as they formerly were) capitalized in letters and the like. The old rule remains that pronouns given a special sense in polite address are capitalized to distinguish them from their normal value: these are (in medieval and Swiss contexts) *Ihr* addressed to a single person; (in early modern contexts) *Er* and *Sie* (feminine singular); and (nowadays) *Sie* (plural). In all of the above the capital is used also in the oblique cases and in the possessive, but not in the reflexive *sich.*

Capitalize adjectives that form part of a geographical name (or are formed from a place name), the names of historic events or eras, monuments, institutions, titles, special days and feast days. Otherwise do not capitalize adjectives denoting nationality:

> *das deutsche Volk* 'the German nation'

or the names of languages in expressions where their use is considered adverbial:

> *italienisch sprechen* 'to speak Italian'

Traditionally, adjectives derived from personal names were capitalized in certain contexts, but according to the new rules all adjectives derived from personal names are to be lower case, except when the name is marked off with an apostrophe:

> *das ohmsche Gesetz* or *das Ohm'sche Gesetz* 'Ohm's Law'

In work titles the first word and all nouns are capitalized, with all other words having a lower-case initial.

12.7.5 Punctuation

There are very specific rules about the placing of commas in German. Do not interfere in the punctuation of quoted matter without reference to the author or the source.

Sentences containing an imperative normally end in an exclamation mark. The traditional practice of ending the salutation in a letter with an exclamation mark—*Sehr geehrter Herr Schmidt!* ('Dear Herr Schmidt')—has largely given way to the use of a comma, after which the letter proper does not begin with a capital unless one is otherwise required.

German rarely employs the en rule in compounds in the way that it is used in English, preferring a hyphen between words:

> *die Berlin-Bagdad-Eisenbahn* 'the Berlin–Baghdad railway'

The en rule is used for page and date ranges (*S.348–349, 1749–1832*): do not elide such ranges. It is also used, with a word space on each side, as a dash.

Quotation marks

German quotation marks (*Anführungszeichen*) take the form of two commas at the beginning of the quotation, and two opening quotation marks (turned commas) at the end („"), or reversed guillemets are used (» ... «). Mark quotations within quotations by a single comma at the beginning and a single opening quotation mark at the end (, '). No space separates the quotation marks from the quotation.

Expect a colon to introduce direct speech. Commas following a quotation fall after the closing quotation mark, but full points go inside if they belong to the quotation.

Apostrophe

The apostrophe is used to mark the elision of *e* to render colloquial usage:

> *Wie geht's?* 'How are things?'/'How are you?'

When the apostrophe occurs at the beginning of a sentence, the following letter does not become a capital:

> *'s brennt!* 'Fire!' (not *'S brennt*)

The apostrophe is also used to mark the suppression of the possessive *s* (for reasons of euphony) after names ending in *s, ß, x, z*:

> *Aristoteles' Werke   Horaz' Oden*

Hyphen

Traditionally, a noun after a hyphen begins with an initial capital:

> *das Schiller-Museum* 'the Schiller Museum'

but the new orthography allows words to be run together:

> *das Schillermuseum*

The hyphen was used to avoid the double repetition of a vowel (*Kaffee-Ersatz*, 'coffee substitute') but not to avoid the similar repetition of a consonant (*stickstofffrei*, 'nitrogen-free'). The new rules no longer require a hyphen—groups of three identical consonants are written out even before a vowel and when *sss* results from the abolition of *ß* after a short vowel:

> *Brennnessel   Schifffahrt*
> *Schlußsatz → Schlusssatz*

It is permissible to make such compounds clearer by using a hyphen:

> *Brenn-Nessel   Schiff-Fahrt   Schluss-Satz*

12.7.6 **Word division**

For the purpose of division, distinguish between simple and compound words.

Simple words

Do not divide words of one syllable. Divide other simple words by syllables, either between consonants or after a vowel followed by a single consonant. This applies even to *x* and mute *h*: *Bo-xer, verge-hen.*

Do not separate *ch*, *ph*, *sch*, *ß*, and *th* (representing single sounds). Correct examples are *spre-chen, wa-schen, So-phie, ka-tholisch, wech-seln, Wechs-ler*. Traditionally *st* was included in this group, but under the new rules it is no longer, and should be divided: *Las-ten, Meis-ter, Fens-ter.*

At the ends of lines, take over *ß*: *hei-ßen, genie-ßen.*

Take over as an entity *ss* if used instead of *ß*, but divide *ss* when it is not standing for *ß*: *las-sen.*

Traditionally, if a word was broken at the combination *ck* it was represented as though spelled with *kk*: *Zucker* but *Zuk-ker, Glocken* but *Glok-ken*. According to the new orthography, the combination *ck* is taken over whole, as it was traditionally after a consonant in proper nouns or their derivatives: *Zu-cker, Glo-cken, Fran-cke, bismar-ckisch.*

Treat words with suffixes as simple words and divide in accordance with the rules above: *Bäcke-rei, le-bend, Liefe-rung.*

Compound words

Divide a compound word by its etymological constituents (*Bildungs-roman, Kriminal-polizei, strom-auf*) or within one of its elements: *Bundes-tag* or *Bun-destag*. Divide prefixes from the root word: *be-klagen, emp-fehlen, er-obern, aus-trinken*.

12.7.7 Numerals

Separate numbers of more than four figures with thin spaces by thousands: *6 580 340*.

A full point after a numeral shows that it represents an ordinal number:

> *14. Auflage* (14th edition)
> *Mittwoch, den 19. Juli 1995* (Wednesday, 19 July 1995)

The full point also marks the separation of hours from minutes: *14.30 Uhr* or *14³⁰ Uhr*.

Germans use Roman numerals rarely: even when citing Roman page numbers, they often convert them into Arabic and add an asterisk: *S. 78** (p. lxxviii). Distinguish this from *1**, denoting the first page of an article that is in fact (say) the third or fifth page of a pamphlet.

12.7.8 Historical and specialist setting

The traditional black-letter German types such as Fraktur and Schwabacher were replaced by the Roman Antiqua in 1941. They are now found only to a limited extent in German-speaking countries, mostly in decorative or historical contexts, or in approximating earlier typography. Any matter to be set in them should be deemed a quotation. Word division should follow the pre-1998 rules, not the new; in particular the *st* ligature should be taken over. The long *s* (ſ) in Fraktur

Table 12.2 **German Fraktur alphabet**

𝕬	𝕬̈	𝕭	𝕮	𝕯	𝕰	𝕱	𝕲	𝕳	𝕴		𝕶	𝕷	𝕸	𝕹	𝕺	𝕺̈	𝕻	𝕼	𝕽	𝕾	𝕿	𝖀	𝖀̈	𝖁	𝖂	𝖃	𝖄	𝖅
A	Ä	B	C	D	E	F	G	H	I	or J	K	L	M	N	O	Ö	P	Q	R	S	T	U	Ü	V	W	X	Y	Z

𝖆	𝖆̈	𝖇	𝖈	𝖉	𝖊	𝖋	𝖌	𝖍	𝖎	𝖏	𝖐	𝖑	𝖒	𝖓	𝖔	𝖔̈	𝖕	𝖖	𝖗	ſ	𝖘	𝖙	𝖚	𝖚̈	𝖛	𝖜	𝖝	𝖞	𝖟
a	ä	b	c	d	e	f	g	h	i	j	k	l	m	n	o	ö	p	q	r	s	s	t	u	ü	v	w	x	y	z

ch	ck	ff	fi	fl	ll	si	ss	st	ß	tz

type is used at the beginnings of words, and within them except at the ends of syllables. The short final *s* (ς) is generally put at the ends of syllables and words.

12.8 Greek

12.8.1 Introduction

Ancient and modern Greek show a remarkable similarity, and much of what follows covers both. Modern Greek may be divided into two forms, **katharevousa** (literally 'purified'), a heavily archaized form used in technical and Church contexts, and **demotic**, the form which is spoken and used in everyday contexts. Demotic has been the official form since 1976, and is employed in official documents.

12.8.2 Alphabet

Ancient and modern Greek are written in an alphabet that consists of twenty-four letters: seventeen consonants and seven vowels (a, ϵ, η, ι, o, υ, ω). Modern Greek is written from left to right, as was ancient Greek from the classical period onwards.

In ancient Greek the 'final' sigma (i.e. the form used at the end of words) must be distinguished from ς stigma [*sic*], which was used for the numeral 6 and in late manuscripts and early printed books for

Table 12.3 **Greek alphabet**

A	α	alpha	a		I	ι	iota	i		P	ρ	rho	r, rh
B	β	beta	b		K	κ	kappa	k		Σ	σ	(ς final) sigma	s
Γ	γ	gamma	g		Λ	λ	lambda	l		T	τ	tau	t
Δ	δ	delta	d		M	μ	mu	m		Υ	υ	upsilon	u or y
E	ϵ	epsilon	e		N	ν	nu	n		Φ	ϕ	phi	ph
Z	ζ	zeta	z		Ξ	ξ	xi	x		X	χ	chi	kh
H	η	eta	ē		O	o	omicron	o		Ψ	ψ	psi	ps
Θ	θ	theta	th		Π	π	pi	p		Ω	ω	omega	ō

στ. Stigma is also used in scholarly work (especially on Latin authors) to denote 'late manuscripts'. In papyri and inscriptions sigma is normally printed Ϲ ϲ ('lunate sigma'), with no separate final form.

Texts of early inscriptions may require Latin *h* (to be italic with a sloping fount), and the letters Ϝ (wau or digamma) and Ϙ (koppa).

In ancient Greek an iota forming a 'long diphthong' with a preceding α, η, or ω is traditionally inserted underneath the vowel: ᾳ ῃ ῳ ('iota subscript'). Some modern scholars prefer to write αι, ηι, ωι ('adscript iota'), in which case accents and breathings should be set on the first vowel; in the case of αι this means that the accent may fall on either letter depending on the pronunciation. When a word is set in capitals, iota is always adscript (i.e. written on the line rather than beneath it); when the word has an initial capital but is otherwise lower case, an initial long diphthong will have the main vowel as capital, the iota adscript lower case; hence ῷ will become ΩΙ in capitals (for the absence of accent and breathing see below), but Ὤι at the start of a paragraph. In modern Greek the iota is omitted even in phrases taken bodily from the ancient language.

12.8.3 **Transliteration**

Whether or not to transliterate ancient or modern Greek must of course depend on the context. In general contexts any use of Greek script will be very off-putting to the majority of people, but readers who know Greek will find it far harder to understand more than a few words in transliteration than in the Greek alphabet. If the work is intended only for specialists, all Greek should be in the Greek alphabet; in works aimed more at ordinary readers, individual words or short phrases should be transliterated:

> *history* comes from the Greek word *historiē*

although longer extracts should remain in Greek script, with a translation. Table 12.3 shows how Greek letters are usually transliterated.

12.8.4 **Accents**

The accents in ancient and modern Greek are acute ´, used on any of the last three syllables of a word; grave `, used only on final syllables; circumflex ˆ, used on either of the last two syllables of a word. The

Table 12.4 **Greek accents**

ʼ	lenis (smooth breathing)	ʺ	lenis acute	῍	circumflex lenis
ʻ	asper (rough breathing)	῎	lenis grave	῝	circumflex asper
		῞	asper acute	¨	diaeresis
´	acute	῝	asper grave	΅	diaeresis acute
`	grave	^	round circumflex	῁	diaeresis grave

diaeresis ¨ is also used, to show that two vowels occurring together do not form a diphthong.

All words of three or more syllables, and most others, carry an accent. Most unaccented words cause the majority of preceding words to take an acute on their final syllable; they are known as **enclitics**, the others (all monosyllables) as **proclitics**. An acute accent on a final syllable or a monosyllable will be found before an enclitic, before punctuation, and in the two words τίς and τί when they mean 'who?' and 'what?'; otherwise it is replaced by a grave, although in modern Greek it is sometimes retained.

Greek uses marks known as **breathings** to indicate the presence or absence of an aspirate at the beginning of a word: they are ʻ (**asper or rough breathing**) and ʼ (**lenis or smooth breathing**). Breathings are used on all words beginning with a vowel or diphthong and also with ρ; in this case, and that of υ and υι, the breathing will nearly always be the asper.

Each of the accents may be combined with either breathing or with the diaeresis; but breathing and diaeresis never stand on the same letter. The accent always stands over the diaeresis; the breathing stands to the left of the acute or grave, but underneath the circumflex. Except in the case of long diphthongs (see above), accents are placed over the second vowel of a diphthong (which is always ι or υ).

Accents and breathings are regularly used when words are set in capital and lower-case style; they precede capitals and are set over lower-case letters. They are omitted when words are set wholly in capitals.

In modern Greek many printers now dispense with breathings and use only a single accent, either a small downward-pointing filled-in triangle or simply the acute; as before, the accent is omitted in capitals, but otherwise precedes capitals and stands over lower-case letters. Monosyllables, even if stressed, do not have an accent, save that ἤ 'or' is distinguished from η 'the' (nominative singular feminine), in traditional spelling ἤ and ἡ respectively. The diaeresis remains in use; however, it is used to show that αϊ and οϊ *are* diphthongs, as opposed to the digraphs αι (pronounced ε) and οι (pronounced ι).

In both ancient and modern Greek a final vowel or diphthong may be replaced at the end of a word by an apostrophe when the next word begins with a vowel or diphthong; occasionally it is the latter that is replaced. Traditionally setters have represented the apostrophe by a lenis; but if the font has a dedicated apostrophe that should be used. Do not set an elided word close up with the word following. It may be set at the end of a line even if it contains only one consonant and the apostrophe or lenis.

12.8.5 Capitalization and punctuation

In printing ancient Greek, the first word of a sentence or a line of verse is capitalized only at the beginning of a paragraph. In modern Greek, capitals are used for new sentences, though not always for new lines of verse.

For titles of works in ancient Greek, it is best to capitalize only the first word and proper nouns, or else proper nouns only. In modern Greek the first and main words tend to be capitalized; first word and proper nouns only is the rule in bibliographies.

In ancient Greek, it is conventional to capitalize adjectives and adverbs derived from proper nouns, but not verbs:

> ῞Ελλην 'a Greek'
> ῾Ελληνιστί 'in Greek'

but

> ἑλληνίζω 'I speak Greek/behave like a Greek'

In modern Greek, lower case is the rule:

> ελληνικός 'Greek (adj.)'

ἑλληνικά 'in Greek'

The comma, the full point, and the exclamation mark (in modern Greek) are the same as in English; but the question mark (;) is the English semicolon (italic where necessary to match a sloping Greek font), and the colon is an inverted full point (·). Use double quotation marks, or in modern Greek guillemets.

12.8.6 **Word division**

In ancient Greek the overriding precept should be that of breaking after prefixes and before suffixes and between the elements of compound words. This requires knowledge of the language, however, since many prefixes cannot be distinguished at sight: ἔν-αυε 'lit' contains a prefix, ἔναιε 'dwelt' does not.

A vowel may be divided from another (λύ-ων) unless they form a diphthong (αι, αυ, ει, ευ, ηυ, οι, ου, υι). Take over any combination of 'mute' (β, γ, δ, θ, κ, π, τ, φ, χ) followed by 'liquid' (λ, μ, ν, ρ), also βδ, γδ, κτ, πτ, φθ, χθ, or any of these followed by ρ; μν; and σ followed by a consonant other than σ or by one of the above groups: ἐλι-κτός, γι-γνώ-σκω, μι-μνή-σκω, κα-πνός, βα-πτί-ζω.

Any doubled consonants may be divided; λ, μ, ν, and ρ may be divided from a following consonant, except in μν. Divide γ from a following κ or χ; take over ξ and ψ between vowels (δεί-ξειν, ἀνε-ψιός).

Modern Greek word division follows ancient principles, but the consonant groups taken over are those that can begin a modern word. Therefore θμ is divided, but γκ, μπ, ντ, τζ, τσ are not.

12.8.7 **Numerals**

Two systems of numerals were in use in ancient Greek. In the older system (the 'acrophonic' system, used only for cardinal numbers), certain numbers were indicated by their initial letters. This was eventually replaced by the alphabetic system, shown in Table 12.5, which could be used of either cardinals or ordinals. The symbols ς and ϡ are known as 'stigma' and 'sampi' respectively.

Modern Greek uses Arabic numerals: if a sloping font is being used they should be set in italic, but with upright fonts they should be set in roman, in both cases ranging. Alphabetic numerals are still employed,

Table 12.5 **Greek numbers**

1	α'	14	$\iota\delta'$	60	ξ'	1,000	$'\alpha$
2	β'	15	$\iota\epsilon'$	70	o'	2,000	$'\beta$
3	γ'	16	$\iota\varsigma'$	80	π'	3,000	$'\gamma$
4	δ'	17	$\iota\zeta'$	90	φ'	4,000	$'\delta$
5	ϵ'	18	$\iota\eta'$	100	ρ'	5,000	$'\epsilon$
6	ς'	19	$\iota\theta'$	200	σ'	6,000	$'\varsigma$
7	ζ'	20	κ'	300	τ'	7,000	$'\zeta$
8	η'	21	$\kappa\alpha'$	400	υ'	8,000	$'\eta$
9	θ'	22	$\kappa\beta'$	500	ϕ'	9,000	$'\theta$
10	ι'	23	$\kappa\gamma'$	600	χ'	10,000	$'\iota$
11	$\iota\alpha'$	30	λ'	700	ψ'	20,000	$'\kappa$
12	$\iota\beta'$	40	μ'	800	ω'	100,000	$'\rho$
13	$\iota\gamma'$	50	ν'	900	λ'		

however, in much the same way as Roman numerals are in Western languages.

12.9 Hebrew

12.9.1 **Alphabet**

The Hebrew alphabet consists exclusively of consonantal letters. Vowels may be indicated by dots or small strokes ('points') above, below, or inside them, but Hebrew is generally written and printed without vowels. Hebrew written without vowels is described in English as 'unpointed' or 'unvocalized'.

Each letter has a numerical value. Letters are therefore often used in Hebrew books—especially in liturgical texts and older works—to indicate the numbers of volumes, parts, chapters, and pages. Letters are also used to indicate the day of the week, the date in the month, and the year according to the Jewish calendar.

Table 12.6 **Hebrew alphabet**

Consonants

Block*	Cursive*	Name	Simplified transcription	Numerical value	Scholarly transcription
א	א	alef	—†	1	ʾ
ב	ב	beit	b	2	b
ב	ב	veit	v		ḇ
ג	ג	gimmel	g	3	g/g̱
ד	ד	dalet	d	4	d/ḏ
ה	ה	hé	h	5	h
ו	ו	vav	v	6	w
ז	ז	zayin	z	7	z
ח	ח	chet	ch, ḥ	8	ḥ
ט	ט	tet	t	9	ṭ
י	י	yod	y, i‡	10	y
כ	כ	kaf	k	20	k
ךכ	ךכ	khaf, khaf sofit	kh		ḵ
ל	ל	lamed	l	30	l
םמ	םמ	mem, mem sofit	m	40	m
ןנ	ןנ	nun, nun sofit	n	50	n
ס	ס	samekh	s	60	s
ע	ע	ʿayin	—†	70	ʿ
פ	פ	pé	p	80	p
ףפ	ףפ	fé, fé sofit	f		p̱
ץצ	ץצ	tsadi, tsadi sofit	ts	90	ṣ
ק	ק	kof	k	100	q
ר	ר	resh	r	200	r
ש	ש	shin	sh	300	š
ש	ש	sin	s		ś
ת	ת	tav	t	400	t/ṯ

Vowels

Form	Name	Form	Name
ֽ	kamats	ֻ	kubutz
ַ	patah	ֲ	hataf patah
ֶ	segol	ֱ	hataf segol
ֵ	tseré	ו	holam
ִ	hirik	ו	shuruk
ְ	sheva		

* Where two forms are given, the second is that used in final position.

† The letters *alef* and *ʿayin* are not transliterated in the simplified system. Where they occur in intervocalic position an apostrophe is used to indicate that the vowels are to be pronounced separately.

‡ Transliterated 'y' as a consonant, 'i' as a vowel.

The consonantal letters are principally found in two different forms: a cursive script, and the block ('square') letters used in printing.

12.9.2 Transliteration

Different systems of transliterated Hebrew may require the following diacritics: $ś$ (and sometimes the acute is also used on vowels to indicate stress); $ā, ē, ī, ō, ū; ê, î, ô, û; ă, ĕ, ŏ$ (in some systems represented by superiors, $^{a\,e\,o}$); $ḥ, ṣ, ṭ, ẓ$ (in older system also $ḳ$ for q); $š; ḇ, ḏ, g, ḵ, p, ṯ$ (less strictly bh, dh, gh, kh, ph, th). Special characters are schwa ə, aleph ʾ, ʿayin ʿ; in loose transliteration from modern Hebrew the latter two may be replaced by an apostrophe or omitted altogether.

12.9.3 Word division

In Hebrew script, words are short enough not to need dividing; transliterated words should be so divided that the new line begins with a single consonant. In loose transliteration, *ts* and combinations with *h* may or may not represent single consonants; when in doubt avoid dividing.

Irish and Scots Gaelic *see* Gaelic

12.10 Italian

12.10.1 **Accents**

The use of accents in the Italian language is not entirely consistent; editors should as a general rule follow the author's typescript. There are two accents, acute and grave. The acute accent is used on a 'closed' *e* and very rarely on a closed *o: perché*, 'because', *né ... né ...* 'neither ... nor ...'. The grave accent is used on the 'open' *e* and *o: è*, 'is', *cioè*, 'that is', *però*, 'but', 'however'. The grave is also used to indicate stress on a final syllable. An alternative convention does exist for *i* and *u*, whereby they are marked with an acute accent: *così* and *cosí* ('so'), *più* and *piú* ('more'). However, in normal, standard Italian it is considered good practice to use the grave accent on all vowels except the closed *e* and, very rarely, *o*.

The appearance in a single text of Italian extracts with several different systems of accentuation may indicate not ignorance or carelessness in the author, but rather scrupulous fidelity to sources. Any discretional accents should be left alone unless the copy-editor is expert in the language and the author is not. There are other respects in which Italian spelling is even now less regulated than, say, French, and zeal for consistency must be tempered by either knowledge or discretion.

Leave capital letters unaccented as a general rule, unless an accent is needed to avoid confusion. The grave accent on an upper-case *E* is marked as an apostrophe:

> *E' oggi il suo compleanno* 'It is his birthday today'

12.10.2 **Abbreviation**

Italian abbreviations are usually set with an initial capital only rather than in full capitals, with no full point following: *An* (*Alleanza Nazionale*), *Rai* (*Radiotelevisione Italiana*). When the expansion does not begin with a capital, neither does the abbreviation: *tv* (*televisione*).

12.10.3 **Capitalization**

Italian uses capital letters much less frequently than English. Capitalize names of people, places, and institutions, and some dates and festivals. Use lower-case for *io* (*I*), unless it begins a sentence. *Lei, Loro,* and *Voi* (polite forms of 'you') and related pronouns and adjectives, *La, Le, Suo, Vi, Vostro,* are often capitalized, especially in commercial correspondence:

> *La ringraziamo per la Sua lettera* 'Thank you for your letter'

When citing titles of works capitalize only the first word and proper nouns:

> *Il gattopardo   La vita è bella*

Roman numerals indicating centuries are generally put in full capitals in both italic and roman:

> *l'XI secolo* 'the eleventh century'

Names of days and months (*lunedì, gennaio*) and languages, peoples, and adjectives of nationality are lower case:

> *Parlo inglese e francese* 'I speak English and French'
> *Gli italiani* 'the Italians'
> *un paese africano* 'an African country'

although the capitalization of the names of peoples (*gli Italiani*) is becoming more common.

12.10.4 **Punctuation**

Italian makes a distinction between points of omission (which are spaced) and points of suspension (which are unspaced). The latter equate with the French *points de suspension*, three points being used where preceded by other punctuation, four in the absence of other punctuation.

Put the ordinary interword space after an apostrophe following a vowel: *a' miei, ne' righi, po' duro, de' Medici.* Insert no space after an apostrophe following a consonant: *l'onda, s'allontana, senz'altro.* When an apostrophe replaces a vowel at the beginning of a word a space always precedes it: *e 'l, su 'l, te 'l, che 'l.*

Single and double quotation marks, and guillemets, are all used in varying combinations. A final full point is placed after the closing

quotation marks even if a question mark or exclamation mark closes
the matter quoted:

> «*Buon giorno, molto reverendo zio!*». 'Good day, most reverend Uncle!'

12.10.5 **Word division**

Do not divide the following compound consonants:

bl	*br*	*ch*	*cl*	*cr*	*dr*	*fl*	*fr*	*gh*	*gl*
gn	*gr*	*pl*	*pr*	*sb*	*sc*	*sd*	*sf*	*sg*	*sl*
sm	*sn*	*sp*	*sq*	*sr*	*st*	*sv*	*tl*	*tr*	*vr*
sbr	*sch*	*scr*	*sdr*	*sfr*	*sgh*	*sgr*	*spl*	*spr*	*str*

Divide between vowels only if neither is *i* or *u*. When a vowel is followed by a doubled consonant, including *cq*, the first of these goes
with the vowel, and the second is joined to the next syllable: *lab-bro*,
mag-gio, *ac-qua*. Apply the same rule if an apostrophe occurs in the
middle of the word: *Sen-z'altro, quaran-t'anni*. In general an apostrophe may end a line if necessary, but in this case it may not, although
it may be taken over along with the letter preceding it.

In the middle of a word, if the first consonant of a group is a liquid (*l*,
m, *n*, or *r*) it remains with the preceding vowel, and the other consonant, or combination of consonants, goes with the succeeding
vowel: *al-tero, ar-tigiano, tem-pra*.

12.11 Japanese

Japanese is expressed and printed in ideographs of Chinese origin
(*kanji*), interspersed with an alphabet-based script (*kana*), of which
there are two versions: the *hiragana* (the cursive form) is used for
inflectional endings and words with grammatical significance, and
the *katakana* (the 'squared' form) is used for foreign loanwords and
in Western names. Both vertical columns running right to left
and horizontal left-to-right layout are used.

The most frequently used system of romanization uses the macron ‾ to
indicate long vowels; syllable-final *n* is followed by an apostrophe
before *e* or *y*. The inclusion of macrons is optional in non-specialist
works, and may be omitted in well-established forms of place names,
such as *Hokkaido, Honshu, Kobe, Kyoto, Kyushu, Osaka, Tokyo*.

12.12 Latin

12.12.1 Alphabet

The standard Latin alphabet consists of twenty-one letters, *A B C D E
F G H I K L M N O P Q R S T V X*, plus two imports from Greek, *Y* and
Z. *A, E, O, Y* are vowels. *I, V* may be either vowels or consonants.

Renaissance printers invented a distinction between vocalic *i, u* and
consonantal *j, v*; many scholars, especially when writing for general
readers, still retain it with *u/v*, distinguishing *solvit* with two syllables
from *coluit* with three (also *volvit* 'rolls/rolled' from *voluit* 'willed'),
but others prefer to use *V* for the capital and *u* for the lower case irrespective of value. (However, the numeral must be *v* regardless of case.)
By contrast, the use of *j* is virtually obsolete except in legal and other
stock phrases used in an English context, such as *de jure*.

In classical Latin the ligatures *æ, œ* are found only as space-saving
devices in inscriptions. They are found in post-classical manuscripts
and in printed books down to the nineteenth century and occasionally
beyond. They should not now be used unless a source containing them
is to be reproduced exactly.

12.12.2 Accents

In modern usage Latin is normally written without accents. In classical Latin the *apex*, resembling an acute, was sometimes used on long
vowels other than *I*, and until recently *ë* was used to show that *ae*
and *oe* did not form a diphthong: *aëris* 'of air' (as opposed to *aeris*
'of bronze/money'), *poëta* 'poet'. Older practice used the circumflex on
long vowels to resolve ambiguity: *mensâ* ablative of *mensa* 'table'; one
may also find the grave accent on the final syllables of adverbs. In
grammars and dictionaries vowels may be marked with the macron
or the breve: *mēnsă* nominative, *mēnsā* ablative.

12.12.3 Capitalization

Classical Latin made no distinction between capital and lower case.
In modern usage proper names and their derivatives are capitalized
(*Roma* 'Rome', *Romanus*, 'Roman', *Graece* 'in Greek') except in verbs
(*graecissare* 'speak Greek/live it up'); the first letter in a sentence may
or may not be capitalized, that in a line of verse no longer so.

In titles of works, one may find (proper names apart) only the first word capitalized (*De rerum natura, De imperio Cn. Pompei*—Oxford's preference), first and main words (*De Rerum Natura, De Imperio Cn. Pompei*), or main words only (*de Rerum Natura, de Imperio Cn. Pompei*), even proper nouns only (*de rerum natura, de imperio Cn. Pompei*). For the treatment of Latin titles within titles see 8.2.7.

12.12.4 Word division

A vowel may be divided from another (*be-atus*) unless they form a diphthong, as do most instances of *ae, oe, ei, au,* and *eu.* When *v* is not used, the correct divisions with consonantal *u* are *ama-uit, dele-uit.* Likewise, a consonantal *i* is taken over (*in-iustus*).

Take over *x* between vowels (*pro-ximus*). Any doubled consonants may be divided; except in *mn,* the letters *l, m, n,* and *r* may be divided from a following consonant. Traditionally, any group capable of beginning a word in either Latin or Greek was not divided: for example *bl, br, ch, cl, cr, ct, dl, dr, gn, gu, mn, ph, pl, pr, ps, pt, qu, th, tl,* and *tr* (many of these are found in such learned English words as *ctenoid, gnomon, mnemonic, pneumonia, psychology,* and *ptomaine*).

However, as in Greek, these rules should be subject to the overriding precept that prefixes and suffixes are separated and compounds divided into their parts. This requires knowledge of the language, as some common prefixes may have different forms in different contexts.

12.12.5 Numerals

Latin, of course, uses Roman numerals, which are described at 11.5. They should generally be set in small capitals. The letter *C* was sometimes used in reversed form in numerals: IↃ 500 (normally written as D), CIↃ 1,000 (otherwise written M).

12.13 Old and Middle English

12.13.1 Alphabet

Old English is the name given to the earliest stage of English, in use until around 1150. Middle English is the name given to the English of the period between Old and modern English, roughly 1150 to 1500.

Several special characters are (or have been) employed in the printing of both Old and Middle English texts:

- the **ash** (*Æ*, *æ*), a character borrowed from the runic alphabet, pronounced approximately as in 'h*a*t'. This character should be printed as a single sort, not two separate letters. There are two types of its italic form, open (*æ*) and closed (*œ*): the open form is to be preferred, as the closed form is easily mistaken for an italic œ ligature (*œ*).

- the **eth** or **edh** (*Ð*, *ð*), sometimes called a 'crossed *d*'. This character is used indiscriminately for the voiced *th* as in 'th*a*t' and the voiceless *th* of 'th*i*n'. There are two (slightly different) types of this letter's lower-case form: one with a straight but angled cross-bar (*ð*), the other with short hooks to the crossbar (*ð*); either is acceptable.

- the **thorn** (*þ*, *þ*), a character borrowed from the runic alphabet, pronounced the same as eth. There are two (slightly different) types of this letter's upper- and lower-case form: the plain form with horizontal serifs, used in Icelandic (*Þ*, *þ*), and the Old English form with a slanted foot serif and a narrower bowl (*þ*, *þ*); each pair is equally acceptable. Authors and editors should ensure that the printer cannot mistake a thorn for a *p* or a wyn (see below). In Old English, furthermore, there is a special character *þ*, *þ* ('that' sign) used as an abbreviation of the word 'that'.

- the **wyn** or **wynn**, formerly called the **wen** (*Ƿ*, *ƿ*), a character borrowed from the runic alphabet to represent the sound of *w*. It is now usual to substitute *w* for the wyn of the manuscript, as it is easily confused with a thorn, though it may be distinguished by the absence of an ascender. Note that a printer may also mistake a wyn for a *p*.

- the **yogh** (*Ȝ*, *ȝ*), a Middle English letter used mainly where modern English has *gh* and *y*. In Old English script the letter *g* was written *ȝ*, *ȝ*, so-called 'insular *g*', and pronounced, according to context, either hard (in the earlier period like Dutch *g* (the voiced equivalent of the German *ach* sound); in later Old English like *g* in *go*) or soft (like *y* in *year*). The Norman Conquest brought with it from the continent the letter *g*, which was pronounced either as in *go* or as in *gentle*; in Middle English it was conventional to use this continental letter for these sounds, but a developed form of the insular shape (ȝ, ȝ) for specifically English values, including the voiceless spirant in *niȝt* 'night' (still heard in Scots *nicht*); a combination of its two most characteristic sounds gave this character the name 'yogh'. Except in special circumstances, Old English ð, ȝ is now represented by *g*; in Middle English the distinction between *g* and yogh must be maintained; ȝ is to be used for yogh in all Middle English work. In some Middle English texts the same shape is also used for *z*. Note that a printer may mistake a yogh for a *g* in one form or a ȝ or *z* in the other.

In printing Old and Middle English no attempt should be made to regularize the use of eth and thorn even in the same word; scribes used both letters at random. Whereas eth had died out by the end of the thirteenth century, thorn continued in use into the fifteenth century, and even later as the *y* for *th* of early Scots printing and in *ye* or *yᵉ* used for *the* and *yt*, *yᵗ*, *yᵃᵗ* for *that*; hence *Ye Olde* was originally read *The Old*.

12.13.2 **Punctuation**

Except in specialized texts, normal modern English punctuation conventions should be applied to Old and Middle English. In manuscripts, editors should not attempt to regularize or correct individual punctuation marks, especially as these marks do not necessarily perform functions equivalent to those of their modern counterparts: in the Old English of the late tenth and eleventh centuries a semicolon was the strongest stop and a full point the weakest. Note that the *punctus elevatus* (⸵), which occurs occasionally in Old English manuscripts and frequently in Middle English manuscripts, is not a semicolon and should not be replaced by one.

12.14 Portuguese

12.14.1 **Introduction**

Brazilian Portuguese differs considerably in spelling, pronunciation, and syntax from that of Portugal, far more so than US English differs from British English. Attempts to achieve agreement on spelling have not been very successful, and important differences in practice have been indicated below.

12.14.2 **Alphabet and spelling**

The letters *k*, *w*, and *y* are used only in loanwords. Apart from *rr* and *ss*, double consonants are confined to European Portuguese: *acção* 'action, share', *accionista* 'shareholder', *comummente* 'commonly', in Brazilian Portuguese *ação*, *acionista*, *comumente*. Several other consonant groups have been simplified in Brazilian Portuguese: *acto*, *amnistia*, *excepção*, *óptico*, *súbdito* (= subject of a king), *subtil* are *ato*, *anistia*, *exceção*, *ótico*, *súdito*, *sutil*.

In Brazilian Portuguese the numbers 16, 17, and 19 are spelled *dezesseis*, *dezessete*, *dezenove* in contrast to European Portuguese *deza-*; 14 may be *quatorze* beside *catorze*.

There are also many differences of vocabulary and idiom, such as frequent omission of the definite article after *todo* 'every' and before possessives.

12.14.3 **Accents**

European Portuguese uses four written accents on vowels: acute, grave, circumflex, and tilde (*til* in Portuguese); Brazilian Portuguese also uses the diaeresis. The acute may be used on any vowel; the grave only on *a*; the circumflex on *a*, *e*, and *o*; the tilde on *a* and *o*. The diaeresis is used on *u* between *q/g* and *e/i* to show that the vowel is pronounced separately.

Normal stress is unaccented; abnormal stress is accented. The rules of accentuation are complex, and cannot be fully described in a work of this type. Normal stress falls on the penultimate syllable in words ending in *-a*, *-am*, *-as*, *-e*, *-em*, *-ens*, *-es*, *-o*, *-os*; in all other cases (including words in *-ã*) the stress falls on the final syllable.

Note the use of the circumflex in words like *circunstância*, *paciência*, and *cômputo*, where *m* or *n* with a consonant follows the accented vowel. In Brazilian Portuguese the circumflex is also used when *m* or *n* is followed by a vowel: *Nêmesis*, *helênico*, *cômodo*, *sônico*. European Portuguese generally has an acute accent, so *Némesis*, *helénico*, *cómodo*, *sónico*. Thus we have *António* in European Portuguese but *Antônio* in Brazilian Portuguese; editors should ensure that any such names are correctly spelled according to their bearers' nationality.

12.14.4 **Punctuation**

The inverted question marks and exclamation marks which are characteristic of Spanish are not normally used in Portuguese.

12.14.5 **Word division**

Take over *ch, lh, nh,* and *b, c, d, f, g, p, t, v* followed by *l* or *r*; divide *rr, ss,* also *sc, sç.* Otherwise divide at obvious prefixes such as *auto-, extra-, supra-,* etc. When a word is divided at a pre-existing hyphen, repeat the hyphen at the beginning of the next line: *dar-lho* is divided *dar -lho.*

12.15 Russian

12.15.1 **Alphabet and transliteration**

Russian is one of the six Slavonic languages written in Cyrillic script (see **Slavonic Languages** at 12.17 for a list of the others). Table 12.7 includes 'upright' (*pryamoĭ*) and 'cursive' (*kursiv*) forms and also a transliteration in accordance with the 'British System' as given in

Table 12.7 **Russian alphabet**

А	а	*А*	*а*	a	Л	л	*Л*	*л*	l	Ч	ч	*Ч*	*ч*	ch
Б	б	*Б*	*б*	b	М	м	*М*	*м*	m	Ш	ш	*Ш*	*ш*	sh
В	в	*В*	*в*	v	Н	н	*Н*	*н*	n	Щ	щ	*Щ*	*щ*	shch
Г	г	*Г*	*г*	g	О	о	*О*	*о*	o	Ъ	ъ	*Ъ*	*ъ*	"
Д	д	*Д*	*д*	d	П	п	*П*	*п*	p	Ы	ы	*Ы*	*ы*	ȳ
Е	е	*Е*	*е*	e	Р	р	*Р*	*р*	r	Ь	ь	*Ь*	*ь*	'
Ё	ё	*Ё*	*ё*	ë	С	с	*С*	*с*	s	Э	э	*Э*	*э*	é
Ж	ж	*Ж*	*ж*	zh	Т	т	*Т*	*т*	t	Ю	ю	*Ю*	*ю*	yu
З	з	*З*	*з*	z	У	у	*У*	*у*	u	Я	я	*Я*	*я*	ya
И	и	*И*	*и*	i	Ф	ф	*Ф*	*ф*	f					
Й	й	*Й*	*й*	ĭ	Х	х	*Х*	*х*	kh					
К	к	*К*	*к*	k	Ц	ц	*Ц*	*ц*	ts					

British Standard 2979 (1958). For a brief discussion of the problems of transliteration see 12.17.1.

12.15.2 Abbreviations

One of the distinctive aspects of non-literary texts of the Soviet period was the extensive use of abbreviations, used to a far lesser extent in the post-Soviet language.

In lower-case abbreviations with full points, any spaces in the original should be kept, for example и т. д., и пр., but с.-д. Abbreviations by contraction, such as д-р, have no points. Abbreviations with a solidus are typically used in abbreviations of unhyphenated compound words.

Abbreviations consisting of capital initial letters, such as OOO 'Ltd', are set close without internal or final points. Commonly used lower-case abbreviations that are pronounced syllabically and declined, for example вуз, are not set with points.

Abbreviations for metric and other units are usually set in cursive and are not followed by a full point; abbreviated qualifying adjectives do have the full point, however (5 *кв. км* etc.).

12.15.3 Capitalization

Capital initial letters are in general rarer in Russian than in English. Capitalize personal names, but use lower-case initial letters for nouns and adjectives formed from them:

> тротскист 'Trotskyite'   марксизм 'Marxism'

and for nationalities, names of nationals, and inhabitants of towns:

> татарин 'Tartar'   англичанин 'Englishman'

Ranks, titles, etc. are also lower case:

> святой Николай 'Saint Nicholas'
> князь Оболенский 'Prince Obolensky'

Each word in names of countries takes a capital:

> Соединённые Штаты Америки 'United States of America'

Adjectives formed from geographical names are lower case except when they form part of a proper noun or the name of an institution:

> европейские государства 'European states'

but

> Архангельские воздушные линии 'Archangel Airlines'

Geographical terms forming part of the name of an area or place are lower case:

> остров Рудольфа 'Rudolph Island'   Северный полюс 'the North Pole'

Capitalize only the first word and proper nouns in titles of organizations and institutions, and of literary and musical works, newspapers, and journals.

Days of the week and names of the months are lower case, but note Первое мая and 1-е Мая for the May Day holiday.

The pronoun of the first-person singular, я = I, is lower case (except, of course, when used at the beginning of a sentence).

12.15.4 Punctuation

Hyphen

The hyphen is used in nouns consisting of two elements:

> интернет-сайт 'website'
> вице-спикер Думы 'The Deputy Speaker of the Duma'

It is also used in compound place names, Russian or foreign, consisting of separable words.

Dash

En rules are not used in Russian typography; em rules set close up take their place. Dashes—spaced em rules—are much used in Russian texts:

> линия Москва — Киев 'the Moscow–Kiev line'
> Волга — самая большая река в Европе 'the Volga is the longest European river'

Dashes are also used to introduce direct speech.

Quotation marks

Guillemets are used to indicate direct speech and special word usage and with titles of literary works, journals, etc.

12.15.5 Word division

Russian syllables end in a vowel, and word division is basically syllabic. However, there are many exceptions to this generalization, most of which are connected with Russian word formation. Consonant groups may be taken over entire or divided where convenient (provided at least one consonant is taken over), subject to the following rules.

- Do not separate a consonant from the prefix, root, or suffix of which it forms a part: род|ной, под|бежать, мещан|ство are correct divisions. Divide between double consonants (клас|сами), except where this conflicts with the preceding rule (класс|ный).

- Do not leave at the end of a line—or carry over—a single letter, or two or more consonants without a vowel: к|руглый, ст|рела, жидко|сть are incorrect. The letters ъ, ь, and й should never be separated from the letter preceding them (подъ|езд).

12.15.6 Numerals

Arabic numerals are used. Numbers from 10,000 upwards are divided off into thousands by thin spaces, and not by commas (*26 453*); below 10,000 they are set closed up (*9999*). The decimal comma is used in place of the decimal point (*0,36578*). Ordinal numbers are followed by a contracted adjectival termination except when they are used in dates (5-й год but 7 ноября 1917 г.).

12.16 Scandinavian languages

12.16.1 Danish, Norwegian, and Swedish

Forms of Norwegian

Norway, which until the middle of the nineteenth century used Danish as its literary language, now has two written languages: **Bokmål** (also called **Riksmål**), a modified form of Danish, and **Nynorsk** (also called **Landsmål**), a reconstruction of what Norwegian might have been but for the imposition of Danish. Each of these has several variants, and the only safe rule for the non-expert is to assume that all inconsistencies are correct.

Alphabets and accents

Modern **Danish** and **Norwegian** have identical alphabets, the twenty-six letters of the English alphabet being followed by æ, ø, å; in their place **Swedish** has å, ä, ö. The letter å, found in Swedish since the sixteenth century, was adopted in Norway in 1907, and in Denmark in 1948; previously these languages used *aa* (cap. *Aa*).

Acute accents are found in loanwords and numerous Swedish surnames, and occasionally for clarity, for example Danish *én* 'one', neuter *ét* (also *een, eet*) as against indefinite article *en, et*. The grave accent
is sometimes used in Norwegian to distinguish emphatic forms.

Capitalization

Until 1948 Danish nouns were capitalized as in German, a practice
also found in nineteenth-century Norwegian. All the languages now
tend to favour lower-case forms, for example for days, months, festivals, and historical events. This also applies to book titles; but periodical and series titles are legally deposited names, complete with any
capitals they may have.

Institutional names are often given capitals for only the first word and
the last; but in Danish and Norwegian some names begin with the
independent definite article, which then must always be included and
capitalized, *Den, Det, De* (= *Dei* in Nynorsk).

Capitalize the polite form of the second person in Danish and Norwegian: *De, Dem, Deres* (Nynorsk: *De, Dykk, Dykkar*). In Danish
capitalize also the familiar second person, *I*, to distinguish it from *i*
('in').

Word division

Compounds are divided into their constituent parts, including prefixes and suffixes. In Danish take over *sk, sp, st*, and combinations of
three or more consonants that may begin a word (including *skj, spj*).
In Norwegian or Swedish take over only the last letter; *ng* representing a single sound is kept back, and in Swedish *x*; other groups that
represent a single sound are taken over (Norwegian *gj, kj, sj, skj*,
Swedish *sk* before *e, i, y, ä, ö*). In Swedish compounds three identical
consonants are reduced to two, but the third is restored when the
word is broken: *rättrogen* ('orthodox'), divided *rätt|trogen*.

12.16.2 Icelandic and Faeroese

Alphabets and accents

In both languages the letter *d* is followed by *ð*. Icelandic alphabetization has *þ, æ, ö* after *z*; Faeroese has *æ, ø*. The vowels *a, e, i, o, u, y* may
all take an acute accent. Icelandic uses *x*, Faeroese *ks*; the Icelandic *þ*
corresponds to the Faeroese *t*.

Capitalization

Icelandic capitalization is minimal, for proper nouns only. In institutional names only the initial article (masculine *Hinn*, feminine *Hin*,
neuter *Hið*) should be capitalized. Faeroese follows Danish practice,
though polite pronouns are not capitalized.

12.17 Slavonic languages

12.17.1 Scripts and transliteration

Of the Slavonic languages Russian, Belarusian, Ukrainian, Bulgarian,
and Macedonian are written in the Cyrillic alphabet, Polish, Czech,
Slovak, Sorbian, Croatian, Bosnian, and Slovene in the Latin. At the
time of writing Serbian is written in either.

See 12.15.1 and Table 12.7 for details of the Cyrillic alphabet. The extra
sorts called for by the languages other than Russian that use Cyrillic
are Belarusian *i* (= *i*) and ў (= *w*); Macedonian ѓ (= *ǵ*), ѕ (= *dz*), ј (= *j*), љ
(= *lj*), њ (= *nj*), ќ (= *ḱ*), and џ (= *dž*); Serbian Ђ, ђ (= *đ*), ј (= *j*), љ (= *lj*), њ
(= *nj*), Ћ, ћ (= *ć*), and џ (= *dž*); and Ukrainian ґ (= *g*), є (= *ye*), і (= *i*), and
ї (= *yi*). In some Macedonian and Serbian fonts cursive *г*, *п*, and *т* are
in the form of superior-barred cursive *ī*, *ū*, and *ūu* respectively.

Transliteration systems are largely similar for those languages written in Cyrillic, but at the time of writing there is still no internationally agreed, unitary system. Of the three currently most favoured
systems, the ALA-Library of Congress, International Scholarly, and
British, the ALA-LC system seems to be gaining ground because of
its increasing use in national and academic libraries, spurred on by
developments in information technology and standardized, machine-
readable cataloguing systems.

Wherever possible, adhere to a single transliteration system throughout a single work. In texts using transliterated Russian, as well as
Belarusian, Bulgarian, and Ukrainian, authors and editors should
avoid mixing, for example, the usual British *ya*, *yo*, *yu*, the Library
of Congress *ia*, *io*, *iu*, and the philological *ja*, *jo*, *ju*. (Note that the
transliteration of Serbian and Macedonian operates according to
different rules.)

12.17.2 Belarusian

In standard transliteration of Belarusian (also called Belorussian), the diacritics ĭ, ŭ, è (or ė, é), and ′ (soft sign) are used. In specialist texts, the philological system requires č, ë, š, ž. The Library of Congress system requires ligatured i͡a, i͡o, i͡u, z͡h. In practice the ligature is often omitted, as many non-specialist typesetters have difficulty reproducing it; this is the case for all languages that employ this system.

12.17.3 Bosnian, Croatian, and Serbian

Linguistic nomenclature in the former Yugoslavia is still very contentious. Serbo-Croat was the main official language of Yugoslavia: although the term Serbo-Croat is still used by some linguists in Serbia and Bosnia–Herzegovina, the ISO has assigned codes to Bosnian, Croatian, and Serbian. Oversimplifying, Bosniaks (Bosnian Muslims) in Bosnia–Herzegovina use Bosnian, Croats in Croatia and Bosnia–Herzegovina use Croat, while Serbs in Serbia and Montenegro and in Bosnia–Herzegovina use Serbian.

The Roman alphabet used for Bosnian and Croatian is the standard *latinica* that is to be used for transliterating Serbian even for lay readers: thus четници will be *četnici* not *chetnitsi*.

The Cyrillic alphabet is ordered а б в г д ђ е ж з и ј к л љ м н њ о п р с т ћ у ф х ц ч џ ш; both in transliterated Serbian and in Croatian, the *latinica* order is a b c č ć d dž đ e f g h i j k l lj m n nj o p r s š t u v z ž.

Diacritics for transliterated Serbian are ć, č, š, ž; special characters are Đ đ.

12.17.4 Bulgarian

The ALA-LC system of transliteration uses the diacritics ĭ, ŭ, and the letter combinations *zh, kh, ch, sh, sht*. It also requires the ligatures i͡a, i͡u, t͡s. The philological system requires č, š, ž.

12.17.5 Czech and Slovak

Czech and Slovak are written using the Roman alphabet, which in Czech is a á b c č d ď e é ě f g h ch i í j k l m n ň o ó p r ř s š t ť u ú ů v y ý z ž; in alphabetizing, ignore accents on vowels and on *d, n*, and *t*. The Slovak alphabet is a á ä b c č d ď e é f g h ch i í j k l ĺ ľ m n ň o ó p r ŕ s š ť ť u ú v y ý z ž; in alphabetizing, ignore acute, circumflex, and accents on *d*, *l*, *n*, *r*, and *t*.

The diacritics used in Czech are *á, é, í, ó, ú, ý, ů, č, ď, ě, ň, ř, š, ť, ž*. The palatalization of *d, t* is always indicated by a háček in upper case (*Ď, Ť*) and in lower case either by a háček (*ď, ť*) or—preferably—a high comma right (*d', t'*). Slovak uses the diacritics *ä, á, é, í, ĺ, ó, ŕ, ú, ý, ô, č, d', l', ň, š, ť, ž*. The palatalization of *d* and *t* is the same as for Czech; that for the Slovak *l* can be either a háček or high comma right in upper case (*Ľ, L'*) and a high comma right in lower case (*l'*).

12.17.6 Macedonian

Macedonian is written in the Cyrillic alphabet, with a transliteration system similar to that used for Serbian. The diacritics used are *ǵ, ḱ, č, š, ž*, and the apostrophe; the letter combinations *lj, nj, dž* should not be broken in word division.

12.17.7 Old Church Slavonic

Also called Old Bulgarian, Old Church Slavonic was written in the Cyrillic alphabet as well as the older Glagolitic alphabet. The regional variants that developed from it are known collectively as Church Slavonic.

The diacritics and ligatures used in the Library of Congress's transliteration of Church Slavonic are *ǵ, f̀, v̀, ẏ, ż, ě, ê, îa, îe, îu, k̂s, p̂s, t̂s, îę, îǫ* (with ogonek or right-facing hook on *e, o*), *ôt, ē, ī, ō, ū, ȳ, ĭ, ę, ǫ* (ogonek). In Russian Church Slavonic, *ja/ya/ia* may correspond to *ę* and *îę, u* to *ǫ*, and *ju/yu/iu* to *îǫ*. The philological system uses *č, š, ž*. Special characters are ' (soft sign), '' (hard sign).

12.17.8 Polish

Polish is written in the Roman alphabet, as in English without *q, v*, and *x*. It employs the diacritics *ć, ń, ó, ś, ź, ż*, and *Ą, ą, Ę, ę* (ogonek, hook right); in addition there is one special character, the crossed (or Polish) *l* (*Ł, ł*).

Alphabetical order is: a ą b c ć d e ę f g h i j k l ł m n ń o ó p r s ś t u w y z ź ż. The digraphs *ch, cz, dz, dź, dż, rz*, and *sz* are not considered single letters of the alphabet for ordering purposes; however, these letter combinations should not be separated in dividing words.

12.17.9 Slovene

Slovene (also called Slovenian) is written in the Roman alphabet and uses the háček on *č, š, ž*; the digraph *dž* is not considered a single letter.

12.17.10 Ukrainian

The philological system requires *č, š, ž, ĭ, ï, ′* (soft sign), and the letter combinations *je, šč, ju, ja*. The Library of Congress system requires ligatured *i͡a, i͡e, i͡u, z͡h*; as with Belarusian, the ligature is often omitted. The Ukrainian и is transliterated as *y*, not *i* (which represents Ukrainian *і*).

12.18 Spanish

12.18.1 Introduction

The Spanish used in Spain and the Spanish spoken in Latin America are mutually intelligible in much the same way that American and British English are. However, there are important differences in vocabulary and usage both between Spain and Latin America and among the Latin American countries—it is a mistake to think that Latin American Spanish is a uniform variant of the language.

12.18.2 Alphabet and spelling

In older works *ch* and *ll* were treated as separate letters for alphabetical purposes, but this is now very dated. The letter *Ñ, ñ* is treated as a separate letter. The letters *k* and *w* are used only in loanwords from other languages and their derivatives.

The only doubled consonants in Spanish are *cc* before *e* or *i*, *rr*, *ll*, and *nn* in compounds. They can be remembered as the consonants appearing in CaRoLiNe. Where an English speaker might expect a double consonant, Spanish normally simply has one, as in *posible* 'possible'.

12.18.3 **Accents**

Normal stress in Spanish falls on either the penultimate or the last syllable, according to complex rules. Normal stress is not indicated by an accent; an acute accent is used when the rules for normal stress are broken. The only other diacritical marks used are the tilde on the *ñ*, and the diaeresis on *ü*, following *g* before *e* or *i*, where *u* forms a diphthong with *e* or *i*. Accents are normally used on capitals.

The accent is used to show interrogative and exclamatory use in the following words:

cuál 'what', 'which'	*cómo* 'how'	*cuándo* 'when'
cuánto 'how many/much'	*dónde* 'when'	*qué* 'what'
quién 'who'		

The accented forms are used in indirect questions. Until recently the demonstrative pronouns *éste* ('this one'), *ése* ('that one'), *aquél* ('that one, further away') with their feminine equivalents, *ésta*, *ésa*, *aquélla* and plurals *éstos/éstas*, *ésos/ésas*, *aquéllos/aquéllas*, were accented. However, the Real Academia has decreed that the accent is not needed when there is no danger of ambiguity. This ruling is not universally accepted and both conventions will be found. The neuter forms *esto*, *eso*, *aquello* are never accented.

12.18.4 **Capitalization**

Capitals are used in much the same way as in English in proper names. Practice differs in titles of books, poems, plays, and articles, where normally the first word and proper nouns are capitalized:

> *Cien años de soledad*
> *La deshumanización del arte*
> *Doña Rosita la soltera, o El lenguaje de las flores*
> *El ingenioso hidalgo don Quijote de la Mancha.*

Capitalize names of high political or religious authorities—when not followed by their first name—and references to God:

> *el Rey   la Reina   los Reyes   el Papa   creer en Dios*

but

> *el rey Carlos III   el papa Juan XXIII*

Roman numerals indicating centuries are generally given in full capitals: *el siglo XI*.

Lower case is usually used for names of posts and titles:

> *catedrático*   *doctora*   *duquesa*   *general*
> *juez*   *ministro*   *presidente*

This may include non-Spanish titles such as *sir* or *lord*: *el embajador británico sir Derek Plumbly*.

Also written in lower case are:

- nouns and adjectives denoting nationalities, religions, and peoples and tribes: *francés, católico, dominicano, oriental, amerindio*
- names of artistic and literary movements: *romanticismo, gótico, surrealismo*
- names of streets and roads: *calle de Hortaleza, avenida de Navarra, puente de Santiago*; but *la Gran Vía*
- names of administrative divisions and geographical features, and cardinal points when they are not part of a name: *provincia de Toledo, estado de Nueva York, condado de Lancashire, cordillera de los Andes, lago Titicaca, el sur de Francia.*

Traditionally names of the days of the week, months, and seasons take a lower-case initial letter, but the use of capitals for these words is now very common and cannot be assumed to be a mistake.

12.18.5 Punctuation

The most obvious differences from other European languages are the inverted exclamation mark and question mark inserted at the place where the exclamation or question begins:

> *¡Mire!* 'look!'   *¿Dónde vas?* 'Where are you going?'

This need not be the start of the sentence:

> *Si ganases el Gordo, ¿qué harías?* 'If you won the jackpot what would you do?'

Quotation marks take the form of guillemets (called *comillas*), set closed up (e.g. *«¡Hola!»*). However, it is more common—especially in fiction—to dispense with *comillas* altogether and indicate speakers by a dash.

Colons are used before quotations (*Dijo el alcalde: «Que comience la fiesta.»*), in letters (*Querido Pablo:*), and before an enumeration (*Trajeron de todo: cuchillos, cucharas, sartenes, etc.*). Points of suspension are set closed up with space following but not preceding them.

12.18.6 **Word division**

The general rule is that a consonant between two vowels and the second of two consonants must be taken over to the next line. The combinations *ch*, *ll*, and *rr* are indivisible and must be taken over: *mu-chacho*, *arti-llería*, *pe-rro*.

The consonants *b*, *c*, *f*, *g*, *p* followed by *l* or *r* must be taken over as a pair: *ha-blar* 'to speak', *ju-glar* 'minstrel'; so must *dr* and *tr*, as in *ma-drugada* 'dawn', *pa-tria* 'fatherland'.

The letter *s* must be divided from any following consonant: *Is-lam*, *hués-ped* 'guest, host', *Is-rael*, *cris-tiano*; similarly *Es-teban* 'Stephen', *es-trella* 'star', even in a compound (*ins-tar* 'to urge', *ins-piración*).

Divide compounds into their component parts, except where they contain *s* + consonant or *rr* (*des-hacer* 'to undo', *sub-lunar*, but *circuns-tancia*, *co-rregir* 'to correct', *inte-rrumpir* 'to interrupt'). Never divide diphthongs and triphthongs; if possible, avoid dividing between vowels at all.

12.19 Welsh

12.19.1 **Alphabet and accents**

The Welsh alphabet consists of twenty-eight letters, alphabetized as *a b c ch d dd e f ff g ng h i l ll m n o p ph r rh s t th u w y*. The letter *j* is used in borrowed words; *k* and *v* are very frequent in medieval texts but are now obsolete.

Rh counts as a separate letter at the start of a word or syllable only, i.e. after a consonant but not a vowel: *route* comes before *rhad* 'cheap', *cynrychioli* 'to represent' before *cynrhon* 'maggots', but *arholi* 'to examine' before *arian* 'money'; *w* is usually, *y* always, a vowel.

All vowels (including *w* and *y*) may take a circumflex. Acute, grave, and diaeresis are also found: most frequent are *á* in final syllables (*casáu* 'to hate') and *ï* before a vowel (*copïo* 'to copy'). The letter with the diaeresis always precedes or follows another vowel.

A word consisting of an apostrophe followed by a single letter must be set close up to the preceding word:

> *cerddai'r bachgen a'i fam i'ch pentref*, 'the boy and his mother used to walk to your village'

12.19.2 Word division

Do not divide the digraphs *ch*, *dd*, *ff*, *ll*, *ph*, *rh*, *th*. Note that *ng* is indivisible when a single letter, but not when it represents *n* + *g*: this happens most frequently in the verb *dangos* 'to show' and its derivatives, compounds ending in *-garwch* or *-garwr* (e.g. *ariangarwr* 'money-lover'), place names beginning with *Llan-* (*Llangefni*, *Llangollen*), and in *Bangor*. Thus *cyng-aneddol* but *a ddan-goswyd*.

Do not divide *ae*, *ai*, *au*, *aw*, *ayw*, *ei*, *eu*, *ew*, *ey*, *iw*, *oe*, *oi*, *ou*, *ow*, *oyw*, *wy*, *yw*, and other combinations beginning with *i* and *w* in which these letters are consonants. The presence of a circumflex or an acute does not affect word division, but it is legitimate to divide after a vowel bearing the diaeresis, as also after a diphthong or triphthong before another vowel. Thus *barddoni-aidd* 'bardic', *gloyw-ach* 'brighter', *ieu-anc* 'young'.

Generally, take back a single consonant other than *h*, except after a prefix (especially *di-*, *go-*, *tra-*): *g-l* but *s-gl* (and so similar groups). A suffix beginning with *i* plus a vowel must be broken off: *casgl-iad* 'collection'.

It is always safe to divide *l-rh*, *ng-h*, *m-h*, *n-h* (but *n-nh*), *n-n*, *n-rh*, *r-r*, and after a vowel *r-h*. Initial *gwl-*, *gwn-*, *gwr-*, and their mutated forms must not be divided, since the *w* is consonantal: *gwlad* 'country', *(hen) wlad* '(old) country', *gwneud* 'to do', *(ei) wneud* 'to do (it)'. *Gwraig* 'woman', *(y) wraig* '(the) woman', cannot be divided.

12.19.3 Mutations and other changes

As in Irish Gaelic, initial consonants are replaced in certain grammatical contexts by others in a process called **mutation**: *cath* 'cat' but *fy nghath* 'my cat', *ei gath* 'his cat', *ei chath* 'her cat'. *Caerdydd* (Cardiff), *Dinbych* (Denbigh), *Gwent* give *i Gaerdydd* ('to Cardiff'), *yng Nghaerdydd* ('in Cardiff'); *i Ddinbych*, *yn Ninbych*; *i Went*, *yng Ngwent*. 'Oxford' is *Rhydychen*, but 'from Oxford' is *o Rydychen*. The full range of mutations is *b* to *f* or *m*; *c* to *ch*, *g*, or *ngh*; *d* to *dd* or *n*; *g* to zero or *ng*; *ll* to *l*; *m* to *f*; *p* to *b*, *mh*, or *ph*; *rh* to *r*; *t* to *d*, *nh*, or *th*.

Initial vowels may acquire a preliminary *h* (*offer* 'tools', *ein hoffer* 'our tools') and changes of stress within a word may cause *h* to appear or disappear and double *n* or *r* to be simplified:

brenin 'king'	*brenhinoedd* 'kings'
brenhines 'queen'	*breninesau* 'queens'
corrach 'dwarf'	*corachod* 'dwarfs'
cynneddf 'faculty'	*cyneddfau* 'faculties'
cynnin 'shred'	*cynhinion* 'shreds'
dihareb 'proverb'	*diarhebion* 'proverbs'

12.20 Yiddish

Yiddish originated in German as spoken by Jews; since the later eighteenth century it has been based on dialects spoken to the east of Germany proper. It is written in an adaptation of the Hebrew alphabet, with extra characters for use in writing the basic German-derived vocabulary, and loanwords taken from surrounding (mostly Slavonic) languages; several other letters are used only in words taken from Hebrew and Aramaic, which are spelled as in their languages of origin.

CHAPTER 13

Law and legal references

13.1 Introduction

Often the standards adopted in the legal discipline are at variance with those of other subjects. Additionally, practices common in one aspect of the law may be unfamiliar in another. However, there is no reason why the following general guidelines cannot be applied across a broad range of legal studies. Given the variety of legal citations in use, this section cannot purport to be wholly definitive, nor to resolve every stylistic point that may occur. Options are given for those aspects of citation on which there is no widespread consensus.

13.2 Typography

13.2.1 **Italics**

Law uses more foreign—particularly Latin—words than many other subjects. For that reason law publishers may deviate from the usage of general reference works when determining which words and phrases to italicize. Only a handful of foreign-language law terms have become so common in English that they are set as roman in general use. Some publishers use this as a basis for determining styles: the well-known 'inter alia' and 'prima facie' are in roman, for example, but *de jure* and *stare decisis* are in italic. Others prefer to set all Latin words and phrases in italic, rather than appear inconsistent to readers immersed in the subject, for whom all the terms are familiar. Regardless of which policy is followed, words to be printed in roman rather than italic include the accepted abbreviations of *ratio decidendi* and *obiter dictum/dicta*: 'ratio', 'obiter', 'dictum', and 'dicta'.

Traditionally, the names of the parties in case names are cited in italics, separated by a roman or italic 'v.' (for 'versus'): *Smith* v. *Jones*. The 'v.' may also match the case-name font, or it may have no full point: any style is acceptable if consistently applied.

13.2.2 **Abbreviations**

There are four possibilities regarding the use of full points in abbreviations:

- there should be no points at all, or no points only in legal abbreviations
- all points should be put in ('Q.B.D.')
- points should be in abbreviations of fewer than three letters ('A.C.')
- points should not appear between or after capitals, but should appear after abbreviations that consist of a mixture of upper- and lower-case letters ('Ont. LJ', 'Ch. D' but 'QBD', 'AC').

References, especially familiar ones, and common legal terms (paragraph, section), may be abbreviated in the text as well as in notes, but all other matter should be set out in full. Where a term is repeated frequently and is unwieldy when spelled out, such as 'International Covenant on Civil and Political Rights', then refer to it at first mention in full, with '(ICCPR)' following it, and thereafter simply as 'ICCPR'. Be careful that the abbreviations chosen do not confuse institutions with conventions (for example, use 'ECHR' for 'European Convention on Human Rights' and 'ECtHR' for 'European Court of Human Rights'). Both the European Court of Justice and the European Court of Human Rights are frequently referred to as 'the European Court': the European Court of Human Rights should always be referred to in full, unless the text in question is specifically about human rights and there is no possibility of confusion.

In cases, use 'Re' rather than 'In re', 'In the matter of', etc. Abbreviate *ex parte* to *ex p.*, with the letter *e* capitalized when it appears at the beginning of a case name but in lower case elsewhere:

> R v. *Acton Magistrates, ex p. McMullen*

When citing a law report, do not include expressions such as 'and another' or 'and others' that may appear in the title, but use 'and anor.' or 'and ors.' in cases such as '*Re P and ors. (minors)*' to avoid the appearance of error. To avoid unnecessary repetition, shorten citations in the text following an initial use of the full name: 'in *Glebe Motors plc* v.

Dixon-Greene' could subsequently be shortened to 'in the *Glebe Motors* case'. In criminal cases it is acceptable to abbreviate 'in *R* v. *Caldwell*' to 'in *Caldwell*'. Where a principle is known by the case from which it emerged, the name may no longer be italicized: for example, 'the Wednesbury principle'.

Law notes tend to be fairly lengthy, so anything that can be abbreviated should be. Thus 'HL', 'CA', etc. are perfectly permissible, as are 's.', 'Art.', 'Reg.', 'Dir.', %, all figures, 'High Ct', 'Sup. Ct', 'PC', 'Fam. Div.', etc., even in narrative notes.

13.2.3 Capitalization

Capitalize 'Act', even in a non-specific reference; 'bill' is lower case except for in the names of bills. Unless it is beginning a sentence, 'section' always has a lower-case initial. 'Article' should be capitalized when it refers to supranational legislation (conventions, treaties, etc.) and lower case when it refers to national legislation.

'Court' with a capital should be used only when referring to international courts such as the European Court of Justice and the International Court of Justice, or for relating information specific to a single court. For instance, in a book about the Court of Appeal, Criminal Division, that court may be referred to as 'the Court' throughout. It is a common shorthand convention in US law to refer to the Supreme Court as 'the Court' and to a lesser court as 'the court'.

A capital may also be used in transcripts where a court is talking about itself, but not necessarily where it refers to itself in a different composition. Thus members of a Court of Appeal would refer to 'a judgment of the Court' when citing a previous judgment by themselves, but to 'that court' when referring to a Court of Appeal composed of others. Where, however, the reference is to a court in general, the *c* should always be lower case.

The word 'judge' should always begin with a lower-case letter, unless it is referring to a specific person's title or the author has contrasted the Single Judge with the Full Court (as in criminal appeals and judicial review proceedings), where they both have specific parts to play and almost constitute separate courts in themselves.

13.3 References

Some legal writers cite others' works without a place of publication, or without first names or initials, for example 'Smith & Hogan *Criminal Law* (10th edn, 2002)'. This is an established convention in at least parts of the discipline, the expectation being that the work will be read by those who are already immersed in the relevant texts. However, editors should not impose it, and if the expected readership is more general or more elementary (as in an undergraduate or introductory text) full references must be given.

Continental and US references (except US case references) should be cited with the date and volume number first, followed by the abbreviation of the report or review name, and then—without a comma in between—the page number.

The names of books and non-law journals and reports should be in italic, following the standard format (see Chapter 8). Abbreviated references to reports and reviews should be in roman—in text, references, and lists of abbreviations. Names of law journals and reports are in roman, the reference following the date:

[2005] 2 All ER 125   (2004) NLJ 14

Abbreviated titles of works are in roman or italic, depending on the style of the expanded version.

Certain textbooks have been accorded such eminence that in references the name of the original author appears in italics as part of the title, for example *Chitty on Contracts* and *Dicey and Morris on Conflict of Laws*. In full references it is not necessary to give the name of the current editor, although the edition number and the date of that edition must be stated.

Abbreviate only titles of extremely well-known books, journals, or reports (for example Smith & Hogan, the NLJ); all others should appear in full. Variations exist in the way that many periodicals are abbreviated or punctuated. Providing authors are consistent such variations are acceptable; in works for non-specialists, readers may benefit from expanded versions of very terse abbreviations.

When the full title of a reports series or a review is quoted—and only the very obscure ones need to be quoted in full—that full title is always in italics. Setting all abbreviated titles in roman does leave some pitfalls, of which one must be wary: 'CMLR', for instance, refers to Common Market Law Reports (which publishes only reports and never articles), while 'CMLRev.' refers to Common Market Law Review. Unfortunately, where authors cite the latter as the former the only clue that they have it wrong is that the reference is to an article.

If a book, journal, report, or series is referred to very frequently in a particular work, certain common abbreviations (such as 'Crim.', 'Eur.', 'Intl', 'J', 'L', 'Q', 'R', 'Rev.', 'U', 'Ybk') may be used; give them in full at their first occurrence but abbreviated thereafter, and include in the List of Abbreviations.

13.4 Citing cases

13.4.1 General principles

Where a specific page within a report or article is referred to, the initial page number should be followed by a comma plus the specific page number, or no comma and 'at' followed by the specific page number: the decision is a matter of personal choice, but should be made consistent throughout a particular work:

> *Ridge* v. *Baldwin* [1964] AC 40, 78–9

or

> ... [1964] AC 40 at 78–9

In reports a date is in square brackets if it is essential for finding the report, and in parentheses where there are cumulative volume numbers, the date merely illustrating when a case was included in the reports:

> *R.* v. *Lambert* [2001] 2 WLR 211 (QBD)
> *Badische* v. *Soda-Fabrics* (1897) 14 RPC 919, HL
> P. Birks, 'The English Recognition of Unjust Enrichment' [1991] LMCLQ 473, 490–2
> S. C. Manon, 'Rights of Water Abstraction in the Common Law' (1965) 83 LQR 47, 49–51

No brackets are used in cases from the Scottish Series of Session Cases from 1907 onwards, and Justiciary Cases from 1917 onwards:

> *Hughes* v. *Stewart*, 1907 SC 791
> *Corcoran* v. *HM Advocate*, 1932 JC 42

Instead, the case name is followed by a comma, as it is in US, South African, and some Canadian cases where the date falls at the end of the reference. It is usual to refer to Justiciary Cases (criminal cases before the High Court of Justiciary) simply by the name of the panel (or accused).

Quote extracts from cases exactly. Do not amend to improve the sense, and clearly indicate if you correct obvious errors. Omitted text should be indicated by ellipses.

13.4.2 Unreported

Cite a newspaper report if there is no other published report. The reference should not be abbreviated or italicized:

> *Powick* v. *Malvern Wells Water Co.*, The Times, 28 Sept. 1993

When a case has not (yet) been reported, cite just the name of the court and the date of the judgment. The word 'unreported' should not be used:

> *R* v. *Marianishi, ex p. London Borough of Camden* (CA, 13 Apr. 1965)

Unreported EU cases are handled differently (see 13.4.4 below).

13.4.3 Courts of decision

Unless the case was heard in the High Court or was reported in a series that covers the decisions of only one court, the court of decision should be indicated by initials at the end of the reference. References to unreported cases, however, should be made in parentheses to the court of decision first (even if it is an inferior court), followed by the date. Reference is not normally made to the deciding judge (for example '*per* Ferris J'), except when wishing to specify him or her when quoting from a Court of Appeal or House of Lords decision. For example:

> *Blay* v. *Pollard* [1930] 1 AC 628, HL
> *Bowman* v. *Fussy* [1978] RPC 545, HL
> *Re Bourne* [1978] 2 Ch 43

Where a case has been included in a report long after it was heard, both the report and hearing dates may be included in the citation so the reader knows there has been no error:

> *Smith* v. *Jones* [2001] (1948) 2 All ER 431

A single 'best' reference should be given for each case cited. For UK cases, the reference should be to the official Law Reports; if the case has not been reported there, the Weekly Law Reports (WLR) are preferred, and failing that the All England Reports (All ER). In certain specialist areas it will be necessary to refer to the relevant specialist series, for example Family Law Reports and Industrial Cases Reports.

13.4.4 European Union

Where it is available, cite a reference to the official reports of the EU, the European Court Reports (ECR), in preference to other reports. If an ECR reference is not available, the second-best reference will usually be to the Common Market Law Reports (CMLR). However, where a case is reported by the (UK) official Law Reports, the WLR, or the All ER, that may be cited in preference to CMLR, particularly if readers may not have ready access to CMLR. If the case is not yet reported it should be cited with a reference to the relevant notice in the *Official Journal*.

The case number should always be given before the name of the case in European Court of Justice (ECJ) cases. Where cases are cited from ECR, an abbreviated reference to the court of decision at the end of the citation is superfluous. When citing from other series of reports, however, it is appropriate to add 'ECJ' or 'CFI' at the end of the citation. Treat Commission Decisions—but not Council Decisions—as cases.

Judgments of the courts are uniformly translated into English from French, sometimes inexactly. If the meanings of such judgments are not clear, refer to the original French for clarification.

13.4.5 European Human Rights

Decisions of the European Court of Human Rights should always cite the relevant reference in the official reports (Series A) and if possible also the European Human Rights Reports:

> *Young, James and Webster* v. *UK* Series A No 44, (1982) 4 EHRR 38

Decisions and reports of the European Commission of Human Rights (now defunct) should cite the relevant application number, a reference to the Decisions and Reports of the Commission series (or earlier to the Yearbook of the ECHR), and—if available—a reference to the European Human Rights Reports:

> *Zamir* v. *UK* Application 9174/80, (1985) 40 DR 42

13.4.6 Other cases

The citation of laws in other jurisdictions is too big a subject to cover in any great detail here. Authors and editors unsure of the relevant conventions should consult *The Bluebook: A Uniform System of Citation* (17th edn, 2000). This is a useful guide to citing legal sources from a wide range of jurisdictions.

13.5 Legislation

13.5.1 UK legislation

A statute's title should always be in roman, even where a US statute is in italics in the original. Older statutes, without a short title, will require the appropriate regnal year (see 11.7) and chapter number. Use Arabic numerals for chapter numbers in Public (General) and Private Acts:

> 3 & 4 Geo. V, c. 12, ss. 18, 19

Use lower-case Roman numerals in Public (Local) Acts:

> 3 & 4 Geo. V, c. xii, ss. 18, 19

Scots Acts before the Union of 1707 are cited by year and chapter: 1532, c. 40. All Acts passed after 1962 are cited by the calendar year and chapter number of the Act; commas before the date were abolished retroactively in 1963. There is no need for the word 'of' except, perhaps, when discussing a number of Acts with the same title (for example, to distinguish the Criminal Appeals Act of 1907 from that of 1904). Provided the meaning is clear, it is permissible even in text to refer to 'the 1904 Act'.

Some UK statutes are almost invariably abbreviated, for example PACE (Police and Criminal Evidence Act) and MCAs (Matrimonial Causes Acts). Where such abbreviations will be familiar to readers they may be used, even in text, although it is best to spell a statute out at first mention with the abbreviation in parentheses before relying thereafter simply on the abbreviation. Use an abbreviation where one particular statute is referred to many times throughout the text.

Except at the start of a sentence or when the reference is non-specific, use the following abbreviations: 's.', 'ss.' (or §, §§), 'Pt', 'Sch.' For example, paragraph (k) of subsection (4) of section 14 of the Lunacy Act 1934 would be expressed as 'Lunacy Act 1934, s. 14(4)(k)'. There is no space between the bracketed items. In general, prefer 'section 14(4)' to 'subsection (4)' or 'paragraph (k)'; if the latter are used, however, they can be abbreviated to 'subs. (3)' or 'para. (k)' in notes.

Statutory instruments should be referred to by their name, date, and serial number:

> Local Authority Precepts Order 1897, SR & O 1897/208
>
> Community Charge Support Grant (Abolition) Order 1987, SI 1987/466

No reference should be made to any subsidiary numbering system in the case of Scots instruments, those of a local nature, or those making commencement provisions.

Quote extracts from statutes exactly. Do not amend to improve the sense, and clearly indicate if you correct obvious errors. Omitted text should be indicated by ellipses.

13.5.2 **European Union legislation**

For primary legislation, include both the formal and informal names in the first reference to a particular treaty:

> EC Treaty (Treaty of Rome, as amended), art. 3b
>
> Treaty on European Union (Maastricht Treaty), art. G5c

Cite articles of the treaties without reference to the titles, chapters, or subsections. As part of a reference, abbreviate 'article' to 'art.', in lower-case roman. Cite protocols to the treaties by their names, preceded by the names of the treaties to which they are appended:

> Act of Accession 1985 (Spain and Portugal), Protocol 34
>
> EC Treaty, Protocol on the Statute of the Court of Justice

References to secondary legislation (decisions, directives, opinions, recommendations, and regulations) should be to the texts in the *Official Journal* of the European Union. The title of the legislation precedes the reference to the source:

> Council Directive (EC) 97/1 on banking practice [1997] OJ L234/3

> Council Regulation (EEC) 1017/68 applying rules of competition to
> transport [1968] OJ Spec Ed 302

While it is always important to state the subject matter of EU secondary legislation, the long official title may be abbreviated provided that
the meaning is clear. For example, the full title

> Commission Notice on agreements of minor importance which do not
> fall under art. 85(1) of the Treaty establishing the EEC [1986] OJ
> C231/2, as amended [1994] OJ C368/20

may be abbreviated to

> Commission Notice on agreements of minor importance [1986] OJ
> C231/2, as amended [1994] OJ C368/20

13.6 International treaties, conventions, etc.

Apart from EU treaties, where the short name usually suffices (see
above), set out the full name of the treaty or convention with the following information in parentheses:

- the familiar name
- the place and date of signature
- the Treaty Series number (if not ratified, the Miscellaneous Series
  number) or, if earlier, other relevant number
- the number of the latest Command Paper in which it was issued
- any relevant protocols.

For example, a reference to the European Human Rights Convention
should be expressed as follows:

> Convention for the Protection of Human Rights and Fundamental
> Freedoms (the European Human Rights Convention) (Rome, 4
> Nov. 1950; TS 71 (1953); Cmd 8969)

A short title will suffice for subsequent references in the same chapter.

References to the Uniform Commercial Code (UCC) and US Restate-
ments should be set in roman, for example 'UCC §2–203'.

13.7 Other materials

13.7.1 Reports of Parliamentary select committees

Refer to such papers by name and number:

> HL Select Committee on European Union 8th Report (HL Paper
> (2000–01) no. 1)

13.7.2 Law Commission

Cite Law Commission reports by name and Commission number,
with the year of publication and any Command Paper number:

> Law Commission, *Family Law: The Ground for Divorce* (Law Com.
> No. 192, 1990) para. 7.41

13.7.3 Hansard

Hansard (not italic) is the daily and weekly verbatim record of debates
in the British Parliament (its formal name being *The Official Report of
Parliamentary Debates*). There have been five series of Hansard: first,
1803–20 (41 vols); second, 1820–30 (25 vols); third, 1830–91 (356
vols); fourth, 1892–1908 (199 vols); fifth, 1909– . It was only from
1909 that Hansard became a strictly verbatim report; prior to that
time the reports' precision and fullness varied considerably, particularly before the third series.

Since 1909 reports from the House of Lords and the House of Com-
mons have been bound separately, rather than within the same
volume. References up to and including 1908 are 'Parl. Deb.', and
afterwards 'HL Deb.' or 'HC Deb.' Hansard is numbered by column
rather than page; do not add 'p.' or 'pp.' before Arabic numbers. Full
references are made up of the series (in parentheses), volume number,
and column number:

> Hansard, HC (series 5) vol. 357, cols 234–45 (13 Apr. 1965)

For pre-1909 citations, use the following form:

> Parl. Debs. (series 4) vol. 24, col. 234 (24 Mar. 1895)

13.7.4 Command Papers

In references, the abbreviations given before the numbers of Command Papers vary according to the time period into which the
paper falls. Consequently they should *not* be made uniform or

changed unless they are clearly incorrect. The series, abbreviations, years, and number extents are as follows, with an example for each:

1st	*(none)*	(1833–69)	1–4,222	(C. (1st series) 28)
2nd	C.	(1870–99)	1–9,550	(C. (2nd series) 23)
3rd	Cd	(1900–18)	1–9,239	(Cd 45)
4th	Cmd	(1919–56)	1–9,889	(Cmd 12)
5th	Cmnd	(1957–86)	1–9,927	(Cmnd 356)
6th	Cm.	(1986–)	1–	(Cm. 69)

The references themselves are set in parentheses.

13.8 Judges' designations and judgments

In text it is correct either to spell out the judge's title (Mr Justice Kennedy) or to abbreviate it (Kennedy J). It is best to follow the author's preference, providing it is consistently applied in similar contexts. It is a matter of house style whether or not the abbreviation takes a full point. The following table shows various titles and their abbreviated forms, where they exist:

Mr Justice	J
Lord Justice	LJ
Lords Justice	LJJ
Lord Chief Justice Parker	Parker LCJ, Lord Parker CJ
The Master of the Rolls, Sir F. R. Evershed	Evershed MR
His Honour Judge (County Court)	HH Judge
Attorney General	Att. Gen.
Solicitor General	Sol. Gen.
Lord ..., Lord Chancellor ...	LC
Baron (*historical, but still quoted*)	B
Chief Baron Blackwood	Blackwood CB
The President (Family Division)	Sir Stephen Brown, P
Advocate General (of the ECJ)	Slynn AG
Judge (of the ECJ)	*no abbreviation*

Law Lords are members of the House of Lords entitled to sit on judicial matters; their names are not abbreviated. Do not confuse them with Lords Justice. 'Their Lordships' can be a reference to either rank, but 'Their Lordships' House' refers only to the Judicial Committee of the House of Lords (its full title). There is in legal terms no such rank as 'member of the Privy Council': the Privy Council is staffed by members of the Judicial Committee.

'Judgment' spelled with only one *e* is correct in the legal sense of a judge's or court's formal ruling, as distinct from a moral or practical deduction. A judge's judgment is always spelled thus, as judges cannot (in their official capacity) express a personal judgement separate from their role. In US style 'judgment' is the spelling used in all contexts.

CHAPTER 14

Science, mathematics, and computing

14.1 General principles

14.1.1 **Official guidelines**

Authors and editors involved in publishing scientific material must be aware of the intended readership and its level of expertise when considering what specialist terminology and stylistic conventions to adopt. Authors of texts involving the 'harder' sciences, such as astronomy, biology, chemistry, computing, mathematics, and technology, commonly employ practices different from those in the humanities and social sciences, particularly in those texts aimed at a specialist readership. Authors should follow the standards common in their discipline, as well as any set out for specific contexts, such as series or journal articles. In general, authors and editors should follow the relevant practices by the Royal Society and the Système International (SI), particularly those for styling symbols and units, which can still vary between specialities within a single subject. (Many units not recognized by SI are still compatible with SI units.) Internal consistency is vital where more than one standard is acceptable, or where recommendations conflict.

If an author has good reason for using a convention different from the norm, they should mention this to the editor early on. As common usage changes more frequently in the sciences than in other disciplines, it is particularly important to clarify variations before editing begins. Many scientific journals have developed their own house style: this will vary according to the subject's conventions and the readership's requirements. Authors should be aware that, for reasons of efficiency and speed, this style may be imposed—often by running the text through a computer template—without the author being consulted. (As a requirement of submission, authors may need to download a template from a publisher's website and incorporate it during writing.)

Authors should avoid introducing a novel notation or non-standard symbols. If non-standard terms are essential to the notation system, authors should consider including a list of symbols in the preliminary matter and supplying the editor with printed examples of each, so that there is no danger of misunderstanding what is intended.

14.1.2 Clarity

Clarity in the presentation and explanation of difficult scientific concepts is to be valued. The principle of maximum clarity underpins most scientific style guidance and should be used to discriminate between alternative solutions to presentational problems.

Authors and editors should take care that copy is clear and unambiguous, and keep any notation inserted by hand to a minimum. When writing by hand or using a keyboard, ensure that the numbers 0 and 1 are distinguished from the letters O and l, single (') and double (") primes are distinguished from single (') and double (") closing quotation marks, and the multiplication sign ($\times$) is distinguished from a roman x. Angle brackets should be distinguished from 'greater than' and 'less than' signs: see 14.6.5. Likewise, ensure that any rules above or below letters or whole expressions are not mistaken for underlining for italic.

There are particular issues of clarity involved in typesetting mathematics which affect the choice of typeface (see 14.6.1).

Scientific illustrations should adhere to the principle of maximum clarity: all unnecessary graphic effects should be eschewed. As far as possible, illustrations and their captions should be self-contained and require no reference to text material to make interpretation of them possible. See Chapter 16.

14.1.3 Numerals

Numbers in general are dealt with in Chapter 11. In scientific work lining figures rather than non-lining or 'old-style' figures should generally be used (0, 3, 6, 9 not 0, 3, 6, 9). In science and mathematics figures are set close up, without a comma, in numbers up to 9999. In larger numbers thin spaces are introduced after each group of three digits to the right or left of a decimal point (*1 234 567.891 011 12*); to permit alignment, spaces are also introduced into four-figure numbers in columnar and tabular work. Decimal points are set on the baseline, not medially. Numerals less than one must be preceded by a zero (0.75), except where specific style guidance allows quantities that never exceed unity (such as probabilities) to be typeset without.

The SI guidelines state that it is preferable to use only numbers between 0.1 and 1000. It is better, therefore, to write *22 km* rather than *22 000 metres*, or *3 mm³* rather than *0.003 cubic centimetres*. Powers of units can be represented exponentially, for example *m²* for square metre and *cm³* for cubic centimetre.

14.1.4 Units

There are internationally agreed abbreviations for many units, including all those in the SI. When an abbreviated unit is used with a number, the number is standardly followed by a space (*10 kg, 1.435 m*);

Table 14.1 **SI units**

1. Base units

Physical quantity	Name	Abbreviation or symbol
length	metre	m
mass	kilogram	kg
time	second	s
electric current	ampere	A
temperature	kelvin	K
amount of substance	mole	mol
luminous intensity	candela	cd

2. Supplementary units

Physical quantity	Name	Abbreviation or symbol
plane angle	radian	rad
solid angle	steradian	sr

3. Derived units with special names

Physical quantity	Name	Abbreviation or symbol
frequency	hertz	Hz
energy	joule	J
force	newton	N
power	watt	W
pressure	pascal	Pa
electric charge	coulomb	C
electromotive force	volt	V
electric resistance	ohm	Ω
electric conductance	siemens	S
electric capacitance	farad	F
magnetic flux	weber	Wb
inductance	henry	H
magnetic flux density	tesla	T
luminous flux	lumen	lm
illumination	lux	lx

in computing contexts, however, the space is generally not used (*3.00GHz*, *1MB*). Table 14.1 shows SI units and their abbreviations.

14.1.5 Punctuation

Traditionally, any formula or equation—whether occurring in the text or displayed—was regarded in every way as an integral part of the sentence in which it occurred, and was punctuated accordingly. Consequently it ended in a full point, and was interspersed with any internal punctuation required by syntax or interpolated text. This style is now considered by many to be too fussy for use with displayed material: instead, no full point ends a displayed formula or equation, and internal punctuation is limited to that in or following any interpolated text. Text set on the same line as a displayed equation which qualifies some aspect of the equation should be spaced off from the equation by at least one em.

14.1.6 Notes

It is good practice in scientific writing for all important information to be worked into the text, leaving only matter of secondary interest in notes, such as references, interpretations, and corrections. Since authors in many technical subjects choose to use an author–date (Harvard) style of references (see Chapter 17), footnotes occur infrequently. If a footnote is needed, however, make every effort to avoid adding the cue to a formula or equation, where it may be mistaken for part of the notation. For this reason superscript numerical note cues are not used except in contexts where equations are sparse. Where non-numerical note cues are required, the cue should be one of the marks of reference († ‡ § ¶ ∥) in that order, repeated as necessary (††, ‡‡, etc.) throughout the work, chapter, or (in older practice) page. The asterisk (*) reference mark used in other disciplines is not found in scientific or mathematical contexts, where that symbol may be assigned special uses. For more on notes and references see Chapter 17.

14.1.7 Eponymic designations

Names identified with specific individuals may be treated in several ways. Traditionally a disease, equation, formula, hypothesis, law, principle, rule, syndrome, theorem, or theory named after a person is preceded by the person's name followed by an apostrophe and *s*:

| Alzheimer's disease | Bragg's law | Caro's acid |
| Gödel's proof | Newton's rings | |

Any variation follows the normal rules governing possessives (see 4.2.1):

| Charles's law | Descartes's rule of signs |
| Archimedes' principle | Chagas's disease |

An apparatus, coefficient angle, constant, cycle, effect, function, number, phenomenon, process, reagent, synthesis, or field of study named after a person is usually preceded by the name alone or its adjectival form:

| Leclanché cell | Salk vaccine |
| Cartesian coordinates | Newtonian telescope |

Eponymic anatomical or botanical parts may incorporate the name either as a possessive (*Cowper's glands, Bartholin's gland, Wernicke's area*) or adjectivally (*Casparian strip, Eustachian tube, Fallopian tube*). Something named after two or more people is known by the bare surnames, joined by an en rule:

Cheyne–Stokes respiration	Epstein–Barr virus
Stefan–Boltzmann law	Haber–Bosch process
Creutzfeldt–Jakob disease	

Particularly in medical use, British technical practice increasingly is to use bare surnames, so as to avoid the possessive's proprietary effect:

| Angelman syndrome | Kawasaki disease |
| Munchausen syndrome | Rous sarcoma |

This is the typical form for toponymic designations:

| Borna disease | Coxsackie virus | East Coast fever |
| Ebola fever | Lyme disease | |

14.1.8 Degrees

Degrees are of three types: degrees of inclination or angle, abbr. *d.* or *deg.*; degrees of temperature, symbol °; and degrees of latitude and longitude, abbr. *lat.* and *long.* (no points in scientific work). For degrees of temperature see 14.1.9.

- A degree of inclination or angle is reckoned as 1/360th of a circle. The degree symbol (°) is set close up to the numeral. Decimal subdivisions of degree are preferred to minute (*1/60 degree*) or second (*1/3600 degree*), as in *60.75°*.

- In geography, degrees of latitude and longitude are the angular distances on a meridian north or south of the equator (**latitude**), or east and west of the prime or Greenwich meridian (**longitude**). They may be expressed in degrees (°), minutes ('), and seconds ("). The degree symbol is set closed up to the figure, for example *40° 42' 30" N 74° 1' 15" W*. In discursive and non-technical contexts there are generally spaces between each item. In display work and technical contexts the figures may be closed up, and the seconds given as decimal fractions, for example *40° 42.5' N 74° 1.25' W*. The *N, S, E*, and *W* (no points) make the addition of *lat.* or *long.* superfluous in most instances, though especially in precise coordinates the reverse holds, with, for example, *Lat. 40.980818, Long. −74.093665*.

- In non-technical writing it is usually best to spell out the word *degree*. Where degrees of inclination and temperature occur in the same writing it may be advantageous to use the degree symbol for one and the word for the other.

14.1.9 **Temperature and calories**

The various common scales of temperature are **Celsius** (or **centi-grade**), **kelvin**, and **Fahrenheit**; in scientific work only the Celsius and kelvin scales are used. Generally, use Arabic numerals for degrees of temperature, but words for degrees of inclination and in ordinary contexts for temperature. The degree symbol (°) is printed close up to its scale abbreviation, when given: *10.15 °C* (not *10.15° C* or *10 °.15 C*); it is not used with the kelvin scale. When the scale is understood and so omitted, the symbol is printed close up to the number: *35° in the shade*. When the symbol is repeated for a range of temperatures it is printed close up to the figure if an abbreviation does not immediately follow: *15°–17 °C*.

- Degree **Celsius** (abbreviation °C) is identical in magnitude to the kelvin. To convert Celsius into kelvin add 273.15. It is the equivalent of degree centigrade, which it officially replaced in 1948. It is used as the common measure of temperature in most of the world outside the US.

- The **kelvin** (abbreviation K) is used in expressing kelvin temperatures or temperature differences: 0 K = absolute zero, or −273.15 °C. It officially replaced degree Kelvin (abbreviation °K) in 1968 as the SI unit of thermodynamic temperature (formerly called 'absolute temperature'). It is used in certain scientific writing.

- Degree **Fahrenheit** (abbreviation °F) is the commonly used temperature unit in the US. The Fahrenheit scale was originally calibrated at the ice (32 °F) and steam points (212 °F).
- The term **calorie** stood for any of several units of heat and internal energy, originally relating to the gram of water and the degree Celsius. The calorie used in food science is actually a **kilocalorie**. Sometimes called a **large calorie**, it is often written with a capital *C* to distinguish it from the **small calorie**. Because of these uncertainties and potential confusions the SI unit of energy, the **joule**, is preferred in all scientific contexts.

14.2 Biological nomenclature

14.2.1 Capitalization of English names

In general contexts the English names of animal or plant species should not be capitalized, unless one of the words is a proper name:

red deer	greater spotted woodpecker	lemon balm
mock orange	Pallas's cat	Camberwell beauty

In specialized contexts such as field guides and handbooks capitalization is more usual, especially in ornithology. A third style is to capitalize only the first word of the compound. In most contexts, however, the use of lower case is still preferable. This could give rise to ambiguities—a little gull could be a particular species or just 'a small gull'—but these are avoidable by careful wording.

14.2.2 Structure of taxonomic groups

In descending order, the hierarchy of taxonomic groups is:

kingdom
phylum (in botany, division)
class
order
family
genus
species

All organisms are placed in categories of these ranks: the domesticated cat, for example, is described in full as Carnivora (order), Felidae (family), *Felis* (genus), *Felis catus* (species). In addition, intermediate

ranks may be added using the prefixes *super*, *sub*, and *infra*, and subfamilies may be further divided into tribes. All taxonomic names are
Latin in form, though often Greek in origin, except for the individual
names of cultivated varieties of plant.

Rules for naming taxonomic groups are specified by the five inter-
national organizations: for animals, the International Code of
Zoological Nomenclature (ICZN); for wild plants and fungi, the
International Code of Botanical Nomenclature (ICBN); for cultivated
plants, the International Code of Nomenclature for Cultivated Plants
(ICNCP); for bacteria, the International Codes of Nomenclature of
Bacteria (ICNB); and for viruses, the International Committee on
Nomenclature of Viruses (ICNV).

14.2.3 Groups above generic level

Names of groups from kingdom to family are plural and printed
in roman with initial capitals (Bacillariophyceae, Carnivora, Cur-
culionidae). The level of the taxon is usually indicated by the ending:
the names of botanical or bacteriological families and orders, for
example, end in *-aceae* and *-ales*, while zoological families and subfamilies end in *-idae* and *-inae* respectively. (Ligatures such as æ and
œ are not now used in printing biological nomenclature.)

14.2.4 The binomial system

Living organisms are classified by genus and species according to the
system originally devised by Linnaeus. This two-part name—called
the **binomial** or **binomen**—is printed in italic, and usually consists of
the capitalized name of a genus followed by the lower-case specific
name. Thus the forget-me-not is *Myosotis alpestris*, with *Myosotis* as
its generic name and *alpestris* as its specific epithet; similarly the
bottlenose dolphin is *Tursiops* (generic name) *truncatus* (specific
name). Specific names are not capitalized even when derived from
a person's name: *Clossiana freija nabokovi* (Nabokov's fritillary),
Gazella thomsoni (Thomson's gazelle).

A genus name is printed in italic with an initial capital when used
alone to refer to the genus. If, however, it also has become a common
term in English for the organism concerned it is printed in roman and
lower case (rhododendron, dahlia, tradescantia, stegosaurus); thus
'*Rhododendron* is a widespread genus' but 'the rhododendron is a

common plant'. Specific epithets are never used in isolation except in the rare cases where they have become popular names (japonica), when they are printed in roman.

Latin binomials or generic names alone may be followed by the surname of the person who first classified the organism. These surnames and their standardized abbreviations are called 'authorities' and are printed in roman with an initial capital: '*Primula vulgaris* Huds.' shows that this name for the primrose was first used by William Hudson; '*Homo sapiens* L.' shows that Linnaeus was the first to use this specific name for human beings. If a species is transferred to a different genus, the authority will be printed in parentheses. For example, the greenfinch, *Carduelis chloris* (L.), was described by Linnaeus but placed by him in the genus *Loxia*.

14.2.5 **Abbreviation**

After the first full mention of a species, later references may be shortened by abbreviating the generic name to its initial capital, followed by a full point: *P. vulgaris, E. caballus*. In some circumstances longer abbreviations are used to prevent confusion: for example, *Staphylococcus* and *Streptococcus* become *Staph.* and *Strep.* respectively.

14.2.6 **Subspecies and hybrids**

Names of animal subspecies have a third term added in italic to the binomial, for example *Motacilla alba alba* (white wagtail), *M. alba yarrelli* (pied wagtail). Plant categories below the species level may also have a third term added to their names, but only after an abbreviated form of a word indicating their rank, which is printed in roman:

> subspecies (Latin *subspecies*, abbreviation subsp.)
> variety (Latin *varietas*, abbreviation var.)
> subvariety (Latin *subvarietas*, abbreviation subvar.)
> form (Latin *forma*, abbreviation f.)
> subform (Latin *subforma*, abbreviation subf.)

So '*Salix repens* var. *fusca*' indicates a variety of the creeping willow, and '*Myrtus communis* subsp. *tarentina*' a subspecies of the common myrtle.

Other abbreviations are occasionally printed in roman after Latin names, such as 'agg.' for an aggregate species, 'sp.' (plural 'spp.') after a genus name for an unidentified species, 'gen. nov.' or 'sp. nov.'

indicating a newly described genus or species, and 'auctt.' indicating a name used by many authors but without authority.

The names attached to cultivated varieties of plants follow the binomial, printed in roman within single quotation marks (*Rosa wichuraiana* 'Dorothy Perkins'). The cultivar name may be preceded by the abbreviation 'cv.', in which case the quotation marks are not used (*Rosa wichuraiana* cv. Dorothy Perkins). The names of cultivated varieties may also appear after variety or subspecies names, or after a genus name alone: for example, the ornamental maple *Acer palmatum* var. *heptalobum* 'Rubrum', and the rose *Rosa* 'Queen Elizabeth'. Names of hybrid plants are indicated by a roman multiplication sign (×): *Cytisus* × *kewensis* is a hybrid species, × *Odontonia* is a hybrid genus. Horticultural graft hybrids are indicated by a plus sign (+*Laburnocytisus adami*).

14.2.7 **Bacteria and viruses**

Bacterial and viral species are further subdivided into strains. The International Committee on Taxonomy of Viruses (ICTV) has developed a system of classifying and naming viruses. The ranks employed for animal, fungal, and bacterial viruses are *family*, *subfamily*, *genus*, and *species*; as yet there are no formal categories above the level of family. Wherever possible, Latinized names are used for the taxa; hence names of genera end in the suffix -*virus*, subfamilies end in -*virinae*, and families end in -*viridae*. Latinized specific epithets are not used, so binomial nomenclature does not obtain. (The ICTV advocates italicizing all Latinized names, but it is Oxford style to italicize only genera and species.) Those genera or higher groups that do not yet have approved Latinized names are referred to by their English vernacular names.

The ranks of genus and species are not used in the taxonomy of plant viruses, which are classified in groups—not families—with the approved group name ending in -*virus*. Existing names employ various combinations of Roman or Greek letters, Arabic or Roman numerals, and superscript and subscript characters. Many names are prefixed with a capital P or lower-case phi (PM2, ϕ6, ϕX, Pf1). It is important therefore to follow carefully the conventions employed in the original name.

14.2.8 **Enzymes**

Enzyme nomenclature has several forms, depending on context. Most enzyme trivial names are based on the name of the type of reaction they catalyse and the name of the substrate or product they are associated with. Most end in *-ase*, though some do not.

A systematic nomenclature has been devised by the International Union of Biochemistry. Each enzyme has a systematic name incorporating its type designation (i.e. group name), the name of its substrate(s), and a unique four-digit numerical designation called the EC (Enzyme Commission) number. For example, the systematic name of glutamate dehydrogenase is L-glutamate:NAD$^+$ oxidoreductase (deaminating), EC 1.4.1.2.

Because systematic names are so unwieldy, they tend to supplement or clarify trivial names rather than replace them. In most contexts trivial names alone suffice, though the EC number and full systematic name should follow at first occurrence.

14.2.9 **Genes**

Conventions for naming genes vary widely among species and also change rapidly. Editors and authors are advised to check the website of the appropriate scientific organization for current nomenclature guidelines.

Gene names are usually printed in italic type, while the names of their protein products are set in roman. Gene symbols (short forms of gene names) are commonly used instead of the full name. Gene names and symbols may be all upper case, all lower case, or set with an initial capital letter depending on the species, whether the allele is wild type or mutant, and whether the gene was named for a dominant or recessive phenotype: for example in fruitfly, *hedgehog* (*hh*) gene, Hedgehog (HH) protein, *Notch* (N) gene named for a dominant phenotype; in arabidopsis, *EXTRA SPOROGENOUS CELLS* (*EXS*) wild-type gene, *exs* mutant allele, EXS wild-type protein.

Genes with related properties (phenotypic or molecular) may be given the same name and different numbers; these are italic and immediately follow the gene name without a space. For example, the symbols denoting the various loci determining the character 'glossy leaf' (symbol *gl*) in maize take the form *gl3*, *gl8*, *gl10*, etc.; three human G protein-coupled receptor genes are designated *GPR1*, *GPR2*, *GPR3*. Different alleles of a gene may be designated by Arabic numerals, which may be hyphenated or superscript, or by superscript gene symbols. A laboratory designation may also be included. In some species normal alleles are followed by a superscript plus sign and defective mutants by a superscript minus sign. For example in budding yeast, allele 7 of arginine auxotroph gene1 is *arg1-7*; in mouse, *rs^{grc}* denotes the grey coat allele of recessive spotting (*rs*); in zebrafish, *cyc^+* represents the wild-type *cyclops* gene and *cyc^{t219}* is a mutant allele identified in Tübingen, Germany.

Each community also has its own convention for designation of genetic markers and transgenic strains.

14.3 Medical terminology

14.3.1 Introduction
Medical writers tend to use abbreviations that combine complex modern, pragmatic, and seemingly antiquated forms:

> HONK (hyperosmolar non-ketotic)
> NMDA (*N*-methyl-D-aspartate)
> $t_{\frac{1}{2}}$ (biological half-life)
> BKA (below-knee amputation)
> LKKS (liver, right kidney, left kidney, spleen)
> NAD (nothing abnormal detected)
> bd (*bis die*, 'twice a day')
> stat (*statim*, 'immediately')
> qqh (*quarta quaque hora*, 'every four hours')

The same abbreviations may be used for different terms: CSF may be *cerebrospinal fluid* or *colony-stimulating factor*. Which of these abbreviations should be employed in a text depends on the type of work and its expected readership.

14.3.2 Antigens
Blood-group antigens are designated by capital letters, sometimes combined with a lower-case letter or letters, such as A, B, AB, O, Rh. Note that while A, for example, is defined as a blood group, *not* blood type, blood is described as being type A, *not* group A.

14.3.3 **Haemoglobin**

The types of normal human haemoglobin are designated Hb A, Hb A_2, and Hb F. Their component globin chains are designated by a Greek letter (α, β, γ, or δ); subscript numerals indicate the number of chains. Abnormal haemoglobins are designated either by letters (C–Q, S) or by the name of the place where they were first identified (e.g. Hb Bart's, Hb Chad).

14.3.4 **Vitamins**

The group of organic compounds that form vitamins may be known by their chemical names or by a single capital letter; those forming part of a group are identified further by subscript Arabic figures (e.g. vitamin B_1). (Dietary minerals are known only by their chemical names.)

14.3.5 **Immunology**

Symbols for human histocompatibility leukocyte antigens are HLA followed by a letter to designate the class (e.g. HLA-A). Symbols for human immunoglobulins are Ig followed by a letter (e.g. IgA). Symbols for many other molecules consist of capital letters to designate the molecule, prefixed by the source, and followed by other designations (e.g. rhIFN-α1, recombinant human interferon-α 1).

14.3.6 **Diseases**

Disease names may be descriptive or eponymic (e.g. *Parkinson's disease*). Derived words do not take a capital letter (e.g. *parkinsonism*). See also 14.1.7 on eponymic designations.

14.3.7 **Drug nomenclature**

In professional or technical contexts, prefer a drug's generic name to its proprietary name, which may differ over time and between countries. Even generic names can vary, however: *paracetamol* is known in the US as *acetaminophen*. To help standardize nomenclature throughout Europe, EC Council Directive 92/27/EEC requires the use of a Recommended International Non-Proprietary Name (rINN) for medicinal product labelling. For the most part, the original

British Approved Name (BAN) and the rINN were the same; where they differed, the rINN is used rather than the BAN:

amoxicillin *not* amoxycillin   riboflavin *not* riboflavine
secobarbital *not* quinalbarbitone sulfadiazine *not* sulphadiazine.

In some cases—where a name change was considered to pose a high potential risk to public health—the old name follows the new for additional clarity:

alimemazine (trimeprazine)
lidocaine (lignocaine)
methylthioninium chloride (methylene blue)
moxisylyte (thymoxamine)

Publishers should impose rINN names as a matter of policy, though editors must be aware that it is still useful in certain contexts or markets, and for certain drugs, to add the original names as a gloss. The British National Formulary (BNF) retains former BANs as synonyms in its publications and, in common with the British Pharmacopoeia, continues to give precedence to the original terms *adrenaline* (in rINN *epinephrine*) and *noradrenaline* (in rINN *norepinephrine*)—though this is not the case in the US or Japan, for example. The BNF website has a complete list of the names concerned.

14.4 Chemistry

14.4.1 Introduction

The International Union of Pure and Applied Chemistry (IUPAC) generates comprehensive advice on chemical nomenclature, terminology, standardized methods for measurement, and atomic weights. By their recommendations, symbols for the elements are set in roman with an initial capital, no point at the end; spelled-out names of chemical compounds are in lower-case roman; and symbols for the elements in formulae are printed in roman without spaces:

H_2SO_4 $Cu(CrO_2)_2$

Table 14.2 shows chemical elements and their abbreviations.

14.4.2 Roman and italic

In certain kinds of name, symbols are printed in italic (O-methylhydroxylamine, *fac*-triamine-trinitrosylcobalt(III)). Italic is

Table 14.2 **Chemical elements**

Element	Symbol	Atomic no.	Element	Symbol	Atomic no.	Element	Symbol	Atomic no.
actinium	Ac	89	hafnium	Hf	72	promethium	Pm	61
aluminium	Al	13	hassium	Hs	108	protactinium	Pa	91
americium	Am	95	helium	He	2	radium	Ra	88
antimony	Sb	51	holmium	Ho	67	radon	Rn	86
argon	Ar	18	hydrogen	H	1	rhenium	Re	75
arsenic	As	33	indium	In	49	rhodium	Rh	45
astatine	At	85	iodine	I	53	rubidium	Rb	37
barium	Ba	56	iridium	Ir	77	ruthenium	Ru	44
berkelium	Bk	97	iron	Fe	26	rutherfordium	Rf	104
beryllium	Be	4	krypton	Kr	36	samarium	Sm	62
bismuth	Bi	83	lanthanum	La	57	scandium	Sc	21
bohrium	Bh	107	lawrencium	Lr	103	seaborgium	Sg	106
boron	B	5	lead	Pb	82	selenium	Se	34
bromine	Br	35	lithium	Li	3	silicon	Si	14
cadmium	Cd	48	lutetium	Lu	71	silver	Ag	47
caesium	Cs	55	magnesium	Mg	12	sodium	Na	11
calcium	Ca	20	manganese	Mn	25	strontium	Sr	38
californium	Cf	98	meitnerium	Mt	109	sulphur	S	16
carbon	C	6	mendelevium	Md	101	tantalum	Ta	73
cerium	Ce	58	mercury	Hg	80	technetium	Tc	43
chlorine	Cl	17	molybdenum	Mo	42	tellurium	Te	52
chromium	Cr	24	neodymium	Nd	60	terbium	Tb	65
cobalt	Co	27	neon	Ne	10	thallium	Tl	81
copper	Cu	29	neptunium	Np	93	thorium	Th	90
curium	Cm	96	nickel	Ni	28	thulium	Tm	69
dubnium	Db	105	niobium	Nb	41	tin	Sn	50
dysprosium	Dy	66	nitrogen	N	7	titanium	Ti	22
einsteinium	Es	99	nobelium	No	102	tungsten	W	74
erbium	Er	68	osmium	Os	76	uranium	U	92
europium	Eu	63	oxygen	O	8	vanadium	V	23
fermium	Fm	100	palladium	Pd	46	xenon	Xe	54
fluorine	F	9	phosphorus	P	15	ytterbium	Yb	70
francium	Fr	87	platinum	Pt	78	yttrium	Y	39
gadolinium	Gd	64	plutonium	Pu	94	zinc	Zn	30
gallium	Ga	31	polonium	Po	84	zirconium	Zr	40
germanium	Ge	32	potassium	K	19			
gold	Au	79	praseodymium	Pr	59			

also used for certain prefixes, of which the commonest are *o*-, *m*-, *p*-, *cis*-, and *trans*- (*o*-tolidine, *p*-diethylbenzene, *cis*-but-2-ene). Retain the italic, but not the hyphen, when the prefix is used as a separate word:

>   the *cis* isomer   position *a* is *ortho* to the methyl group

The prefixes *d*-, *l*-, and *dl*- are no longer used for labelling stereo-isomers, which are expressed either by small capitals or by symbols: D-(+), L-(−), and DL-(±) respectively; for example 'DL-lactic acid', '(+)-tartaric acid'. In each case the hyphens must be retained, although not when expressing their absolute configuration.

14.4.3 Formulae and structural drawings

When expressing formulae, the order of brackets normally follows that in mathematics: { [( )] }. Parentheses are used to define the extent of a chemical group, as in $(C_2H_5)_3N$; square brackets are used to denote, for example, chemical concentration in complex for-mulae: $[H_2SO_4]$. This sequence will vary in certain circumstances, for example in the use of square brackets in denoting coordination com-pounds:

> $K_3[Fe(CN)_6]$ $[Ni(CO)_4]$

In organic chemical nomenclature, it is usual to write a formula as a series of groups:

> $CH_3COC_2H_5$ RCH_2COOCH_3

If, for purposes of explanation, it is necessary to divide off the groups, the dots representing single bonds should be set as medial, not on the line:

> $CH_3 \cdot CO \cdot C_2H_5$ $R \cdot CH_2 \cdot COOCH_3$

In most other contexts they can be dispensed with altogether, although dots in formulae of addition compounds cannot be dispensed with:

> $Na_2CO_3 \cdot 10H_2O$

Indicate a double bond by an equals sign ($CH_3CH{=}CH_2$) not a colon, and a triple bond by a three-bar equals sign ($CH_3C{\equiv}CH$), not a three-dot colon. In chemical equations 'equals' is shown by a 2-em arrow (⟶) rather than a conventional equals sign.

Authors should expect that any formulae or structural drawings will need to be treated as artwork; for details see Chapter 16.

14.4.4 **Superscripts and subscripts**

Superscripts and subscripts need not occur only singly, and need not follow what they modify. In specifying a particular nuclide, the atomic (proton) number is printed as a left subscript ($_{12}$Mg). Similarly, the mass (nucleon) number of an element is shown with its symbol and printed as a left superscript (^{235}U, ^{14}C)—not to the right, as formerly. If it is given with the name of the element no hyphen is necessary (uranium 235, carbon 14).

In inorganic chemical nomenclature the relationship between the superscripts and subscripts surrounding a chemical symbol is important: superscript expresses the electrical charge and subscript the number of atoms for each molecule. These should be staggered so as to indicate the ions present ($Na^+_2CO_3{}^{2-}$ (sodium carbonate) but $Hg_2{}^{2+}Cl_2{}^-$ (dimercury(I) chloride)). A medial dot is used to indicate coordinated species ($CuSO_4 \cdot 5H_2O$). Ionic charge is shown by a right superscript ($SO_4{}^{2-}$). Indicate complex ions by square brackets: $K^+_3[FeCl_6]^{3-}$.

Indicate oxidation states by a small-capital Roman numeral, set in parentheses close up to the spelled-out name, for example 'manganese(IV)'; or by a superscript Roman numeral set in capitals to the right of the abbreviated name, for example 'Mn^{IV}'.

Atomic orbitals, designated s, p, d, f, g, are roman, and can have subscript letters with superscript numbers attached (d_{z^2}, $d_{x^2-y^2}$).

Formerly a hyphen was inserted to indicate that a spelling with *ae* or *oe* was not to be construed as a digraph (*chloro-ethane*). This is no longer the case: all such combinations are run together as one word (*chloroethane*), which is as well because ample hyphenation may exist elsewhere (*1,1-dibromo-2-chloroethane*).

14.5 Computing

14.5.1 **Terminology**

The influence of the US on the computing field has resulted in US spelling being adopted for much of the standard vocabulary, such as *analog*, *disk*, *oriented*, and *program* rather than *analogue*, *disc*, *orientated*, *programme* (but note *compact disc*, *laser disc*). Other spellings not forming part of computing terminology should be normalized to British spelling for books intended wholly or mostly for the UK market.

The names of both procedural and functional programming languages vary in treatment. They may be styled in even full capitals (COBOL, PASCAL) or—particularly where ubiquitous—even small capitals (COBOL, PASCAL), although this style is considered old-fashioned by many. Alternatively they may be styled with an initial capital and lower case (Cobol, Pascal). Logically, capitals are used for acronyms and upper- and lower-case for the rest, though this is not universally observed, often through an attempt to impose consistency on all language names. While it is acceptable to style different language names differently, ensure that the same style is adopted for the same language throughout a work.

14.5.2 **Representation**

The text of a computer program may be presented in a work in several ways: in whole or in part, displayed or run into text. Not being a prose extract in the traditional sense, any such program is treated rather like an equation, with no minimum size and no small type needed for display.

Where the features of the program require character-literal syntax and precise line breaks, display, indentation, spacing, or special sorts, these must be reproduced exactly. It is wise to insert any lengthy code directly from the source rather than retype it, which can introduce error. For clarity it is often useful to set any selected material in a distinctive typeface—a sans-serif font, or a monospace typewriter font like Courier. (It is common to use a font that approximates the form found on the relevant terminal or printout.)

```
< body bgcolor = "#000033" text = "#000033"
       link ="#FF0000" vlink ="#66CC33" alink ="#FFFF00"
            onLoad ="MM_displayStatusMsg ('welcome');
            return
       document.MM_returnValue" >
```

Where text is complicated or frequent it may be as well for authors to provide it as print-ready copy—for example an ASCII printout—to be inserted into text.

If the font chosen to indicate programming-language text is sufficiently different from the font used for normal text, it is unnecessary to delimit it further by quotation marks, even when run into text. If, however, quotation marks are needed, note that computing practice matches standard British usage in the relative placement of punctuation and quotation marks. The punctuation falls outside the closing quotation mark, so that in citing parts of

```
begin real S; S : = 0;
    for i : = 1 step 1 until n do
        S : = S + V[i];
    x : = S
end
```

in text, the punctuation does not interfere with the syntax: 'begin real S;', 'S := 0;', and 'x := s'. This style, which would be imposed naturally in British publishing, should also be imposed in US computing texts, though not extended to normal quotations. US computing books can also reserve British-style single quotation marks for programming-language text, using double quotes for normal quotations.

In-text or displayed formulae and equations are best described and set so far as possible according to the rules governing mathematics. Any visual representations of structures or hierarchical classifications (flow charts, data-flow diagrams, screen shots, tree grammars, Venn diagrams) will be treated as artwork (see Chapter 16).

14.5.3 Computing symbols

Mathematical references in computing contexts are usually treated in the same way as in other texts using such references, although the sense of, for example, some logic symbols may differ from standard practice. In programming, the different types of bracket have various specific uses and order, depending on the language. In computing, the **solidus** (/) is used as a separator, as with directory names. When a **backslash** (\) separator is used, the solidus can be called a **forward slash** to differentiate it further.

Other symbols have various context-specific functions: the asterisk, for example, is a Kleene star in BNF, a multiplication sign in Fortran, and a substitute for ∩ in Pascal.

In some computing languages a combined colon and equals sign := is used as the assignment symbol ('gets' or 'becomes'); in others ::= means 'is defined as' and :- means 'if'. Each of these symbols constitutes a single unit and must be set close up, with space either side:

> {A[x] := y, B[u,v] := w}.
>
> ⟨decimal fraction⟩ ::= ⟨unsigned integer⟩

Tags are enclosed by angle brackets, < >: note that the narrow angle brackets ⟨ ⟩ generally employed in technical contexts should not be used here.

Other symbols with unique meanings include the following:

@	'at' sign, display point
=..	a Prolog predicate
↑	up or return
!	cut, comment, 'bang', negation
==	equality
\=	not equal
°	composition
*	asterisk, superscript star, Kleene star
**	exponentiation
−−	comment
<>	less–greater
<=	subset
=>	superset
+	plus, union
⁺	superscript plus, Kleene cross
|	'pipe': used for joining commands together

14.6 Mathematics

14.6.1 Introduction

Mathematics was traditionally regarded as one of the most difficult types of material to typeset. In a mathematical equation each letter represents a quantity or operation, but the style (bold, italic, script, sans serif) and the relative positioning and sizes of the symbols (subscript, superscript) also convey important information. The diversity of sorts required and their precise disposition on the page posed very serious problems for typesetters in the days of mechanically controlled typesetting systems. With the advent of specialist word-processing/typesetting programs those mechanical constraints have been eliminated. The author and editor have now taken over the type-setter's role and must work together in new ways.

Some typefaces are not suited to setting mathematics and should be avoided: sans-serif faces often suffer from indistinguishable characters (l, I, 1 are common examples). Subscripts and sub-subscripts must be legible and the distinction between roman, italic, bold, and sans serif clear even in one isolated character. Plain serifed faces such as Times and Computer Modern are generally to be favoured for mathematical work. The choice of typeface should be carried through to headings and labelling of figures where maths may occur. The typography of equations should not be altered to conform with design specifications for headings and labels.

14.6.2 Notation

The established style is to use roman type for operators and certain numerical constants, and to label points in a diagram, italic for letters expressing a variable, and bold for vectors and matrices. Each description should be represented by a single symbol: avoid using abbreviated words. Speed, accuracy, and economy will be achieved if authors can follow, or mark, their notation in this way. Here are some specific guidelines:

- It is common to set the headword of definitions, theorems, propositions, corollaries, or lemmas in capitals and small capitals, with the remaining text of the heading in italic. The full text of the proof itself is set in roman.

- Avoid starting a sentence with a letter denoting an expression, so that there is no ambiguity about whether a capital or lower-case letter is intended.

- Most standard abbreviations, for example 'log(arithm)', 'max(imum)', 'exp(onential function)', 'tan(gent)', 'cos(ine)', 'lim(it)', and 'cov(ariance)', are set in roman, with no full points.

- Make clear the distinction between a roman 'd' used in a differential equation ($\mathrm{d}x/\mathrm{d}y$), the symbol ∂ for a partial differential, and the Greek lower-case delta (δ). Authors should preclude further potential for confusion by avoiding an italic d for a variable.

- The exponential 'e' always remains in roman; sometimes it may be preferable to use the abbreviation 'exp' to avoid confusion. The letters i and j are roman when symbolizing imaginary numbers, and italic when symbolizing variables.

- In displayed equations, the integral, product, and summation symbols ($\int \Sigma \Pi$) may have limits set directly above them (upper limit) or below them (lower limit). In running text, place these after the symbol wherever possible (as in the first example) to avoid too great a vertical extension of the symbol:

$$\int_a^b x^2\,\mathrm{d}x \quad \sum_{m=0}^{\infty} \quad \prod_{r\geq 1}$$

- Missing terms can be represented by three dots which are horizontal (...), vertical (:), or diagonal ($\cdot\cdot$), as appropriate. Include a comma after the three ellipsis dots when the final term follows, for example x_1, x_2, ..., x_n.

14.6.3 Symbols

Operational signs are of two types: those representing a verb ($= \approx \neq \geq$) and those representing a conjunction ($+ - \supset \times$). All operational signs take a normal interword space of the line on either side; they are not printed close up to the letters or numerals on either side of them. Set a multiplication point as a medial point ($\cdot$); it should be used only to avoid ambiguity and is not needed between letters, unless a vector product is intended. A product of two or more different units may be represented as N m (with a fixed thin space between the units) or N·m but not Nm.

Any symbol that involves printing a separate line of type should be avoided when an alternative form is available. So, for angle ABC, prefer $\angle ABC$ to

$\widehat{ABC}$,

and for vector r, prefer **r** (in bold) to $\vec{r}$.

A colon used as a ratio sign—as in, for example, 'mixed in the proportion $1\!:\!2$', '$2\!:\!4 \propto 3\!:\!6$'—has a thin space on either side of it, not a normal space of the line.

No more than one solidus should appear in the same expression; use parentheses to avoid ambiguity: J K^{-1} mol^{-1} or J/(K mol), but not J/K/mol.

Omit the vinculum or overbar—the horizontal rule above the square-root sign: $\sqrt{2}$ is sufficient for $\sqrt{2}$. (Where necessary for clarification the extent covered by the rule may be shown by parentheses.)

Similarly,

$$\sqrt{\left(\frac{x^2}{a^2} + \frac{y^2}{b^2}\right)}$$

is sufficient for

$$\sqrt{\left(\frac{x^2}{a^2} + \frac{y^2}{b^2}\right)}$$

The mechanical difficulty of setting vinculum rules means that they were formerly considered to be poor printing practice and were avoided by various measures. No such constraints apply to computer-aided typesetting systems, although they may still be best avoided in tightly leaded text.

14.6.4 Superscripts and subscripts

Reserve superscript letters for variable quantities (set in italic); reserve subscript letters for descriptive notation (set in roman). Asterisks and primes are not strictly superscripts and so should always follow immediately after the term to which they are attached, in the normal way.

When first a subscript and then a superscript are attached to the same symbol or number, mark the subscript to be set immediately below the superscript in a 'stack'. If it is necessary to have multiple levels of superscripts or subscripts, the relationships must be made clear for the typesetter.

Wherever possible, it is customary—and a kindness to the reader's eyesight—to represent each superscript or subscript description by a symbol rather than an abbreviated word. Those subscript descriptions that are standardly made up of one or more initial letters of the word they represent are set in roman type.

14.6.5 Brackets

The preferred order for brackets is { [( )] }. When a single pair of brackets have a specific meaning, such as $[n]$ to denote the integral part of n, they can, of course, be used out of sequence. The vertical bars used to signify a modulus— $|x|$ —should not be used as brackets.

Two further sorts of brackets may be used: double brackets $[\![\ ]\!]$ and angle brackets $\langle\ \rangle$. Angle brackets are used singly in Dirac bra and ket notation and in pairs they may be used to indicate the value of a quantity over a period of time, but they can also be used generally. Note that in science and mathematics 'narrow' angle brackets are used; standard 'wide' angle brackets $<\ >$ signify 'less than'/'greater than'. Double brackets can be placed outside, and narrow angle brackets inside, the bracket sequence, and are handy for avoiding the rearrangement of brackets throughout a formula or, especially, a series of formulae. Thus for comparison's sake the formula

$$\{1 + [2(a^2 + b^2)(x^2 + y^2) - (ab + xy)^2]\}^2 =$$
$$[\![1 + \{[(a + b)^2 + (a - b)^2](x^2 + y^2) - (ab + xy)^2\}]\!]^2$$

is perhaps better put

$$= \{1 + [(\langle a + b\rangle^2 + \langle a - b\rangle^2)(x^2 + y^2) - (ab + xy)^2]\}^2$$

14.6.6 Fractions, formulae, and equations

Displayed formulae three or four lines deep can be reduced to a neater and more manageable two-line form in almost all instances. Formerly this action made typesetting simpler and so was desirable. Now the quest for clarity of meaning may overrule the desire to save space and 'tidy up' equations. Simplification remains desirable for equations embedded in text material that would otherwise require extra leading to be introduced.

For example,

$\dfrac{a}{b}$ can be written as a/b, and $\left|\dfrac{x - 1}{3}\right|$ as $|(x - 1)/3|$.

Simple fractions such as $^7/_2$, $^x/_3$, $^{a+b}/_4$ can be written as $\frac{1}{2}\pi$, $\frac{1}{3}x$, $\frac{1}{4}(a+b)$.

Work can be reduced and appearance improved by writing such a formula as

$$\lim_{n\to\infty}\left[1 - \sin^2\frac{\alpha}{n}\right]^{\frac{-1}{\sin^2\frac{\alpha}{n}}} \quad \text{in the form} \quad \lim_{n\to\infty}[1 - \sin^2(\alpha/n)]^{-1/\sin 2(\alpha/n)}$$

Displayed formulae are usually centred on the page. If there are many long ones, or a wide discrepancy in their length, it may be better to range them all left with a 1- or 2-em indent.

If it is necessary to break a formula—whether displayed or run-in—at the end of a line, it should be done at an operational sign, with the sign carried over to the next line. If an equation takes up two or more lines it should be displayed, with turnover lines aligned on the operational sign (preferably =):

$$\mu_0 = 4\pi \times 10^{-7} \text{ H m}^{-1}$$
$$= 12.566\ 370\ 614\ 4 \times 10^{-7} \text{ H m}^{-1} \tag{2.1}$$

Any equation referred to at another point in the text should be numbered; any numbered equation should be displayed. It is usually better to include the chapter number in front of the sequence number, such as 2.1 for the first equation in chapter 2. If, however, the total number of equations is very small, it is possible to use a single sequence of numbers throughout the text. As illustrated above, these numbers are enclosed in parentheses and set full right, aligned on the same line as the final line of the equation.

14.6.7 Mathematical symbols

π	pi
∞	infinity
$=$	equal to
$\neq$	not equal to
$\equiv$	identically equal to
$\not\equiv$	not identically equal to
$\approx$	approximately equal to
$\not\approx$	not approximately equal to
$\simeq$	asymptotically equal to
$\not\simeq$	not asymptotically equal to
$\sim$	equivalent to, of the order of
$\not\sim$	not equivalent to, not of the order of
$\propto$	proportional to
$\rightarrow$	approaches
$>$	greater than
$\not>$	not greater than
$<$	less than
$\not<$	not less than
$\gg$	much greater than
$\ll$	much less than

$\geq$	greater than or equal to
$\leq$	less than or equal to
( )	parentheses
[ ]	square brackets
{ }	curly brackets, braces
< >	angle brackets
⟨ ⟩	narrow angle brackets
⟦ ⟧	double brackets
$\wedge$	vector product
$\varnothing$	the empty set
+	plus
−	minus
$\pm$	plus or minus
$\mp$	minus or plus
$ab, a\cdot b, a \times b$	a multiplied by b
$a/b, a \div b, ab^{-1}$	a divided by b
a^n	a raised to the power of n
$|a|$	the modulus (or magnitude) of a
$\sqrt{a}, a^{1/2}$	square root of a
$p!$	factorial p
'	minute, prime
"	second, double prime
°	degree
$\angle$	angle
:	ratio
::	proportion
$\therefore$	therefore, hence
$\because$	because
$\exp x, e^x$	exponential of x
$\log_a x$	logarithm to base a of x
$\ln x, \log_e x$	natural logarithm of x
$\lg x, \log_{10} x$	common logarithm of x
$\sin x$	sine of x
$\cos x$	cosine of x
$\tan x$	tangent of x
$\sin^{-1} x, \arcsin x$	inverse sine of x
$\cos^{-1} x, \arccos x$	inverse cosine of x
$\tan^{-1} x, \arctan x$	inverse tangent of x
$\int$	integral
Σ	summation
Δ	delta
Π	product
Δx	finite increase of x
δx	variation of x
dx	total variation of x
$f(x)$	function of x

14.7 Astronomy

14.7.1 Conventions

Most current astronomy texts follow those recommendations for style set out by the International Astronomical Union (IAU), though other styles may be found, especially in older works. Ensure consistency within a given work, preferring modern to older styles except when reproducing earlier texts.

Capitalize *Earth*, *Moon*, and *Sun* only in contexts where confusion with another earth, moon, or sun may occur. *Galaxy* is capitalized only when it refers to the Milky Way, although *galactic* is lower case in all contexts. While *minor planet* is preferable to *asteroid* in technical usage, *asteroid belt* is an accepted astronomical term.

14.7.2 Stellar nomenclature

Galaxies, nebulae, and bright star clusters can be designated by names (*Crab Nebula*, *Beehive Cluster*, *Sombrero Galaxy*) or by numbers in a catalogue such as that of Messier (*M1*, *M104*) or the New General Catalogue (*NGC 1952*, *NGC 4594*).

The eighty-eight constellations have been assigned official names and a three-letter roman abbreviation (no point) by the IAU, so that Andromeda is *And*, Corona Borealis is *CrB*, and Sagittarius is *Sgr*. Many bright stars within these constellations have traditional names (*Sirius*, *Canopus*, *Castor*, and *Pollux*), though astronomers tend to favour the Bayer letter system, in which Greek letters are allotted in alphabetical order by brightness as seen from Earth. The letter is followed by the genitive form of the constellation name, each capitalized (*Alpha Centauri*, *Beta Crucis*, *Gamma Orionis*).

CHAPTER 15

Lists and tables

15.1 Lists

15.1.1 **General principles**

Lists arrange related elements of text in a linear, structured form. Lists may be displayed or run into text; their characteristics are explicit when they are displayed (see 15.1.4), but should be no less rigorously applied when they are embedded in the text (see 15.1.3). Lists may be broken across pages, whereas most tables should not be broken unless their size makes a break unavoidable.

15.1.2 **Arrangement of items**

Regardless of presentation, the text should make it clear what the elements of a list have in common. An open-ended list should specify at least three items, which are sufficiently similar to show how the list might continue: *French, Spanish, Portuguese, etc.* A list comprising examples introduced by *includes*, *for example*, or *such as* should not end tautologically in *etc.*

Lists should be grammatically consistent and balanced; for example, *the zookeeper fed the elephant, a lion, and llamas* unsettles the reader because it is inconsistent in its use (or lack) of articles. Depending on context and emphasis, the first item alone may have an article (*what colours are the legs, eye, and bill?*), all the items may have no article (*deciduous trees include oak, ash, sycamore, and maple*), or the article for each item may be repeated to emphasize its separateness:

> The government does not yet appear to have given much consideration to balancing the needs of the research community, the taxpayer, and the commercial sectors, for which it is responsible.

A list that is very complex, or just very long, may need to be broken off and displayed (see 15.1.4).

15.1.3 **Lists in running text**

A list occurring as part of a sentence or sentences (a **run-on** or **in-text** list) follows the same rules governing any other sentence. A straightforward list within a single sentence needs no numbers or letters to aid the reader:

> Rabbits are divided into four kinds, known as warreners, parkers, hedgehogs, and sweethearts

House style will dictate whether the serial, or Oxford, comma (see 4.3.5) is used before the final list item; in the examples below, the first has it, the second does not:

> Markets are held every Tuesday, Thursday, and Saturday
> A bridge provides passage over obstacles such as rivers, valleys, roads and railways

It is usually acceptable to arrange into lists information where each element has only a few simple components, so long as these are treated unambiguously; notice in the following example that each element has the same structure:

> Animals with specific medical problems that may be helped by special diets, for example renal disease (restricted protein and phosphorus), inflammatory bowel disease (select protein, limited antigen), or diabetes mellitus (high fibre), should be fed the most appropriate diet for their condition.

For a discussion of the use of commas and semicolons in run-on lists see 4.4.

Information in many run-on lists may equally be displayed (see below), or presented as simple 'open tables' (see 15.2.7).

15.1.4 **Displayed lists**

There are three kinds of displayed list: lists marked by numbers or letters, lists with bulleted points, and simple lists with no markers. The purpose of a display is to draw the reader's attention and to make the material easy to find, consult, and digest; displaying also has the effect of breaking up the text. It is important to establish an underlying logic that determines whether lists are run on or displayed. End punctuation may vary: full points if list items are sentences; commas or semicolons at the discretion of author or editor; full point at the end of the last item. Omit 'and' and 'or' at the end of the penultimate point in a displayed list.

The preceding sentence can end with a full point or a colon (but no dash). Items that are complete sentences generally start with capitals and end in full points:

- Fino is a pale and delicate dry sherry of medium alcohol that is best drunk well chilled as an aperitif.
- Manzanilla is a very dry fino, considered to be the best, and is only produced in Sanlúcar de Barrameda on the coast.
- Amontillado is nuttier and fuller-bodied than the fino, between 17 and 18 degrees of alcohol.
- Oloroso is darker and more fragrant, containing between 18 and 20 degrees of alcohol.
- Cream sherries are sweeter and range from the lighter-tasting pale creams to the darker and velvety varieties that make a great after-dinner drink.
- Palo Cortado is a cross between an oloroso and an amontillado, and is very rare as it occurs spontaneously in only a small percentage of fino barrels when the yeast does not form properly.

Sentence fragments are usually lower case, with no end punctuation except for the final full point, for example:

Legislation will be effective only if it is:
- closely monitored
- comprehensive
- strictly enforced.

Where possible, choose a system and be consistent; however, in a publication with many diverse lists it may be better to allow both types rather than to impose an artificial uniformity.

15.1.5 Numbers, letters, and bullets

When elements of a list are cited in text, or when it is desirable to show the order or hierarchy of the points being made, numbering the items clarifies the sense. Letters or numbers in italic or roman may be used in run-on or displayed lists. In run-on lists lower-case letters or Roman numerals are often used; they should be in parentheses:

Problem-solving helps to: (*a*) define the problem; (*b*) divide it into manageable parts; (*c*) provide alternative solutions; (*d*) select the best solution; and (*e*) carry it out and examine the result.

In displayed lists numbers are often used; they may be in roman or bold, with or without a following point, depending on the design decisions made:

1. Activities and action happen extremely quickly when in a product-recall situation. It is suggested that a number of blank copies of the product-recall coordinator's log be held, allowing data to be recorded directly on to this document.

2. The log is a key document and it is extremely important that it is maintained at all stages during the product-recall process.

3. Information in the log must be accurate, clear, and concise.

4. In the product-recall coordinator's absence the log's continued maintenance must be given priority by the Incident Management Team.

There are no hard-and-fast rules about the sequence of number styles in lists of more than one level. In Oxford style Arabic numbers at the first level are followed by italic lower-case letters in parentheses, followed by lower-case Roman numerals in parentheses—1 (*a*) (i) (ii) (iii) (*b*) (i) (ii) (iii) 2 (*a*) (i) (ii) (iii) (*b*) (i) (ii) (iii), etc. But a hierarchy that ran 1 (i) (*a*) (*b*) (*c*) (ii) (*a*) (*b*) (*c*), etc., would be no less acceptable. More complex lists might require, in addition, upper-case letters and Roman numerals above the Arabic numerals in the hierarchy. Numbered sections and subsections are discussed in 1.3.5 and 1.3.6.

If there is no reason for items to be hierarchical, a typographical symbol such as a bullet is used:

> The moons closest to Jupiter are:
> - Metis
> - Adrastea
> - Amalthea
> - Thebe
> - Io
> - Europa.

Bullets may be ranged left or indented, with an en space separating them from the item. Each typeface has a standard bullet size, so there is normally no need to specify this.

15.1.6 **Simple lists**

Material may also be displayed in simple lists with neither numbers nor bullets:

9.00	arrive at meeting point
9.15	coach leaves
10.30	motorway stop (20 minutes)
11.30	arrival at destination

1.00   lunch in the picnic area
3.45   return to coach
4.00   coach departs for home
5.15   motorway stop (20 minutes)
6.30   arrive home.

15.2 Tables

15.2.1 General principles

A table is a set of data systematically displayed in rows and columns. Tables are best used for information that is too complex to be presented clearly in a list or in running text, and particularly for information intended for comparison, either within a single table or between similar tables.

Tables may be numbered by chapter or section in the order in which each is mentioned (*Table 1.1*, *Table 1.2*, etc.), or if there are only a few tables they may be numbered in a single sequence throughout the text. Frequent or large tables may be better placed at the end of the chapter or as an appendix to text; tables in an appendix are numbered separately. Unlike lists, tables should not be broken across pages unless their size makes a break unavoidable; open tables (15.2.7) are the exception to this principle.

Consider whether tabular presentation is the clearest means of setting out the material. It might be more digestibly presented in a few sentences, or as a figure or graph. Two or more tables might be better merged, or a large one split up. The information must be relevant to the textual argument and correspond to what the text describes. It should not merely repeat the text. The order of elements in the table should be transparent; if no other order can be imposed on the table as a whole, alphabetical or numerical order may be best.

Omit vertical rules in tables—presentation is clearer and less cluttered without them. Horizontal rules should be kept to a minimum, although head and tail rules are included in most cases.

Most word-processing programs have a tool to create and edit tables; whether typesetters can import the result into their own page make-up system depends on their software and expertise. Some prefer data presented as columns separated by one tab, rather than in table cells. If your publisher cannot provide guidance about preparation, be prepared for the fact that tables may be rekeyed. It is essential that hard copy should accompany electronic files, in case intended alignment is lost. Drawn elements within a table, such as chemical structures, may need to be treated as artwork. When in doubt, flag problematic tables or seek advice from the publisher.

Tables are treated as separate elements during page make-up, so should be extracted from the text and presented in a separate sequence. When material is presented in electronic form tables are generally gathered in one or more separate electronic files, although they may sometimes be grouped at the end of the document. The approximate position of tables should be clearly flagged—by a cue in the margin of hard copy or by a cue on a separate line in an electronic text, for example:

<<TABLE 1>>

All tables should be cited in the text. Citations may be of the style *Table 2.1 summarizes the planning processes*, or in the passive form *The planning processes are summarized (Table 2.1)* ... Avoid positional references such as 'the table above' or 'the following table', as the final paginated layout is likely to be different from that in the script.

Running heads can be set normally over full-page **portrait** (upright) or **landscape** (turned or broadside) tables, or they can be omitted; consistency is important.

15.2.2 **Table headings**

Tables have headings, which are positioned above the table, consisting of the table number and a title, which may use minimal or maximal capitalization according to the style of the work as a whole; no full point is needed after the table number or at the end of the heading.

When units are the same throughout the table they may be defined in the heading, for example:

Table 15.1 Price of apples, by region, 1954–1976 ($/ton)

The heading may also be used to expose the logic behind the order in which the material is presented in the table, for example:

Table 8.1 Tree and shrub species used in hedging (ordered by frequency of use)

15.2.3 Column and row headings

The length of headings should be reduced to a minimum, so any repeated information should be removed to the table heading. Similar
tables should be treated similarly. Capitalize only the first word and
proper names in each heading; do not include end punctuation. Do
not number headings unless the numbers are referred to in text. Spans
in headings must not overlap: *1920–9, 1930–9, 1940–9* rather than
1920–30, 1930–40, 1940–50.

Units, where needed, are usually in parentheses, and should not be
repeated in the body.

Column headings with common elements can be combined over a
'straddle' or 'spanner' rule (see Table 15.1).

Table 15.1 **Per cent of deaths from cancer attributable
to smoking, 1975 and 1995**

Country	Male		Female	
	1975	1995	1975	1995
Australia	39	32	4	14
Finland	46	37	1	4
France	33	38	0	2
Hungary	36	53	5	15
UK	52	40	12	20
US	42	43	10	25

Source: *Oxford Textbook of Medicine*, 4th edn, vol. 1
(Oxford University Press, 2003).

Totals may be set off by a space or a rule (see Table 15.2). The word
'Total' may be formatted differently from the body.

Table 15.2 **New Zealand casualties 1939–1945**

Branch	Deaths	Wounded	Prisoners	Interned	Total
Army	6,839	15,324	7,863	—	30,026
Navy	573	170	54	3	800
Air Force	4,149	255	552	23	4,979
Merchant navy	110	—	—	—	—
TOTAL	11,671	15,749	8,469	149	36,038

Source: R. Kay (ed.), *Chronology: New Zealand in the War, 1939–1945* (Wellington, 1968).

Row headings (also called stub or side headings) may or may not have a heading like other columns. If they do have a heading, ensure that it is appropriate and relevant to all of the stubs. Where row headings turn over to another line, data should be aligned consistently with either the last or the first line of the side heading.

15.2.4 **Body of table**

The body of a table is simply the tabular data introduced and ordered by the columns and stub. Where data drawn from a variety of sources has to be recast to allow comparison, ensure that this does not introduce inaccuracy or anachronism, or distort the material's integrity, especially if the source is in copyright.

The unit(s) used in the table should suit the information: for example, national agricultural production figures may be easier to compare if rounded to 1,000 tons. Rounding also saves space, but editors should not make wholesale changes without querying them with the author. Tables intended for comparison should ideally present their data consistently in similar units. Ensure that abbreviations are consistently applied from one table to another, and that all units and percentages are defined. Exclude end punctuation. Set mathematical operators (+, −, >, etc.) close up to the following digits. Ensure that minus signs (−) are distinguished from hyphens and from em rules (—) at their first occurrence in each table. Add zeros in front of decimal points if omitted; the exception may be probability values, for example p<.05, as house styles vary.

Familiar abbreviations are acceptable, such as %, &, country abbreviations, and those well known in the reader's discipline. Ambiguous abbreviations such as *n/a* ('not applicable' or 'not available') and unfamiliar abbreviations must be explained in the notes (see 15.2.5): the reader should be able to understand the table independently of the text. Repeat information rather than use ditto marks. Em rules or en rules are often used in empty fields, but can indicate either 'no data' or 'not available', so it may be better to specify which is the case.

Turn-lines in simple items in columns are indented 1 em, with no extra vertical space between items (see for example column 2 in Table 15.3). Turn-lines in discursive or run-on items (for example data in a chronology) can be set full left in a column as panels or blocks of text, not

Table 15.3 **Beaufort wind scale**

Force	Description of wind	Mean wind speed (*knots*)	Specification for use at sea
0	calm	less than 1	Sea like a mirror
1	light air	1–3	Ripples with appearance of scales are formed, but without foam crests
2	light breeze	4–6	Small wavelets, still short but more pronounced; crests have a glass appearance and do not break
3	gentle breeze	7–10	Large wavelets; crests begin to break; foam of glassy appearance, perhaps scattered white horses
4	moderate breeze	11–16	Small waves becoming longer; fairly frequent white horses
5	fresh breeze	17–21	Moderate waves, taking a more pronounced long form; many white horses are formed
6	strong breeze	22–7	Large waves begin to form; the white foam crests are more extensive everywhere (probably some spray)
7	moderate gale *or* near gale	28–33	Sea heaps up and white foam from breaking waves begins to be blown in streaks along the direction of the wind
8	fresh gale *or* gale	34–40	Moderately high waves of greater length; edges of crests begin to break into spindrift; foam is blown in well-marked streaks
9	strong gale	41–7	High waves; dense streaks of foam; crests of waves begin to topple, tumble, and roll over
10	whole gale *or* storm	48–55	Very high waves with long overhanging crests; the resulting foam is blown in dense white streaks; the sea takes a white appearance; the tumbling of the sea becomes heavy and shock-like; visibility affected
11	storm *or* violent storm	56–63	Exceptionally high waves at sea; the sea is completely covered with white patches of foam; visibility affected
12+	hurricane	64 and above	The air is filled with foam and spray; sea completely white with driving spray; visibility very seriously affected

Sources: Smithsonian Institution, *Smithsonian Meteorological Tables* (1966); Hydrographer of the Navy (UK).

indented, with a space between each item (see for example column 4 in Table 15.3).

Related figures in a single column should have the same number of decimal places. Unrelated figures may have a different number of decimal places, but only if reflecting different levels of accuracy. Editors should check with the author before rounding them to a common level. Percentage totals may vary slightly above or below 100 per cent as a result of rounding.

When statistical matter within each column is unrelated, align it on the left with the column heading (see Table 15.4). Optionally, the longest line can be designed so that it is centred under the heading, if the result suits the material better.

When statistical matter within the columns is related, align it so that the longest item aligns with the column heading and other items align with the decimal point or with the final digit on the right (see Table 15.5).

Table 15.4 **Comparison of four forests with infection present**

	Forest			
	Black	**New**	**Sherwood**	**Speymouth**
Age	20	43	35	69
Area sampled, acres	6.9	11.2	7.5	27.6
No. of trees	10,350	4,702	2,650	945
No. of infected trees	163	98	50	23
Infected trees, %	1.63	0.9	20.3	10.7
Chi-square for observed values	7.83	11.09	4.98	too small

Table 15.5 **Working days lost through strikes per 1,000 workers, six countries, 1960–1999 (annual averages)**

	1960–4	**1971–5**	**1980–4**	**1990–5**	**1995–9**
France	352	232	90	36	98
Germany	34	57	50	17	1
Italy	1,220	1,367	950	148	33
Japan	302	188	10	3	2
United Kingdom	242	1,186	480	29	23
United States	722	484	160	33	13

Source: S. Ackroyd et al. (eds), *Oxford Handbook of Work and Organization* (Oxford University Press, 2005), derived from: J. Davies, 'International Comparisons of Labour Disputes in 1999', *Labour Market Trends*, 109/4; D. Bird, 'International Comparisons of Industrial Disputes in 1989 and 1990', *Employment Gazette*, 99/12; *Employment Gazette*, 90/2; *Department of Employment Gazette*, 79/2.

15.2.5 Notes to tables

Notes fall directly beneath the table to which they refer; they are not incorporated with the text's footnote system. Set notes to table width, normally one size down from table size. General notes, notes on specific parts of the table, and probability values should appear in this order; source notes may go first or last provided they are treated consistently. Ensure that notes to a table cannot be mistaken for text recommencing after the table. General and source notes are uncued and often preceded by *Note*: and *Source*: respectively. The reference structure of source notes matches that used elsewhere in the work.

Each note should generally begin on a new line and end with a full point (see Table 15.6), although notes of a kind can run on, separated by semicolons, to save space:

CI = confidence interval; OR = odds ratio; SD = standard deviation

Mark specific notes with a system of indices different from that used in the text (for example * † §), as in Table 15.6, or superscript letters or numbers (italic or roman). Cues in a table read across; for example, a cue in the last column of the first row precedes a cue in the first column of the second row.

Probability values may be indicated by a system of asterisks, in which case the convention should be explained in a note: '*p < .05; **p < .01; ***p < .001'. Editors should not impose other symbols in this case.

Table 15.6 **Issues of the de luxe edition of *Ulysses*, copies 1–1,000**

Copies	Paper	Price		
		France (FF)	UK (£/s./d.)	USA ($)
1–100*	Holland handmade	350	7/7/-	30
101–250	Verge d'Arches	250	5/5/-	22
251–1,000†	linen	150	3/3/-	14

* Autographed by Joyce.

† This issue, the cheapest of the three, was still 5–7 times costlier than the average book.

15.2.6 Presentation on the page

Tables may be placed on the page in portrait or landscape format. Authors are not responsible for determining the format in which tables will be set. A wide table may fit a page's measure if the arrangement of column and stub heads is reversed, but editors should consult the author first. Do not rearrange similar or related tables into differing structures.

Large portrait and landscape tables may be presented over two or more pages of text. Indicate on hard copy preferred places where a large table may be split. Headings do not need to be repeated where continued tables can be read across or down a facing page. If the table continues on a verso page, however, mark on hard copy which headings need to be repeated. Do not repeat headings in electronic files that will be imported into DTP software. Insert a 'continued' line, such as 'Table 2 *cont.*', only if the table turns over to a verso page, not if it extends over facing pages. When several continued tables are given in succession, a short form of each table's title can be helpful.

15.2.7 **Open tables**

Open tables, also called tabulated lists, are very simple tables with few elements. Used for presenting small blocks of information and having no number, title, or rules, they have more impact and accessibility than a run-on or displayed list (see 15.1.3, 15.1.4) but less formality than a full table. Particularly in non-technical work, or in texts having no other tables, an open table can serve as a convenient halfway house between list and table, offering data in a readily assimilated visual form. An open table typically has only column heads or a stub— any table with both column heads and stub requires the structure of a formal table, and should be set as such. Do not mix formal and open tables for related matter.

Unlike formal tables, open tables may be freely broken across pages. An open table may be introduced by a colon, but cannot then be moved unless the preceding text is reworded accordingly, which may pose layout problems for the typesetter. An example of an open table follows:

Types of food affected by *Clostridium botulinum* are shown below.

Strain type	Food	Disease caused
A	Vegetables, meat, and fish conserves	Human botulism in western USA

| B | Prepared meat, silage, feed | Human botulism in eastern USA and Europe |
| C | Spoiled vegetables, maggots | Thought not to be implicated in human botulism |

Significance:

Botulism is caused by toxin(s) produced by *Cl. botulinum*, and high numbers of cells are necessary for toxin to be present in the food.

CHAPTER 16

Illustrations

16.1 General principles

16.1.1 **Introduction**

Images enhance publications of all kinds, from fairy tales to technical manuals. They may be, for example, diagrams, graphs, photographs, or drawn or painted artwork, essential to the delivery of the ideas in the publication or cosmetic and decorative. They may be integrated (that is, embedded in the text) or separated off in a section of their own; they may be an integral part of the design of the page or in some sense an addition to the text that has to be accommodated to support the textual argument. Illustrations may or may not have a title, they may be referred to by number in the text or by reference to their position, or they may simply be juxtaposed with the relevant material.

The two main forms of image are **line** (see 16.3) and **tone** (see 16.4), both of which may be black and white or colour. Originals are typically supplied as black-and-white drawings, tone photographs, and colour transparencies. Alternatively, images may be created or stored in electronic format (see 16.2).

An illustration is an image together with its explanatory **caption**, also called **underline**, **cutline**, or **legend**. **Figures** are illustrations integrated into and surrounded by text. **Plates** are illustrations separated from the text; uncommon today, they are usually high-quality images that benefit from being printed in a section or sections of glossy art paper.

16.1.2 **Numbering and citing illustrations**

Figures may be numbered by chapter or section in the order in which each is mentioned; if there are only a few, they can be numbered in a single sequence throughout the text. Figures in an appendix are numbered separately. Maps may be included in the same sequence with other illustrations or, if many, numbered separately.

A reference to an illustration out of sequence should include the word 'see'; a reference to one in sequence need not. Such references may be variously styled: in roman, italic, or bold; abbreviated or in full (*Fig.* or *Figure*, *Illustration* or *Illus.*, *Example* or *Ex.*); with or without an initial capital. Consistency is most important, whichever style is adopted. Illustrations can be mentioned actively:

> Figure 1.1 shows the large intestine of the rabbit

or passively:

> The rabbit's digestive system (Figure 1.1) is specially adapted to absorb chlorophyll

Images do not have to be cited in the text, but if they are not they need a unique identification system for production purposes, and clear page make-up instructions.

Numbered plates use a sequence separate from illustrations in the text, with Arabic or Roman numerals, for example, *Plate I*, *Plate II*, *Plate III*, etc. *Plate* is not usually abbreviated.

Avoid positional references (such as *the figure above* or *the following illustration*) before page layout, as the configuration may change. If the illustrations are unnumbered it may be necessary to insert guidance for the reader (*opposite*, *far left*) after page make-up. Identify all original artwork clearly with the title of the work (a short form will do), identification number (*Fig. 1.1*, *Plate I*, etc.) and an arrow pointing to the 'top' (where confusion might occur). Never use ballpoint pen on the back of photographs, as the impression will show on the other side; use a soft pencil, a chinagraph pencil, or printed sticky labels. Never attach anything with staples or a paper clip, or use sticky tape on the front.

16.1.3 Page make-up

The typesetter or designer is usually responsible for putting artwork in the appropriate place, ideally following, but within two pages of the first mention of the figure in the text; the proofreader should check this. The exceptions are plate sections, which will be inserted by the printer in the most convenient place for subsequent collation. To help the layout process, mark the approximate position of figures with a cue in the margin of hard copy or on a separate line in electronic text, for example:

<<FIGURE 1>>

This is essential guidance if the illustrations are not cited but their relationship to the text is nonetheless important.

Page design often dictates that pictures appear at the bottom or top of a page, or may bleed over the cut edge. Illustrations that have to be set landscape should always be placed with the head of the illustration turned to the left, whether on a recto or verso page. Running heads and page numbers are generally omitted from full-page illustrations in books; if more than two sequential pages have no running head, however, the page number is usually included, except in plate sections that are added by the printer during binding so are not paginated in with the text.

16.2 Graphics files

Authors and editors should appreciate that the requirements for printed and on-screen images are very different: in print, resolution determines image quality and scaling determines image size, but on-screen the reverse is true. The commonest error is to supply images that look acceptable on-screen but are not of a high enough resolution for the final, printed image size. One solution is to reduce the image size (to improve the image quality), but that may not be desirable. Seek advice before scanning pictures, therefore, and supply sample files and hard copy.

Typesetters will accept a limited number of graphics formats—usually restricted to TIFF or JPEG bitmaps or EPS vector art. Images created in word-processing, spreadsheet, or presentation software may be in-compatible with typesetting software: supply unmarked hard copy that can be scanned into a graphics package, as otherwise it will not be possible to harmonize editorial style of, for example, lettering in diagrams with that in the text.

Be aware that as computer printers and monitors use different models for reproducing colour, it will not be possible to print identical colours to those viewed on-screen.

Illustrations are treated as separate elements during page make-up, so graphics files should be presented separately and never embedded in the text. Captions should be numbered and listed at the end of the document or in a separate file.

16.3 Line figures

Line images can be graphs, charts, plans, diagrams, maps, cartoons, pen-and-ink studies, and woodcuts—typically, any image that has no continuous tone (see 16.4) and cannot be typeset. Unusual symbols and characters such as hieroglyphs or structural formulas should be produced separately as uncued and uncaptioned artwork and inserted into text during page make-up. However, if there is a lot of this material discuss it with the publisher, as it can be time-consuming and comparatively expensive to prepare such pages.

16.3.1 **Scaling**

The final dimensions of the artwork will depend on the format of the text, and whether the text is to be in one or two columns. Usually the editor or designer will decide the final size—the editor is likely to be more aware of the significance of an image or its parts but not of difficulties in page make-up; the designer will be able to integrate the image in the page more effectively but might crop or scale it inappropriately.

Space should be allowed for the caption, and between the illustration and the text or adjacent figures. When illustrations span a two-page spread, ensure that nothing important is lost in the gutter where the two pages join.

If calculating percentage reduction or enlargement, each linear dimension will be reduced *to* (say) 67 per cent of its original length—not reduced *by* 67 per cent. If scaling in one dimension (width/depth) is critical, check that the other dimension still fits after enlargement/reduction. Similar illustrations need to be in proportion, especially when being compared. Cropping may mean the image does not have to be reduced as much; it should be marked on a photocopy or overlay. Be aware of possible restrictions on the use of copyright images (see 16.5.2 and Chapter 20).

Consideration should also be given to the size of lettering, weight of lines, and density of tints or hatching to ensure that they do not merge or disappear after reduction (see also 16.3.2).

16.3.2 **Labelling (lettering) and shading**

The traditional process is that authors provide roughs, which are copy-edited and sent to an illustrator for redrawing, at which stage any changes can be made. However, line artwork is often now produced by authors using graphics packages, and the publisher may not want to have it redrawn, in which case the changes that can be made will be restricted—for example, it may not be practical to match editorial style in the text with that of the labels in diagrams.

Check that final-size characters are large enough to remain sharply defined on printing. Most often this means using a typeface no smaller than 8 points (with 9-point linefeed) or, on drawings destined for a 67 per cent reduction, 12 points (with 14-point linefeed). Line widths should usually be ½ point after reduction or enlargement (final size) or ¾ point before 67 per cent reduction. Helvetica or a similar sans-serif font is commonly used.

Labels on line artwork to be redrawn may be indicated on a photocopy, as the original may be scanned to capture the image without redrawing from scratch. Ensure ambiguous characters such as *1*, *l* and *I* are clearly marked. An accompanying electronic file listing each label on a separate line may be helpful, especially when labelling is heavy. If lettering would obscure the relevant item, leader lines pointing out the relevant features may be used. These should preferably be straight and horizontal, although this is often not practicable, and may or may not have arrowheads (be consistent). Figure 16.1 shows the use of leader lines.

Spelling, hyphenation, symbols, and abbreviations for units should match those in the captions, and should follow the stylistic conventions used in the text.

Labels are set in lower case, usually with an initial capital for the first word only (and for proper names, of course). There should be no full point at the end of the label.

A tint is shading made up of fine dots, like a photograph. Tints are expressed as a percentage of black. Solid black is really 100 per cent

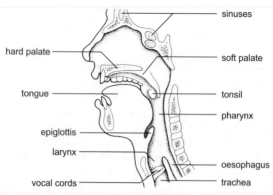

Figure 16.1 **Nose, mouth, and throat**

tint; white is 0 per cent tint. For all line work, tints should be added by using specialist computer software. Authors can supply the basic line artwork, drawn in black, which the publisher can scan in and add tints to. The lowest viable tint for book production is 15 per cent; the highest viable is 80 per cent. (The limitations of the print process make any tint above 80 per cent appear as black.) At least a 20 per cent difference in tint value is required to achieve contrast between areas of different tint, such as three areas with shading tinted at 20 per cent, 40 per cent, and 60 per cent. Do not use solid black for any large area, as it is difficult for the printer to avoid the ink offsetting on to the opposite page, or showing through on to the backing page.

16.3.3 Key

The key or legend explains the symbols or tints used. It is usually physically part of the figure, although if it is simple it may be included as part of the caption, provided the key's elements can be typeset or described. Where letters and numbers (A, B, C, (*a*), (*b*), (*c*), 1, 2, 3, I, II, III) are used to pinpoint parts of a figure, these can be referred to directly in the caption, as shown below:

Reconstruction of a Greek *trapetum* from Olynthus, for crushing olives. A solid column (1) stands in the middle of a large circular basin of lava (2). A square hole on top of this column holds an upright pin (3) fastened with lead. A wooden beam (4) fits over the pin and carries two heavy plano-convex millstones (5), turning on the centre pivot.

16.3.4 **Maps**

Ensure there are no unnecessary features that distract the reader; information must be relevant and presented in a clear and uncluttered fashion. The level of detail should relate to the reasons why the reader will consult the map: for instance, the names of small towns or minor rivers are not needed if the purpose is to pinpoint capital cities or major waterways. When a map is to be (re)drawn by the publisher, the artist will need the following included on a rough sketch or copy:

- scale—a bar scale is most appropriate. It is useful to include both SI and non-SI readings.
- orientation—unless otherwise stated, north is assumed to be at the top (usually the top of the page unless the map will be set landscape).
- labels—geographical and political features in upper and lower case, listed by category. The spelling of place names must agree with the text. Supply copy for any key or note to appear on the map, as well as a caption.
- area for inclusion—indicate cropping (if necessary), either to allow for enlargement of an area or to minimize peripheral features.
- distinctions between areas—best shown by tints and hatching, either throughout the area or along its boundary.
- features—must be easily distinguishable by line weights and treatment of lettering: for example, towns may be presented in roman upper and lower case, rivers in italic, and countries and regional features in capitals.
- projection—if known, state the type of projection used for the original.

16.3.5 **Graphs**

The horizontal (x) and vertical (y) axes should be labelled: they are commonly marked with a quantity and units in parentheses. The labels should be parallel to the axis, reading from bottom to top for the y axis (Figure 16.2). They should be concise, and consistent with the text and the caption.

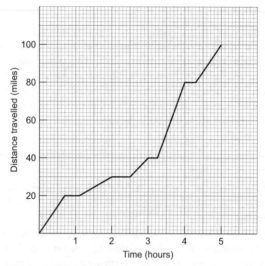

Figure 16.2 **Simple graph**

The intervals in the axis divisions should be consistent, unless it is a logarithmic scale. The numbers differentiating the divisions preferably should be horizontal for both axes, although if space is limited on the x axis, labels can be turned. The numbers do not have to start at zero.

Extra rules other than the x and y axes may be deleted. Arrowheads can be drawn at the ends of axes to indicate a trend but are superfluous if the axis has a scale.

Frequency distributions may be represented as vertical or horizontal bars or columns of continuous data (bars touch) or discrete data (bars separated). The bars must be of the same width and any shading explained in a key or in the caption (see Figure 16.3).

16.4 Tone figures

Continuous tone illustrations are usually photographs, with or without imposed labels (as is often the case in scientific and technical publishing), but may also be drawn and painted artwork, as in children's

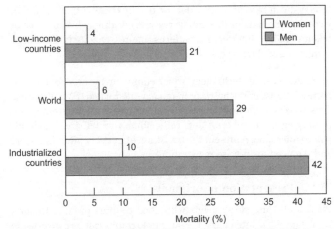

Source: D. Simpson, *Doctors and Tobacco: Medicine's Big Challenge* (Tobacco Control Resource Centre, 2000), derived from R. Peto et al. (eds), *Mortality from Smoking in Developed Countries 1950–2000* (Oxford University Press, 1994).

Figure 16.3 **Estimated percentage of all cancer deaths due to smoking, 1990**

stories. As the preparation and printing of continuous tone images differs from the reproductive processes for text, anyone involved in publishing illustrated works needs some insight into production processes to deal effectively with them.

16.4.1 Screening

Tone originals differ from line artwork in having transitions of tone—imagine the difference between a wash drawing and a pen-and-ink study to appreciate the difference. To simulate these subtleties in print, the picture is screened, or broken up into a series of dots of various shapes and size, the resulting image being known as a **half-tone**. This was formerly done by reflecting light from the original through an actual screen to burn dots on to film; now scanners use a virtual screen, but the same standard screen rulings—from coarse to fine, depending on the final quality required—are used.

Colour tones are screened for each process colour (cyan, magenta, yellow, black). Ink of each colour is applied to the paper in separate stages during the printing. Half-tones that have already been

screened can be reproduced 'dot-for-dot' by treating them as if they
were line originals, or they can be rescreened, although steps must be
taken to reduce interference patterns (moiré). Quality is likely to be
compromised, however, so it is better to scan originals.

Computer-to-plate technology, which eliminates the need for film, has
boosted the use of stochastic or frequency-modulated (FM) screening.
This process produces high-quality colour images at lower resolutions
by varying the number of dots rather than the dot size. Randomly
placed microdots represent the transition of tones, eliminating moiré
and the need for precise registration.

16.4.2 Presentation of originals

Black-and-white glossy prints with good contrast produce the best
results on the printed page. Colour photographs can be converted to
black and white, but some quality may be lost, resulting in a rather
'muddy', low-contrast appearance.

Labels and cropping (masking) should be marked on a photocopy or
an overlay (such as tracing paper attached to the back): press *lightly*
so as not to make any impression on the print. Mark any areas that
should not be obscured by labelling, or where detail is particularly critical. Use scale bars on the image rather than magnification sizes in the
caption.

Present composite pictures—that is, illustrations with more than one
part—as individual photographs, clearly identified and accompanied
by a photocopy or sketch showing how the illustration is to be set out.
Do not paste up original photographs in position.

For colour work most publishers require 35 mm (mounted) or larger-
format colour transparencies, although high-resolution digital files
(usually of 300 dpi resolution) are becoming common. They can reproduce from colour (glossy) prints if slides are not available, but some
contrast will be lost. Previously screened illustrations (see 16.4.1) and
photocopies reproduce poorly.

16.5 Captions

16.5.1 Presentation

Purely decorative images may not require explanation, but for the most part illustrations require captions, which should indicate the essential content of the illustration. They should be concise and extraneous information should be removed: for example, delete the words *The diagram shows* ... when the representation is obvious. Captions and legends go beneath (sometimes beside) the image, whereas table headings go above. Captions traditionally end with a full point, whether they are full sentences or not. Remove or reduce labelling on the figure where possible by including explanations in the caption, as in Figure 16.4.

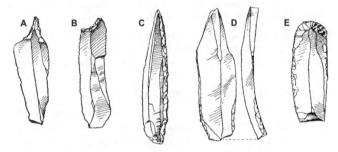

Figure 16.4 **Upper Palaeolithic blade tools in flint. (A) Solutrean piercer or 'hand drill', Dordogne. (B) Magdalenian concave end-scraper or 'spokeshave', Dordogne. (C) Gravettian knife point, Dordogne. (D) Magdalenian burin, Dordogne. (E) End-scraper, Vale of Clwyd, Wales.**

Present captions as a separate list, either at the end of the document or in a separate file. Do not integrate them with the text or attach them to illustrations, although they can be added to roughs, especially if the illustration will occupy the whole page, as this will help the artists scale the figure. Make a separate list of captions for illustrations in a plate section. The captions of unnumbered illustrations should be marked with the relevant unique identifier (see 16.1.2), which should be circled on the hard copy so that it is not typeset.

Check that spellings, hyphenation, and symbols correspond to those used in the figure and in the text. The typesetter may not be able to set symbols used in a figure; these can be placed in a key, as part of the artwork.

Either the editor or designer should specify whether captions are to be set to the width of the figure or to full measure, and whether turn-lines are to be ranged left, indented, or centred.

Terms such as *above*, *below*, *top*, *bottom*, *left*, *right*, and *clockwise* can serve to pinpoint elements in an illustration, or components of a group of illustrations. These may be set in italic, bold, or roman when used as labels, either before or after the subject:

> Fig. 1. *Left to right*: Benny Goodman, Teddy Wilson, Lionel Hampton, and Gene Krupa.
>
> Fig. 2. Relationship of hormonal changes to (**top**) development of a fertile egg; (**centre**) changes in the lining of the uterus; and (**bottom**) hormonal control of both processes.

Use of *Figure* or *Fig.* and punctuation after the figure number can vary (see examples in 16.5.2) but must be consistent. An en space is usually inserted when there is no punctuation after the figure number.

16.5.2 **Permissions and acknowledgements**

Permission must be obtained in good time from the copyright holder to reproduce any illustrations from published sources. Where there is any doubt (as, for example, when a modified version of an illustration is to be used) it is prudent, as well as courteous, to ask for permission. For more information see Chapter 20.

If captions are very long it is best to include the illustrations' sources or copyright information in a list of illustrations rather than in the caption itself, unless the copyright holder instructs otherwise. If the illustrations are drawn from only a few sources one can acknowledge the sources in a separate note, either following the list itself or in a separate acknowledgements section. See also 1.2.11 and 1.2.12.

Where individual works of art or other creative pieces (manuscripts, designed objects, etc.) are reproduced, the caption should name the maker and the work, give the date of the work, and provide a location. If only part of a work is shown the picture should be identified as a detail.

The order of elements in a caption can vary but must be imposed uniformly. When acknowledgements are included in the caption they are placed at the end, run on after the text or on a new line; alternatively, source information can be included as a reference. The following examples show some of the possible styles of caption:

Fig. 1. George V and Queen Mary when they were Duke and Duchess of York, at York House, 1895. Royal Archives, Windsor Castle. Copyright reserved. Reproduced by gracious permission of Her Majesty the Queen.

Figure 2: James Brown (*left, with cape*) and the Famous Flames during the recording of the *Live at the Apollo* album. *Courtesy PolyGram/Polydor/Phonogram Records.*

Figure 3 'The Learned Pig relating his Adventures', engraving by R. Jameson, 1 July 1786. By permission of the Houghton Library, Harvard University.

Fig. 4: 'Oh, for heaven's sake! Twenty years from now, will it matter whether the italics are yours or his?' Drawing by Joe Mirachi, © 1981 The New Yorker Magazine Inc.

Fig. 5 Simplified bearing capacity configuration (from Menzies, 1976a).

CHAPTER 17

Notes and references

17.1 General principles

Publications of many kinds employ pointers within the main body of the text to refer the reader to explanatory or additional material either on the same page or elsewhere in the work. Academic publications in particular need an apparatus to provide references to support, and sometimes to clarify and amplify, what is said in the text. It is of course the responsibility of the author to ensure that the text is properly supported by appropriate sources, that the sources are correctly quoted or interpreted, and that the citations are accurate and complete. It is, however, the duty of the editor to ensure that the references in a work are presented in a clear and consistent manner. The reader may well see sloppy references as symptoms of generally careless scholarship.

The systems commonly adopted vary greatly between disciplines, and there may be considerable variation even within a single discipline, according to the preferences of particular publishers, editors, and authors. Furthermore, as in other aspects of editing, practice changes over time, and new styles may be taken up very unevenly. The most traditional system employs numbers, letters, or symbols as cues to direct the reader to notes which are printed either at the foot of the page to which they relate (**footnotes**) or in a group at the end of the text (**endnotes**). Alternatively, in what is known as the **author–date** or **Harvard** system, the cues may take the form of an author's name and date of publication (or in the **author–number** or **Vancouver** system simply a reference number) within parentheses that enable the reader to identify the work in a list of full references at the end of the text. Various permutations are possible. In some ways life is made easier for both author and editor if a commonly recognized system is adopted, but agreed adaptation to the needs of a particular work can prove beneficial. What matters most is that the necessary information should be conveyed to the reader clearly and economically.

The primary function of scholarly annotation is to identify for the reader the sources of what is said in text. This may be the location of a verbatim quotation or—just as important in an academic work— the basis for a statement by the author. Simple references of this kind can be accommodated by systems that use brief parenthetical references in the text to take the reader to a consolidated bibliography (see 17.3 and 17.4). Such references are particularly well suited to scientific publications, but they are also used in the social sciences and increasingly in the humanities. In the humanities it is normally notes that are the essential feature of the supporting apparatus. Notes are a convenient vehicle not only for complex bibliographical citations but also, for example, for acknowledgements, further discussion, supporting original text, and bibliographical surveys (see 17.2.1). Notes may be used in conjunction with a bibliography or more selective suggestions for further reading, or with a list of abbreviations of frequently cited sources (see 17.2.6).

17.2 Footnotes and endnotes

17.2.1 The use of notes

An apparatus based on notes is normal in the humanities, where more is often needed than a simple link to a consolidated list of printed sources. For example, manuscript sources are more easily cited in notes than in the systems of parenthetical reference used in scientific publications. Different sources, or versions of a source, may be compared and evaluated in a note. If a quotation is given in translation in the text the original may perhaps be given in a note, or conversely (this may be scrupulous scholarly practice where doubt is possible about the correctness of a translation, but it should not be adopted routinely without good reason). It is sometimes helpful to include in a note a brief survey of the literature on a particular topic, or a summary of a debate, though authors should be discouraged from needlessly transforming notes into bibliographies. Author's acknowledgements also fit neatly into notes. Also, notes can perform special functions in scholarly editions of original texts, where they may, for instance, supply variant readings from different manuscripts.

The flexibility that makes notes such a useful tool can be abused. Authors sometimes include in notes further discussion of a question raised in the text, or of some related issue. While this cannot be outlawed altogether, it should be avoided wherever possible. For the most part, if a point is important and relevant enough to be discussed at all it should be dealt with in the text. Notes should be kept as short as possible, and inessential material excluded. The best place for extensive but essential ancillary matter that cannot be accommodated in the text may be an appendix. The main function of notes (other than those in editions of texts) remains the clear and concise presentation of necessary references.

17.2.2 **Footnotes or endnotes?**

Notes may be either **footnotes**, printed at the foot of the page to which they relate, or **endnotes**, printed in a single sequence at the end of the text. In multi-author volumes and journals that employ endnotes they should be printed at the end of an individual chapter or article; otherwise they are normally placed at the end of the book, in a separately numbered sequence for each chapter.

Some categories of note, like those that explain the meaning of words in the text or provide variant readings, have an especially strong claim to be placed at the foot of the page. Footnotes are in general much more convenient for the reader, who can keep track of them without the annoying disruption of flipping back and forth between text and notes in the course of reading. The setting of notes at the foot of the page is of course more typographically complex and demanding than is placing them together at the end of the text.

17.2.3 **Numbering and placement**

The reader is referred to a footnote or endnote by a cue in the text. This normally takes the form of a superior Arabic number. The cue is placed after any punctuation (normally after the closing point of a sentence). If, however, it relates only to text within parentheses it is placed before the closing parenthesis. The cue is repeated at the start of the note. Notes cued in the middle of a sentence are a distraction to the reader, and cues are best located at the end of sentences:

He was a genuine Shropshire lad, as John H. Johnston reminds us.[51]

> Bergonzi quite correctly notes, 'Owen's attitude to the "boys" or "lads"
> destined for sacrifice has some affinity with Housman's.'[55]
> (Hopkins wrote defensively to Bridges: 'When you read it let me know
> if there is anything like it in Walt Whitman; as perhaps there may
> be, and I should be sorry for that.'[29])

Characters other than Arabic numerals may be used for note cues
when there are relatively few notes in a sequence. In mathematical or
scientific contexts, for example, superior lower-case letters may be
used to avoid confusion with superscript numbers in technical notation. Lower-case Roman numerals may also serve as note cues, as can
reference marks (the traditional order is *, †, ‡, §, ¶, ‖, repeated in
duplicate as **, ††, and so on as necessary). Occasionally different
types of cue are employed on the same page for parallel sequences of
notes serving different purposes.

Traditionally footnotes were numbered in a sequence that restarted
on each page, but now it is normal for them to be numbered continuously through each chapter or article. This allows the numbers in the
author's copy to remain unchanged at typesetting; internal cross-
references to notes thus do not require correction on proof, and passages of text may even be located by reference to numbered notes (*Ch.
6 at n. 17*). Continuous numbering of footnotes through an entire
book is to be avoided, as it can generate too many three-digit cues
and may require extensive correction if a note is deleted or added at
proof stage. Whether numbered page by page or chapter by chapter
note cues must appear in strict numerical sequence; the same number
must not be used twice within a sequence, even if the content of the
note is the same.

An initial note consisting entirely of acknowledgements may be placed
before the numbered notes and cued with an asterisk; the asterisk is
sometimes placed at the end of the chapter or article title, sometimes
at the end of the first sentence of text. On the whole it is best to avoid
placing note cues in headings or subheadings. An initial uncued note
may be used to provide the original location of a reprinted chapter or
article.

A note giving the source for a displayed quotation is best placed at the
end of the quotation itself rather than at the end of the preceding text.
Where there are multiple quotations from or references to a particular
source the locations should be given in a single note after the last

quotation or reference, provided no other citation intervenes. The page numbers should be in the same order as the quotations or statements to which they relate, not rearranged into numerical sequence. If there are repeated citations of a single source (but no other) over several paragraphs it may be best to provide a separate note for each paragraph. The notes in three such successive paragraphs might, for example, be:

> 6. *Windham's Green Book*, 25, 17, 31.
>
> 7. Ibid. 87, 95, 103–5.
>
> 8. Ibid. 150, 75, 279.

Furthermore, where it can be done without ambiguity, it is good practice to group references to different sources in a single note after several sentences or at the end of a paragraph. The nature of the source will generally indicate to which statement in the text it relates, and any doubt may be removed by a parenthetical word or phrase after the references or by an introductory phrase before several related references. The editorial effort required is justified by the reduction in the number of notes and the improved readability of the text.

> Not even the best endowed colleges had incomes approaching those of such great Benedictine houses as ... Westminster or Glastonbury ... New College's estates probably yielded revenues of a similar magnitude to the Augustinian abbey of Oseney. ... The estate income of All Souls ... was probably slightly lower for example than that of Bolton Priory in Yorkshire, which supported merely fifteen canons ... The college by contrast remained close to its statutory complement of a warden and forty fellows.[30]
>
> > 30. D. Knowles and R. N. Hadcock, *Medieval Religious Houses: England and Wales* (1953), 80 (Westminster), 66 (Glastonbury), 149 (Oseney), 128 (Bolton); I. Kershaw, *Bolton Priory* (1973), 186; Cobban, 'Colleges and halls', 609.

17.2.4 Layout of notes

The layout and typography of notes is subject to considerable variation. Footnotes in particular are usually set in smaller type than text. A note should begin with a capital initial and end with a full point. It may or may not contain grammatically complete sentences. Abbreviated forms (for example for the months of the year) and symbols that would not be acceptable in open text may be appropriate within citations in notes. Various forms of punctuation and wording may be used to group citations and to indicate how they relate to material in the text or to related questions; what is most efficient in any context is a matter for editorial judgement. Sometimes the word 'see' is printed in roman type when it directs the reader to material outside the present work but in italics when it refers to another place within the same work; this is not necessarily a helpful convention, and can seem strange when the two forms occur close together. The common abbreviation 'cf.' (Latin *confer*) means 'compare', and thus is not quite the same as 'see'.

The number preceding the note may be superscript or on the line:

> [40] Mokyr, *Why Ireland Starved*, 26.
> 40. Mokyr, *Why Ireland Starved*, 26.

Whether or not a point is needed after a number on the line is a design issue.

17.2.5 Forms of citation

Full guidance on the form of bibliographic citations is to be found in Chapter 18. For the most part the same considerations govern entries in a bibliography and citations in notes, with the important exception that in notes an author's initials precede rather than follow the surname. Consistent systems for the formulation of notes are essential, but abstract rules should not be followed too slavishly: much can depend on editorial judgement in presenting particular references as clearly and economically as possible.

Author and short title

In addition to general bibliographic rules there are conventions, relating especially to multiple citations of the same work, that are intended to promote brevity and clarity within notes. Unless it is included in a list of abbreviations (see 17.2.6), full bibliographic details of a published work or the location of an unpublished source should be given when it is first cited in an article or book, and repeated at its first citation in any subsequent chapter in the same book. Subsequent citations should take a very abbreviated form, typically the author's surname and a shortened title of the work. The short title should be accurately extracted from the full title (not a paraphrase) and should be as brief as is compatible with the unambiguous identification of the work. Rather longer forms may be advisable if works of similar title are cited. Short titles alone may be used for works cited with no named author. It is a matter of judgement whether an editor's name should be repeated with the title of an edited text. Short forms may also be devised for the multiple citation of unpublished sources whose full forms are unduly lengthy.

When a work is cited more than once within, say, two or three pages, the author's surname may suffice without even a short title after the first citation (provided, of course, that no other work by the same author or another author of the same name intervenes). Once a short form has been established, the author's initials or the full title should not be reintroduced in later citations in the same chapter.

> 5. R. J. Faith, *The English Peasantry and the Growth of Lordship* (1997).
>
> 73. Faith, *English Peasantry*, 49–50 and *passim*.
>
> 74. Faith, 202.

A system may now be encountered in a journal in which a consolidated list of full references to published works is printed at the end of an article, and in the footnotes even the first citation of each work is given in short form. This arrangement, which gives the reader a convenient list of sources while making the notes more concise, has much to commend it in a journal, though it might prove unwieldy and unhelpful to the reader if applied to a whole book, especially one with extensive annotation.

Location within a work

Locations within a work should generally be given in the shortest unambiguous form. Publishers will have their own conventions for the various fields in which they produce books or journals. Lower-case Roman numerals were traditionally used for volume numbers, but Arabic numerals are now common; either system should be applied consistently. Roman page numbers must be retained and not converted to Arabic. Volume and page numbers may be linked by a point, consistently either closed up or spaced off. Abbreviations for pages or volumes (*p.*, *pp.*, *vol.*, *vols.*) are not strictly necessary in most cases, but they should be included before Arabic or Roman numerals if there is a risk of confusion as to what element is being cited. This is in fact very uncommon, though sometimes care must be taken to make it clear that numbered items not pages are being cited. If a work has numbered columns rather than pages there is no need to use the abbreviation *col.* in citations, as there will be no ambiguity when the reader consults the source. Likewise compound locations consisting of several numbers (whether Arabic, lower-case Roman, or small capitals, depending on house style or general convention) may reasonably be used with no explanation of the elements they represent (book, chapter, paragraph, question, or whatever) if there will be no ambiguity in the source itself.

> *Letters and Journals of Robert Baillie*, 2.110
> Brett-Smith, 1.xxviii–xxix
> *English Historical Documents*, i, 2nd edn, ed. D. Whitelock (London, 1979), no. 191
> *Liber de caesaribus*, v.39.20

Authors sometimes feel obliged to give the overall pagination of articles or chapters they cite in addition to the particular passage to which they are referring. This is no more logical or helpful than citing the total pagination of a book, and is an unnecessary complication of a citation.

For the treatment of abbreviations and contractions of terms such as 'page', 'chapter', and 'volume' see Chapter 10. The use of 'f.' after a page number to indicate 'and the following page' should be replaced with an explicit two-page span (*15–16*, not *15 f.*). A page number followed by 'ff.' to indicate 'and the following pages' should also be converted to a precise span if possible, but this form is acceptable when it is difficult for the author (or editor) to identify a final relevant page. The spacing, if any, before the abbreviation (*23ff.* or *23 ff.*) is a matter of house style; Oxford traditionally uses a thin space between a number and a following 'f.' or 'ff.', and between a number and a following 'n.' or 'nn.' in the absence of a subsequent note number (when a note number is included, normal space of the line is used: *23 n. 5*). When specific notes are cited, 'note' may be abbreviated to 'n.' and 'notes' to 'nn.' It is best to avoid punctuation between page number and note number. In the third of the following examples the notes cited contain information additional to that given in the text:

> Marx, *Manifesto*, ed. Feuer, 37 n. 4.
> Kleinhans, 'Marxism and Film', 106 ff.
> K. McRoberts, *Misconceiving Canada* (Toronto: OUP, 1997), 12 and nn. 37–8.

A reference to another place within the work itself may be included in a note if it will be genuinely helpful to the reader, but such internal cross-references should be added judiciously, and not simply because a topic happens to be discussed at more than one point. A reference to a particular page may be entered on copy with zeros in place of exact figures (*see 000–0 above, see 00 below*) with the relevant folios of the copy noted in the margin. The correct printed page numbers will have to be substituted at proof stage. This adds to the cost of production and introduces the real risk that the page number will be inserted incorrectly or not at all. Citations of complete chapters, sections, or other subdivisions avoid these difficulties but may be less helpful to the reader.

Abbreviations

Many abbreviations are used in note references, to aid or direct the reader as succinctly as possible. For the most part, a lower-case abbreviation that begins a note is capitalized, whether or not the note is a complete sentence. A handful of common abbreviations are, however, exceptions to this rule: *c.*, e.g., i.e., l., ll., p., pp. generally remain lower case:

> 20. *c.*1344, according to Froissart.
> 21. e.g. service outside the jurisdiction.
> 22. i.e. Copyright, Designs & Patents Act 1988, §4.
> 23. p. 7.
> 24. ll. 34–44 (Miller edn).

Certain Latin words or their abbreviations are commonly used to make citations in notes more concise; only the most frequently encountered are mentioned here. Some can indeed be helpful, but must be deployed with care. These Latin abbreviations are normally set in roman rather than italic type; full forms are italicized as shown below. The abbreviations should be capitalized at the start of a note.

• The word *ibidem*, meaning 'in the same place', is normally abbreviated to 'ibid.', occasionally to 'ib.' The form 'in ibid.' is thus incorrect. Bibliographically, 'ibid.' means 'in the same work', or 'in the same place within that work', as in the immediately preceding citation (either in the same or the preceding note). 'Ibid.' cannot be used if any other reference comes between the two citations of the same work. 'Ibid.' with no further qualification must be taken to mean exactly the same place as in the preceding citation. If a different location within the same work is intended 'ibid.' may stand for the work and as much of the location as has not changed (for example a volume number), and is followed by the new location. It is important to check that late changes to notes have not inserted new citations in positions that invalidate the original use of 'ibid.' A comma is sometimes placed between 'ibid.' and a following page number or other location, but this is not generally necessary:

[2] *The Letters of Lewis Carroll*, ed. M. N. Cohen (1979), 2.476.

[3] Ibid. 473.

[4] C. M. Blagden, *Well-Remembered* (1953), 117.

[5] Ibid.

[6] *Letters*, ed. Cohen, 2.759.

[7] Blagden, 116.

[8] Ibid. 117.

[41] *Gesetze*, ed. Liebermann i. 88–123; for the date see ibid. iii. 65.

- The abbreviations 'op. cit.' (*opere citato*, 'in the cited work') and 'art. cit.' (*articulo citato*, 'in the cited article') were once commonly used in place of a work title, normally after an author's name. In fact they are of little use. If the work title in question is evident the author's name alone is sufficient; if not, a short title is more helpful. These forms are best avoided.

- The abbreviation 'loc. cit.' (*loco citato*, 'in the cited place') is often misunderstood and misused. It can represent only a specific location within a work and is therefore of extremely restricted usefulness. It may occasionally save the repetition of a long and complex location involving multiple elements that cannot easily be compressed, but most often the repeated location (for example volume and page) will be no longer than 'loc. cit.' itself.

- *Idem* (commonly but not always abbreviated to 'id.') means 'the same person', and is often used in place of an author's name when works by the same author are cited one after the other. This is perhaps an excessive saving of space. Furthermore there are grammatical complications, as the form of the Latin pronoun varies with gender and number. While a male author is *idem* (id.) a female must be *eadem* (ead.); multiple female authors are *eaedem* (eaed.) and multiple authors of whom at least one is male are *eidem* (eid.). An author's gender is not always known, and editors cannot always be relied upon to apply the correct forms. All in all, it is as well to repeat an author's name in a new citation.

- The word *passim* may be placed after a span of pages, or a less specific location, to indicate that relevant passages are scattered throughout the overall location.

Other Latin forms may be encountered. They may be genuinely useful in certain contexts, but it is often a kindness to the reader to replace them with English equivalents. For example 'under' can often be substituted for 's.n.', 's.v.', or 's.a.' (*sub nomine, sub verbo, sub anno*); *supra* may be replaced with 'above' and *infra* with 'below'. The form *(et) seq.* should be replaced with a two-page span in the same way as 'f.' and *(et) seqq.* treated like, or changed to, 'ff.' (see above).

17.2.6 **Bibliographical abbreviations**

A list of bibliographical abbreviations is often printed in a book's preliminary matter, or at the start of a bibliography. An abbreviated citation assigned in this way will be used every time the work is cited in a note, even at its first citation in a chapter. Whether or not it is worth including such a list in a volume will depend not only on how often particular works are cited in the volume as a whole but also on how many works are cited frequently in more than one chapter. If a work is cited very many times in one chapter it will routinely be reduced to author or author and title after its first citation; a more irregular abbreviation of a complex source may be explicitly introduced at its first mention in a chapter:

> Bede, *Historia ecclesiastica gentis Anglorum* (hereafter *HE*)
> St John's College, Cambridge, archives (hereafter SJC)

If a source abbreviated in this way is cited in no other chapter in the volume an entry in an overall list of abbreviations may be superfluous.

17.3 Author–date system

An apparatus for references known as the **author–date** (or **Harvard**) system is normal in the physical sciences and related fields, and is also used extensively in the social sciences. It is not based on notes but relies on brief parenthetical references in the text to take the reader to the appropriate point in a consolidated list of full citations, generally known as the reference section. A reference section includes only those works that are cited in the text; a more general list of works of related interest should be called *Bibliography* or *Further Reading*. This is an economical method of citing straightforward published sources.

It is possible to combine this arrangement with a separate sequence of footnotes or endnotes for explanatory or discursive matter:

> *text*
>
> a stoutly republican coalition that retained none the less a great deal of the administrative style of the old regime (see Stookey 1974). It was replaced by a government with a different style,[2] a style ... not forgotten or revoked.
>
> *endnote 2*
>
> The usual explanation of the timing of the coup is that it forestalled a Ba'athist plot. That this was no simple question ... we shall see when we quote the speeches given at a tribal meeting soon afterwards.
>
> *reference section*
>
> Stookey, R. W., 1974. 'Social Structure and Politics in the Yemen Arab Republic', *Middle East Journal*, 28/3: 248–60; 28/4: 409–19

In extreme cases where multiple references (and multiple authors) render a sentence unreadable, and the problem cannot be resolved by rewriting, a group of references may be relegated to a footnote. Bracketed author–date references to a bibliographic list are sometimes included within footnotes.

17.3.1 Reference section

In the author–date system the full references are listed alphabetically in a section at the end of the text (either chapter by chapter or in a consolidated list at the end of the book). As in bibliographies, authors' initials generally follow their surnames. To facilitate linking with the short references given in the text the date of publication immediately follows the authors' names. The styling of these references can vary considerably; scientific and medical publishers, for example, may use very different conventions from those adopted in the humanities. For further guidance see Chapter 18.

17.3.2 References in text

A typical reference in the text consists of an author's name and date of publication enclosed within parentheses (or occasionally square brackets), with or without a comma separating name and date, according to the style adopted. The reference is placed immediately after the statement to which it relates. If this happens to be at the end of a sentence the closing parenthesis precedes the closing point (but a reference at the end of a displayed quotation follows the closing punctuation). If the author's name is given in open text it need not be repeated in the parentheses, where the date alone suffices. Several references may be included within the same parentheses, separated by semicolons:

> *text*
> While there was an extraordinary sense of optimism among people establishing their own farms in the early years of independence (Unwin 1994), this is rapidly withering away.
> *reference section*
> Unwin, T. (1994), 'Structural Change in Estonian Agriculture: From Command Economy to Privatisation', *Geography*, 79, 3: 246–61.
> *text*
> For years, most textbooks referred to the five stages of economic integration as defined by Balassa (1961).
> *reference section*
> Balassa, Bela (1961), *The Theory of Economic Integration*. London: Allen and Unwin.
> *text*
> They are also used to detect segmental hypermobility (Magarey 1988; Maitland 2001).
> *reference section*
> Magarey, M. E. 1988 'Examination of the Cervical and Thoracic Spine'. In: R. Grant (ed.) *Physical Therapy of the Cervical and Thoracic Spine*, pp. 81–109. Churchill Livingstone: New York.
> Maitland, G. 2001 *Maitland's Vertebral Manipulation*, 6th edn. Butterworth–Heinemann: Oxford.

Multiple authorship is very common in scientific publication. Each work should have a consistent convention as to how many authors' names are given in full and what number, if any, should be reduced to 'et al.' (sometimes italicized) after the name of the first author (see Chapter 18). Some publishers use 'et al.' to shorten references in text even when the names are given in full in the corresponding entry in the reference section. Either an ampersand or 'and' should be used consistently to link dual authors or the last two of multiple authors, even though in the reference section they may be separated by a comma:

text

One of the biggest successes of the 1960s was transformed into an albatross hanging from the neck of an embattled Community (Rosenblatt et al., 1988).

reference section

Rosenblatt, Julius et al. (1988), *The Common Agricultural Policy of the European Community*, International Monetary Fund, occasional paper 62, November.

text

Prototypical birds, for instance, seem to be birds of average size and average predacity (Rips et al., 1973).

reference section

Rips, L. J., Shoben, E. J., and Smith, E. E. (1973). 'Semantic Distance and the Verification of Semantic Relations'. *Journal of Verbal Learning and Verbal Behaviour* 12: 1–20.

text

It has been estimated that the human eye can discriminate no fewer than 7.5 million just noticeable colour differences (Brown and Lenneberg 1954).

reference section

Brown, R., and Lenneberg, E. H. (1954). 'A Study in Language and Cognition'. *Journal of Abnormal and Social Psychology* 49: 454–62.

If the reference section contains works by authors of the same surname their initials may be retained in the in-text reference to distinguish between them. If there is more than one work by an author in a single year they are distinguished by lower-case letters (normally but not always italic) appended to the year in the parenthetical reference and in the list. The dates of several works by a single author are separated by commas. Occasionally a parenthetical reference may be introduced by terms like 'see', 'see also', or 'cf.':

text

a diverse body of work has emerged which focuses on the 'governance' of socio-economic systems (see Jessop 1995a, 1997)

reference section

Jessop, B. (1995a) 'The Regulation Approach, Governance and Post-Fordism', *Economy and Society*, 24, 3: 307–33.

Jessop, B. (1995b) 'Regional Economic Blocs', *American Behavioral Scientist*, 38, 5: 674–715.

Jessop, B. (1997) 'The Governance of Complexity and Complexity of Governance', in A. Amin and J. Hausner (eds) *Beyond Markets and Hierarchy*, Aldershot: Edward Elgar.

How to style references to works that do not fit into the normal pattern of author and title is a matter for editorial judgement. A reference to an anonymous work, for instance, may place either 'anon.' or a short title before the date of publication; reference to a work produced by a corporate body may similarly use either the work title or the name of the body. A reference to an unsigned item in a periodical may use its title and date. The crucial point is that all in-text references should be styled consistently with the reference section and should enable the reader easily to identify the source there. A personal communication or an interview with the author may be so described in a parenthetical reference, but need not be included in the reference section:

> *text*
> By this time, industry had come to play a leading role (World Bank 1993).
> *reference section*
> World Bank (1993) *Vietnam: Transition to the Market*. Washington, DC: The World Bank.
> *text*
> in Uppsala 'the main aim is to create sustainable development, although there is no true consensus as to what this means' (Peterson, pers. comm.).
> *appendix: Informants*
> Agneta Peterson, environmental planning officer, Uppsala municipality.

Broadly speaking, articles in scientific disciplines are shorter than those in the humanities, and often it is not necessary to specify a location within in-text references; locations are more commonly cited in references in the social sciences. When a location is given it is usually separated from the date by a colon. 'Ibid.' may be used parenthetically to refer to the preceding reference:

> *text*
> a point admirably discussed by Pitt-Rivers (1977: 101, 110) ... (ibid. 119).
> *reference section*
> Pitt-Rivers, J. R., 1977. *The Fate of Shechem*. Cambridge Studies in Social Anthropology 19. Cambridge: Cambridge University Press.

17.4 Numbered references

Some scientific publications use the **author–number** (or **Vancouver**) system. Like the author–date (Harvard) system, this employs very brief references in text as pointers to a full list of citations. In the reference section each work is assigned a number, either in a single overall sequence or with a separate sequence for each contributor in a multi-author work. In the text the author's name is followed by the number of the work, either as a superscript figure or in parentheses:

> *text*
>
> It is also being used to relieve phantom limb pain, menstrual cramps, and other types of chronic pain, including migraine (Grinspoon and Bakalar 2).
>
> *reference section*
>
> 2. Grinspoon L., Bakalar J. B. *Marijuana: The Forbidden Medicine.* London: Yale University Press; 1993.

A related system numbers the citations in a single sequence and dispenses with authors' names in the references in text; these consist simply of superscript numbers or numbers in parentheses or square brackets, multiple references being separated by commas. This arrangement has a superficial resemblance to endnotes, but the reference numbers do not necessarily occur in numerical sequence in the text, where any one may be repeated several times:

> *text*
>
> Issues of risk, choice, and chance are central to the controversy over the MMR vaccine that erupted in the UK in 1998 and has continued into the new millennium.[1]
>
> *reference section*
>
> 1. Fitzpatrick M. *MMR and Autism: What Parents Need to Know.* London: Routledge, 2004.
>
> *text*
>
> The inter-individual variability in VO_2 measured at a given speed and rate can be as high as 15% [18]
>
> *reference section*
>
> 18. Nieman, D. C. *Exercise Testing and Prescription*, 5th edn. New York: McGraw-Hill, 2003; 90.

The late addition or removal of a reference from a numbered list may require more or less extensive correction of the numbers in the reference section and the in-text citations.

CHAPTER 18

Bibliography

18.1 General principles

18.1.1 Introduction

Bibliography, specifically **enumerative bibliography**, is the discipline of citing reference matter in a consistent and accurate manner, so as to provide enough key material for readers to be able to identify the work and locate it in a library. Bibliographies occur in all types of publication, and are found in most non-fiction works (though depending on the type of publishing they may not be headed *Bibliography*—see 1.4.4).

The structure of bibliographic citations is determined by the referencing system in use in the publication concerned. In general publishing and academic publishing in the humanities, bibliographic citations are ordered (very broadly speaking):

> author, title, place of publication, date of publication

This form supports the use of footnotes or endnotes for referencing (see 17.2). In these types of publishing the bibliographic list is likely to include works that are not referred to in the text.

Academic publishing in the sciences and social sciences uses **author–date** references in the text to source quotations and references to other authorities (see 17.3); this form requires bibliographic citations ordered:

> author, date, title, place of publication

In these types of publishing the bibliographic list often includes only those works that are referred to in the text; the correct heading for such a list is not *Bibliography* but *References*.

A variation on the author–date system is the **author–number** system (see 17.4).

18.1.2 **Placement within a publication**

Citations are conventionally found in two different parts of an academic work:

- **Note citations** appear in footnotes and endnotes.
- **Bibliography citations** form a list of works that is usually placed at the end of a publication before an index.

In the interests of simplicity it is best to keep stylistic differences between note citations and bibliography citations to a minimum. The following distinctions are useful, however:

- Note citations will frequently require a specific volume and/or page number. Apart from page ranges to identify the start and end of chapters in books or articles in journals, bibliography citations will usually cite a work in its entirety.
- In bibliography citations, if an author or editor is cited before the title the surname should appear first, aiding the reader in navigating through a list. In note citations this is an irritant that reduces readability, and should be avoided:

    note citation
    Joe Bailey, *Pessimism* (London, 1988), 35.
    bibliography citation
    Bailey, Joe, *Pessimism* (London, 1988).

Except when it is necessary to clarify a difference between the two types of citations, examples in this chapter follow bibliography style.

18.1.3 **Arrangement and ordering of a bibliography**

A bibliography is normally ordered alphabetically by the surname of the main author or editor of the cited work. It is sometimes advantageous to subdivide longer lists, for example by subject or type of work. A typical division is that of primary and secondary sources; also, a separate list of manuscripts and documents may be made. A bibliography of primary sources is sometimes more historically interesting if ordered chronologically, or more practical if arranged by repository. For ordering in the author–date system see 18.5.

Alphabetization follows the same principles as in indexing (see Chapter 19); ignore all accents (index *Müller* as *Muller*, not *Mueller*) and treat *Mc* as *Mac* and *St* as *Saint*. See 6.1.8 for the indexing of names with prefixes.

Single author

Entries by the same author may be ordered alphabetically by title, ignoring definite and indefinite articles, or chronologically by year, the earliest first, and alphabetically within a single year. Alphabetical order is advisable when many works by one author are cited, but chronological order may be preferred if it is important to show the sequence of works. In second and subsequent works by the same author replace the name with an em rule or rules: Oxford style is to use a 2-em rule followed by a fixed thin space before the title or next element in the citation, with no punctuation after the rule:

> Rogers, C. D., *The Family Tree Detective* (Manchester, 1983).
> —— *Tracing Missing Persons* (Manchester, 1986).

Works edited by an author are listed in a separate sequence following all works written by him or her, singly or with co-authors; works edited in collaboration are arranged according to the same rules as for multiple authors. Alternatively, it is possible to list all publications associated with a single person in a single sequence, ignoring the distinction between author and editor.

More than one author

It is usual to alphabetize works by more than one author under the first author's name. Names of authors common to subsequent works are replaced by as many em rules as there are authors' names. Oxford style is to use 2-em rules for each name, as explained above, with a thin space after each rule and without punctuation.

When there is more than one citation of the same author, group references within these two categories:

- works written by a single author
- works written by the same author with any co-authors, in alphabetical order by surname of the co-author:

> Hornsby-Smith, Michael P., *Roman Catholic Beliefs in England* (Cambridge, 1991).
> —— *Roman Catholics in England: Studies in Social Structure since the Second World War* (Cambridge, 1987).
> —— and Dale, A., 'Assimilation of Irish Immigrants', *British Journal of Sociology*, xxxix/4 (1988), 519–44.
> —— and Lee, R. M., *Roman Catholic Opinion* (Guildford, 1979).
> —— —— and Turcan, K. A., 'A Typology of English Catholics', *Sociological Review*, xxx/3 (1982), 433–59.

18.1.4 Bibliographic elements

As a general rule, it is important for citations in a bibliography to be consistent in the level of detail provided. Inconsistency is a form of error and will reduce the overall integrity of an academic publication. Moreover, readers should be able to infer reliably that an absence of information from one citation but not another reflects the bibliographic detail available from the texts being cited.

For published matter, the key elements required for a 'complete' citation are:

- person or persons responsible for the work
- title of the work or serial
- the edition being used, if not the first edition
- place and date of publication.

Some citations require further details: these will be covered in the various sections that follow. A decision to include other details (for example number of volumes, series title, or publisher) should be applied consistently to all citations.

For non-published material, such as manuscripts and electronic sources, there are fewer established conventions, and publishers are more open to whatever is provided, so long as the style is followed consistently and does not jar unnecessarily with the general pattern applied to published matter.

The means by which a reader distinguishes one element from the other is by its order within the citation, its typography, and its surrounding punctuation. It is therefore important to ensure that each part of the citation is presented correctly, and in the appropriate place.

All bibliographic information must be taken from the cited work itself, and not from a secondary source such as a library catalogue or other bibliography. Additional information not supplied by the work should generally appear within square brackets.

18.2 Books

18.2.1 Introduction

A complete book citation must include author or editor details, title, edition information (if an edition other than the first edition is cited), and date and place of publication:

> Robert Demaus, *William Tyndale: A Contribution to the Early History of the English Bible*, new edn, rev. Richard Lovett (London, 1886).
>
> R. W. Watt, *Three Steps to Victory* (London, 1957).
>
> Enid Bagnold, *A Diary Without Dates* (2nd edn, London, 1978).

18.2.2 Author's name

Best practice, especially in the humanities, is to cite the author's name as it appears on the title page (the same applies to all personal names, whether of authors or others); some authors insist on being known by their initials while others object to their forenames being cut down. Applying this practice requires the discipline of noting the form as it appears in the book, and not relying on secondary sources, such as library catalogues and other bibliographies. When compiling very large bibliographies (especially for multi-author works where different contributors may have adopted different practices), systematically reducing forenames to initials is sometimes more practical.

The author's name should appear at the start of the citation. In bibliography citations the surname is given first, followed by a comma and the given names or initials:

> Bailey, Joe   Eliot, T. S.

Names that are best left unabbreviated and in natural order in bibliography citations include:

- medieval compound names that conjoin a personal name with a toponym, occupation, patronymic, or epithet:
  > Hereward the Wake   Aelred of Rievaulx
- pseudonyms that lose their sense if altered:
  > Dotted Crotchet   Afferbeck Lauder
- names given as initials only, even if the full name is known:
  > G. E. C.

In a list, such examples would all be ordered by their first element.

If works of one author are cited under different names, use the correct form for each work, and supply a former name after a later one in parentheses; add a cross-reference if necessary:

Joukovsky, F., *Orphée et ses disciples dans la poésie française et néolatine du XVIe siècle* (Geneva, 1970).

—— (= Joukovsky-Micha, F.), 'La Guerre des dieux et des géants chez les poètes français du XVIe siècle (1500–1585)', *Bibliothèque d'Humanisme et Renaissance*, xxix (1967), 55–92.

Unless the author's preference is known to be otherwise, when citing British names that include particles keep the particle with the surname only if it is capitalized. For foreign names follow the correct usage for the language or person in question:

De Long, George Washington   Goethe, Johann Wolfgang von
Musset, Alfred de

Titular prefixes (*Sir, Revd, Dr, Captain*, etc.) are not needed unless their removal would mislead:

Wood, Mrs Henry, *East Lynne*, 3 vols (London, 1861).

Standard Oxford style is for all names that precede the main title to be given in full and small capitals:

JOHN OF SALISBURY, *Historia Pontificalis*, ed. Marjorie Chibnall (Oxford, 1986).

Two or more authors

With two or three authors (or editors), cite in the order that appears on the title page. Either the first cited name only, or all names before the title, may be inverted so that the surname appears first. Whichever style is chosen must be applied consistently:

King, Roy D., and Morgan, Rodney, *A Taste of Prison* (London, 1976).
King, Roy D., and Rodney Morgan, *A Taste of Prison* (London, 1976).

When there are four or more authors, works in the humanities usually cite the first name followed by 'and others', or 'et al.' (from Latin *et alii* 'and others', though note that 'et al.' generally appears in roman type):

Stewart, Rosemary, and others, eds, *Managing in Britain* (London, 1994).

In some scientific journals, where it is not unusual for several names to be identified with an article or paper, the policy can be to cite up to six or seven authors before reducing the list to a single name and 'and others'.

Pseudonyms

Cite works published under a pseudonym that is an author's literary name under that pseudonym:

> Eliot, George, *Middlemarch* (New York, 1977).
> Twain, Mark, *A Connecticut Yankee at King Arthur's Court* (Harmondsworth, 1971).

In some contexts it may be useful to add a writer's pseudonym for clarification when a writer publishes under his or her real name:

> Dodgson, C. L. [Lewis Carroll], *Symbolic Logic* (Oxford, 1896).

Conversely, an author known by his or her real name may need to be identified when he or she occasionally publishes under a pseudonym:

> Afferbeck Lauder [Alistair Morrison], *Let Stalk Strine* (Sydney, 1965).

If the bibliography contains works under the author's true name as well as a pseudonym, the alternative names may be included in both cases to expose the identification:

> Coulange, P. [J. Turmel], *The Life of the Devil*, tr. S. H. Guest (London, 1929).
> Turmel, J. [P. Coulange], 'Histoire de l'angélologie du temps apostolique à la fin du Vᵉ siècle', *Revue d'Histoire et de Littérature Religieuse*, iii (1898), 299–308, 407–34, 533–52.

Anonymous

For texts where the author is not known, in bibliography citations *Anon.* or *Anonymous* may be used, with like works alphabetized accordingly:

> Anon., *Stories after Nature* (London, 1822).

Do not use *Anon.* for note citations; simply start the citation with the title:

> *Stories after Nature* (London, 1822).

If the author's name is not supplied by the book but is known from other sources, the name may be cited in square brackets:

> [Balfour, James], *Philosophical Essays* (Edinburgh, 1768).
> [Gibbon, John], *Day-Fatality, or, Some Observations on Days Lucky and Unlucky* (London, 1678; rev. edn 1686).

18.2.3 Editors, translators, and revisers

In books comprising the edited works of a number of authors, or a collection of documents, essays, congress reports, etc., the editor's name appears first followed by *ed.* (standing for 'editor'; plural *eds* or *eds.*) before the book title:

> Dibdin, Michael, ed., *The Picador Book of Crime Writing* (London, 1993).
>
> Ashworth, A., 'Belief, Intent, and Criminal Liability', in J. Eekelaar and J. Bell, eds., *Oxford Essays in Jurisprudence*, 3rd ser. (1987), 6–25.
>
> Bucknell, Katherine, and Nicholas Jenkins, eds, *W. H. Auden, 'The Map of All My Youth': Early Works, Friends, and Influences* (Oxford, 1990).

Some styles, including Oxford, insert 'ed.' and 'eds' within parentheses:

> SAMPSON, RODNEY (ed.), *Early Romance Texts: An Anthology* (Cambridge, 1980).

Editors of literary texts (or of another author's papers) are cited after the title; in this case *ed.* (standing for 'edited by') remains unchanged even if there is more than one editor:

> Hume, David, *A Treatise of Human Nature*, ed. David Fate Norton and Mary J. Norton (Oxford, 2000).

For note citations, when an author is responsible for the content of the work but not the title (for example letters collected together posthumously), and the author's name appears as part of that title, there is no need to repeat the author's name at the start of the citation:

> *The Letters of Percy Bysshe Shelley*, ed. F. L. Jones (Oxford, 1964).

rather than

> Shelley, Percy Bysshe, *The Letters of Percy Bysshe Shelley*, ed. F. L. Jones (Oxford, 1964).

As with editors, translators and revisers are named after the title and are introduced respectively by *tr.* or *trans.* ('translated by'), *rev.* ('revised by'):

> Albert Schweitzer, *The Quest of the Historical Jesus*, tr. William Montgomery (n.p., 1910).

Translators or revisers whose contribution is sufficiently substantial for them to count as joint authors are named after the original author.

18.2.4 Organization as author

In the absence of an author or editor, an organization acting in the role of author can be treated as such. Do not use *ed.* or *tr.* in these instances:

Amnesty International, *Prisoners Without a Voice: Asylum Seekers in the United Kingdom* (London, 1995).

18.2.5 Titles and subtitles

In general the treatment of titles in bibliography matches that of work titles mentioned in text (see Chapter 8). Always take the title from the title page of the work being cited, not the dust jacket or the cover of a paperback edition, and never alter spelling in order to conform to house style. Punctuation in long titles may be lightly edited for the sake of clarity.

Consider truncating long and superfluous subtitles, but not if that would significantly narrow the implied scope of a work. Subtitles are often identified as such on the title page by a line break or a change in font or font size; in a bibliography a subtitle is always divided from the title by a colon.

Capitalization

In most bibliographic styles traditional capitalization rules are applied to titles (see 8.2.3). In practice the choice between upper and lower case is usually instinctive, and unless the exact form is of bibliographic or semantic relevance your primary guide should be to style a title sensibly and consistently throughout a work.

> *The Importance of Being Earnest: A Trivial Comedy for Serious People*
> *Twenty Years After*
> *Moby-Dick, or, The Whale*

Capitalization of foreign titles follows the rules of the language (see Chapter 12); however, the treatment of the first word of a title, subtitle, or parallel title conforms to the style used for English-language titles.

Titles within titles

Titles within titles may be identified by quotation marks. Always capitalize the first word of the nested title; this capitalized word is regarded in some styles as sufficient to identify the subsidiary work:

> Grigg, John, *The History of 'The Times'*, vi (1993).
> O'Conor, Roderick, *A Sentimental Journey through 'Finnegans Wake', with a Map of the Liffey* (Dublin, 1977).
> Grigg, John, *The History of The Times*, vi (1993).

The convention of using roman instead of italic to identify nested titles is established but not recommended; see 7.6. For a further discussion of titles within titles see 8.2.8.

Foreign-language titles

Works should be cited in the form in which they were consulted by the author of the publication that cites them. If the work was consulted in the original foreign-language form, that should be cited as the primary reference; a published English translation may be added to the citation if that is deemed likely to be helpful to the reader:

> J. Tschichold: *Typographische Gestaltung* (Basle, 1955); Eng. trans. as *Asymmetric Typography* (London, 1967).

Conversely, if a work was consulted in translation, that form should be cited; the original publication may also be included in the citation if that would be helpful (as it will be if the two forms of the title differ significantly):

> R. Metz, *A Hundred Years of British Philosophy*, ed. J. H. Muirhead, trans. J. W. Harvey (1938) [Ger. orig., *Die philosophischen Strömungen der Gegenwart in Grossbritannien* (1935)]

When it is helpful to include a translation of a foreign-language title for information, the translation follows immediately after the title in roman, within square brackets. Translations of this kind are not maximally capitalized:

> Nissan Motor Corporation, *Nissan Jidosha 30nen shi* [A 30-year history of Nissan Motors] (1965).

18.2.6 Chapters and essays in books

The chapter or essay title, which is generally enclosed in quotation marks and conforms to the surrounding capitalization style, is followed by a comma, the word *in*, and the details of the book. When citing a chapter from a single-author work there is no need to repeat the author's details:

> Ashton, John, 'Dualism', in *Understanding the Fourth Gospel* (Oxford, 1991), 205–37.

The placement of the editor's name remains unaffected:

> Shearman, John, 'The Vatican Stanze: Functions and Decoration', in George Holmes, ed., *Art and Politics in Renaissance Italy: British Academy Lectures* (Oxford, 1993), 185–240.

Quotation marks within chapter titles and essay titles become double
quotation marks:

> Malcolm, Noel, 'The Austrian Invasion and the "Great Migration" of
> the Serbs, 1689–1690', in *Kosovo: A Short History* (London, 1990),
> 139–62.

See 9.2 for more on quotation marks.

If an introduction or foreword has a specific title it can be styled as a
chapter in a book; otherwise use *introduction* or *foreword* as a descriptor, without quotation marks:

> Gill, Roma, introduction in *The Complete Works of Christopher
> Marlow*, 1 (Oxford, 1987; repr. 2001).

18.2.7 Volumes

A multi-volume book is a single work with a set structure. Informing
readers of the number of volumes being cited is a useful convention
that, if followed, must be applied consistently. The number of volumes
is provided before the publication information, using an Arabic
numeral. In references to a specific volume in a set, however, the number is usually styled in lower-case Roman numerals, although this
style may vary: capital or small capital Roman numerals, or Arabic
figures, may also be used.

There are two ways of citing a particular location in a multi-volume
work: the entire work may be cited and the volume and page location
given after the date(s) of publication; or the single relevant volume
may be cited with its own date of publication, followed by the relevant
page reference. Note in the examples below the use of Arabic and
Roman numerals for different purposes:

> Edmond Vander Straeten, *La Musique aux Pays-Bas avant le XIXe
> siècle*, 8 vols (Brussels, 1867–88), ii, 367–8.
> Edmond Vander Straeten, *La Musique aux Pays-Bas avant le XIXe
> siècle*, ii (Brussels, 1872), 367–8.

When the volumes of a multi-volume work have different titles, the
form is:

> Glorieux, P., *Aux origines de la Sorbonne*, i: *Robert de Sorbon* (Paris,
> 1966).
> Ward, A. W. and A. E. Waller, eds, *The Cambridge History of English
> Literature*, xii: *The Nineteenth Century* (Cambridge, 1932), 43–56.

If only the volume title appears on the title page the overall title should still be included, either as directed above or within square brackets after the volume title:

> David Hackett Fischer, *Albion's Seed: Four British Folkways in America* [vol. i of *America: A Cultural History*] (New York, 1989).

18.2.8 Series title

A series is a (possibly open-ended) collection of individual works. In book citations, a series title is optional but useful information. It always appears in roman type, fully capitalized, and before or within the parentheses that hold publication information. Most, but not all, series are numbered; the volume numbers in the series should follow the series title:

> Stones, E. L. G., ed. and tr., *Anglo-Scottish Relations, 1174–1328: Some Selected Documents*, Oxford Medieval Texts (Oxford, 1970).
>
> Dodgdon, J. McN., *The Place-Names of Gloucestershire*, 4 vols, English Place-Name Society, 38–41 (1964–5).

18.2.9 Place of publication

Publication details, including the place of publication, are usually inserted within parentheses. The place of publication should normally be given in its modern form, using the English form where one exists:

> The Hague (*not* Den Haag)   Munich (*not* München)
> Turin (*not* Torino)

Where no place of publication is given *n.p.* ('no place') may be used instead:

> Marchetto of Padua, *Pomerium*, ed. Giuseppe Vecchi (n.p., 1961).

It is sufficient to cite only the first city named by the publisher on the title page. While other cities from which that imprint can originate may also be listed there, it is the custom for publishers to put in first place the branch responsible for originating the book. (For example, an OUP book published in Oxford may have *Oxford · New York*; one published in New York reverses this order.)

18.2.10 Publisher

The publisher's name is not generally regarded as essential informa-tion, but it may be included if desired; in the interests of consistency

give names of all publishers or none at all. The preferred order is place
of publication, publisher, and date, presented in parentheses thus:

> (Oxford: Oxford University Press, 2005)

Publishers' names may be reduced to the shortest intelligible unit
without shortening words (for example, *Teubner* instead of *Druck
und Verlag von B. G. Teubner*), and terms such as *Ltd*, *& Co.*, and
plc can be omitted. University presses whose names derive from their
location can be abbreviated (*Oxford: OUP*; *Cambridge: CUP*; etc.),
providing this is done consistently.

18.2.11 **Date**

The use of parentheses around a date in a bibliographic citation implies publication. See 18.4 and 18.6 for dates of unpublished works.
Always cite the date of the edition that has been consulted. This date is
usually found on the title page or the copyright page; for older books it
may appear only in the colophon, a publishing device added to the last
page of the book. Dates given in Roman numerals should be rendered
into Arabic numerals.

When no date of publication is listed, use the latest copyright date.
When multiple dates are given ignore the dates of later printings and
impressions, but when using a new or revised edition use that date. If
no date can be found at all, use *n.d.* ('no date') instead. Alternatively, if
the date is known from other sources, it can be supplied in square
brackets:

> C. F. Schreiber, *A Note on Faust Translations* (n.d. [*c.*1930])

Works published over a period of time require a date range:

> Asloan, John, *The Asloan Manuscript*, ed. William A. Craigie, 2 vols
> (Edinburgh, 1923–5).

When the book or edition is still in progress, an open-ended date is
indicated by an en rule:

> W. Schneemelcher, *Bibliographia Patristica* (Berlin, 1959–).

Cite a book that is to be published in the future as 'forthcoming'.

18.2.12 **Editions**

When citing an edition later than the first it is necessary to include
some extra publication information, which is usually found either on

the title page or in the colophon. This may be an edition number, such as *2nd edn*, or something more descriptive (*rev. edn, rev. and enl. edn*).

Placement

As a general rule, edition details should appear within parentheses, in front of any other publication information:

> Baker, J. H., *An Introduction to English Legal History* (3rd edn, 1990).
> Denniston, J. D., *The Greek Particles* (2nd edn, Oxford, 1954).

When the edition being cited is singularly identified with a named editor, translator, or reviser the editor's name appears at the head of the citation; the edition number directly follows the title and is not placed inside the parentheses that contain the publication details. This establishes that earlier editions are not associated with that editor:

> Knowles, Elizabeth, ed., *The Oxford Dictionary of Quotations*, 5th edn (Oxford, 1999).

Citing more than one edition

Sometimes it is useful to include details of more than one edition. When this information is limited to publication details (edition, date and place of publication, and publisher) the information can remain within a single set of parentheses. When more information is needed (e.g. when a later edition has a different title and editor) it is clearer to close off the parentheses, insert a semi-colon, and continue:

> Denniston, J. D., *The Greek Particles* (1934; 2nd edn, Oxford, 1954).
> Denniston, J. D., *The Greek Particles* (Oxford, 1934; citations from 2nd edn, 1954).
> Berkenhout, John, *Outlines of the Natural History of Great Britain*, 3 vols (London, 1769–72); rev. edn, as *A Synopsis of the Natural History of Great Britain*, 2 vols (London, 1789).

18.2.13 Reprints, reprint editions, and facsimiles

Reprint and facsimile editions are generally unchanged reproductions of the original book, perhaps with an added preface or index. It is always good practice to include the publication details of the original, especially the publication date if a significant period of time has elapsed between the edition and its reprint.

If the reprint has the same place of publication and publisher details as the original, these need not (though they may) be repeated. Best

practice is to arrange the citation so that a reading from left to right
follows the chronology of the work:

> Gibbon, Edward, *Decline and Fall of the Roman Empire*, with
> introduction by Christopher Dawson, 6 vols (London, 1910; repr.
> 1974).
>
> Allen, E., *A Knack to Know a Knave* (London, 1594; facs. edn, Oxford:
> Malone Society Reprints, 1963).
>
> Joachim of Fiore, *Psalterium decem cordarum* (Venice, 1527; facs.
> edn, Frankfurt am Main, 1965).
>
> Smith, Eliza, *The Compleat Housewife, or, Accomplished
> Gentlewoman's Companion* (16th edn, London, 1758; facs. edn,
> London, 1994).

Reprints that include revisions can be described as such:

> Southern, R. W., *Saint Anselm: A Portrait in a Landscape* (rev. repr.,
> Cambridge, 1991).

Title change

A changed title should be included: the parentheses that hold details
of the original publication are closed off and the reprint is described
after a semicolon in the same fashion as for a later edition with an
altered title (see above):

> Hare, Cyril, *When the Wind Blows* (London, 1949); repr. as *The Wind
> Blows Death* (London, 1987).
>
> Lower, Richard, *Diatribæ Thomæ Willisii Doct. Med. & Profess.
> Oxon. De febribus Vindicatio adversus Edmundum De Meara
> Ormoniensem Hibernum M.D.* (London, 1665); facs. edn with
> introduction, ed. and tr. Kenneth Dewhurst, as *Richard Lower's
> 'Vindicatio': A Defence of the Experimental Method* (Oxford, 1983).

18.2.14 Translations

In a citation of a work in translation, the original author's name comes
first and the translator's name after the title, prefixed by 'tr.' or 'trans.':

> Bischoff, Bernhard, *Latin Palaeography: Antiquity and the Middle
> Ages*, tr. Dáibhí Ó Cróinín and David Ganz (Cambridge, 1990).
>
> Martorell, Joanat, *Tirant lo Blanc*, tr. with foreword by David H.
> Rosenthal (London, 1984).

Details of the original edition may also be cited:

> José Sarrau, *Tapas y aperitivos* (Madrid, 1975); tr. Francesca
> Piemonte Slesinger as *Tapas and Appetizers* (New York, 1987).

18.3 Articles in periodicals

18.3.1 Introduction

A complete periodical citation requires author or editor details that relate to the article being cited, the article title, the journal title, volume information, date, and page range:

> Schutte, Anne Jacobson, 'Irene di Spilimbergo: The Image of a Creative Woman in Late Renaissance Italy', *Renaissance Quarterly*, 44 (1991), 42–61.

Authors' and editors' names in periodical citations are treated the same as those for books.

18.3.2 Article titles

Titles of articles—whether English or foreign—are usually given in roman within single quotation marks; in some academic works quotation marks are omitted altogether. Quotation marks within quoted matter become double quotation marks:

> Halil Inalcik, 'Comments on "Sultanism": Max Weber's Typification of the Ottoman Polity', *Princeton Papers in Near Eastern Studies*, 1 (1992), 49–72.
>
> Pollard, A. F. 'The Authenticity of the "Lords' Journals" in the Sixteenth Century', *Transactions of the Royal Historical Society*, 3rd ser., 8 (1914), 17–39.

Titles of journals, magazines, and newspapers appear in italic with maximal capitalization, regardless of language. If the title starts with a definite article this can be omitted, except when the title consists of the word *The* and only one other word:

> Downing, Taylor and Andrew Johnston, 'The Spitfire Legend', *History Today*, 50/9 (2000), 19–25.
>
> Drucker, Peter, 'Really Reinventing Government', *Atlantic Monthly*, 275/2 (1995), 49–61.
>
> Greeley, A. W., 'Will They Reach the Pole?', *McClure's Magazine*, 3/1 (1894), 39–44.
>
> Henry James, 'Miss Braddon', *The Nation* (9 Nov. 1865).

See also 8.2.7.

18.3.3 Periodical volume numbers

Volume numbers are usually styled as Arabic numerals, but whatever you choose must be applied consistently: do not follow what is used by the journal itself.

Volumes usually span one academic or calendar year, but may occasionally cover a longer period of time. When a volume is published in issues or parts, some journals will separately paginate each issue, so that each new issue starts at page 1. Other publications paginate continuously through each volume, so that the first page number of a new issue continues from where the preceding issue left off. It is important to include issue numbers when citing separately paginated journals, because volume number and page number alone will not adequately guide a researcher to the appropriate location within the journal run. Although issue numbers are superfluous with continuously paginated journals, best practice is to include issue numbers nevertheless: the information is not in error, the citation remains consistent with neighbouring journal citations, and in formulating the citation there is no need for you to determine which pagination system the journal follows at any given time (some journals switch from one system to another over the history of their publication).

Part or issue numbers follow the volume number after a solidus:

> Neale, Steve, 'Masculinity as Spectacle', *Screen*, 24/6 (1983), 2–12.
> Garvin, David A., 'Japanese Quality Management', *Columbia Journal of World Business*, 19/3 (1984), 3–12.

Magazines and newspapers are often identified (and catalogued) by their date, rather than a volume number:

> Lee, Alan, 'England Haunted by Familiar Failings', *The Times* (23 June 1995).
> Putterman, Seth J., 'Sonoluminescence: Sound into Light', *Scientific American* (Feb. 1995), 32–7.

Some publishing houses prefer to distinguish magazine and newspaper publications from academic journals by not inserting the date between parentheses:

> Blackburn, Roderic H., 'Historic Towns: Restorations in the Dutch Settlement of Kinderhook', *Antiques*, Dec. 1972, 1068–72.

Always follow the form used on the periodical itself: if the issue is designated *Fall*, do not change this to *Autumn*, nor attempt to adjust the season for the benefit of readers in another hemisphere, as the season forms part of the work's description and is not an ad hoc designation.

Series

Where there are several series of a journal the series information should appear before the volume number:

Moody, T. W., 'Michael Davitt and the British Labour Movement, 1882–1906', *Transactions of the Royal Historical Society*, 5th ser., 3 (1953), 53–76.

New series can be abbreviated either to 'new ser.' or NS in small capitals. Avoid OS, which can mean either 'original' or 'old' series:

Barnes, J., 'Homonymy in Aristotle and Speusippus', *Classical Quarterly*, new ser., 21 (1971), 65–80.
Barnes, J., 'Homonymy in Aristotle and Speusippus', *Classical Quarterly*, NS 21 (1971), 65–80.

18.3.4 **Page numbers**

As with chapters and essays in books, it is customary to end the citation with a page range showing the extent of a periodical article. This is particularly important when a through-paginated journal is cited without issue numbers, as it aids the reader in finding the article in a volume that has no single contents page. The page extent is also useful as an indicator of the scale and importance of the article.

18.3.5 **Reviews**

Reviews are listed under the name of the reviewer; the place of publication and date of the book reviewed are helpful but not mandatory:

Ames-Lewis, F., review of Ronald Lightbown, *Mantegna* (Oxford, 1986), in *Renaissance Studies*, 1 (1987), 273–9.

If the review has a different title, cite that, followed by the name of the author and title of the book reviewed:

Porter, Roy, 'Lion of the Laboratory', review of Gerald L. Geison, *The Private Science of Louis Pasteur* (Princeton, 1995), in *TLS* (16 June 1995), 3–4.

18.4 Theses and dissertations

Citations of theses and dissertations should include the degree for which they were submitted, and the full name of the institution as indicated on the title page. Titles should be printed in roman within single quotation marks. The terms *dissertation* and *thesis*, as well as *DPhil* and *PhD*, are not interchangeable; use whichever appears on the title page of the work itself. The date should be that of submission; it should preferably not be placed within parentheses:

Hill, Daniel, 'Divinity and Maximal Greatness', PhD thesis, King's
College, London, 2001.

Universities and institutions must always be cited using their full,
official form, so as to avoid potential confusion between similar-
sounding names (for example *Washington University* and *University of Washington*).

18.5 Citations to support author–date referencing

The foregoing sections have presented bibliographic citations in the
form used in general and academic humanities publishing. As explained in 18.1.1 and in Chapter 17, where the author–date referencing
method is in use bibliographic citations are reconfigured so that the
publication date appears at the head after the author's name (this is
the formula that the reader, trying to trace a work referenced in the
text, will seek):

Lakoff, R. (1975). *Language and Women's Place*. New York: Harper
and Row.

A reference list in this system is ordered:

- alphabetically by author (for complications where multiple authors
  are named see 18.1.3)
- multiple works by a single author (or by the same combination of
  authors) are ordered chronologically by year of publication
- multiple works published in the same year are ordered
  alphabetically by title, ignoring definite and indefinite articles.

Author–date references in the text must be able to identify each work
uniquely by means of the author's surname and date of publication
alone. Where more than one work by a particular author or authors is
published in a single year, it follows that some further identifier is
needed to distinguish them. In this case the dates of publication are
supplemented by lower-case letters, which are used in the in-text references:

Lyons, J. (1981a), *Language and Linguistics: An Introduction*
(Cambridge: Cambridge University Press).
—— (1981b), *Language, Meaning and Context* (London: Fontana
Paperbacks).

18.6 Manuscript and other documentary sources

18.6.1 Introduction

Conventions for citing manuscripts and archival material are less well established than those for published works, partly because it is often necessary to formulate citations in a way that addresses the qualities and subject matter of the particular material at hand. When establishing how best to order and describe manuscript sources ensure that each citation:

- is consistent with others of the same kind
- conforms with the basic bibliographical principles that control the ordering of elements for citing published matter (authors are cited before titles, and titles before dates)
- includes the repository where the manuscript is stored, and, if possible, a shelf mark, piece number, or other unique identifier that allows the manuscript to be located within that repository.

The different elements that constitute a manuscript citation will normally fall into one of two categories:

- details that *describe* the item (author, title and/or descriptor, and date)
- details that *locate* the item (name and location of repository, collection name and/or shelf mark, page or folio number(s)).

Treat author details as for book details (see 18.2.2.).

18.6.2 Titles and descriptors

When a manuscript has a distinct title it should be cited in roman, in single quotes. General descriptors appear in roman only, and usually take a lower-case initial:

> Chaundler, Thomas, 'Collocutiones', Balliol College, Oxford, MS 288.
> exchequer accounts, Dec. 1798, Cheshire Record Office, E311.

Depending on the readership and function of the bibliography, descriptors are not always necessary; sometimes a shelf mark is enough for an informed reader to comprehend the general nature of what is being cited. For example, in a specialist historical text it may be sufficient to provide piece numbers for documents in the Public Record Office without naming the collection to which they belong:

> PRO, FO 363   PRO, SP 16/173, fo. 48

18.6.3 Dates

Dates follow description details and are not enclosed in parentheses:

> Smith, Francis, travel diaries, 1912–17, British Library, Add. MS 23116.
> Bearsden Ladies' Club minutes, 12 June 1949, Bearsden and Milngavie District Libraries, box 19/d.

18.6.4 Repository information

The level of information required to identify the place accurately will depend upon the stylistic conventions of the work in which the citation occurs, the anticipated readership of the publication, and the size and general accessibility of the repository being cited. Repositories of national collections and archives may not require a country or city as part of the address. Some repositories include enough information within their name to render further address details otiose. If one particular repository is to be cited many times, consider creating an abbreviation that can be used in its place, with a key at the top of the bibliography, or group like citations together as a subdivision within the list.

In English-language publications names of repositories are always roman with upper-case initials, regardless of the conventions applied in the language of the country of origin:

> Bibliothèque Municipale, Valenciennes, MS 393
> Biblioteca Nazionale Centrale, Florence, cod. II.II.289

18.6.5 Location details

Any peculiarities of foliation or cataloguing must be faithfully rendered: a unique source is permitted a unique reference, if that is how the archive stores and retrieves it. For archives in non-English-speaking countries, retain in the original language everything— however unfamiliar—except the name of the city. Multiple shelf-mark numbers or other numerical identifiers should not be elided:

> Bodleian Library, Oxford, MS Rawlinson D. 520, fol. 7
> Paris, Bibliothèque Nationale de France, MS fonds français 146
> Koninklijke Bibliotheek, The Hague, handschriften 34C18, 72D32/4

18.7 Audio and audiovisual materials

18.7.1 Introduction

Broadcasts and recordings are often difficult to deal with because no universally accepted form of citation exists. Moreover, the ordering of elements within a citation may differ according to the content of the recording or the purpose for which it is cited: sound recordings, for example, might be best listed under the name of the conductor, the name of the composer, or even the name of the ensemble. As with all citations, sufficient information should be given to enable the reader to understand what type of work it is, and how to find it.

18.7.2 Audio recordings

Essential elements to include are title, recording company and catalogue number, and, if available, date of issue or copyright. Other useful information includes details of performers and composers, specific track information, recording date (especially if significantly different from date of issue), authorship and title of any sleeve notes that accompany the recording, and the exact type of recording (e.g. wax cylinder, 78 rpm, compact disc). The following examples show an appropriate style for presenting such information:

> Carter, Elliott, *The Four String Quartets*, Juilliard String Quartet (Sony S2K 47229, 1991).
> Davis, Miles, and others, 'So What', in *Kind of Blue*, rec. 1959 (Columbia CK 64935, 1997) [CD].
> Vitry, Philippe de, *Philippe de Vitry and the Ars Nova*, Orlando Consort (Amon Ra CD-SAR 49, 1991) [incl. sleeve notes by Daniel Leech-Wilkinson, 'Philippe de Vitry and the 14th-Century Motet'].

Audio recordings that combine different works without a clear single title may require more than one title:

> Dutilleux, Henri, *L'Arbre des songes*, and Peter Maxwell Davies, *Concerto for Violin and Orchestra*, André Previn, cond., Isaac Stern, violin, and Royal Philharmonic Orchestra (CBS MK 42449, 1987).

In recording numbers a hyphen rather than an en rule is the norm. Where a range of such numbers is given they should never be elided:

> Lightnin' Hopkins, *The Complete Aladdin Recordings* (EMI Blues Series CDP-7-96843-2, n.d.) [2-vol. CD set].

18.7.3 **Films and broadcasts**

When citing audiovisual and broadcast media, the three key elements that need to be included are:

- title of the film or programme (italic), or a description of what the item is (roman):

    The Empire Strikes Back   interview with Claire Noon

- broadcasting or production details, including a date: a reader is more likely to approach the producer or distributor than a library to acquire a copy of the cited item

- short description of the medium, unless this is already made clear by the context or a heading within the bibliography.

Depending on the rarity of the cited item, if the work is known to be available from an accessible archive then including repository and location details may be desirable:

> *Casablanca*, Michael Curtiz, dir. (Warner Brothers, 1942) [film].
> *Desert Island Discs*, Sue Lawley with Jan Morris (BBC 4, 16 June 2002) [radio interview].

18.8 Websites and other electronic data

18.8.1 **General principles**

The basic template for citing electronic references might include some, or all, of the following classes of information (not always necessarily in this order):

- author's or editor's name
- title of the article or other subsection used (roman in quotes)
- general title or title of the complete work (italic)
- volume or page numbers (when citing electronic journals that have no volumes the date may be cited here)
- general information, including type of medium (in square brackets)
- date on which the material was created or on which it was published or posted (day month year, in parentheses)
- institution or organization responsible for maintaining or publishing the information (roman, with maximal capitalization)

- address of electronic source (within angle brackets)
- pagination or online equivalent
- date accessed.

Examples are shown below:

> Quint, Barbara, 'One Hour to Midnight: *Tasini* Oral Arguments at the Supreme Court', *Information Today* [online journal], 18/5 (May 2001). <http://www.infotoday.com/newsbreaks/ nb010330-1.htm> accessed 1 July 2001.
>
> *The Bibliographical Society* [website] <http://www.bibsoc.org.uk/> accessed 1 Oct 2004.

Electronic books, journals, magazines, newspapers, and reviews should be treated as much as possible like their print counterparts, with the same style adopted for capitalization, italics, and quotation marks. It is sometimes less straightforward to fit the pertinent information into the categories normally associated with print publications, such as author, title, place and date of publication, and publisher. Aspects such as pagination and publication date may differ between hard-copy and electronic versions, so the reference must make clear which is meant.

Where print versions exist they can—but need not—be cited; similarly, citing electronic versions of printed media is not mandatory. To provide the reader with both does, however, offer all possible options for following up a reference. Authors should always give precedence to the most easily and reliably accessible form: for example, journal references drawn from back issues available on a CD-ROM should be cited with the journal itself as the source rather than the CD-ROM, unless the CD-ROM is the best way to access it (as for particularly old or obscure periodicals). When making citations for references with more than one online source, choose the one that is most likely to be stable and durable.

18.8.2 **Media**

Where the context or content of a citation does not make obvious the format or platform in which the data are held, give additional clarification (typically in square brackets):

> [CD-ROM]   [newsgroup article]   [abstract]

There is no need to add *online* or *available from* to the citation, since this will be apparent from the inclusion of an address.

When citing references to sources accessible only through a fee, subscription, or password (as for many databases, online periodicals, or downloadable electronic books), include the source (typically a URL) and information on how it is accessed.

18.8.3 **Addresses**

Electronic addresses should be inserted within angle brackets < >:

     <http://www.oxfordreference.com>

It is necessary to retain the protocol prefix *http://* in Internet addresses, since other protocols, such as FTP and telnet, exist.

If citing the whole of a document that consists of a series of linked pages, give the highest-level URL; this is most often the contents or home page. Give enough information to allow the reader to navigate to the exact reference. Many sites provide a search facility and regularly archive material; the search function will provide the surest method of reaching the destination.

If citing a long URL is unavoidable, never hyphenate the address at a line break, or at hyphens. Divide URLs only after a solidus or a %; where this is impossible, break the URL *before* a punctuation mark, carrying it over to the following line. Where space allows, setting a URL on a separate line can prevent those of moderate length from being broken.

Time and dates

Up to four dates can be significant in providing a complete citation for an electronic source:

- the date the information was originally **created**, released, or printed; this is of special interest when citing electronic reprints of previously published material

- the date the information was originally **posted** or made available electronically: mainly of relevance when citing large online reference works

- the date the information was **last updated** or revised: rarely required

• the date you last **accessed** the information: always record this and
include it in your citation.

It is rarely necessary to include more than two of the above dates, and
usually the access date, and maybe the last updated date, will suffice.

Internet (World Wide Web) sites

> Strunk, William, *The Elements of Style* (Geneva, NY, 1918; pubd
> online July 1999) <http://www.bartleby.com/141> accessed 14
> Dec 1999.

Online books

> Maury, M. F., *The Physical Geography of the Sea* [online facsimile]
> (Harper: New York, 1855), Making of America digital library
> <http://moa.umdl.umich.edu/cgi/sgml/moa-idx?notisid
> =AFK9140> accessed 1 Sept. 2004.

Online journal articles

> 'University Performance, 2001 League Tables: Firsts and Upper
> Seconds', *Times Higher Education Supplement*, Statistics page
> (published online 31 May 2001) <http://www.thesis.co.uk/
> main.asp> accessed 31 May 2001.

Online databases

Note that, depending upon context, it may not be necessary to include
a URL for a well-known database:

> Gray, J. M., and G. Courtenay, *Youth Cohort Study* [computer file]
> (1988), Colchester: ESRC Data Archive.
> 'United States v. Oakland Cannabis Buyers' Cooperative' [online
> database; 2001 US Supreme Court case], US LEXIS 3518, LEXIS/
> NEXIS, accessed 14 May 2001.

Online reference sources

> Philip Hoehn and Mary Lynette Larsgaard, 'Dictionary of
> Abbreviations and Acronyms in Geographic Information Systems,
> Cartography, and Remote Sensing', UC Berkeley Library <http://
> www.lib.berkeley.edu/EART/abbrev.html> accessed 25 July
> 2001.
> 'Knight Bachelor', *Encyclopaedia Britannica Online* (2002) <http://
> www.britannica.com/eb/article?eu=46863> accessed Nov. 2002.

Personal communications

A wide range of electronic sources are, in practical terms, difficult
or impossible for readers to retrieve from the original source cited.
In this they are akin to personal correspondence, or papers or records

held privately. Email messages are the most frequently cited type of personal communications. Specify the email address and, where necessary, the recipient(s):

Patterson, Deborah, 'Revised medical report' [email to Janet Wills] (11 Aug. 2004) <dr.dp@nhs.mailserve.org.uk> accessed 2 Dec. 2004.

CD-ROMs

Morris, Peter and William Wood, *The Oxford Textbook of Surgery*, 2nd edn [Windows CD-ROM] (Oxford: OUP, 2001).

CHAPTER 19

Indexing

19.1 Introduction

A good index enables the user to navigate sensibly through the work's main topics and facts. How long it need be to accomplish this depends on the size and complexity of the work and the requirements and expectations of the readership. In general, a short index for a general book can account for as little as 1 per cent of the text it catalogues, while an exhaustive index for a specialist book can take up as much as 15 per cent. Although extremely short indexes are of limited use to a reader, it does not necessarily follow that a long index is better than a short one; those preparing an index should familiarize themselves with the indexes of related works in the field, and consult their editors regarding an agreed length.

Since an index normally requires proof pages before it can be started, it is chronologically one of the last publishing stages involving the author. The index is nevertheless a vital component of the work, and one that directly affects the text's usefulness for the reader. This chapter provides some general guidance on producing and checking an index. In many cases an author will be responsible for producing the index; however, professional indexers are available for this purpose, who are skilled at choosing, compiling, and ordering an index's content and should certainly be considered for a large or important work.

An index's intricate structure and unintuitive content mean that errors introduced during typesetting are comparatively easy to make and difficult to catch; consequently, indexes should be submitted electronically where possible, to enable direct setting from the file.

19.2 What to index

19.2.1 General principles

The indexer's job is to identify and analyse concepts treated in the text so as to produce a series of headings based on its terminology; to indicate relationships between concepts; to group together information that is scattered in the text; and to synthesize headings and subheadings into entries. All items of significance (names, places, concepts) should be entered, with correct page numbers and spelling. The needs of the user of the index should always be kept in mind, particularly in terms of what and where things will be sought: for example, in all but the most technical books an entry for *humankind* or *mankind* will be more helpful than one for *homo sapiens*.

Usually a single index will suffice: subsidiary indexes should not be provided without good reason, or without being agreed with the editor beforehand.

Indexes are made up of individual **entries**, each comprising a **headword** and some indication of where that word may be found in the text, by way of either one or more references (to a page, section, clause, or some other division) or a cross-reference to another headword. Entries complicated enough to require further division may have **subentries**; the entries within which they fall are sometimes called **main entries** to distinguish them. In all but the most complex indexes, subentries within subentries (sub-subentries) should be avoided; if they are used, however, they should occur with relative frequency.

In some works it is desirable to highlight those references which include the principal discussion of a headword, and this is usually indicated by the use of bold type:

> miners **245–7**, 257, 346

Editors of multi-author works must ensure as far as possible that contributors' terminology and sources have been standardized to a single form throughout a work: the index may otherwise require frequent cross-references to guide the reader between variants.

19.2.2 Main entries

Main entries are those most likely to be first sought by the reader, and should be in a form that anticipates where the reader will look for them. They should be concise, and consist of nouns modified if necessary by adjectives, verbs, or other nouns; unless house style dictates otherwise, they should start with a capital letter only if the word is capitalized in the text. Choose either the singular or plural form of a word if both are found in the text, though where unavoidable both can be accommodated through parentheses: *cake(s)*. If singular and plural forms have different meanings, both forms may be used in the index.

Ignore passing or minor references that give no information about the topic. Do not include entries from the preface, contents, introduction, and other preliminary matter unless they contain information not found elsewhere that is relevant to the subject of the work. There is no need to index bibliographies or reference lists. There is usually no need to augment an entry's heading with supplementary information from the text, though in some cases a gloss or other clarification in parentheses may prove necessary.

Use cross-references or subentries where a single reference spans ten or more pages, or where lengthy strings of page numbers threaten to clutter the layout. An array of unqualified or undifferentiated page numbers several lines deep is tiresome and unhelpful to users, who will have to spend too much time trying to locate the information they seek. Any string should ideally be reduced to six or fewer numbers. For example,

> habitat loss 83–5, 100–7, 114–16, 117–18, 121–2, 125–9

can be broken down into:

> habitat loss:
>   from development 83–5, 100–7
>   from erosion 125–9
>   from logging 114–16
>   in Asia 117–18
>   in England 121–2

If it is necessary to create main entries that echo the title or subtitle of the book, ensure that these are succinct. In biographies or collections of letters, keep subentries relating to the subject to a reasonable minimum, confining them to factors of relevance.

19.2.3 Subentries

Subentries are used chiefly to analyse a complex subject heading made up of two or more discrete categories:

life:
    beginnings of 2, 98
    DNA's role in 5–7, 10, 12–13
    and inorganic matter 7, 10, 28–9, 48
    as process, not substance 10, 11
    understanding 240–1

Run together a simple heading with no general page references and only one category:

life, beginnings of 2, 98

Sub-subentries can most effectively be bypassed by denesting the subentry containing the sub-subentry into a separate main entry of its own, cross-referring to it as necessary. For example, in the following

moorlands:
    enclosure 198, 200, 201
    industries 201, 205
        charcoal-burning 197
        coalmining 201
        tin-mining 197
    roads 201

the subentry *industries* under *moorlands* can be changed to a cross-reference '*see also* industries', leading to a headword entry with subentries of its own.

It may not always be possible, or practical, to use subentries and sub-subentries to avoid long strings of page numbers in an exhaustive index—such as one containing numerous references to authors of cited publications, a separate index of authors, or an index of musical works.

An index is not intended to be an outline of the entire text: there should not be a subentry for every page number, and a list of sub-entries all with the same page number should be condensed.

19.2.4 Notes

Notes should be indexed only if they give information not found elsewhere in the text. When there is a reference to a topic and a footnote to that topic on the same page, it is usually sufficient to index the text reference only. See 19.6.

19.2.5 **Cross-references**

Cross-references are used to deal with such things as synonyms, near-synonyms, pseudonyms, abbreviations, variant or historical spellings, and closely related topics; they fall into two classes. The first, introduced by *see*, directs attention from one possible entry to a synonymous or analogous one, under which the references will be found:

Canton, *see* Guangzhou
farming, *see* agriculture
Dodgson, C. L., *see* Carroll, Lewis
Severus, Sextus Julius, *see* Julius Severus

The second, introduced by *see also*, extends the search by directing attention to one or more closely related entries or subentries. Two or more cross-references are given in alphabetical order, separated by semicolons:

birds 21, 88–9; *see also* chickens
clothing 27, 44–6, 105–6; *see also* costume; millinery
housing 134–9, 152; *see also* shelter, varieties of
tread depth 109; *see also* routine maintenance; tyre condition,
indicators

Do not cross-refer to an entry that takes up the same space occupied by the cross-reference itself. In

authors, *see* writers
writers 25, 36–8

the reader would find it easier if the page references were repeated after both headwords (a 'double entry'). Equally, do not cross-refer simply to the same references listed under a different heading, nor bewilder the reader by circular or redundant cross-referring:

authors 25, 36–8, 50; *see also* writers
writers 25, 36–8, 50; *see also* authors

There must be no 'blind' cross-references: in other words, ensure that every cross-reference is to an existing entry. Cross-references to general areas rather than specific headwords are often in italic:

authors, *see under the individual authors*

In addition to inversion of proper names (see 19.3.2), wherever an entry (or subentry) consists of more than one word a decision must be made as to whether another entry in inverse form is also needed. As long as the first word is one that users will look for, the direct form of entry is better:

> right of expression
> secondary education
> trial by jury

If the second and later words in the heading are also words that may be looked for, then additional inverse headings (and cross-references) can be made:

> education, secondary
> expression, right of
> jury trials

Inverse headings are not made automatically for every multiword heading. The selection will depend on the context: for example, the heading *education, secondary* above is not needed if *education* is the subject of the whole text.

Terms such as names of organizations are often referred to in the text in an abbreviated form. The indexer must decide whether to make an entry under the shortened form or at the spelled-out version of the term. It is generally agreed that widely known terms such as UNICEF and NATO can be indexed in their shortened forms without cross-references from the spelled-out forms. However, the indexer will need to decide how much cross-referencing is appropriate for the likely users of the index. It may be helpful to include the full form in parentheses after the shortened version:

> OUP (Oxford University Press)
> Oxford University Press, *see* OUP

A double entry may also be used:

> OUP (Oxford University Press)
> Oxford University Press (OUP)

although if space is an issue a cross-reference is more economical.

19.3 Alphabetical order

19.3.1 Systems of alphabetization

The two systems of alphabetizing entries are **word by word** and **letter by letter**, with minor variations in each. The British Standard (BS ISO 999: 1996) advocates word-by-word indexing, which is the system usually employed in general indexes in Britain. Letter-by-letter indexing is preferred in British encyclopedias, atlases, gazetteers, and some dictionaries, and is more common in the US.

The word-by-word system alphabetizes compound terms (those that consist of more than one word or element) up to the first word space and then begins again, so separated words precede closed compounds (e.g. *high water* comes before *highball*). Hyphens are treated as spaces, and the two parts of a hyphenated compound are treated as separate words, except where the first element is not a word in its own right (e.g. *de-emphasis, iso-osmotic, proto-language*).

In the letter-by-letter system alphabetization proceeds across spaces, with separated (and also hyphenated) words being treated as one word.

In both systems the alphabetization ignores apostrophes, accents and diacritics. Parenthetical descriptions are also ignored: *high* (light-headed) is treated as a simple entry (i.e. as *high* alone would be). Alphabetization continues until a comma indicates inverted order: for instance, *High, J.* is treated as *High* for alphabetization, although if there were several instances of *High*, the form *High, J.* would come after *High* alone and also after *High, B.*; *Bath, order of the* would come before *Bath bun* and *Bath chair*.

In both systems, Oxford style when dealing with entries where the alphabetized term is identical is to order them as follows:

people:	New York, mayor of
places:	New York, US
subjects, concepts, and objects:	New York, population
titles of works:	*New York, New York*

Thus in the example below *High, J.* comes first, as the name of a person. Science-related texts and some dictionaries and directories may reverse the order of these classes, so that lower-case words (things) appear before capitalized words (people):

barrow, long	Barrow, Isaac
bell, Lutine	Bell, Gertrude

It can be argued, however, that many index users will not be aware of these conventions, so it is sometimes considered better to arrange identical entries in normal alphabetical order.

The example below demonstrates alphabetization in the word-by-word and letter-by-letter systems:

Word by word	Letter by letter
High, J.	High, J.
high (light-headed)	high (light-headed)
high chair	highball
high-fliers	highbrow
high heels	high chair
High-Smith, P.	Highclere Castle
high water	high-fliers
High Water (play)	high heels
highball	highlights
highbrow	Highsmith, A.
Highclere Castle	High-Smith, P.
highlights	high water
Highsmith, A.	*High Water* (play)
highways	highways

In both systems, letter groups are treated as one word if—such as
NATO and *NASA*—they are pronounced as such. Otherwise, the
word-by-word system lists all sets of letters before any full word,
ignoring any full points:

Word by word	Letter by letter
I/O	I/O
IOU	iodine
IPA	IOU
i.p.i.	Iowa
IPM	IPA
i.p.s	IP address
IP address	Ipanema
Ipanema	i.p.i.
iodine	IPM
Iowa	i.p.s.

Definite and indefinite articles at the beginning of entries are transposed in both systems:

> *Midsummer Night's Dream, A*
> *Vicar of Wakefield, The*

In works written in English, foreign words are conventionally alphabetized by ignoring accents and diacritics, so for example *ö* and *ø* are
treated as *o*. Some information on alphabetization in languages other
than English is given in Chapter 12.

19.3.2 **Names**

Personal names are generally given in inverted form to bring the significant element (the surname) forward: so *Meynell, Alice* rather than *Alice Meynell*.

Where people bear the same surname, initials are conventionally listed before full names; a name with a title that is otherwise identical with one without should follow it:

Meynell, A.
Meynell, Dr A.
Meynell, Alice
Meynell, F.
Meynell, Sir F.
Meynell, W.
Meynell, W. G.

List names prefixed with *Mc*, *Mac*, or *M^c* as if they were spelled *Mac*:

McCullers
MacFarlane
McFingal
McNamee

Personal names given only by surname in the text require a fuller form in the index, even if mentioned only in passing: *Shepard's illustrations* is therefore expanded to the headword *Shepard, E. H.* Bare surnames should be avoided wherever possible: particularly for specialist subjects an author should anticipate inserting missing names in an index generated by an indexer, or checking for accuracy those the indexer supplies.

Personal names in a single numbered (usually chronological) sequence should be recorded in that sequence in spite of any surnames or other additions. Beware the omission of a number, especially of *I*; if others in the sequence appear duly numbered, restore the number when listing. Hence Frederick Barbarossa should become *Frederick I Barbarossa* and precede Frederick II. Where appropriate—especially for the period before *c.*1300—index people by their given names, with their titles, offices, etc. provided with suitable cross-references. Note again that descriptions in parentheses are disregarded for the purposes of alphabetization:

Henry
Henry (of France), archbishop of Reims
Henry, chaplain

Henry I, count of Champagne
Henry (the Lion), duke of Saxony
Henry, earl of Warwick
Henry II, emperor and king of Germany
Henry IV, emperor and king of Germany
Henry I, king of England
Henry II, king of England
Henry, king of England, the young king
Henry, scribe of Bury St Edmunds
Henry, son of John
Henry de Beaumont, bishop of Bayeux
Henry of Blois, bishop of Winchester
Henry Blund
Henry of Essex
Henry the Little
Henry de Mowbray
Henry Fitz Robert

Treat *St* as if it were spelled *Saint*, for both personal and place names.
In alphabetical arrangement, saints considered in their own right as
historical figures are indexed under their names, the abbreviation *St*
being postponed:

Augustine, St, bishop of Hippo
Margaret, St, queen of Scotland
Rumwald, St, of Kings Sutton

When a place or a church is named after a saint, or the saint's name
complete with prefix is used as a surname, alphabetize it under
the word *Saint* as if spelled out, not under *St*. Thus for example *St
Andrews, Fife, St Peter's, Rome*, and *St John, Olivier* are all treated
as if they were written *Saint* —:

Saint, J. B.
St Andrews, Fife
St Benet's Hall
St James Infirmary
St John-Smythe, Q.
Saint-Julien
St Just-in-Roseland

When the saint's name is in a foreign language, alphabetize its abbreviation under the full form in that language: thus *Ste-Foy* is alphabetized as *Sainte-Foy*.

Foreign names are treated in the form familiar to the reader, so there
is a comma in *Bartók, Béla* even though in Hungarian the surname

comes first. Some information on alphabetizing non-English names is
given at 6.1.8 and 6.1.9.

Alphabetize natural geographical features according to whether the
descriptive component forms part of the name:

  Graian Alps
  Grampians, the
  Granby, Lake
  Granby River
  Gran Canaria
  Grand, North Fork
  Grand, South Fork
  Grand Bérard, Mont
  Grand Canyon
  Grand Rapids
  Grand Ruine, La
  Grand Teton

Always retain the component if it is part of the official name:

  Cape Canaveral
  Cape Cod
  Cape of Good Hope
  Cape Horn

Where confusion may result—in atlases, for example—cross-
references or multiple entries are common.

19.3.3 Scientific terms

If the first character or characters in a chemical compound is a prefix
or numeral, such as O-, s-, cis-, it is ignored for alphabetizing but taken
into account in ordering a group of similar entries. For example, '2,3-
dihydroxybenzene', '2,4-dihydroxybenzene', and 'cis-1,2-dimethyl-
cyclohexane' would all be found under D, and the abbreviation
'(Z,Z)-7,11-HDDA', expanded as 'cis-7,cis-11-hexadecadien-1-yl
acetate', would be alphabetized under H. In chemical notation disre-
gard subscript numerals except when the formulae are otherwise the
same:

  vitamin B_1
  vitamin B_2
  vitamin B_6
  vitamin B_{12}

Greek letters prefixing chemical terms, star names, etc. are customarily spelled out (and any hyphen dropped): for example, α Centauri, α
chain, and α-iron are alphabetized as *Alpha Centauri, alpha (α) chain*,

and *alpha iron*. However, Greek letters beginning the name of a chemical compound are ignored in alphabetization: for example, 'γ-aminobutyric acid' is spelled thus but alphabetized under *A* for *amino*, not *G* for *gamma*.

19.3.4 Symbols and numerals

There are two systems for alphabetizing symbols and numerals: the British Standard advises listing them before the alphabetical sequence, but they are also commonly arranged as if spelled out, alphabetizing '=' as *equals*, '£' as *pounds*, '→' as *implies*, '&' as *ampersand*, '1st' as *first*, and '7' as *seven*. An ampersand *within* an entry is best treated either as if spelled out as *and* or ignored.

Before the alphabetical sequence	As if spelled out
1st Cavalry	1st Cavalry
2/4 time	*42nd Street*
3i plc	3i plc
42nd Street	2/4 time

Where the names of symbols may be problematic, it may be helpful to give an umbrella heading for symbols (for example *rules of inference, linguistic symbols, coding notation*) in addition to alphabetical listings. Whichever system is followed, maintain consistency throughout.

19.3.5 Subentries

Arrangement of subentries should normally be alphabetical by key words (but see 19.4), ignoring leading prepositions, conjunctions, and articles in alphabetical ordering. Ensure that subentries are worded so that they are unambiguous and 'read' from or to the headword in a consistent pattern. Arrange subentries beneath related or similar headwords in parallel. Cross-references given as subentries fall at the end of all other subentries:

    monasticism 20–3, 69, 131, 158, 202
       cathedrals 112
       churches 206
       and mission 89, 90, 94, 134
       reform 112–14
       in Spain 287
       see also ascetism; religious orders

19.4 Non-alphabetical order

Some matter will call for ordering on some basis other than alphabetical, such as numerical, chronological, or hierarchical. Where this matter forms part only of an occasional group of subentries within an otherwise alphabetical index it may be ordered as necessary without comment; however, where a significant amount needs to be included in the form of headwords it should be placed in a separate index where similar elements can be found and compared easily. Never arrange entries or subentries themselves by order of page references, as this is of least help to the reader.

Chronological ordering is useful in arranging entries or subentries, for example arranged according to the life and times of the subject in a biography rather than the order of reference in the work:

> dynasties, early:
>   Legendary Period (prehistoric) 1–33, 66, 178
>   Xia (*c.*2100–1600 BC) 35–60, 120
>   Shang (*c.*1600–*c.*1027 BC) 61–84
>   Zhou (*c.*1027–256 BC) 12, 85–100, 178
>   Quin (221–207 BC) 109–35
>   Han (206 BC–AD 220) 132, 136–7, 141
> Hart, Horace:
>   birth 188
>   apprenticeship 192, 195
>   in London 195–9
>   in Oxford 200, 201–60
>   retirement 261
>   illness and death 208, 277–9

Subjects may sometimes be ordered according to some recognized hierarchical system of classification (e.g. *BA, MA, MPhil, DPhil* or *duke, marquess, earl, viscount, baron*). Indexes of scriptural references are arranged in their traditional order rather than alphabetically.

19.5 Presentation of indexes

19.5.1 **Style**

Index matter is set in small type, one or two sizes down from text size, usually set justified left (ragged right) in two or more columns.

Typically, the running heads are *Index* on both recto and verso, though two or more indexes can be differentiated according to their title, such as *Author index, General index, Index of first lines*.

Begin each entry with a lower-case letter unless it is for a word that is capitalized in the text. Carefully check hyphenation, italics, spelling, and punctuation for consistency with the text. Instructions for cross-referring (*see, see also*) should be italicized. However, 'see' and 'see also' commonly appear in roman when they are followed by italicized text:

> Plutarch's *Lives*, see *Parallel Lives*; *see also* biographies; Dryden
> Poema Morale, see *Selections from Early Middle English*
> *Poetics*, see Aristotle

In Oxford style there is an en space between the entry and the first page number; there is no need to put a comma between them, though formerly this style was commonplace. If an entry end with a numeral (*B-17, Channel 13, M25, uranium 235*), add a colon between it and the page reference. Separate an entry from a following cross-reference with a comma:

> earnings, *see* wages

Separate multiple cross-references from each other with semicolons:

> earnings, *see* income; taxation; wages

There is no punctuation at the end of entries, apart from the colon used after a headword when there are no page numbers but instead a list of subentries:

> earnings:
>   income 12, 14–22, 45
>   taxation 9, 11, 44–9
>   wages 12–21, 48–50

19.5.2 Layout

The first or only index in a work typically begins on a new recto, though subsequent indexes can begin on a new page.

The samples below show the two basic styles of typographic design for indexes, the subentries being either **set out** (or **indented**) or **run on** (or **run in**). The set-out style uses a new (indented) line for each subentry; it is therefore clearer than the run-on style, though it takes up more room. In the set-out style, avoid further subdivision of subentries if possible, as this can result in complicated and space-wasting structures. In the run-on style, subentries do as the name suggests: they run on and are separated from the main entry—and each other—by a semicolon. They are indented appropriately to distinguish them from the heading. Take particular care that the arrangement is logical and consistent, since the style's density makes it more difficult to read.

Set out	Run on

shields 4, 78, 137, 140
  heraldic designs 82
  kite-shaped 199
  round 195
  Viking 43, 44, 53
	shields 4, 78, 137, 140; heraldic
	  designs 82; kite-shaped 199;
	  round 195; Viking 43, 44, 53

ships/shipping 22, 68, 85, 230–52
  design and navigation 6
  pirate 23
  spending on 59
  see also galleys; longships; piracy
	ships/shipping 22, 68, 85, 230–52;
	  design and navigation 6; pirate 23;
	  spending on 59; *see also* galleys;
	  longships; piracy

shipyards 234	shipyards 234

Which style a publisher chooses depends on the length and number of subentries in the final index copy, and the conventions of related works. In any case, index copy must be submitted for setting with all entries and subentries in the set-out form for markup: it is easier for the typesetter to run these on afterwards, if necessary, than it is to set out an index from copy that was presented in the run-on format.

Turn-lines or turnovers (where text runs to more than one line of typescript) should be indented consistently throughout, and in set-out style should be indented more deeply than the deepest subheading indentation. To save space, sub-subentries—where unavoidable—are generally run on even in otherwise set-out indexes.

When an entry breaks across a page—most especially from the bottom of a recto to the top of a verso—the heading or subheading is repeated and a continuation note added during typesetting:

  shields (*cont.*)
  Viking 43, 44, 53

19.6 Number references

In references to pagination and dates, use the smallest number of figures consistent with clarity: see 11.1.4.

Be as specific as possible in your references. For this reason, do not use section or clause numbers instead of page numbers unless they are frequent and the entire index is to be organized that way. Avoid using 'f.' and 'ff.'; give instead the first and last pages of the material: *123–5*, for example, denotes one continuous discussion spanning three pages, whereas *123, 124, 125* denotes three separate short references. Avoid using *passim* ('throughout'). Avoid indexing a whole chapter; where this is impossible, cite the page extent, not *Ch. 11*.

Give references to footnotes and endnotes in the form '*word* 90 n. 17' for one note and '*word* 90 nn. 17, 19' for two or more; each has a full point and a space after the abbreviation. There is no need to give the note number where there is only one note on the page cited; in such cases it is Oxford style to insert a thin space between page number and 'n.' (a thin space also separates the page reference and the abbreviation where 'f.' and 'ff.' are unavoidable).

To provide the most effective help to the reader, a general index serving more than one volume must include the volume number as part of each page reference, regardless of whether the pagination runs through volumes in a single sequence or begins anew with each volume. Volume numbers may be styled in Roman numerals, often in small capitals, separated by a full point: '*word* III. 90'. Indexes to a group of periodicals may have both the series and volume number as part of the page reference.

It is usual to mark figures denoting references to illustrations in italic or bold, or with some typographic symbol (such as an asterisk or dagger), and provide an introductory note at the start of the index in the form *Italic/bold numbers denote reference to illustrations*. Some authors use a similar treatment to flag passages that are particularly significant or include definitions; again, explain this practice at the start of the index.

CHAPTER 20

Copyright and other publishing responsibilities

20.1 Introduction

This chapter is not intended to provide legal advice, but as a general guide to copyright and other related areas, with emphasis on the position in the UK. It should alert readers to matters on which help may need to be sought from their publisher or legal adviser.

20.2 UK copyright

20.2.1 General principles

Copyright is a property right that attaches to an 'original' literary, dramatic, musical, or artistic work: examples of these are books, letters, drawings, book layouts, and computer programs. It arises when a work is created in permanent form such as in writing, or by visual, audio, or electronic means. Copyright belongs to the creator of the work unless the work is made in the course of employment, when it will generally belong to the employer. In the UK the test of 'originality' is low: for example, a train timetable can attract copyright protection. In many other countries, such as France and Germany, a higher degree of originality is generally required for copyright protection, as a copyright work is expected to demonstrate some aspect of the author's 'personality'. Broadly, copyright protects the expression of ideas, not ideas themselves, although the two do converge: for instance, incidents in a story have been protected.

In the UK the Copyright, Designs and Patents Act 1988 ('Copyright Act 1988') established the copyright period for most of types of work to be the life of the author plus fifty years from the end of the year in which the author died. From 1 July 1995 this was increased to the life of the author plus seventy years. Reference books, multi-author works, and other works with no named author are also covered by the Act, and it can be very difficult to establish whether they are still in copyright.

A separate copyright, belonging to the publisher and lasting for twenty-five years from the end of the year of first publication, also exists. This right attaches to the typographical arrangement of a literary, musical, or dramatic work, irrespective of whether the underlying content of the work is still in copyright. This provides the publisher with protection from unauthorized photocopying of the printed page.

As from 1995, a new right akin to copyright was introduced. This right, called 'publication right', arises where a previously unpublished work is first published after the expiry of copyright. It lasts for twenty-five years from the end of the year of first publication.

Copyright confers on its owner the exclusive right to authorize certain acts in relation to their work, including copying, publishing, and adapting. Copyright owners can give third parties the right to use their works by licensing or assigning the work. Licensing means allowing a third party to use the work in a specified way, for example in a certain territory, for a certain length of time, in a specified language, or on a specific medium, or a combination of these. Generally, assigning a work means that the work is permanently given away. Copyright owners will usually only deal with their works in this way in return for financial compensation. This may be a one-off fee or royalties (which are payments linked to sales of the work). Authors' agreements with their publishers often provide that copyright transferred to the publishers revert to the author in certain circumstances, such as if the publisher allows the work to go out of print.

Copyright is infringed if the whole or a substantial part of the work is copied. Although the amount used will be relevant, the test is qualitative rather than quantitative. If the essential element of a work is copied, even if this constitutes only a small part of the work quantitatively, copyright will be infringed.

If an author or editor adapts or adds to a copyright work, and in so doing exercises sufficient skill and care, then a new copyright can arise in the revised work. Nevertheless, if the revised work incorporates a substantial part of the original work without the consent of the copyright owner, copyright in the original work will be infringed.

A joint copyright work is one in which the contributions of two or more authors are commingled. A collective work is one in which the contribution of each author, and initially the copyright for it, is separate from that of the other author(s). One party to a joint copyright cannot alone give consent binding on their co-authors to use a joint work.

Copyright is subject to national frontiers. Different copyright periods apply, and acts of infringement that take place outside the UK are not generally actionable in the UK. As a general rule, proceedings have to be brought in the jurisdiction in question.

20.2.2 Illustrations

Illustrations an author wishes to include, but that are not their own work, are governed by laws similar to those for writing. In the main, the copyright for a painting belongs to the artist, and continues with their heirs or anyone to whom they have transferred their copyright until seventy years after their death. Hence although the owner of the painting may sell it, they may not generally reproduce it without the artist's permission. The same law applies to commissioned works, with copyright belonging to the creator and not the commissioner. Copyright in pictures is quite complex and a specialist picture researcher may be needed to determine what may and may not be done with images. For example, although works of art are on show in a public place and are themselves often out of copyright, permission to reproduce must sometimes be sought from the gallery that owns or displays them. Also, the photographer of a painting can hold their own copyright in the photograph they have taken.

20.2.3 Fair dealing

The Copyright Act 1988 contains a list of various activities which permit substantial parts of a copyright work to be reproduced without the copyright owner's permission, in certain circumstances. Of most relevance to authors and publishers are the various 'fair dealing' exceptions. In general, when reproducing a substantial part of a work using one of these 'defences' sufficient acknowledgement needs to be given. The forms of fair dealing are use for purposes of non-commercial research or private study, or, provided the work has already been made available to the public, fair dealing for the purposes of criticism or review, or of reporting current events. Photographs are excluded from the fair dealing provisions relating to the reporting of current events.

The amount of a work that can be copied within the fair dealing limits varies according to the particular circumstances of the works in question. Issues to take into account include whether the work could be considered by potential purchasers to constitute a substitute for the other work, and the number and extent of the proposed quotations or extracts in the context of the work in which they are to be incorporated. Trade practice may also be relevant. Various guidelines have been issued, for example by the Society of Authors, but these are not legally binding and are by way of general guidance only. As a general rule, copyists must reproduce the minimum necessary to achieve their purposes.

Separate provisions exist for dealing by librarians and for copying for the purposes of educational instruction or examination.

In summary, therefore, there are two steps to determining whether the use of a work infringes the copyright in it. It must be established whether a substantial part of the work has been used. If so, one must consider whether such use constitutes fair dealing.

20.2.4 **Moral rights**

Under the Copyright Act 1988, authors have four basic 'moral rights'; many other countries extend similar 'moral rights' to their authors. The rights apply to works entitled to copyright protection, and ownership of copyright is a separate issue: authors can sell their copyright without affecting their moral rights, which cannot be assigned. (The Act itself gives specific information about when and to whom the rights do and do not apply, and how the right of paternity is asserted in the case of non-literary works.) The rights are:

- **the right of paternity**: the right to be identified as the work's author. This needs to be asserted, as it does not exist automatically; it lasts for the same period as the copyright period.
- **the right of integrity**: the right to protest against treatment that 'amounts to distortion or mutilation of the work or is otherwise

prejudicial to the honour or reputation of the author'. (Thus something done that is prejudicial to the author's honour or reputation will not generally be actionable unless there is *also* some modification to the work itself, although the context in which a work is placed can constitute a 'treatment'.) The right does not need to be asserted, as it exists automatically; it lasts for the same period as the copyright period.

- **the right of false attribution**: the right not to have a literary, dramatic, musical, or artistic work falsely attributed to one as author. This right lasts for twenty years after the person's death.

- **the right of privacy of photographs and films commissioned for private and domestic purposes**.

Many publishers affirm the author's moral rights as a matter of course, usually on the title verso.

The rights of paternity and integrity do not extend to works reporting current events, or to works where an author contributes to a periodical or other collective work of reference. In such cases the work may be trimmed, altered, and edited without the author's approval, subject to the general laws of copyright and any contractual obligations which may be owed to the authors.

20.2.5 Database rights

In the EU a separate right, akin to copyright, which protects databases has existed since 1998. This right, which arises automatically, can exist alongside copyright in a database. Database right arises where a collection of data or other material is created which: (*a*) is arranged in such a way that the items are individually accessible; and (*b*) is the result of a substantial investment in either the obtaining, verification or presentation of the data. Database right is infringed by the extraction and/or re-utilization of the whole or a substantial part of the contents of the database.

Database right lasts for fifteen years from making, but if publication takes place during this time, the term is fifteen years from publication.

20.3 Copyright conventions

Most countries give copyright protection to foreign works under international copyright treaties, such as the Berne and Universal Copyright Conventions referred to below. Anomalies exist in the treatment afforded in different countries, however, for example because the qualification requirements and rules on ownership and duration differ.

20.3.1 **Berne Convention for the Protection of Literary and Artistic Works**

Most industrialized countries are signatories to the Berne Convention, including the UK, the US, and Russia. The Berne Convention does not require registration of copyright and there is no obligation to include a copyright statement or to use the © symbol (although doing so is good practice in any event).

20.3.2 **Universal Copyright Convention**

To claim copyright protection in signatories to the Universal Copyright Convention, the following formality must be complied with: the symbol ©, the name of the copyright owner, and date of first publication must appear in a prominent place in every copy of the work published with the authority of the copyright owner. There is no requirement to register the copyright. Very few countries are parties to the Universal Copyright Convention and not to the Berne Convention, and so in most of the world, to obtain copyright protection this © wording is not required, although, as said above, its use is good practice in any event.

Having said that there is no requirement to register copyright, in some countries, such as the US and China, it can be advisable to do so to avoid potential enforcement problems.

20.4 Permissions

20.4.1 **What needs permission**
As explained above, unless the fair dealing provisions apply the copyright owner's permission needs to be obtained when a substantial part

of a copyright work is to be copied. Such permission may sometimes only be given on payment of a fee. Most publishers expect authors to secure permissions to reproduce any copyrighted work in their text.

There can be no hard-and-fast rules to allow authors to gauge when they have taken a 'substantial part' of a work. As stated above (see 20.2.1), substantiality is a qualitative measure and calculating the arithmetic proportion copied does not assist. An extract may be deemed to be a substantial part of a work, and therefore infringing, even where only a small part of the work have been taken. Careful consideration must always be given to the amount copied from a qualitative viewpoint. For example, one author was found to have infringed the copyright of another when he copied one page from a long book, and a thirty-two-line poem was deemed to have been infringed by the unauthorized use of four lines. If in doubt authors should seek guidance from their editor/publisher.

20.4.2 Requesting permission

In requesting permission, authors should describe the work in which the material is to be included, specifying the author, the title, the publisher, and the type of work, so the copyright owner understands where, and in what circumstances, their material will appear. Authors should give the copyright owner specific information about the work in which the material originally appeared, to aid identification.

Authors should make clear if they are translating, redrawing, or modifying copyright material. Care should be taken to request all the rights needed. Note that the rights for different territories may be separately owned. Also, care needs to be taken when issuing a new edition of a work to check whether the original permissions cover the new edition as well.

Crown copyright publications include Bills and Acts of Parliament, Command Papers, Reports of Select Committees, Hansard, non-parliamentary publications by government departments, naval charts published by the Ministry of Defence, and Ordnance Survey publications. The rules relating to Crown copyright are different from the general rules on copyright. Guidance can be obtained from Her Majesty's Stationery Office.

20.4.3 **Acknowledgements**

This section sets out general industry practice relating to acknowledgements. It applies where the copyright owner does not impose
specific provisions relating to the acknowledgement. For details on
setting out acknowledgements see 1.2.11.

The acknowledgement should identify: (*a*) the author of the work
(remembering that under the fair use provisions, it is the author
who has to be acknowledged, not the copyright owner—who could
be different); and (*b*) the work by its title or other description.

The acknowledgement should be placed where practicable or logical,
given the quantity and variety of material to be acknowledged. When
an entire chapter or section is being reproduced, practice is for it to
appear as an uncued note at the foot of its first page. When a smaller
extract or series of extracts is being reproduced, details are generally
listed in an acknowledgements section, either in the preliminary matter or—especially with anthologies or collections—at the end of the
work.

Acknowledgement of permission to reproduce illustrations, figures,
or tables is generally incorporated in or appended to a list of illustrations, or added to an acknowledgements section in the preliminary
matter of the work. For illustrations, acknowledgements are often set
as part of the caption; for figures and tables they are often set in a
separate note below the caption under the heading *Source*.

General practice is to credit the source, providing the elements in an
acknowledgements format along these lines:

> [author], from [title of copyrighted text] [edition, if other than the first],
> [year of publication], © [copyright proprietor—this can be the author or
> another party]. Reprinted [*or* Reproduced] by permission of [usually a
> publisher or agent].

The publisher's name alone is generally given, without the address,
city, or country. When it is in a foreign language it should not generally be translated, although romanization from a non-Roman
alphabet is usually acceptable. When copyright illustrations are acknowledged, use *reproduced* instead of *reprinted*.

Wording, capitalization, and punctuation can generally be standardized, although not where the copyright holder specifies a particular

form of words for the acknowledgement, or its position. An acknowledgement list may be prefaced by *We are grateful for permission to reproduce the following material in this volume*, to save space and avoid repetition.

As a general rule, permission should be obtained for *all* copyright material in an anthology, regardless of length. The result is usually a separate acknowledgements section, placed either in the preliminary pages or at the end of the book, before the index. Normally an acknowledgement must be in the exact form specified by the copyright holder and not standardized; reprint and copyright years must be given in full where indicated.

In some situations copyright owners cannot be located, despite real efforts having been made to trace and contact them. When this happens the author needs to decide whether to omit the extract or to include it and risk being the subject of a copyright infringement action. If the author chooses to include the extract, a 'disclaimer' at the end of the acknowledgements section should be included, for example:

> There are instances where we have been unable to trace or contact the copyright holder. If notified the publisher will be pleased to rectify any errors or omissions at the earliest opportunity.

It is important to understand that such a disclaimer is not a defence to copyright infringement; if an author chooses to include such material, however, the disclaimer together with the evidence of efforts made to trace and contact the copyright owners may mitigate the adverse consequences if a copyright owner should subsequently object.

20.5 Defamation

A defamatory statement is one that injures the reputation of another person by exposing that person to hatred, contempt, or ridicule, or is disparaging or injurious to that person in their business, or lowers a person in the estimation of right-thinking members of society generally. **Libel** is making a defamatory statement in permanent form (e.g. in writing); **slander** is making a defamatory statement in temporary form (e.g. in speech).

In essence an allegation is defamatory if it is untrue and a person's reputation is damaged by it. The claimant need not be named but must be identifiable. The defamatory statement need not be direct; it may be implied or by way of innuendo. A company has a reputation but can only sue if it can demonstrate that an allegation has resulted in financial loss. However, directors of a company—if named or identifiable—might be able to sue for untrue allegations made against the company, even if no financial loss has been suffered.

The dead cannot be libelled, but care must be taken to ensure that in statements about the dead the living are not defamed by association.

The author's intention is irrelevant in determining whether a statement is defamatory. A defamed person is entitled to plead any meaning for the words used that a 'reasonable' person might infer.

The clearest defence against a defamation action is that the statements can be proved to be true by direct first-hand evidence. It is no defence to a libel action that the defamatory statements have been published previously, although this might affect the level of damages payable.

Criticism or other expressions of opinion can be defended as fair comment provided the subject matter of the comment is one of public interest, the facts underlying the expression of opinion are true, the comment is one which an honest person could hold, and the statement is 'comment' rather than 'fact'.

20.6 Negligent misstatement

If an author makes a statement negligently (without due care) in circumstances where it is likely and reasonable that the reader will place reliance on it, in some, limited, circumstances, the reader could sue the author/publisher. It is not possible to exclude liability for death or personal injury caused by such negligence. It is for this reason that care needs to be taken when, for example, giving information about DIY or other potentially dangerous activities. A publisher will generally require the author to provide warranties in the author contract that any instructions contained in the book are accurate.

20.7 Passing off

'Passing off' occurs where a misrepresentation is made which causes damaging confusion. Passing off in publishing can arise in various different ways. Most disputes involve similar titles—especially series titles where customers may buy individual books on the strength of the series name—or similar jacket design, where books from different publishers have a similar appearance, logo, or brand. More specific examples include giving the impression that a biography has been authorized by its subject, or that a sequel was authorized or written by the author of the original book.

20.8 Trade marks

It is sometimes necessary to refer to a registered trade mark in a work. When referring to a trade mark care should be taken not to give the impression that it is being used with the approval of its owner. A registered trade mark is indicated by the symbol ®; ™ indicates rights that are claimed but not registered.

20.9 The Internet

It is a common misconception that copyright does not apply to material which appears on the Internet. This is untrue: copyright and other laws apply to works put on the Internet as much as printed publications. Hence, copying material from a website can constitute copyright infringement as much as copying material from a book, and the considerations set out earlier in this chapter apply. An added complication of posting to and using material from a website is the issue of jurisdiction: if a work is written in France, posted on to the Internet from a cybercafe in Germany with an ISP based in Ireland, and read by someone in Australia, ascertaining which country's laws apply can be problematic. A detailed analysis of this issue is beyond the scope of this book.

20.10 Blasphemy, obscenity, racial hatred, and official secrets

Publishing a work which contains contemptuous, scandalous, or insulting material relating to the Christian religion is a criminal offence, punishable by a fine or imprisonment. Note that only the Christian religion is covered by this law and that merely attacking Christianity is not blasphemy: the attack would be blasphemous only if it were contemptuous or insulting.

It is also an offence to publish an obscene work. A work is deemed to be obscene if its overall effect is to deprave or corrupt its readers. Lewd or repulsive material is not necessarily obscene: to be obscene the material must constitute a menace to public morals.

By publishing works which could stir up racial hatred publishers could commit another offence. Racial hatred means hatred against groups of people who are defined by their colour, race, nationality, or ethnic or national origins. A work could stir up racial hatred if it contained threatening, abusive, or insulting material, and if there was either an intention to stir up racial hatred or it was likely that the work would do so.

It is also an offence to publish certain types of material if publication could damage national security or interests: cases on this point have related to memoirs by former workers for the Foreign Office or members of the intelligence agencies.

Appendices

Proofreading marks

Below is a list of the most commonly used proofreading marks. See also the British Standard Institution's BS 5261-2: *Copy Preparation and Proof Correction—Part 2* (2005), which may be obtained from the BSI.

Instruction	Mark in text	Mark in margin
Correction is concluded	None	/ or ⅄
Insert matter indicated in the margin	⅄	New matter followed by ⅄
Insert additional matter identified by a letter in a	⅄	Ⓐ⅄; write matter to be inserted at any convenient position on the page, preceded by the corresponding letter Ⓐ
Delete	/ through a single character or ⊢——⊣ through multiple characters to be deleted	♒
Close up and delete space between characters or words	◠ connecting characters	◠
Substitute character(s)	/ through a single character or ⊢——⊣ through multiple characters	New character(s) followed by /
Substitute or insert full point or decimal point	/ through character or ⅄ between characters	⊙/ or ⊙⅄
Substitute or insert colon	/ through character or ⅄ between characters	⊙/ or ⊙⅄
Substitute or insert semicolon	/ through character or ⅄ between characters	;/ or ;⅄
Substitute or insert comma	/ through character or ⅄ between characters	,/ or ,⅄
Substitute or insert solidus (oblique)	/ through character or ⅄ between characters	⊘/ or ⊘⅄

Instruction	Mark in text	Mark in margin
Substitute or insert character in superior (superscript) position	/ through character or ⋏ between characters	⋎ or ⋏ under character, e.g. ⋎ or ⋏
Substitute or insert character in inferior (subscript) position	/ through character or ⋏ between characters	⋏ or ⋏ over character, e.g. ⋏ or ⋏
Substitute or insert opening or closing parenthesis, square bracket, or brace	/ through character or ⋏ between characters	(/) / or (/) / or { / } /
Substitute or insert hyphen	/ through character or ⋏ between characters	⊢⊣ / or ⊢⊣ ⋏
Substitute or insert rule	/ through character or ⋏ between characters	Give the size of rule ⊢1 em⊣ / or ⊢4 mm⊣ ⋏
Set in or change to bold type	∿∿∿ under character(s) to be set or changed	∿∿∿ /
Set in or change to bold italic type	∿∿∿ under character(s) to be set or changed	∿∿∿ /
Set in or change to italic	— under character(s) to be set or changed	⊔ /
Change bold to roman type	Encircle character(s) to be changed	∿∿∿ /
Change bold italic to roman type	Encircle character(s) to be changed	⫫ /
Change italic to roman type	Encircle character(s) to be changed	⊣ /
Set in or change to capital letters	☰ under character(s) to be set or changed	☰ /
Change capital letters to lower-case letters	Encircle character(s) to be changed	≢ /
Set in or change to small capital letters	═ under character(s) to be set or changed	═ /
Set in or change to capital letters for initial letter and small capital letters for the rest of the word	☰ under initial letter and ═ under rest of the word	☰═ /
Change small capital letters to lower-case letters	Encircle character(s) to be changed	≢ /
Start new paragraph	⌐	⌐ /

Instruction	Mark in text	Mark in margin
Run on	⌒	⊃/
Transpose characters or words	⎍ around and between characters or words	⎍/
Transpose lines	⎍ around and between lines	⎍/
Transpose a number of lines	① ② ③ around and between lines	To be used when the sequence cannot be clearly indicated otherwise. Each line to be transposed should be numbered
Invert type	Encircle character to be inverted	⊙/
Centre	⸤/⸥ enclosing matter to be centred	⸤/⸥
Insert or substitute space between characters or words	⋏ between characters or / through characters	Y⋏ or Y/
Reduce space between characters or words	⏉ between characters or words affected	⏉/
Equalize space between characters or words	⏉ between characters or words affected	⋎/
Close up to normal interlinear spacing	(each side of column, linking lines)	⌒/ Linking symbols are placed in the margins
Insert space between lines or paragraphs	⟩– or –⟨ each side of column between lines	Marginal marks extend between lines of text
Reduce space between lines or paragraphs	⟵ or ⟶ each side of column between lines	Marginal marks extend between the lines of text
Take over character(s), word(s), or line to next line, column, or page		Textual mark surrounds matter to be taken over and extends into the margin
Take back character(s), word(s), or line to previous line, column, or page		Textual mark surrounds matter to be taken back and extends into the margin
Insert or substitute em space, en space, thin space, or fixed space	�□ (em), ⊠ (en), ⍭ or ⍖ (thin), ⍬(fixed)	�□/, ⊠/, ⍭⋏, ⍖⋏, ⍬⋏
Indent	⌐	⌐/ (verticals indicate alignment)

Instruction	Mark in text	Mark in margin
Cancel indent	⌐	⌐/ (verticals indicate alignment)
Move matter specified distance to the right	enclosing matter to be moved to the right →	⊏/
Move matter specified distance to the left	← enclosing matter to be moved to the left	⊐/
Correct vertical alignment	‖	‖/
Correct horizontal alignment	Single line above and below misaligned matter, e.g. misaligned	=/
Correction made in error. Leave unchanged	under characters to remain – – – – – – – –	✓/
Remove extraneous mark(s) or replace damaged character(s)	Encircle mark(s) to be removed or character(s) to be changed	✗/
Wrong font. Replace by character(s) of correct font	Encircle character(s) to be changed	✗/
Query something in the text	Encircle word(s) affected	?/

Glossary of printing and publishing terms

accent a mark on a letter that indicates pitch, stress, or vowel quality.

acknowledgements (US **acknowledgments**) a statement at the beginning of a book expressing the author's or publisher's gratitude to others for ideas or assistance or for permission to use copyright material.

afterword a short concluding section in a book, typically written by someone other than the author.

appendix (also **annex**) a section of subsidiary matter at the end of a book or document.

Arabic numeral any of the numerals 0, 1, 2, 3, 4, 5, 6, 7, 8, 9; cf. **Roman numeral**.

artwork 1 illustrations, figures, photographs, or other non-textual material. **2** typeset material supplied to the printer in electronic form.

ascender a part of a letter that extends above the level of the top of an x (as in b and d).

ASCII American Standard Code for Information Interchange, used as a standard format in the transfer of text between computers.

back matter another term for **end matter**.

bibliography a list of books or other texts that are referred to in a work or that contain material of related interest, typically printed as an appendix.

blad a promotional booklet of pages from a forthcoming book.

bleed (of an illustration or design) be printed so that it runs off the page.

block capitals plain capital letters.

block quotation another term for **displayed quotation**.

bold (also **boldface**) a style of type with thick strokes, as **here**.

camera-ready copy material that is in the right form and of good enough quality to be reproduced photographically on to a printing plate.

caption a title or brief explanation accompanying an illustration, in particular one shown beneath or beside the image.

cancel a new page or section inserted in a book to replace the original text.

caret a mark ^, ʌ used to indicate a proposed insertion in a text.

case-bound (also **cased**) (of a book) hardback.

cast-off a typesetter's estimate of the number of pages a given amount of copy will make given the specified design.

catchline an eye-catching line of type, such as a slogan or headline.

collate 1 assemble folded sections of a book in the correct sequence ready for binding. **2** verify the number and order of the sheets of a book. **3** bring together proof corrections from different sources and put all the corrections on to a single master copy of the proof.

colophon a publisher's emblem, usually appearing on the title page of a book.

composition the preparation of a text for printing by setting up characters mechanically or by applying its design and layout electronically.

compositor a person who arranges type or keys material for printing.

copy matter to be printed, in particular the text of the publication in paper form before or after it is marked up by the copy-editor.

copy-edit prepare the text for typesetting by checking its consistency and accuracy and identifying elements requiring special attention during the publishing process.

copyright the exclusive legal right to print, publish, perform, film, or record literary, artistic, or musical material.

copyright page another term for **title page verso**.

corrigenda (singular **corrigendum**) a list of errors in a printed book that is fixed to or printed in the book.

credits acknowledgements expressing gratitude for permission to use images.

CRC short for **camera-ready copy**.

cue a number, letter, or symbol placed in the text to direct the reader to a footnote or endnote.

dele mark (a part of a text) for deletion.

descender a part of a letter that extends below the level of the base of an x (as in g and p).

desktop publishing the production of printed matter by means of a printer linked to a desktop computer.

diacritic an accent or similar sign which is written above, below, or through a letter to indicate pitch, stress, or vowel quality.

digraph 1 a combination of two letters representing one sound, as in ph and ey. **2** another term for **ligature**.

displayed quotation a quotation that is broken off from the text to begin on a new line, often set in smaller type.

drop capital (also **drop initial**) a large capital letter at the beginning of a section of text, occupying more than the depth of one line.

DTP short for **desktop publishing**.

dummy a mock-up of a book or the layout of a page.

duotone a half-tone illustration made from a single original with two different colours.

dust jacket another term for **jacket**.

edition a version of a book at its first publication and at every following publication for which more than minor changes are made.

em a unit for measuring the width of printed matter, originally reckoned as the width of a capital roman M in the typeface in use.

embedded another term for **run on**.

em rule (also **em dash**) a long dash (—).

en a unit of horizontal space equal to half an em and originally reckoned as the width of a capital roman N in the typeface in use.

en rule (also **en dash**) a short dash (–), used in particular to elide ranges of figures.

end matter (also **back matter**) material that supplements the text and is placed after it.

endnote a note printed at the end of a book or section of a book.

endpaper a leaf of paper fixed to the inside of the cover at the beginning or end of a hardback book.

epigraph a quotation placed at the beginning of a volume, part, or chapter.

epilogue an author's short concluding comment on the text.

errata slip (singular **erratum slip**) a list of errors and their corrections inserted in a book.

even working a situation whereby the text of a book fits neatly into the allotted number of pages so that there are no blank pages at the end.

face short for **typeface**.

fascicle (also **fascicule**) a separately published section of a very long book.

figure an illustration (often a diagram or other line drawing) that is integrated into the text.

filmsetting the setting of material to be printed by projecting it on to photographic film from which the printing surface is prepared.

flush aligned with the left- or right-hand edge of the text.

flyleaf a blank page at the beginning or end of a book.

folio 1 an individual leaf of paper, either loose as one of a series or forming part of a bound volume. **2** the page number in a printed book.

font (also **fount**) a set of type of one particular face and size.

footer a running foot.

footnote a note printed at the bottom of a page.

foreword a recommendation of the work written by someone other than the author, printed before the main text.

frontispiece an illustration that faces the title page.

front matter another term for **preliminary matter**.

full out aligned (or 'flush') with the left- or right-hand edge of the text.

galley proof a printer's proof in which the typographic design is applied but the material is not paginated and illustrations, figures, etc. are not in place, traditionally supplied in the form of long single-column strips.

gathering a group of signatures or leaves bound together in the production of a book.

gutter the blank space between facing pages of a book or between adjacent columns of type.

hair space a very thin space between characters, as, for example, between numerals and units of measure.

half-title the first page of the preliminary matter of a book, bearing only the work's title.

half-tone a reproduction of an image in which the various tones of grey or colour are produced by variously sized dots of ink.

hard hyphen an ordinary hyphen that is keyed and appears whether the word containing it is split across the end of a line or not; cf. **soft hyphen**.

header a running head.

heading a title at the head of a page, a section of a book, or a table.

headword a word which begins a separate entry in a reference work.

hot metal an old typesetting technique in which type is newly made each time from molten metal, cast by a composing machine.

HTML Hypertext Markup Language, a standardized system for tagging text files to achieve font, colour, graphic, and hyperlink effects on World Wide Web pages.

imposition the layout on the quad sheet of the pages of a publication so that when the sheet is printed and folded they will fall in the correct order.

impression a particular printed version of a book, especially one reprinted with no or only minor alteration.

imprint the name and other details of a book's publisher.

inferior another term for **subscript**.

ISBN International Standard Book Number.

ISSN International Standard Serial Number.

italic a sloping style of type like *this*.

jacket (also **dust jacket**) a removable paper cover, generally with a decorative design, used to protect a book.

justified (of text) adjusted so as to fill the width of the text area and align at the left and right margins.

kern a part of a printed character that overlaps its neighbours.

kerning adjustment of the spacing between characters in a piece of text.

landscape a format of printed matter which is wider than it is high; cf. **portrait**.

leaders a series of dots or dashes across the page to guide the eye.

leading 1 the amount of blank space between lines of print. **2** the distance from the bottom of one line of type to the bottom of the next.

leaf a single sheet of paper, forming two pages in a book.

legend 1 another term for **caption**. **2** the wording on a map or diagram that explains the symbols used.

letterpress printing from a hard raised image under pressure.

ligature a character consisting of two or more joined letters (e.g. æ, œ, fi, ffl).

line artwork graphic material, such as a map, diagram, or graph, consisting of solid lines or other shapes on a white background, as opposed to a **half-tone**.

linefeed the distance from the bottom of one line of type to the bottom of the next; the leading.

Linotype® an old kind of composing machine producing lines of words as single strips of metal.

lithography printing from a flat surface treated to repel the ink except where it is required for printing.

lower case small letters as opposed to capital letters (**upper case**).

margin the white space around the text area on a page.

markup the process or result of correcting text in preparation for printing.

minuscule of or in lower-case letters.

Monotype® an old kind of typesetting machine which casts type in metal, one character at a time.

moral rights the right of an author or artist to protect the integrity and ownership of their work.

note a piece of explanatory or additional information printed at the end of a section or in the end matter of the publication (**endnote**) or at the foot of the page (**footnote**).

octavo (abbrev. **8vo**) a size of book page that results from folding each printed sheet into eight leaves (sixteen pages).

offprint a printed copy of an individual article or essay that originally appeared as part of a larger publication.

offset a method of printing in which ink is transferred from a plate or stone to a uniform rubber surface and from that to the paper.

opening a double-page spread (see **spread**).

orphan the first line of a paragraph set as the last line of a page or column, considered undesirable.

overmatter material that cannot be accommodated in a work.

Oxford comma another term for **serial comma**.

page proof a printer's proof of a page to be published.

Pantone® a system for matching colours, used in specifying printing inks.

parentheses (also **parens**) round brackets ( ).

PDF Portable Document Format, a file format for capturing and sending electronic documents in exactly the intended format.

pica a unit of type size and line length equal to 12 points (about ⅙ inch or 4.2 mm).

pitch the density of typed or printed characters on a line.

plate 1 a sheet of metal, plastic, etc. bearing an image of type or illustrations from which multiple copies are printed. **2** a photograph or other illustration that is separated from the text, especially one on superior-quality paper.

point a unit of measurement for type sizes and spacing, in the UK and US traditionally 0.351 mm, in Europe 0.376 mm, now standardized as $\frac{1}{72}$ in. (0.356mm).

portrait a format of printed matter which is higher than it is wide; cf. **landscape**.

preliminary matter (also **prelims**) the pages preceding the main text of a book, including the title page, title page verso, contents page, and preface.

preface a section in the preliminary matter where the author sets out the purpose, scope, and content of the book.

proof a trial impression of typeset text, which is checked for errors before final printing.

proofread read proofs, mark any errors, and make a final check of the material.

quad sheet the large sheet of paper that is printed with text and then folded and cut to produce separate leaves.

quarto (abbrev. **4to**) a size of book page resulting from folding each printed sheet into four leaves (eight pages).

ragged right (of text) justified only at the left margin, with the result that the width of lines is variable.

range (with reference to type) align or be aligned, especially at the ends of successive lines.

ream 500 (formerly 480) sheets of paper.

recto the right-hand page of a spread, having an odd page number; cf. **verso**.

register 1 the exact correspondence of the position of colour components in a printed positive. **2** the exact correspondence of the position of printed matter on the two sides of a leaf.

reprint a republication of a book for which no corrections or only minor corrections are made.

roman an upright style of type used for text that requires no special emphasis or distinction.

Roman numeral any of the letters representing numbers in the Roman numerical system (I or i = 1, V or v = 5, X or x = 10, etc.); cf. **Arabic numeral**.

round brackets parentheses ( ).

running head (or **running foot**) a book title, chapter title, or other heading which appears at the top (or bottom) of every page or spread.

running sheets a set of unbound pages that are checked to ensure that the correct order has been achieved.

run on (also **run in**) continued on the same line as the preceding matter, rather than broken off or displayed.

sans serif a style of type without serifs.

serial comma (also **Oxford comma**) a comma used after the penultimate item in a list of three or more items, before 'and' or 'or'.

serif a slight projection finishing off a stroke of a letter, as in T contrasted with T.

signature 1 a group of pages formed by folding a single sheet. **2** a letter or figure printed at the foot of one or more pages of each sheet of a book as a guide in binding.

small capitals capital letters which are of the same height as a lower-case x in the same typeface, as in THIS STYLE OF TYPE.

soft hyphen a hyphen inserted automatically into a word when it is divided at the end of a line of text, sometimes shown as the symbol -.

special sort a character, such as an accented letter or a symbol, that is not normally included in a font.

spread (also **double-page spread**) a pair of pages (left-hand and right-hand) exposed when a book is opened at random, in particular a pair of pages designed as an entity, as in an illustrated book; cf. **opening**.

stet (literally 'let it stand') an instruction on copy or a proof to indicate that an alteration has been made in error and should be ignored.

subscript (of a letter, figure, or symbol) written or printed below the line.

superscript (also **superior**) (of a letter, figure, or symbol) written or printed above the line.

table an arrangement of data in columns and rows.

text area the part of the page in which the text and images of the book are accommodated; the area inside the margins.

title page a page at the beginning of a book containing the complete title and subtitle of the work, the name of the author or editor, and the publisher's name.

title page verso the verso of the title page, on which is printed the statements and clauses that establish the copyright of the material, the identity of the work, and its publication history.

turn-line (also **turnover**) **1** the part of a line of verse or quoted material, a bibliographical citation, etc. that has to be carried over on to a new line. **2** the last line of a paragraph.

type 1 characters or letters that are printed or shown on a screen. **2** a piece of metal with a raised letter or character on its upper surface, used in letterpress printing.

typeface a particular design of type.

typescript the text of a publication in paper form.

typeset arrange or generate the type or data for a piece of text to be printed.

typographic specification (also **type spec**) the designer's definition of the format, layout, and typography of the publication.

typography 1 the style and appearance of printed text. **2** the process of setting and arranging text in type for printing.

Unicode an international encoding system by which each letter, digit, and symbol is assigned a unique numeric value that applies across different platforms and programs.

upper case capital letters as opposed to small letters (**lower case**).

verso the left-hand page of a spread, having an even page number; cf. **recto**.

widow a last word or short last line of a paragraph falling at the top of a page or column, considered undesirable.

x-height the height of a lower-case x, considered characteristic of a given typeface or script.

XML Extensible Markup Language, a system which allows users to define their own customized markup languages, especially in order to display documents on the World Wide Web.

Index

The index entries appear in word-by-word alphabetical order.
Page references in italics indicate illustrations.